About the author

Will Brodie is a writer and image-maker from Melbourne, Australia. He co-wrote *One Week At A Time: A Supporter's Diary of AFL season 1995* with Matthew O'Connor and he is the author of the novel *Suburban Tours* (2009). He worked as a producer, editor and writer for theage.com.au between 2004 and 2014, reporting on the Australian Ice Hockey League between 2011 and 2014. His work can be found at willbrodie.com and fineartamerica.com/profiles/will-brodie.

REALITY CHECK

Travels in the Australian Hockey League

Will Brodie

Combiner Publishing
Melbourne 2015

COMBINER PUBLISHING
Melbourne 2015

First published in Melbourne, Australia in 2015 by Combiner Publishing
ABN 57 542 448 004

National Library of Australia Cataloguing-in-Publication entry

Creator: Brodie, Will, 1967- author.

Title: Reality check : travels in the Australian Ice Hockey League / Will Brodie (author)

ISBN: 9780646932040 (paperback)

Subjects: Melbourne Ice (Hockey team)
Melbourne Mustangs (Hockey team)
Australian Ice Hockey League.
Hockey teams--Victoria--Melbourne.
Hockey--Australia.

Edited by Sue Harvey.
Designed by Marija Ercegovac
Photography by Will Brodie, Mark Bradford, Jack Geraghty, Tania Chalmers, Andrew Mercieca, Paul Rewell, Reverend William A Stewart, Peter Podlaha, Ben Southall, Ben Quiggin

Dewey Number: 796.962099451

Some passages of this work were previously published at theage.com.au
This work features UK English spelling.

willbrodie.com

CONTENTS

MAP OF AUSTRALIAN HOCKEY*

Melbourne to Perth:
2724 kilometres, 1692 miles
Estimated driving time:
36 hours.
Flying time:
3 hours 54 minutes

Melbourne to Adelaide:
654 kilometres., 406 miles
Estimated driving time:
8.5 hours.
Flying time:
1 hour 19 minutes

Melbourne to Sydney:
714 kilometres, 443 miles
Estimated driving time:
10 hours.
Flying time:
1 hour 23 minutes

Melbourne to Canberra:
467 kilometres, 290 miles
Estimated driving time:
7 hours.
Flying time:
1 hour 5 minutes

Melbourne to Newcastle:
823 kilometres, 511 miles
Estimated driving time:
12 hours.
Flying time:
1 hour 31 minutes

* As of January 2014

Perth

Perth Thunder

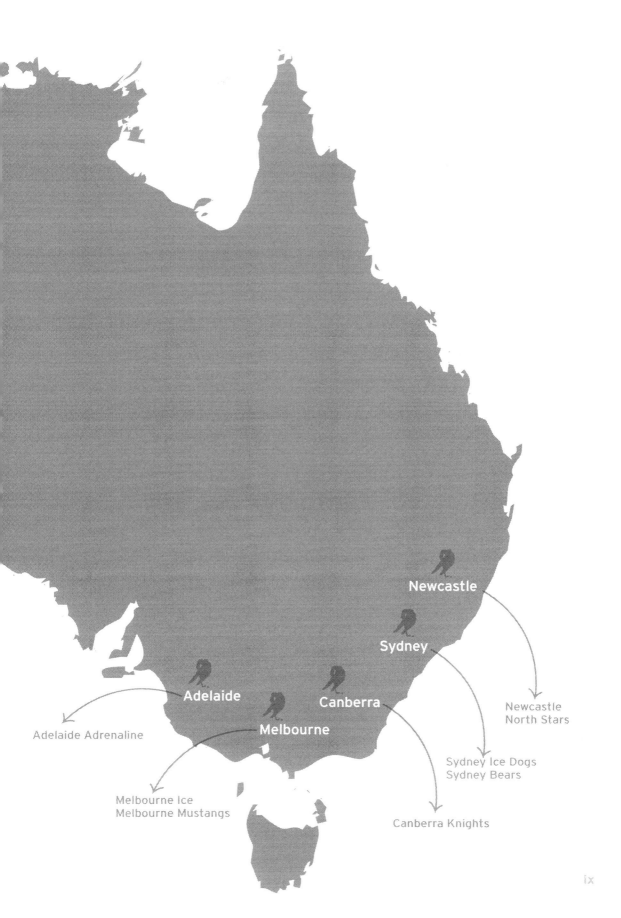

Newcastle

Sydney

Adelaide

Canberra

Melbourne

Adelaide Adrenaline

Newcastle
North Stars

Sydney Ice Dogs
Sydney Bears

Melbourne Ice
Melbourne Mustangs

Canberra Knights

KEY CHARACTERS

Pat O'Kane
Melbourne Mustangs forward
(American import)

Matt Armstrong
Melbourne Ice forward
(Canadian import)

John Belic
Melbourne Mustangs president

Robert Bannerman
AIHL Commissioner

James Morgan
ATC Productions chief

Brad Vigon
Melbourne Mustangs coach

Jack Wolgemuth
Melbourne Mustangs
defenceman (American import)

Jamie Bourke
Melbourne Mustangs forward

Joey Hughes
Melbourne Mustangs forward

Vinnie Hughes
Melbourne Mustangs
defenceman

Andrew McDowell
Melbourne Mustangs vice-
president, Ice Hockey Australia
vice-president

Emma Poynton
Melbourne Ice president

Fraser Carson
Mustangs goalie

Tom Harward
Melbourne Ice team manager

Nathan Walker
Australian NHL prospect

Mark Rummukainen
captain, Canberra Knights,
CBR Brave

Peter Chamberlain
CBR Brave chairman

Jaden Pine-Murphy
Melbourne Ice goalie

Paul 'Jaffa' Watson
ATC Productions commentator;
former Melbourne Ice coach

Lliam Webster
Melbourne Ice captain

Tommy Powell
Melbourne Ice forward

Viktor Gibbs-Sjodin
Melbourne Mustangs forward
(Swedish import)

Johan Steenberg
Melbourne Ice goalie coach

Shane Rose
Sydney Ice Dogs president

Stan Scott
Perth Thunder coach, president
and general manager

Jeff Smith
Melbourne Ice defenceman
(Canadian import)

Josh Puls
Melbourne Ice patron and past
president

James Meredith
Melbourne Ice trainer

Ian Webster
Melbourne Ice insider; former
Ice team manager; father of
Lliam

Tim Johansson
Melbourne Ice forward (Swedish
import)

Austin McKenzie
Melbourne Ice forward

Mathieu Ouellette
CBR Brave forward (Canadian
import)

Anton Kokkonen
CBR Brave forward (Finnish
import)

Stephen Blunden
CBR Brave forward (Canadian
import)

Jeff Grant
Melbourne Mustangs
defenceman (American import)

Simon Barg
Sydney Ice Dogs forward
(Canadian import)

Andrew Petrie
Sydney Ice Dogs coach

Jeremy Brown
Melbourne Ice forward

Daniel Palmkvist
Sydney Bears goalie (Swedish
import)

Ryan O'Handley
Adelaide Adrenaline coach

Vlad Rubes
Sydney Bears coach; former
coach of Australia

Mick Burslem
Melbourne Mustangs equipment
manager

Andrew Fitzgerald
Melbourne Mustangs forward

Mark "Chuck" Connolly,
Melbourne Mustangs assistant
coach

Petri Pitkanen
CBR Brave goalie

Garry Dore
Newcastle North Stars coach
and general manager; Hunter
Ice Skating Stadium general
manager and part-owner

Sean Jones
Melbourne Mustangs captain;
housemate of Pat O'Kane

Luke Read
Sydney Bears back-up goalie

Jonathan Cornford
rink-builder and junior coach

Chris Kubara
father of Sydney Ice Dog Tyler
Kubara

Ric Del Basso
Perth Thunder defender

For Australian hockey.

Introduction

Yes, there is ice hockey in Australia. It has been played here since 1904, a tenacious minor sport nurtured in a handful of rinks by a cabal of dedicated devotees. Today, visionary optimists say a recent surge in popularity has left the game poised on the brink of emergence from the Australian sporting underground. Pessimist realists say it will remain obscure, unable to overcome its usual obstacles. As you will read, there is plenty of evidence to support either contention.

As a child, I played a hundred games of hockey (aficionados drop the word 'ice'). My parents are both Canadian and the youth of that nation are put on skates before they walk; to do otherwise is considered child abuse. But I was born and raised in Melbourne, Australia, and it was in that city's humble rinks that my love of hockey was fostered. I first skated at the St Moritz rink when I was three, attending my dad's Blackhawks training, where I met my first best friends, Glenn and Tim Grandy, the sons of Charlie, a legend of the Australian game. Blackhawks folk helped raise me and form my character, but in 1981 I badly damaged my knee and when I recovered, books and writing and music held as much appeal as playing combative sports. I became a watcher.

I used to have dreams in which I was playing, eerie reminders of a neglected passion, but my life changed and the small but vibrant Victorian hockey scene of my youth shrank to one rink, the oldest and tiniest, at suburban Oakleigh. I meant to get back to hockey but never did. Since I last played, Glenn Grandy became a Victorian, New South Wales and Australian representative and Melbourne Ice pioneer. He is now president of the Blackhawks, still plays defence in the seniors and has logged close to a thousand games.

My absence from hockey had grown to 30 years when my brother Craig took me to a Melbourne Ice game at the newly opened, state-of-the-art Icehouse near the Melbourne CBD in 2011. Watching the Ice forwards rush towards us early in that game, Craig and I held our breath, anticipating the final pass, our nervous systems exhilarated. We turned to each other and said, "How good is this?!"

It was good, very bloody good. The Australian Ice Hockey League (AIHL) was providing the best, most competitive hockey ever seen down under, featuring crisp passing, an

THE FIRST RINK IN AUSTRALIA WAS BUILT OVER A **COLD** STORAGE PLANT IN 1903 IN ADELAIDE. THE FIRST ORGANISED MATCH WAS PLAYED IN 1906 AT THE MELBOURNE GLACIARIUM BETWEEN LOCAL SKATERS AND A TEAM FROM THE CREW OF A UNITED STATES WARSHIP, THE USS BALTIMORE.

absence of goonery, and packed houses in a clean, modern venue complete with a proper grandstand. Previous Melbourne rinks of my acquaintance had provided stands that were not grand, or even good. Paltry stands. Ignoble stands. Dingy, rough concrete and plywood terraces used as makeshift seats by hardy, blanket-packing family members of hockey players. There had been no such thing as fans. At that first Icehouse game, I realised I was back in love with hockey. I became a rapt weekly visitor, then I began writing about what I felt was as good a sporting experience as any on offer in sports-mad Melbourne for my employer theage.com.au, the website of the Melbourne *Age* newspaper. That meant getting to know Ice's rink-mate, the Melbourne Mustangs, only a couple of years old and headed by a president, John Belic, who was happy to admit "mistakes had to be made" for his club to learn. "We have learnt a lot!" he joked gleefully of his new club's formative years.

Then I flew to Newcastle to watch the thrilling 2012 AIHL grand final between the Newcastle North Stars and the Melbourne Ice. Entranced by the atmosphere in that smaller, more intimate venue, and inspired by stories of the league's other, more idiosyncratic rinks, I determined to visit them all. Fulfilling that ambition led to the writing of this book, in which I witnessed games at each AIHL team's rink. I'm rapt to be back in the hockey world, and happy to be helping to spread the word to newcomers, 99 per cent of whom love the spectacle and return to watch it again. But for most of the world, Australian hockey remains a mystery. So here is a primer.

The Australian national team, ranked 34 in the world, plays five times a year, usually overseas, in April, in

Division Two of the World Championships. The AIHL season runs between April and September in Newcastle (North Stars), Sydney (Bears and Ice Dogs), Canberra (Knights), Adelaide (Adrenaline), Perth (Thunder) and Melbourne (Ice and Mustangs).

Games are played over two fifteen-minute periods and a third of 20 minutes, rather than the three 20-minute periods played everywhere else. Rink costs are blamed, but the suspicion remains that some clubs cannot afford to carry the extra players who would be required if three proper length periods were played. Teams play under International Ice Hockey Federation (IIHF) rules, under which fighting is punished by game misconducts and suspensions.

If scores are tied after regular time expires, a shootout determines the result. Teams receive three points for a win, two points for a shootout win and one point for a shootout loss. Each AIHL team is allowed six imports on its roster, four of whom can play in any one game. They are usually stars from minor professional hockey in North American and Europe, and invariably lead the league scoring charts and goalie statistics at the end of the season. There are hundreds of well-performed internationals desperate to experience the AIHL, and the import selection process takes clubs months.

The eight teams contest a 28-game season aiming to make a final four. Hockey is usually played over at least best of three finals, and best of seven at the highest professional level, but in Australia there are two sudden-death semi-finals – first versus fourth and second versus third on the Saturday, followed by a winner-takes-all grand final the following day. The teams are competing for the Goodall Cup, previously awarded to the senior Australian men's state champion team, a trophy variously regarded as either the third- or fifth-oldest piece of silverware in the entire sport.

The league's knockout format resembles the hockey tournament at the Winter Olympics, which is fitting because the entire league is amateur. Referees get a minor stipend, but the players get no payment, nor do the league's administrators. The league's main commissioner Robert Bannerman doesn't take a cent from his position, and like every player, coach and staff member, he has to balance his hockey duties with his paid employment. Off the ice, the league depends on the largesse of hockey-loving volunteers.

In 2010, James Morgan, a tech-savvy new fan with a background in amateur theatre, began live streams of Ice games on the internet. James's crew morphed, quick-smart, into a professional sports broadcast company, ATC Productions. In 2012, Ice allowed a camera crew of hockey-fan film-makers from Resolution Media to follow the team during what turned out to be its third consecutive championship-winning season. The resulting lovingly crafted six-part documentary *Ice: Road To Threepeat* aired repeatedly on Fox Sports, opening up an interest in the league now filled by ATC, which produces coverage of a game of the week for the Pay TV network. ATC also provides livestreams for Ice and the Mustangs on the internet, helps other clubs set up their own livestream services, and is a sponsor of the league, but still does not prosper directly from its altruistic ventures.

The AIHL began in 2001 with Adelaide Avalanche, the Sydney Bears and the Canberra Knights. The West Sydney Ice Dogs, Newcastle North Stars and Melbourne Ice joined in 2002, and the Central Coast Rhinos and Brisbane Blue Tongues in 2005. The Rhinos departed in 2009 and the Blue Tongues, by then playing out of the Gold Coast, were forced out due to rink issues in 2013. The Melbourne Mustangs joined in 2011 and Perth Thunder in 2012. The AIHL is by far the longest-lived of many attempts at a national competition in Australia.

Given the huge distances between many of the teams, and the need to get players back for their day jobs, plane travel is used as much as buses, much to the delight of minor-pro imports who are accustomed to endless cross-country bus trips in the northern hemisphere, and all but two games are played on Saturdays and Sundays.

The sport has little national mainstream media coverage aside from the weekly replay of the game of the week on Fox Sports, and for three years my articles on theage.com.au, though Canberra and Newcastle are well covered by local agencies. Newspapers rarely cover the game, even its elite professional iteration the NHL (National Hockey League), and the free-to-air electronic media generally shuns the sport unless it is to show fighting. Social

THE GOODALL CUP WAS FIRST CONTESTED IN 1909 IN MELBOURNE BETWEEN NEW SOUTH WALES AND VICTORIA, MAKING THAT TROPHY ONE OF THE OLDEST IN INTERNATIONAL HOCKEY.

media has proved a boon to Australian hockey, offering fans great access and clubs cheap means of spreading their message, but the vast majority of the Australian populace remain ignorant about the sport.

So what was the state of play of this unique league at the start of 2014? The Sydney Ice Dogs had claimed the 2013 title after beating Melbourne Ice (who had won the three previous titles) in a tough, tight semi-final, then dominating perennial contenders the Newcastle North Stars in the final. Perth Thunder, in their second year of existence, had defied the odds, yet confirmed insider predictions, by making the finals. The Mustangs, Melbourne's newer team, had begun getting their house in order under new coach Brad Vigon, a former Ice player and assistant coach, and they just missed the playoffs. Adelaide Adrenaline, a perennial powerhouse, had narrowly missed the finals, and were expected to fight back strongly in 2014. The Canberra Knights, possessed of a rabid fan base despite never having made the finals, won just two games in 2013. The Sydney Bears remained

competitive for the majority of the season, but their crowds were moderate and they ended up with only seven wins.

The consensus is that the standard of play in the league has improved by 10 per cent a year since 2010, and clubs are becoming more 'professional' about their import selection, training, preparation and road trips. Australian hockey fans have always said that once decent venues were built and a proper league put in place, Australians would fall in love with hockey. Pace, skill under pressure, big hits – hockey had everything Australians love in their passionately followed football codes.

Crowd numbers outstripped the wildest hopes of hockey officials from the day the Icehouse opened, and rates of interest in adult hockey programs skyrocketed in Melbourne. The sport faces big issues, as you will see, but its fragile national league is thriving as never before.

This book is the story of the 2014 AIHL season and the sights and sounds I found at its quirky outposts. It features the Melbourne clubs more strongly than any others because my interstate journeys ended up giving me greater insights into the

teams I travelled with than those I visited, Melbourne Ice and the Melbourne Mustangs graciously having offered me unfettered access on three trips each. I have tried to reveal key voices from each club, but like the players, coaches and officials I spoke to, I had a day job throughout this project, so inevitably this work features more insights from the two Melbourne rivals.

My observations are abetted by the acumen of two expert and friendly guides: Melbourne Ice's Canadian import Matt Armstrong, and Melbourne Mustangs' American import Pat O'Kane.

This book does not claim to be the definitive account of the AIHL or of hockey in Australia, but I believe I have caught the league, and Australian hockey, at a fascinating point in their history. I hope that you enjoy reading this chronicle as much as I enjoyed researching and writing it, for this hockey enclave is generous, creative, passionate and fun-loving, and it deserves celebration.

DECEMBER 2013

SATURDAY THE 7TH

Where do you start a book about hockey in Australia?
Langwarrin.

It is a suburb a long way from the centre of Melbourne, the big city at the south-eastern end of the Australian mainland. It is more than an hour beyond the inner city of that sports-loving metropolis, well beyond its ageing but constantly renovated bayside suburbs, and even a fair way inland from the end of the train line at Frankston. Langwarrin is the quintessential sprawl suburb: maturing housing estates, shopping centres rooted in grey car-park seas, and horse paddocks. It's a long way from the epicentre of hockey in North America, and many thousands of miles from Hollis, New Hampshire, the hometown of 24-year-old Mustangs forward Pat O'Kane, who is the reason I'm catching trains and cabs to the deep south-east of my hometown.

Pat O'Kane, 43 kilometres from the Icehouse.

The internet assures me Langwarrin (the 257th best suburb in greater Melbourne, according to homely.com), is only 43 kilometres from the Melbourne CBD, but by the time we've crossed Boggs Creek and meandered the curving estate streets off Cranbourne-Frankston Road, I feel like I could be in another dimension. There are none of the trams, cafes and music venues I'm accustomed to out here, and not a hint of hockey. But once I find the right number on the right modest family dwelling, there is Pat.

It's an invigorating experience, encountering so fit a young man in person. Minus all his hockey gear and the high heels of skates, Pat is surprisingly short. Hockey website Elite Prospects gives him away as five feet seven inches (171 centimetres). He has the hollow-cheeked face of the super-fit – the taut, no body-fat presence I have only previously experienced when interviewing highly-paid, sports-science-ruled professional Australian footballers. Pat plays as an amateur here, but he is clearly a pro.

He is also a Nice Guy, by his own admission. Though fiercely competitive, he is "more likely to congratulate an opponent on a good hit than retaliate". "I like to beat them, not fight," he says. And education and career mean as much to him as his beloved hockey. Pat says he was raised well by affluent professionals and has been "incredibly fortunate" to travel and remain a student for so long. He mentions that his folks see opportunities in Asia for him if he studies in Melbourne. For now, Pat is keen to enjoy the journey as much as look forward to that possible destination, but he acknowledges that responsibilities beckon. Implicit is the expectation that he will make the most of his advantages. "I came for the hockey, I'm staying for everything else," he says, when asked why he's playing a second season down under. "Everything else" is a Master's degree in International Business at Monash University, work as an integration aide at Cranbourne Secondary College, and formerly, coaching development-league hockey at Melbourne's second rink at Oakleigh. It also means 'family-like' relationships with Mustangs captain Sean Jones and Sean's wife Sheree, his landlords and housemates, and with back-up goalie Fraser Carson's clan in Cranbourne. He shares Sunday dinner with the Carsons every week.

Pat's attitude to Langwarrin is revealing. He genuinely enjoys living here on the fringes. He is not a big-city guy. Hollis, population 7684, in Hillsborough County, New Hampshire, is a "town village" with one set of traffic lights. The biggest city in New Hampshire, Manchester, is occupied by just 110,209 mostly white, predominantly Christian Americans. Boston, Massachusetts is only an hour away if he needs a major metropolis, but it doesn't sound like he indulges very often. Pat feels at home here in the leafy, semi-rural suburb rated "safe and sound", and "clean and green" and a little prone to snake sightings. (It is also reportedly prone to hoon-driving on blackspot roads by teenagers, and lacks nightlife and public transport.) He is effusive about his outer-suburban neighbours and workmates. He has none of the snobbery of the inhabitants of major cities about their outliers. Pat takes people as he finds them. This is the privilege of the visitor, but also a reflection of his values. He finds everyone welcoming. "Even the tradies, who have a foul mouth!" he says. And, once you adapt, the language is not really offensive. Well, not to a Nice Guy. Looking through his eyes, Australian are outgoing, welcoming, and genuine.

Pat is the sort of impressive young man who can use the word "respect" without inviting cynicism. He admits without embarrassment, that he is not cut out for manual labour. There is little irony, no self-pity and not a hint of laziness about him. He is down-to-earth and laughs frequently, appearing fit in mind as well as body, a good advertisement for his upbringing. What are his doubts, his demons? I wonder, this first get-to-know-you revealing no vices or torments. I might have to probe his teammates for an annoying habit, a quirk. So far, no person in Australian hockey has had anything but praise to offer about Pat O'Kane.

The pacy leftie was a major part of the Mustangs' coming-of-age after arriving in April 2013. In hiring Pat that year, as well as his former Assumption College teammate Kevin Glanzman, Albertan-born goalie Jon Olthuis and goal-scoring Alaskan defenceman Jack Wolgemuth, the Mustangs provided role models for their young squad, as well as elite on-ice talent. Everyone I speak to in Australian hockey emphasises that imports must be "good citizens" as well as decent scorers or stoppers. Nice Guys. Bad influences are a cancer, and horror stories of stars who abused hospitality and left early, or were kicked out, are cited as reasons for wasted seasons.

Pat says four-year Melbourne Ice imports Jason Baclig and Matt Armstrong – both of whom have put down roots in Melbourne after initially coming for a single year – were a "big reason" he came to play in the AIHL; he initially knew nothing about Australia and Australian hockey. Melbourne Ice's livestreams of matches and the fly-on-the-wall documentary *The Ice: Road to Threepeat* helped publicise the league. It may not have hurt that Jason, even smaller than Pat, thrived here. Despite professing a keen rivalry with Ice, Mustang Pat says "they're both great players and great guys". He likes to talk to imports from other clubs and compare notes about the expatriate experience.

In 2013, the Mustangs improved sharply, rising from near the bottom of the league to within a whisker of making the playoffs. They were a team transformed with their fit kids skating out games and rising in confidence, Pat forming a potent partnership with reformed local bad boy Jamie Bourke, and with Jack Wolgemuth launching penetrating rushes from defence. They finally toppled big brother Melbourne Ice in the last local derby of the season. Their fan base, brashly orange and happily rowdy, also grew noticeably.

Pat says he can't wait to continue the surge of the Mustangs. There is an obvious togetherness at work – he lights up talking about how enjoyable it was playing for the "tight group" that was the 2013 Stangs, most of whom are his age or younger. But he surprises me with a few of his admissions. He prefers right wing to centre, considers himself a playmaker rather than a scorer – despite his 30 goals and 21 assists in 28 games in 2013 – and he hates taking penalty shots (all too often necessary in the AIHL, where all ties immediately go to the shootout). He says he "blacks out" when confronted by them, and shoots straight at the goalie's chest, supposedly aiming for the five-hole. It is the admission of a high achiever, exaggerating a weakness out of proportion.

While his time playing in Melbourne is fun, it is also a mission. He really wants to help build this fledgling club, and play his part in spreading the hockey gospel in Australia. He wants something he can tell his grandkids about when he is back surrounded by the forests of New Hampshire - the thickest in the union - after his travels cease. As for many talented, but not elite North Americans, playing days come to an abrupt halt when the competitor is past college age, but reaching his prime. If Pat had been finishing his schooling at home he would not have kept playing hockey.

This is his last hurrah, at 24. In Australia. In Langwarrin.

Pat O'Kane plays every game as if it is his last.

SUNDAY THE 15TH

It's just a get-together skate, not even an official training session, but the low-key off-season gathering of Mustangs at the Icehouse this Sunday night is momentous. I had been tipped off about what was to come, as had Pat O'Kane, but many Mustangs players would have been shocked when Melbourne Ice icons Joey and Vinnie Hughes, formerly arch-rivals, laced up and joined them as prospective teammates.

After three championships in succession, two captained by canny defenceman Vinnie, and featuring the stick-handling and scoring virtuosity of Joey, Melbourne Ice and the Hughes brothers parted company midway through the 2013 season. The reaction from all parties was muted, in public at least, diplomacy overcoming what must have been high emotions, but it could not have been easy for the club or the Hughes men. It was not even made clear whether there had been a sacking or a resignation. The club mentioned discipline breaches. Vinnie seemed to have walked because blood is thicker than water.

This would be the first time such high-profile players had changed AIHL clubs in Melbourne. Joey was named the 2011 finals Most Valuable Player, a right-winger with years of experience in professional and college hockey in North America, long a national representative, and a brilliant talent at the peak of his powers at 29 years of age. And 32-year-old defenceman Vinnie inspired hand-held banners from devoted Ice fans which read simply "Love #9". He had been with the club since its inception, playing 161 games with Ice since 2002. In the tight-knit Australian hockey community, opponents often work together or play together in junior or representative teams, both calming and intensifying the rivalry between the Mustangs and Ice. Off the ice, many of the players are friends. On the ice, the fierce desire to usurp mates or stick it to a former team is undeniable. The sell-out derbies will now be even more passionately contested.

Not surprisingly, the Hughes news hit social media fast, and reactions were plentiful. I saw mostly conciliatory messages, the general tone being that it would be a shame if such hockey talent was lost to Australian hockey. But there was also ugly abuse.

Joey, once the AIHL's most penalised player, had suffered a lengthy suspension in 2012, as had Vinnie. In a league in which fighting guarantees an automatic ejection from the game, the North American style of Joey's passionate but volatile hockey could be problematic.

After three straight championships, Ice had changed coach, captain and president in 2013, before it further lost depth and stability with the departure of the Hughes brothers. It remained a strong club and team, and played a gallant semi-final, but it struggled to topple the top two teams,

Vinnie and Joey Hughes celebrate Melbourne Ice's third consecutive championship, 2012.

the Sydney Ice Dogs and the Newcastle North Stars. There was a sense of inevitability about talk of disunity which circulated following a respectable, but not victorious end to Ice's season.

But what of the challenge for the Mustangs? The league's rules haven't changed. Joey will still have to control himself. Vice-president Andy McDowell is optimistic. "We have had countless meetings with Joey, and he seems to be a bit more relaxed, he wants to play, and he wants to let his hockey do the talking. It's a challenge for us, however we reckon with Brad [Vigon, head coach and ex-Ice player], and the set-up we now have, we will give him a chance. Let's face it; where else does he go if he wants to play? If we can pull it off successfully, it gives us some depth to seriously challenge."

With Pat O'Kane, Jamie Bourke and Joey Hughes, the Mustangs now have three elite scoring forces. Vinnie Hughes is a very handy addition in a league light on for quality defencemen, and brings proven leadership to a youthful club. Depending on the imports both clubs signed over summer, the balance of power in Melbourne might be even up even further in 2014.

TUESDAY THE 17TH

The sky is cloudless, and a 40-degree day is imminent, the extreme heat afflicting cricket's Third Test in distant Perth finally reaching Victoria from across the desert. Australia is struggling to prise out the remaining English batsmen in order to claim the Ashes.

And there are sled dogs at the Icehouse. I know this because I've called Melbourne Ice star, Ottawa native, and Icehouse employee Matt Armstrong to confirm his interest in this project. "I thought I'd seen it all in this job," is Matt's merry slant on the apparition of Arctic snow dogs in the Melbourne summer. Yep, as I enter the Icehouse, amid the plink and plop of the public rink's skating music, there is the unmistakable yelp and yap of excited canines. Icehouse technician and former Mustangs team manager Ken McCoy helps wrangle the huskies off the ice and stops for a chat. Ken is hopeful gun defenceman Jack Wolgemuth will return to the Mustangs this season, despite being only a 50:50 prospect when he departed at the end of the 2013 season. "I saw him on Facebook today at a tournament up in Alaska, wearing the Mustangs helmet," Ken says. "I'm going to tell him he has to return the helmet – in person. And if he's come all that way, he may as well stay and play!" Jokes aside, Ken admits that it's hard for such recruits to commit to the amateur AIHL. "He was doing some work for Andy McDowell [Mustangs hockey operations manager] last year ... but it probably cost him to be out here."

Pat O'Kane is at the gym when he answers my call. He says he feels uncomfortable if he misses a session. He is rarely uncomfortable. Five days a week, unfailingly, he undertakes a body-toning regime he has followed since he was sixteen. Two years ago, he had a personal trainer friend devise a four-month schedule of exercises that prepares him for hockey seasons. Two days after the Mustangs' final game of 2013, Pat started his pre-season regime.

The AIHL season is very short by international hockey standards – just 28 games. In North America or Europe, the demanding fixture would leave less time for gym sessions. When I ask Pat about his comparative lack of ice time in Australia for both games and practice sessions, he says "There is always something you can do. Shoot a thousand pucks at your garage door ..." Or get to the gym.

I ask Pat what chance he thinks Jack Wolgemuth is to return to the Mustangs in 2014. "He loved it out here – who wouldn't?" Pat says. "But Jack is 29, at the age when you have to start life, start work." In North America, there are not that many options for players not of NHL standard once they move out of the college competitions. Pat said he tried out for a Federal League team but it was "just like *Slapshot*": the prospect of endless bus trips and rampant thuggery from cynical, "washed-up" players, and owners keen to spark crowd interest with controversy and violence. He was offered a contract as soon as he tried out, but declined. Pat, small but solid, doesn't judge others who use their fists as much as their skills, and he doesn't think fighting should see a player automatically kicked out of a game as it is under international rules in the AIHL.

But his future lies in international business, not the backwaters of American hockey, living pay cheque to pay cheque, dodging head-hunters. Pat and Jack have made the most of their hockey-playing youth, playing the game they love in places they didn't know had competitive hockey. Jack Wolgemuth left behind girlfriend Natalie to play for the Mustangs in 2013. She visited for three weeks mid-season. "That's not going to fly this season!" Pat says.

Aside from a Skype session with his family in New Hampshire, Pat will share the festive season with his local "families". He is off to Bali during the Christmas break, the most common Aussie holiday rite of passage. I wonder if there are gyms there, whether the routine stops in an even more relaxed country.

JANUARY 2014

MONDAY THE 13TH

AIHL commissioner Robert Bannerman has undertaken a trip into hockey's heartland during his off-season. He tells me via the phone from Sydney that he received a warm welcome from NHL International and the Calgary Flames, Los Angeles Kings and Chicago Blackhawks. "We face the same challenges as the NHL, just on a vastly different scale," Robert says of his meetings with the senior executives he encountered. Far from treating him as irrelevant, coming from such a distant, minuscule market, the executives were keen to compare notes and share tips and information.

Robert Bannerman, middle, with Luc Robitaille and Kelly Cheeseman of the LA Kings.

In the short term, his goals for the AIHL are the same as they have been for years. Raise awareness of the sport; find new fans and convert fans of the sport into fans of the league; continue to improve the product so new revenue streams can help it develop further.

Robert, who came to Australia nine years ago to enjoy sun and surf, is less athletic these days. But he is productive. "I'm not good at sitting still despite my figure!" he says. Like AIHL players, he is an unpaid volunteer. Many of the people helping the AIHL can only do so because they have flexible work situations. The workload is not sustainable for long – work or family obligations inevitably intervene. For now, the league is lucky enough to have a group of energetic young professionals able to find time for AIHL administration.

THURSDAY THE 16TH

Matt and Sara Armstrong's inner-city lifestyle is completely at odds with Pat's semi-rural experience in Langwarrin. Their apartment is in a modern high-rise structure minutes from the Icehouse, alongside the Yarra River, a wrist shot from the Melbourne CBD. The sleek building is both central and secluded. It possesses mercifully efficient air-conditioning, put to use this night in their first hardcore Aussie heatwave. It is far from cluttered, reflecting the fact that Sara is an "anti-hoarder", and that Matt "lived out of a suitcase" for six years.

Matt and Sara Armstrong at home with an Ice star; Matt at his workplace and home rink, the Icehouse; the "grinder" in action.

The Armstrongs serve me a fine Aussie cabernet sauvignon, and we sit at the kitchen counter, talking hockey and life for long enough that Matt will miss his habitual gym session the next morning. No enjoyment goes unpunished when you are on a strict fitness regime.

Matt says he sees a lot of himself in Melbourne Mustangs rival Pat O'Kane. "He reminds me of myself ... way back when I was playing in Holland. I was fresh out of school, hungry and loving the game, and having fun doing it." There are a lot of similarities between the two AIHL imports. Both shoot left, work out in the gym every day, and are considered role models by the club and league. Both are also different players in Australia than in North America. Matt is a scoring forward rather than a "third-line grinder with a chip on his shoulder". "I was never a finesse player," he says. His smooth skating and proficient stick-handling for Ice make this a surprising revelation. But there are telling differences between the two imports. Armstrong, 31, has spent years as a travelling pro, playing in five countries on three continents, and is keen to play on. Pat, 24, is already near the end of his hockey journey.

The shoulder issue Matt endured on the eve of last year's AIHL finals was the first major injury setback he has experienced in his four seasons in Australia. He appears to be in his prime as a player, having adapted to a less physical style of game. (After being sat down for fifteen minutes of penalties in one of his first outings down under, Matt says he decided it was easier on his team and his body if he stopped trying to make as many big hits.) The best part of a decade as a pro hockey player has provided many such lessons. There is a decisive pragmatism about Matt. Time is not for wasting. "You can lose that job in a moment. It can be your job one day and ... not your job the next day," Matt says of the life of the minor-pro player.

Matt is looking at his career from the other end to Pat, and it helps him appreciate his unexpectedly prolonged Australian experience, and why Pat is enjoying his turn down under. "It's funny when you come here, you're not making money from playing hockey which kind of releases the pressure. It's not as if it's your job. You come here because you want to be here. It creates a bit more of a fun atmosphere to play in. I think that's why Pat can do whatever he wants out there. If you're trying things and you're being creative and they don't work out sometimes, you'll still get a game. I think it probably allows you to be the player you want to be."

Matt was on skates "out of the womb" and playing hockey for many hours a day from the age of four on outdoor rinks in Orleans, Ottawa, using gear handed down from his competitor, teammate and older brother Mike. It is the Canadian hockey myth writ large – a love of the game forged in the great, very cold, very white outdoors. Like most pond hockey tragics, his dream was to play in the NHL. And there was a moment in time when it was a possibility. "It was back in major bantam when I was coached by my first agent and he said I had the skills to go somewhere in hockey and potentially could go to the OHL [Ontario Hockey League] or the NCAA [American college system]. You don't know at that point, but it was a stepping stone in the right direction. It was my first year in the OHL and I played for the Kitchener Rangers. It took me about half a season to get going, then we made a bit of a run and we got into the playoffs. I was playing well at the time, so I was moved up to the second line and so I piqued some interest from scouts who were watching and I was rated in the sixth round in the NHL draft."

He says that ranking is "something to show my kids one day". But when European prospects were added to the draft assessment for the first time, Matt was pushed back to the ninth round, and he never got picked up. It was a tough time for a young man in love with the game and unsure of other ambitions: he attended college for two years without nailing down an alternative career path. "I didn't know what to do really. I had to have surgery [on a tailbone cyst] that year. Pretty much since my first year in the OHL, every summer I had a surgery. I tried different doctors, but the same situation every time." The difficult-to-treat condition, which dogs him to this day, meant he was always starting behind rivals who had the head-start of an off-season preparation.

With his slim NHL prospects gone, Matt began earning a living in one of the most psychologically exacting ways possible, as a hockey professional in leagues beneath the pampered top flight. His profile on the Elite Prospects statistics site tells some of the story - a stellar stint in Holland and brief journeys to the IHL (International Hockey League} and SPHL (Southern Professional Hockey League) in America. The lists and statistics don't reveal that to get better jobs in Europe he had to get gigs in American leagues on his CV. Numbers don't tell of gruelling journeys to fruitless try-out camps; broken promises from coaches about higher paid opportunities in better grades; the need to adapt from a low-profile role-playing "grinder" to the scoring focus of an entire organisation; caustic coaches; and enforced absences from wife Sara. But Matt is thankful for what his talents have brought him. "It's not so much the hockey, it's being able to travel with the hockey, experiencing different things, seeing different countries. It's really different when you live with locals for a time period, really taking in the culture, as opposed to backpacking and just seeing the sights of the city."

It was that attitude which meant he was keen to pursue a chance to play for no money at all in the amateur Australian Ice Hockey League. "One of my roommates back in university [Trevor Hocking] went to Australia first and then he went on to Europe. I met him in Germany and he mentioned things about Australia and gave me an insight. I approached Newcastle first about coming to Australia and they were pretty keen about me coming. Then they found out I had a girlfriend, and they weren't keen about bringing females into the team, or as a couple. So that year I didn't make it out there. But the following year I approached Ice and things kind of worked out." Ice, by then focused family values, was a good fit. "They were excited about it. They didn't want young guys coming out here and getting on the piss, going out partying. They liked the fact that I was in a relationship and I was coming out here to play hockey."

Unlike in Germany, where the prospect of a gig in a higher, better paying division was dangled before Matt and Sara, Ice did not promise anything it could not deliver. "They didn't say anything except to come out and play. We paid for the flight to get

SARA ARMSTRONG SAYS WOMEN CONSIDERING TRAVELLING WITH A SPORTING PARTNER NEED TO UNDERGO THEIR "OWN ADVENTURE" AND DEVELOP THEIR OWN INTERESTS. "I DON'T THINK SOMEBODY CAN COME HERE FOR THE HOCKEY ALONE," SHE SAYS. IT IS NOT UNEXPECTED ADVICE FROM A DUAL DEGREE-HOLDER WITH EXPERIENCE IN EVENT MANAGEMENT. SARA IS, HOWEVER, KEEN TO HELP MATT SPREAD THE HOCKEY GOSPEL. "WE JUST WANT IT TO REACH AS WIDE AN AUDIENCE AS POSSIBLE. IT'S SUCH A GREAT GAME AND MELBOURNE PARTICULARLY AND AUSTRALIA HAS SUCH A GREAT SPORTING CULTURE, AND EVEN THOUGH IT'S A MINOR SPORT, I THINK THERE IS A PLACE FOR HOCKEY HERE." SARA SAYS BECAUSE OF THAT CULTURE, IT WASN'T HARD MAKING THE TRANSITION FROM MONTREAL TO MELBOURNE. "I THINK IT'S THE WAY OF LIFE HERE IS ALSO QUITE SIMILAR. MONTREAL PEOPLE ARE ABSOLUTELY ICE HOCKEY MAD. IT REMINDS ME A LOT OF THE FOOTY CULTURE HERE. REALLY THE WHOLE CITY STOPS WHEN ONE OF THE GAMES IS ON, WHICH IS REALLY COOL AND THERE'S SORT OF A BUZZ AROUND THE CITY. WE LOVE THE WAY OF LIFE HERE. PEOPLE GO FROM ONE THING TO THE NEXT AND EACH SEASON BRINGS SOMETHING NEW AND FUN THAT YOU CAN GET INVOLVED IN."

ourselves here and they paid it back progressively throughout the year. Minor things [were paid for] that everyone else gets, socks and pants ..."

For imports in the AIHL, the experience of playing, travelling and living in Australia is the "payment". Matt sees playing in Australia as a good option for a North American pro. He can keep fit and in good touch during his off-season, without over-stressing his body, and gain the experience of living down under. The standard of the hockey in Australia was a surprise to Matt. "I thought it was going to be worse than it was. I didn't come in with any expectations. I just wanted to come and see Australia, have some fun and see how it goes." But he finds it hard to compare the standard of the AIHL with a North American league. "It's a tough one. Because there's four imports on every team, the first line on every team is quite good, then it really falls off. It's hard to compare with a team back home. But I'd say our team was very strong because of our good local players – we didn't fall off as much. Back home you play four lines and in situations you drop down to two or three, but here it's often just two lines then you gradually look to the third line."

Matt marvels that he has spent four years with one club. Melbourne Ice is now the team he has played for the longest, in a lengthening career. This in a place he knew nothing about, a country where he hadn't known hockey was played before receiving Trevor's recommendation. He says he would be "playing beer league with his brother" if he had gone home instead of staying in Australia. "The lifestyle here is outstanding and the quality of living is amazing. It does come with a price tag, but ..." It doesn't hurt that Sara has parlayed her two psychology degrees into rewarding jobs in Melbourne. But when I ask Matt if the Armstrongs would have stayed so long without good occupational prospects for both of them - they are into their fifth AIHL season, and are keenly seeking Australian Permanent Resident status – he can't be sure. "We both love the city for what it is, jobs aside ... the no snow is a good thing as well!"

Matt is another who has noted the annual improvement in the standard of the AIHL. "I can only speak for myself, from 2010, but just to see where it's come to, from then to now, and the potential for where it should go is really exciting." Matt arrived in the first season the Ice played at the Icehouse, and has seen first-hand the effect of such a modern facility. "It would be nice to see all of the teams in this league in a situation like Melbourne Ice. If you create a good environment for ice hockey it will grow." The Icehouse is also Matt's employer. He has devised a hockey school program where his skills and genial nature are having a huge impact on the fans who fall in love with the game after seeing an AIHL fixture and want to learn how to play.

There is a downside to this idyllic hockey adventure. Ice's desire to be a true community club engenders a sense of ownership from fans and volunteers which can occasionally become cloying. President Emma Poynton is trying to clamp down on parents and fans making uninvited excursions into the dressing room and "superfans" have had to be gently discouraged from joining team breakfasts on the road. Social media, a boon to the league, can be problematic for players. And sometimes the fabric of a close-knit family becomes frayed. In an amateur setting, administrators cannot shape a team via trades. Players not under pressure for their position can become complacent. Simple clashes of philosophy can become personal. Gossip can flourish. The Armstrongs admit they have learnt to be "friendly, rather than friends" with people they meet. Matt says they have "learned big lessons about who to trust". Sara says it is a "miracle" that Ice won their third championship in 2012, given some of the divisions behind the scenes, which then bedevilled 2013. Playing a "minor" sport is akin to living in a scenic small town. Pettiness accompanies the sublime. However, after all the hard yards he has endured, Matt Armstrong (usually known as "Army"), knows things have overwhelmingly fallen his way in Melbourne. "It's great that I can work and still have a really passionate involvement in the game. There's not too many people that can work and also play in a situation like this."

Get Matt talking about the upcoming season, and his philosophy is clear: ignore the negatives, don't make excuses, and have fun. It's the only way to win. "Last year was a funny year. It was a bit of a rollercoaster, with personnel leaving; we had a new coach ... different factors. You can put your finger on various things, penalties and this and that. But we just didn't get it done last year and I think we probably learnt the lesson." Matt believes Ice need a couple of good import defencemen and an import goalie to be a title contender. He thinks the Mustangs will also need another good goalie after they thrived with import Jon Olthuis in net in 2013. He figures the Sydney Ice Dogs, who have key imports achieving residency, should again be the team to beat.

If permanent residency is granted to the Armstrongs, Matt can consider a job outside the Icehouse and hockey. If he becomes naturalised, he says he would "start life". It is the same phrase Pat used about a career beyond hockey. Matt's prospective choice of post-hockey career is illuminating. He wants to be a fire-fighter. He says it requires teamwork, leadership, fitness and it is "never the same day to day". Sounds like hockey!

TUESDAY THE 21ST

The potential goalie-go-round in the AIHL is now spinning faster after the surprise retirement of Newcastle net-minder Olivier Martin was confirmed by the North Stars. Nova Scotia-born Olivier recorded the league's best goals against average (2.45) last year. The two teams with the best goalies of the year – Newcastle and the Sydney Ice Dogs (Anthony Kimlin) – played off for the 2013 title. Olivier had played the past two seasons with the North Stars after playing with Adelaide from 2004 to 2011. (He also had a four-game stint with Newcastle in 2005.) He was an Australian representative, and goalie with Adelaide Adrenaline's championship-winning team in 2009, and his departure at just 25 years of age highlights the reality of life in the AIHL: despite the fact that players are unpaid, they have and need a professional attitude.

Olivier tells Ellie-Marie Watts from the Newcastle website that after relocating to Sydney for work, and seeking accreditation as an architect, he knew he couldn't commit 100 per cent to the North Stars. "Hockey is something that I have played all my life and what I love doing most," he says. "There will be an adjustment period and I will miss it. Unfortunately some drastic decisions had to be made for my future. Being a goaltender makes it that much harder to not be committed 100 per cent and it would be unfair for the organisation, my teammates and the fans who come to support us [if I played]."

The importance of social media to the AIHL was underscored by his departure, which evoked an emotional response from fans. "The responses I got on Twitter and Facebook were overwhelming and probably made my decision even harder," Martin said. "I knew it would create some discussion but not to the extent it did. I do want to thank everyone who reached out, it does mean a lot."

Jack Wolgemuth, attacking defenceman, in full flight for the Mustangs.

FRIDAY THE 24TH

"Ohhhhh yeahhhhh baby WOOOOOOO."

"YES YES YES YES YES YES YES YES YES YES YES YES YES YES YES YES YES YES YES YES YES YES YES YES YES YES YES YES YES YES YES."

"And here was me thinking Christmas had already come .... Whoooooooooooo."

These Facebook exclamations sum up the response of Melbourne Mustangs fans to the news that high-scoring defenceman Jack Wolgemuth will be returning to play with the orange horses in 2014. Anchorage, Alaska native Wolgemuth, 29, scored 43 points for the Stangs in 2013, after playing two seasons for the Mississippi Surge in the Southern Professional Hockey League. Jack not only sets up play and scores himself, he stays out of the penalty box. At six foot three inches (190 centimetres), he adds much-needed muscle in front of his goalie. The Mustangs are starting to put together a potentially formidable squad.

THURSDAY THE 30TH

Genial Mustangs vice-president Andy McDowell is a busy man. After he greets me warmly in the grandstand above the bench at Mustangs training, he is not long without an interruption from a prospective new player, his social media manager Myles Harris, or ebullient president John Belic. He's an old-school Aussie, however: you are his entire focus when he gets the chance to chat. He looks you in the eye.

'Andy' is an apt name for McDowell. He is Mustangs vice-president AND hockey operations manager AND Ice Hockey Australia vice-president AND a former (local club) Blackhawks president AND husband to timekeeper Lynette ... And, like many Mustangs volunteers, he is also a parent of players – defenceman Mike and forward Brendan. Some see parents acting as administrators as a no-no for a club. Not the Mustangs. The president, vice-president and last year's team manager all have offspring in the squad.

Andy says the club was formed because there weren't enough opportunities for young Victorian players to play in the AIHL. "We had the rink and we had kids getting heartbroken because there was only one team – Melbourne Ice. It's not their fault, but it just wasn't enough ... We had this huge traffic jam. When we opened the rink we had guys ready to explode, so hand on the heart, the time was right. The minute they opened this rink I said, 'We'll have two teams.' " At that stage, Andy was Ice Hockey Victoria boss – he can be seen in a photo of Melbourne Ice after they became the first Victorian team to win the Goodall Cup the year the Icehouse opened, 2010.

At this first Mustangs' on-ice session of the season, which doubles as a first tryout session, there are over 40 skaters. It doesn't excite Pat O'Kane, who knows his quality ice time will be minimal, but it thrills John Belic. He sees the numbers as (further) validation of the Mustangs venture. "They said there weren't enough players for two teams in Melbourne!" he loudly repeats, beaming.

Andy sees the experience of people like John and himself as essential not just for clubs, but for the sport in Australia. "When you have been involved for as long as I have ... it becomes clear that you're bringing something to the table, you're bringing some experience and you're bringing some effort. You're not someone who has decided you want a label."

Andy played over 200 games for the Blackhawks in league and rec. league hockey – with fewer games played per season than in major hockey centres that takes some doing. He loved it. But he left the sport due to familiar factors – life responsibilities colliding with bad ice times. "I really gave up hockey in the end because I got made manager at work and the 10.30 until midnight training twice a week at Dandenong was killing me. With the 60 hours at work and hockey, I was getting really tired and I thought I needed a rest." That rest lasted fifteen years. Then he took his young boys to watch his younger brother Simon play. They "absolutely loved it" and his path back to hockey was almost immediate. Eventually he became vice-president of Ice Hockey Victoria; then spent five years as president of that body. Last year, he was asked to assist at Ice Hockey Australia, and his evolution from burly goalie to senior administrator was complete. Little wonder Andy believes he brings necessary insights, experience and expertise to his roles. "That's what the sport must have, isn't it? The sport must have people who have their heart and soul into it."

He is not impressed by newcomers who ignore the hard-won wisdom of locals. "Generally the Canadians, we call on their knowledge and expertise. [But] there's no doubt that the best Canadians are the ones who have been here 20 years. Because you do get some guys who have been here five minutes and we say 'hang on, hang on, we tried that twenty years ago and it doesn't work in this country and this is why it doesn't'. " Andy says administrators have to understand the grassroots club structure of Australian hockey, and welcome parents sacrificing their time for their kids to play "because there aren't another 400 kids vying for that spot. We're in a position in this country where we have to encourage and make parents feel warm and fuzzy."

Andy first got into hockey thanks to some pretty skaters. He believes it was at the end of Year 9 in 1976 when his friend Mark Baker made the fateful choice on behalf of his gang to go to Ringwood's Iceland rink, in pursuit of four cute girls, instead of playing golf. Andy said OK, despite not being able to skate. "Once we got into it, it became an obsession, we went crazy. My whole family got involved," he says. He is still obsessed, hockey and family entwined for him and the Mustangs.

Among those skating at this training session are Joey and Vinnie Hughes. Pat O'Kane and Matt Armstrong have played golf with Joey recently, a competitive but apparently jovial experience. Pat says Joey won the worst jacket competition. "Does that make him a winner or a loser?" he asks. In Australia, that means a winner, of course. Of his new teammates, Pat says: "They just want to play hockey. And that's all we want them to do. We don't want to know about what went on [at Melbourne Ice]."

Pat introduces me to his best mate, goalie Fraser Carson, who is fresh back from conceding only a single goal from a 53-shot game against Iceland at the under-20 world championships. "I was at his home more than him recently!" Pat says, referring to his mandatory Sunday dinner at the Carson family home. "I need it!" Fraser is as short as Pat, when I take a picture of the pair, Fraser gallantly offers to remain a step below in order to appear shorter. It's not an ideal build for a modern goalie, but he is clearly a prospect. He is wearing shorts and thongs, still not feeling the

MUSTANGS GOALIE FRASER CARSON, JUST NINETEEN, FIRST TRAVELLED TO CALGARY, CANADA AS A FOURTEEN-YEAR-OLD, AND LATER PLAYED AT COLLEGE IN CANTON, NEW YORK, FOLLOWING HIS HOCKEY DREAMS. BUT HE BELIEVES IT IS NO LONGER AS VITAL FOR YOUNG AUSTRALIANS TO PLAY OVERSEAS, BECAUSE IMPROVED COACHING AND IMPORTS ARE LIFTING THE STANDARD OF LOCAL JUNIOR DEVELOPMENT. THE ACROBATIC GOALIE SAYS THAT TALENTED JUNIORS GET PLENTY OF ICE TIME, AT LEAST IN MELBOURNE, CITING TEAMMATE MATT STRINGER, WHO PLAYS LOCAL HOCKEY ON FRIDAY NIGHTS FOR THE BRAVES, COACHES THE MUSTANGS COLTS, AND TRAINS AND PLAYS FOR THE MUSTANGS, OFTEN A SIX-DAY-A-WEEK COMMITMENT. "THEY'RE NOT GETTING PAID, BUT IT'S LIKE THEIR FULL-TIME JOB," FRASER SAYS. HE DECIDED NOT TO PLAY FOR HIS LOCAL TEAM THIS YEAR, BUT HE STILL COACHES JUNIORS, SOMETIMES RIGHT BEFORE HIS OWN GAMES. KNEE SURGERY WAS CAUSE FOR CAUTION, BUT HIS MAIN CONCERN WAS WITH HIS AIHL OUTPUT. "WITH THE MUSTANGS NOT CHOOSING TO GO WITH AN IMPORT GOALIE IT PUT A LOT MORE PRESSURE ON ME AND MIKEY [JAMES] SO WE NEEDED TO FOCUS A LOT MORE ON THE MUSTANGS."

chill rinkside, but his knees are feeling the impact of five games in little more than a week. Pat, wearing shorts and a singlet, is trying to get his head around Melbourne's heatwave, featuring multiple days above 40 degrees Celsius. He has never experienced anything like it.

This being an ice rink in Melbourne, the Icehouse surface is in high demand. Since I arrived at 7.30 pm, I have watched speed-skaters end their circulations and drag off their huge blue board pads. Then an under-20 national junior league team trained for a brisk hour. This league is Andy McDowell's baby, and he considers it vital to help develop kids out of local leagues yet to be picked up by AIHL teams. Then followed the crowded Mustangs session, surprisingly taut and upbeat given the sluggish first session I watched from the comparatively threadbare Ice two weeks prior. After all this, Ice are due to hit the ice at 10.30 pm. Matt Armstrong, still dressed in his Icehouse blue, has been killing time upstairs watching his rivals. Ice President Emma Poynton has been buying up sessions unused by speed-skaters in a bid to get more pre-season ice time. Andy says the Mustangs stayed at one session per week, declining an offer of extra sessions at 11 pm Mondays.

New Ice team manager Tom Harward, returning to the sport after a long absence, emits a wry grin at that. "Nothing's changed in 40 years!" he mutters. Tom returned because his old Ringwood Rangers teammate Sandy Gardner was coaching Ice. Sandy has since been replaced as coach, which has made Tom's initial dealings with Ice "awkward". He is enthusiastic about the proposal for a rink at distant south-eastern suburb Pakenham, having seen the plans. It is much closer to his home. He won't get to sleep until 1.30 am tonight. Andy McDowell says the Pakenham proposal really could come to fruition. But anyone involved with Australian hockey knows that for every dream or rumour of a new rink, for every blueprint, analysis and reasoned argument, ten fall through.

Andy is adamant that the grand Melbourne Ice–initiated vision of a hockey-first rink is not going to eventuate. Former Ice president Andy Lamrock pushed it, but the proposal may live and die with his involvement. Melbourne, despite the Icehouse, or perhaps because of the boom it has created, needs more rinks, as it has for 30 years, and it needs to find a way to make them sustainably profitable and hockey-friendly. The entire sport in Australia is currently caught between big picture optimism and survival mode, struggling for ice-time, still engaged in the endless fight for money and awareness.

The raucous Mustangs practice session flies past under the huge banners proclaiming Melbourne Ice's three consecutive titles, and on the wall facing the grandstand, depicting Ice players. The full-colour, ten-metre-high posters are highly impressive. But the keen observer might notice that left-handed Matt Armstrong has lined up as a right-hander, and right-hander Dylan Moore as a leftie. This impish improvisation on the part of Ice players reminds me why I like this league: these guys are here for fun. They love the game and sacrifice a lot to play it at a good level. But it's a pleasure, or should be. It could be that the team having the most fun this season will win the championship.

The Mustangs attracted a crowd in pre-season.

Pat O'Kane and Fraser Carson escape Melbourne's heatwave.

FEBRUARY 2014

WEDNESDAY THE 12TH

There's another game in town. It is the Canada v USA exhibition series run successfully last year in Melbourne and Sydney, and this year expanding to Perth and Brisbane. Promoters Craig Douglas, a Kiwi entrepreneur, and Winnipeg-born Kerry Goulet, "Stop Concussions" campaigner and a fifteen-year pro in Europe, added a handful of NHL players to a mainly American Hockey League roster, and put temporary rinks into Melbourne's Hisense Arena (7000 capacity), and Sydney's Allphones Arena (20,000 capacity). They sold out Melbourne twice, and memorably filled Allphones last year. But it's not an easy way to make a buck. Last year I saw the moment the Zamboni ice cleaning machine went through the ice at Hisense, at the press conference the day before the event. That gash led to hours of toil and improvisation for organisers. They rigged an oversized buggy from the nearby tennis centre with towels and water tanks to get the surface cleaned between periods. The hockey was a little contrived in the first game, players understandably tentative given the ice and their tenuous "rivalry". But they put on a great show in the second of the high-scoring encounters. And the Sydney experience – 20,000 watching a hockey game in Australia! – was apparently a major success.

Kerry Goulet mostly speaks to me about the concussion message – he is the co-author of *Concussed* with NHL head injury victim and former star Keith Primeau – but he is the wrangler of the hockey talent for the series, and this year he has the perfect inclusion to his roster: twenty-year-old Australian Nathan Walker is going to play for "America" during the upcoming series in July. A feisty forward who left home at thirteen to play in the Czech Republic in a bid to further his hockey, the leftie is playing for Washington Capitals American Hockey League affiliate team the Hershey Bears in Pennsylvania. Kerry admits there has been criticism of the naming of an Aussie to play for a nominally American team, but it is an exhibition game after all. And very few of us have seen Nathan play live. He has played nine games for Australia, mostly overseas, and only three for his local team the Sydney Ice Dogs.

"The kid's gone the extra mile to make it to the National Hockey League," Kerry says. His coach thinks he's got a good chance to make it next year ... what a great story!" Kerry says Nathan, despite being less than six feet tall, can make it to the NHL as a third-liner. The first thing I noticed about the exhibition series players was that they were all taller than most AIHL players. In fact, some of the better forwards in the Australian league are skilful but smaller North Americans, who thrive under the AIHL rules and the comparative dearth of accomplished local defencemen. "What he does possess is he's a great skater, which is really important in the National Hockey League," Kerry says. "I got to see him practice, he's got really good vision, he communicates well and he's not intimidated. And I think that's probably being here and going to Europe to play in a pretty high level league at a pretty young age. The Washington Capitals said they're really going to look at him seriously as being part of their organisation for a long time to come."

In Melbourne this year, the international exhibitions series plays at Rod Laver Arena, centrepiece venue of the tennis Australian Open, capacity 14,820. Promoter Craig Douglas wants to ramp up the theatrics. "I want to bring a bigger entertainment product this time. I know that we're promoting an ice hockey game between two rival nations and that's fantastic. I have very little control over how that actually operates. But what I can control is the entertainment package which runs around it."

The series aims to appeal to the uninitiated who are looking for something different and are prepared to pay quite heavily for it. It also represents a big opportunity for local hockey to get its hooks into new fans. I ask Craig and Kerry if they have considered having an AIHL curtain-raiser for their event. Mustangs President John Belic has made the same inquiry. Craig has decided not to do so, because of labour costs, the risk to the ice surface, and concerns about how much hockey a casual fan could take in one hit. Hopefully the league can gain more traction off the series in 2014, after endorsing the concept in 2013. Hockey-hungry expats and curious Aussie newcomers ought to know that an affordable, hard-fought league is played under their noses, all winter, every year.

Nathan Walker is a keen attendee at Sydney AIHL games in the northern hemisphere off-season.

SUNDAY THE 23RD

It is Canada v USA at the Winter Olympics, a knock-out semi-final, something you can only possibly see every four years. I stayed up with the help of Northcote's one 3 am licensed bar, then proceeded to the CBD's Imperial Hotel for the telecast. Decisions made with the assistance of wine often lack wisdom, but I got lucky this time. As soon as I arrived at Melbourne's self-appointed hockey pub and saw every second person wearing a Team Canada jersey, it felt ridiculous that I had considered not catching a cab into the city in the middle of the night to watch this game. The pub has been taken over by Melbourne's Canucks. There are no Americans in evidence. The Canadians talk among themselves, but somehow know when to look up, telepathically reading the play despite the commentary being inaudible. There is some unease when the computer feed pixelates early in the first period, but soon enough the free-to-air feed kicks in, and the crowd gets to witness Canada's defensive virtuosity without further interruption.

My preview of this contest became the first ever front-page ice hockey story on theage.com.au because my mate Jon McDonald, a recent hockey convert, was running that part of the site. A Chicago businessman had made a huge billboard which announced "Loser gets Bieber". The hilarious picture of that billboard, featuring Canada and America fighting to avoid ownership of boy star Justin Bieber, sold the story into prominence on a mainstream Australian media site. By whatever means ...

Matt Armstrong is at the telecast, in a jovial, playful mood, feigning outrage over my use of "off the record" quotes in the story. I had painted him as the representative of Canadian modesty and reserve when asked about this contest, contrasted with Pat's American confidence, an old cliché unknown to most Aussies.

Australian Rules football fans have an exasperated catchcry when their team over-possesses the ball: "Kick the bloody thing!" Tonight I notice the Canadian version, exclaimed when they feel their team is dallying with the puck: "Too much mookin aboot!" The tension of holding a one-goal lead all game is eased by the surety of the Canadian defence. There are few real scoring chances, and goalie Carey Price deals with those easily. Canada win 1-0. The gathering, some magical apparition of the night, appears to be settling in for a long session. I flee upon the final whistle, trying to preserve some remnant of normality from the weekend.

MONDAY THE 24TH

Matt Armstrong and Ice teammate Jason Baclig were hosting a function at the Icehouse for last night's Winter Olympics hockey final against Sweden, but I had to decline their invitation, my job permitting no fuzziness on Monday mornings, the busiest part of my week. Social media pictures reveal a rugged-up mob paying rapt attention to the big screen. I watched at my girlfriend's house, the sound down low. Able to watch without interruption, I found the defensive mastery and teamwork of the Canadians mesmerising. So often the Swedes could barely get to centre ice before being stripped of the puck. So often, when they did, they faced a wall of four Canadians. It looked like the Canucks had an extra skater. It was inspiring that such well-heeled professionals could come together like this, so selflessly. I ended the telecast believing that regardless of whether I knew all the tactical nuances of hockey, I had just seen it played at its highest level. By teaming in such an airtight system, the Canadians reconfirmed their status as the nation that most loves hockey.

WEDNESDAY THE 26TH

It is the kind of news one dreads in a minor sport. Canberra Knights boss and Phillip Swimming and Ice Skating Centre manager John Raut has announced that the Knights have been wound up and will not take their place in the AIHL in 2014, six weeks before the start of the season. He cites a lack of local players and rising costs for the decision, which ends the tenure of one of the league's pioneer clubs, and ends the Knights' existence at 33 years of age. "We were offered an extra two import places for this season, but it wouldn't have solved the situation because the local talent we have is two or three years away before we have the numbers so we can field a competitive team," Raut tells the *Canberra Times*.

Knights captain Mark Rummukainen concedes that the team had declined in recent seasons. "When I came into the team it was a fight to get into the team, a fight for ice time, and the last couple of years it's definitely dropped off," he says. "Last year it was a case of if you can play, you're on the team. I've got two young kids, so I could play for the national team and hang the skates up after that." *Canberra Times* columnist Ian Warden described the news as "a pang of sadness, hitting us like a flying puck in the midriff ... Some of us, veteran sportsgoers in this city, will always maintain that the Knights' matches at Phillip were the best sports events we ever knew here."

AIHL deputy commissioner Alex Lata said it was disappointing to lose the Knights from the competition given the fantastic crowd support the team enjoys. "It's a bit of a shock," she said. "Canberra fans are renowned around the league for being very passionate and determined. We definitely want to have a presence in Canberra." Despite being one of the foundation teams in the league in 2000, the Knights have never made the finals. In 2013, they won only twice, and mid-season suffered a 16–0 loss to the Melboure Ice when their travelling ranks were threadbare. They won four times from 24 attempts in 2012. Despite this, they have maintained a legendary following at what Warden described as their "crazily intimate, dilapidated, working-class home venue". Warden wrote: "In recent times the venue was always filled with devotees ... a full venue echoes and throbs with noise and you can smell the bogan camaraderie of your fellow fans."

THURSDAY THE 27TH

There is something going on here. In August 2013, in response to a huge social media outcry, the league overturned a decision not to livestream the AIHL finals. Now, in less than a day, social media has helped promote a campaign in which more than $10,000 has been pledged by members of the hockey community to help keep the Canberra Knights afloat. The campaign is being spearheaded by player Mark Rummukainen, who obviously reflected upon the situation and felt there was hope to save the club. The ginger-haired veteran has been all over the airwaves mobilising belief in Canberra's ability to put together players, finances and rink time - the three necessities rightly demanded by the league – in order to continue in the competition, despite owner John Raut's decision to pull the pin.

The media coverage has revealed how fondly the club is considered by its region. After initial scepticism about whether they would be able to get it together in time, shared in all likelihood by the AIHL, the campaign is giving the players a chance of putting together a team. It could be that a shake-up was necessary, and the structure of the club, seemingly far too reliant on John Raut's individual input, long ago needed overhauling. Now that he has relinquished responsibility, it seems there are plenty of folk with money and time they want to devote to the club.

Mark Rummukainen is making all the right noises on radio, talking of forming a committee to run the club like a business. Suddenly it seems ludicrous that the most passionately followed team in the AIHL could die. The news ticker at the bottom of the Fox Sports screen is reporting the potential revival. Facebook is abuzz with it. It is a sad story turned hopeful in a day. I pledge my offering, sharing the news by means official and personal. A day ago I was almost resigned to the Knights being out. Now I am going to be disappointed if they are not resurrected. A day is a long time in social media sport.

Being a Knights goalie was always a busy job.

Canberra was one of the three foundation AIHL clubs.

The Knights scored 51 goals and conceded 181 goals in 2013. They lost their last 23 games.

Canberra fans
are willing to
improvise to get
a view of the
action.

MARCH 2014

SATURDAY THE 1ST

Matt Armstrong's response to the Canberra bombshell: "It's never good when a team folds. It's just a shame because they had so much potential to be a good club. I think with a bit of money and some good hockey management they could have been a powerhouse. They get such great support from their fans, it's awesome. I hear it's not over yet."

Matt is right. It is far from over. Three days after the fight to save the Knights began, there is $20,000 pledged, there has been a deluge of fan support announced on social media, and the prospect of a Canberra team remaining in the league appears a real possibility.

AIHL Commissioner Alex Lata says "there is a very limited window for resolution of the issue," but there is snowballing momentum. The league is discussing the proposal with Canberra players today.

The terms of AIHL licences are unambiguous. A team must be able to compete satisfactorily for the entire season; it must be financially stable; and it must have guaranteed ice times for matches and practice. These strictures mean the Knights players have to move quickly to guarantee they have a viable playing roster, new financial backing, and a good relationship with rink manager John Raut, the former owner of the Canberra Knights. The season begins on April 12, and most clubs have already purchased their flights and accommodation for the season ahead, including their scheduled trips to Canberra. John Raut is maintaining his right to the Knights moniker and colours, saying he may want to re-enter that team in the future. So the new group will also have to come up with a name, logo and uniforms. Minute-by-minute, decisions are being made that will determine whether the league has eight teams or seven in 2014.

Naturally, the plight of the Knights dominates AIHL discussions. But there is other news. Sydney Ice Dogs 2013 AIHL finals Most Valuable Player Anthony Kimlin, currently in Canada playing for the Whitby Dunlops, won't be playing this season due to study commitments. The Dogs have signed 22-year-old Timothy Noting, who has been playing in the Swedish first and second divisions. Ice Dog head coach Ron Kuprowsky is unfazed "Losing an Australian goalie like Anthony is a setback; however, with Tim taking over in net and with Bert [Robert Malloy] getting his permanent residency and opening a spot for another import, this is something we can absorb," he tells the club's website.

FRIDAY THE 7TH

Canberra was one of the main reasons I wrote this book. I had heard so much about its "feral" fans and the great atmosphere at its rink that I came up with the idea to travel to each AIHL venue and write about them. Melbourne Ice's 2012 import defender Doug Wilson Jnr, told me - and the superb *Threepeat* documentary - that he came to Australia to experience the variety of small-time hockey in all its rawness. This meant outdoor bucket urinals at Gold Coast, and intimately delivered abuse in Canberra. When I assumed that highly skilled but diminutive Ice centre Jason Baclig would dislike the comparatively cramped confines of the Canberra rink, he put me straight, saying he enjoyed the challenge of playing on the smaller rink. Former Ice captain Vinnie Hughes told me of having bourbon thrown on him while he battled for a puck on the boards. He said it laughing. The *Threepeat* makers insisted it was a must-see rink. When I interviewed John Raut last year, he said he turned fans away at every home game and made money regardless of how the team was performing. He dreamed of opening up the venue to fit more of them in.

Visiting Canberra to watch the Knights became my priority, and when I expanded that desire into a plan to visit every rink, Canberra was the trip I thought of as the centrepiece. Why and how did the nation's mild-mannered capital, artificially created, isolated, bureaucratic, home to administrative and political fly-ins, develop such a love for its hockey team? After the amazing events of the past week, my piqued curiosity has peaked.

The Canberra Knights are no more. All hail the AIHL's newest team, Canberra (CBR) Brave.

Yesterday the other seven clubs, on the recommendation of the AIHL commissioners, voted to grant the new Canberra club a provisional licence. Within days of the Knights' demise, a new team, with a potentially more democratic and sustainable structure, featuring new players and a remarkable $28,000-plus in donations – from as far afield as Norway and Canada - has been born. It is an entity created by Knights players, in a biblical three days, which retains the 2014 fixtures of the Knights. The show goes on, as planned, with eight teams, and only the reinstatement of a Queensland team is needed to make the league truly national. (Sorry, Tasmania, but you need a full-sized rink first.)

The new club will wear the navy blue and yellow colours customary to its region and play out of the Knights' former home, the Phillip Swimming and Ice Skating Centre. Four sponsors are lined up and soon to be released memberships are expected to be heavily subscribed, ensuring the entity can turn a profit in its first season. Allinsure director Peter Chamberlain and Jamie Wilson, owner–director of advertising agency Coordinate, are running the club after offering their services to team captain Mark Rummukainen. "If we can bring the entertainment value to the game and engage the community, then I think this will be a team that will be around for a long time," Jamie tells the *Canberra Times*. Mark, who originally considered retirement, is thrilled with the rebirth. "The league said we could have six imports if we couldn't field a strong team, but with the proposal we put forward the league feels we'll be competitive and we feel the same way."

Newcastle hockey stalwart Pete Lambert, a former AIHL commissioner, has always insisted that hockey in Australia is best served by the "community model", in which sizeable regional population centres feel they have ownership of a team; local media take a crucial interest; and sponsors see a reason to associate with the team and derive a benefit from its local links. Fans are highly engaged because the players and administrators are in their community. This was borne out in the reaction to the Knights' demise. It was front-page news on the *Canberra Times*.

It was prime-time talkback fodder on Canberra breakfast radio. Neither would happen in Melbourne or Sydney if the entire league was swallowed by a croc during a cyclone watched by naked film stars. There are many other 'minor' sports as worthy of attention as local hockey. But in Canberra, the demise of a national sporting team is a big issue. Local media covered the story eagerly, and around the rest of Australia, social media filled in the gap and publicised the team's plight, then its stirring renaissance, enabling fans to comment, support and contribute.

Modern communications technology offers unprecedented opportunities to smaller sports. Whatever else its faults, cyberspace has great reflexes, and more room than a newspaper. The passionate response, particularly on Facebook, convinced the organisers they would sell memberships, get volunteers and bums-on-seats, and establish a more professionally structured, membership-based club. Ideas about junior development, sponsorship, team name and logo, and organisation of all the above, occurred online.

The best things about modern media just saved a team for its passionate fans and its league. I get to go to Canberra to see why it so loves its hockey. This book keeps its centrepiece. Thank you, nerds and geeks, thank you. God bless the internet.

SATURDAY THE 15TH

Each day, a new development in Canberra. Today the logo for the Brave is unveiled. And a professional, streamlined, dynamic capital "B" it is, not surprisingly, with new board member Jamie Wilson, an advertiser in charge of its creation. Jamie is behind the branding of the Canberra tourism strategy, under the abbreviation CBR – confident, bold, ready. 'CBR' is also the designation increasingly used by ACT folk on social media when they refer to their major city. Hence the new team will officially be known as the CBR Brave.

Elsewhere, already formed teams are completing preparations for the opening matches of the season. A Sunday scrimmage will determine the final cuts to the long-honed Mustangs squad. Ice, who have had their places determined for weeks, are about to undergo their pre-season camp at Mt Buller, where president Emma Poynton has an involvement with a ski lodge.

Perth Thunder announce the FINAL BOARDING CALL for their 2014 season memberships. New South Wales teams the Sydney Bears, Newcastle North Stars and reigning AIHL champions Sydney Ice Dogs are playing the Wilson Cup pre-season tournament with a game at each of their venues over the next three weeks. The Dogs seem to be taking social media awareness too far, referring to themselves on Facebook as the "Official Sydney Ice Dogs Page" That would give new meaning to a team being "good on paper".

Canberra of course are still finalising their squad. Two Finnish imports have been signed and 25 skaters are vying for places at training. New Chairman Peter Chamberlain says an announcement is imminent on further imports, some of whom may not make it before the start of the season. Two Canadians living in Canberra are among those skating with the team.

News out of Adelaide is scarce. Given they were the other club possibly facing financial difficulties a couple of months ago, such media silence is a little disconcerting. The last club so out of date with their communications was the now defunct Canberra Knights. But the league assures me Adrenaline are all systems go.

MONDAY THE 17TH

Talking on the phone to CBR Brave Chairman Peter Chamberlain, who has worked 90 hours a week on establishing the new club, it is obvious that two things have saved ice hockey's national league presence in the nation's capital: a handful of motivated, creative individuals and widespread love for the team and the sport. Peter, still in full-tilt club-creation mode, talks about the saga day-by-day, like a disaster-recovery general.

Day Six is D-Day. The phone hook-up with the AIHL commissioners commences at 8 pm. Peter Chamberlain begins speaking at 8.01. At 8.02, the final pages of co-administrator Jamie Wilson's submission reach his hands. The presentation, planned to run for an hour, runs for nearly three. It is impressive and thorough enough that the league response is, "You've answered every question and more." Its recommendation to admit the new team to the AIHL will be endorsed by voting clubs on Day Seven.

On Day Seventeen, Chamberlain is still swamped, and he admits that the initial rush of ideas and adrenaline "was not the hard part". The work has just begun, with uniforms to be ordered, imports to be finalised and arranged, a website to be built, memberships to be sold, a more sustainable club structure to be implemented. An entire club has to be built from scratch, though it already has a supporter base and players.

Peter Chamberlain and Jamie Wilson and Mark Rummukainen are so busy that tasks prioritise themselves. There can be no fine-tuning of junior development, governance and the nuances of the limited guarantee company that has been created before the team is put together and the season started. Peter is committed to running the commercial entity in the short-to-medium term, but he aims to have a fully-paid general manager to take over many of the day-to-day activities of the club at some stage, not something done elsewhere in the league. In some ways, such a goal speaks to why the Brave is likely to work – new blood, fresh ideas. Peter and Jamie are successful entrepreneurs in their thirties. "You can't run things the way they were run 30 years ago," Peter says.

There is energy, enthusiasm and a can-do attitude. There is also expert financial acumen, marketing knowledge, and negotiating prowess. This latent expertise was there all along and went untapped. The demise of the Knights could prove to be the luckiest bounce of the puck that ice hockey in the ACT has experienced since the resourceful John Raut established the Knights 33 years ago.

The reasons why the name "Brave" was chosen expose a mindset that should give the sport a massive kick-start in Canberra. "We loved the idea of the Melbourne Heart, the modern name, the modern logo, rather than pitching an animal or one of these other things that has been done. Jeez, you've got this group of five or six senior players who've gone 'we are not going to lie down, we want our team, we want our hockey'. And they were really brave about putting their hand up and going to the league and saying 'we'd like to apply for this licence'. And you look at all the community and all the people who chipped in money to the pledge page, not knowing if they'd actually get a team at the end of it. It's a pretty brave thing to do. Then the sponsors who have come on board. And also the board members and the volunteers who have put all this time into it. It's very brave thing to do. So we thought [Brave] just encapsulated the spirit of the team, the spirit of the organisation."

FRIDAY THE 21ST

For a time in the 1980s, Mustangs coach Brad Vigon was considered one of the best hockey players in California. He tells me this on the phone as he drives back from a sales meeting in rural Gippsland. The next thing he tells me is that being the best player in California in his time "didn't amount to a whole hill of beans". Upbeat, lively Brad is forthright. No false modesty, no skiting. He has the verbal demeanour of someone keen to get things done, sans frills. He mentions his status as an in-demand junior with good skills to make a point about the potential of hockey in Australia. "Hockey was very much at that time like it is here in Australia, it wasn't very popular at all, it was as far down the ladder of sports as you could get."

The advent of Wayne Gretzky changed all of that. Brad says that when the Great One came to the Los Angeles Kings, hockey "exploded" in the west. The Kings had previously played to half-filled houses. These days there is a rink "every twenty minutes" and the best players in California are playing in the NHL and are among the best players in the world. Brad is devoted to improving the standard of home-grown hockey in Australia, and the sport's low status here is something he is familiar with from his formative days in Los Angeles. "There's lots and lots of professional players who have retired to Los Angeles who have taken on coaching gigs or run hockey development schools." Brad believes the first similar ventures in Australia – including the Next Level hockey school run by internationally experienced Mustangs recruit Joey Hughes – are an important element in lifting standards. Providing and protecting opportunities for young locals in the national league is also on his agenda.

He is critical of AIHL teams who play two lines, leaving few opportunities for their up-and-comers to do much but dump the puck in a corner and get off the ice, enabling the imports and higher profile Aussies to dominate. His dream is to create a local team capable of thriving without any imports, an almost unbelievable notion at present. But he is walking the walk. This year the Mustangs will be the only team to suit up Australians in goal – Pat O'Kane's Sunday night dinner mate, nineteen-year-old Fraser Carson – and Michael James. Most teams are going the route of the import goalie. Melbourne Ice, having lost promising local Dahlen Phillips to the travel bug for a year, opted for a Swede, Gustaf Huth to join Kiwi Jaden Pine-Murphy. The reigning champs the Sydney Ice Dogs lost local superstar Anthony Kimlin and hired another Swede, Tim Noting. Sydney, Perth, Adelaide and Canberra will use an import berth on a net-minder. Brad believes that only the bottom two teams should be allowed to sign a non-Australian goalie. He says the Mustangs, who had finished in that position in 2012, needed the much-admired Canadian Jon Olthuis in 2013. But this year they will back diminutive Fraser as their number one goalie.

Competitive they may be, but the Mustangs are all about developing the sport as much as their team, and if the local kids don't get opportunities, Brad says, the sport won't grow. After all, the Mustangs exist because of people who believed more opportunities were needed for young Victorian players; junior development is in their DNA. Brad is also concerned about the impact of players gaining permanent residency, which enables a team to sign another import, removing more opportunities for locals. He says if Matt Armstrong and Jason Baclig are naturalised, and Ice adds another elite import duo, they will be unbeatable. Brad knows the scene – he played with Ice between 2003 and 2010, and was a playing assistant coach in his final two seasons.

He appears to be a man born to coach; he is keen to teach, tactically adept, a confident orator. But his coaching career, in fact his whole Australian hockey venture, is a result of happenstance and fluke, the way he tells it. When his Australian-born wife wanted to move home after five

Brad Vigon, left, with assistant coach Mark "Chuck" Connolly.

Brad Vigon says as a kid he was "hockey-obsessed and hyper-focused".

years in LA, Brad was content, as long as there was some sort of hockey he could play. It had been eleven years since he had played professionally, and he intended to continue playing beer league. Having discovered there was a team in Melbourne, Brad arrived after a partying holiday in South America to ask when tryouts commenced. They started that day. Out of shape and jet-lagged, he suited up, having ignored then Ice boss Mark Weber's urging not to try because there were already 24-would-be imports who had paid their way to Melbourne to compete for the six available import slots. Hopeful of a non-contact session of flow drills, Brad's worst nightmare unfolded fifteen minutes into the session when coach Sandy Gardner, in a bid to cull the squad, ordered scrimmage. Sandy wanted to see "who was tough, who could hit". Brad faced "60 guys trying to murder each other" after eleven years of non-contact social hockey. He took it as a sign and decided to retire once and for all if not picked up. When his name was not read out at the end of that brutal week, Brad figured his skills had gone unnoticed amidst the hits festival. But he made a fateful decision to "just check" with Sandy. And sure enough, the coach had been referring to Brad by the wrong name. He was in, and went on to play 68 games over seven years for Ice.

Brad insists his coaching career was also accidental. A rule demanded that Victorian AIHL players turn out for a local club. Brad was so dismayed by the shemozzle that was Sharks training that he suggested some drills. Pretty soon he was coaching, and the Sharks went from cellar-dwellers to champions. "I wasn't planning to coach, it just happened to fit," Brad says. Tactically astute Brad was called upon to run Ice training drills while still a player, a combination he said did not work. "It's nearly impossible to be a good player-coach; something gets taken away from." By the end of his Ice career as a playing assistant coach, Brad "didn't really want to be there" and dreaded heading to the rink. He took a year away from the game. For someone who moved to Canada when seventeen to further his game, "hockey-obsessed and hyper-focused on being the best he could be", becoming the only American in the leagues in which he played, this was a turning point.

Brad admits that he had "always looked over the fence at the Mustangs". The club full of youngsters was a perfect fit. He loves coaching, but says the enjoyment level is mostly determined by the group of players at one's disposal. "With this group it is purely a coaching role where I get to mentor and teach. And it's not only about what you're doing on the ice, it's about how you carry yourself off the ice as a person, and these guys are soaking it up … It's been super fulfilling for me as a coach." Brad says it makes all the difference having young guys who want to learn and are willing to listen. He admits he was surprised by the team's "fantastic" progress in his first season as coach in 2013. "If we had won one more game, as long as culturally we were going in the right direction, I would have looked at it as a completely successful year.

Brad says the club had previously failed to do "due diligence" when recruiting its imports. "They kind of looked at the [professional] resumes and said 'holy shit, get this guy a ticket!' I said we had to go with young guys who are going to be hungry. We know they might not be as good as some others we could sign, but they will be a good influence on our guys. So we wanted to make sure we got the right people more than getting the exact ideal players." The Mustangs thus chose college-educated players, even if their hockey credentials were inferior to professionals from competitions like the Central and East Coast leagues. "But it turned out that not only were these guys super fantastic players but they were even better people and it was a really good lesson for our young guys. Pat … you know that guy is probably going to be a Pope one day, he's that good a guy, and Jack [Wolgemuth] is similar."

"I really do love it," Brad says of coaching the Mustangs, and helping build a sustainable club. "I am extremely, unbelievably excited about the season ahead."

FRIDAY THE 28TH

In Melbourne, a sporting town, everything is defined by footy, and compared to it. "Footy" means Australian Rules Football, the code unique to Australia, and most followed in its southern states. Conversation is rarely too far from the game, even if it is to criticise the sport. It dominates in the way the NFL now rules American sport.

That cultural ubiquity is a crucial missing element for new Ice coach Brent Laver. It was a realisation he came to in Red Deer, Alberta, Canada. "I remember sitting in a bar at Red Deer and I'm talking to a 75-year-old guy who's telling me the breakout which he thinks works best, that sort of thing, it was an incredible time." Brent discussed the minutiae of the game with this "hockey god" as part of a "hockey sabbatical" he undertook after his wife's employer extended a North American trip. "I felt like I went to uni in hockey … when you're just immersed in the culture, you run into someone at the supermarket and she sees you've got a Calgary hat on and you end up talking about the Flames."

Most footy fans enjoy hockey when they see it live, and many hockey players have grappled with both games. Brent was one of them. He played representative hockey as a junior at the same time he was forging a career as a professional footballer. He played one step below and a lot of income away from the highly professional Australian Football League. He stepped away from hockey at 30 when his son was born, and returned to the sport, like me, only in recent years, by chance, after running into an old teammate who urged him to take in an AIHL game at the newly opened Icehouse. "And we've walked in … I think we both just stopped and went 'Holy Shit!' and we just looked around and had big smiles on our faces. The standard, the intensity, the vibe … we just couldn't believe it. As kids who grew up on promises of new rinks it was just like walking into hockey heaven, it was amazing."

Brent believes that "things follow in a progression for a reason". As soon as he saw AIHL hockey at the Icehouse, he wanted to be involved. Initially, he was a supporter and sponsor. Then he met Ice coach Paul "Jaffa" Watson, who had coached the Victorian junior state team when Brent was captain. Brent says he still uses "Jaffaisms" in his business life. "He's just such a quality human being," he says of Jaffa, who won three consecutive AIHL titles with Melbourne Ice. That led him further into the inner ranks, and his expertise was sought by Ice as an assistant coach midway through 2013. When then coach Sandy Gardner was not reappointed, Brent was named Ice coach, four years after returning from the hockey wilderness.

The similarity with rival Brad Vigon is undeniable. Both mentors are enthusiastic and gregarious. They are also both concerned with more than wins and losses. And they are humble. Brent says he has a lot to learn and he refuses to accept that he was an "elite" talent as a junior. "Within our little fishbowl, maybe in the upper end ... I played as high as I could here as a younger guy." He played senior hockey at seventeen, but says he probably wasn't good enough to play for Australia by his mid-20s.

Brent coached hockey and footy at junior level as a relatively young man. But most of his confidence as a coach comes from his ability as a "man manager". And he honed those skills at work, not play. "I started a business with my cousin when I was pretty much out of school. I've never really had a boss. I've never had a job interview. So I was lucky enough to learn a lot of real life lessons from the building of a business. What I do on a Tuesday and a Thursday and a weekend with hockey is so closely aligned to what I do at work; I'm pretty lucky in that sense." The crossover between life and sport goes both ways. Brent has used counsellors Leading Teams, most known for their work with AFL clubs, in his business. And he has used the sports psychologist from Hawthorn, the 2013 AFL premiers, to devise the pre-season sessions that helped Melbourne Ice players produce the "core values and behaviours" that will govern their 2014 season. "I didn't want it to be something that we gave them. It needed to be something that they owned, especially with this the group in a real state of flux. You've got your guys getting to the top end, you've got your young guys coming up through and there's this middle section that's not really there."

Brent's half-season as an assistant coach last year gave him an insight into the effects of Ice's success on its younger players. He said when current stalwarts Lliam Webster and Tommy Powell were learning their trade as kids in the Ice team, "there were no expectations". "They were playing at Oakleigh. If they had a win it was outstanding; if they had a loss it was status quo. If they missed a pass, there weren't six, seven hundred people staring at them. There was no-one walking around with a Melbourne Ice hoodie or hat on, and that's the environment we're now expecting these guys to come up through." This scrutiny was "tying up the self-esteem" of some young players, he says. "It's almost frightening for them to make a mistake. We're trying to have a real emphasis on turning out good citizens that can go out and use the experiences that they're having at Melbourne Ice. The ultimate goal in an amateur sport apart from winning is that your people end up being really good human beings. Still chase your dream but be very much aware of what is going on around you." Brent has seen too many mates who put everything into hockey, got to 30 and realised: "I'm not in the NHL, I'm not earning a pay packet, what am I going to do now?"

Brent says he has a dialogue with his opposite number Brad Vigon at the Mustangs. "We both understand there is a bigger picture. We need the Melbourne Mustangs to be strong. The Mustangs need Melbourne Ice to be strong." He agrees with Brad that local goalies need support and says Ice had planned to start a local before his wanderlust intervened. Brent vows he will play three lines all year, as the Mustangs do, the third consisting of younger players. "They will be given a chance to learn and grow."

Brent is not just keen to develop his players. The plan is for his young New Zealand goalie Jaden Pine-Murphy to go to a Swedish club at the end of the season. That club will send a coach in exchange. "In this state and in this country in a lot of areas the players are ahead of the coaches." Brent is looking forward to "up-skilling" by watching and listening to a more experienced coach, and getting reviews and critical analysis of his own work.

Two players he admits are more knowledgeable than himself are Ice's veteran imports Jason Baclig and Matt Armstrong. "We're just so lucky to have those two. Jason I probably got to know a bit more intimately last year as captain. Matt I started to develop more of a relationship with towards the end of last year. Matt and I talk a couple of times a week now. He's just been outstanding. I'll call the boys in and he will come right up to my left and he'll be really close – and you'll feel the whole group come in." Brent gets "buy-in" from as little as an Armstrong nod, which "lifts his currency" as a coach.

Brent is striving to improve his hockey knowledge, seeking mentors, poring over game tapes. But he is confident his "man management" delivers values that his club cherishes. He will reward effort, not results, as part of the club's key objectives. Before having coached an AIHL game, he says he will be "forever indebted" to the club and its players for the support they have shown him and the effort they have put in. "The people that give back, you just can't do enough for them. If we can make you a better person it's worth 20 Goodall Cups."

Brent Laver with son Jacob at a Melbourne ice family day.

Natural leader: Brent, far left, captaining Victoria in 1994.

SUNDAY THE 30TH

The voice coming down the line from Pennsylvania is unmistakably Australian, but by rights it should have a European twist and more of a North American twang. Australian hockey star Nathan Walker has been living and travelling in Europe and North America since he was thirteen. In the past two years, the NHL prospect has played in the Czech Republic, and Youngstown, Ohio. He now plies his wares for the Hershey Bears, the first-ever Aussie in the American Hockey League. "I think I've got into the habit now that I'm not going stay in one place for a very long time," the 20-year-old says on a rare day off in Hershey. I always go home in the summertime, so it's not like I am going to be staying somewhere for years and years. It gets a little too much at some points but then again it's nice to be moving around and seeing other parts of the world."

Nathan, economical with his words but not shy, seems inured to external pressures which might faze a less-travelled youngster. On the tantalising possibility of an NHL career: "You kind of know what kind of player you are and so do the coaches, and you've just got to do what you can do and hopefully a team can see you and then you might have a chance to go and play in the NHL." On being a role model to Australian fans and kids: "At the end of the day I'm just another hockey player in the world that's trying to make it. So I try not to think about that too much."

Nathan does however get a kick out of helping Australian youngsters, running clinics when he gets back in town. "It's awesome. I love doing that. I did that [clinics] when I was a kid. And I always said to myself that if I had a chance to teach other kids what I know, and my knowledge of the game, then I'm definitely going to do that." If one of those kids shows enough talent, he concedes that the tyro might have to emigrate. "We just don't have the funding for it and the ice time. It's not a major priority in sport ... to be an ice hockey player there. You're on the ice twice a week, which doesn't really give you that much. Whereas if you head overseas you have a chance to get on the ice every day of that week."

Nathan uses his seven days a week on the ice to improve his "hockey awareness". "It's really an honour to get to play with some of these guys that I'm playing with right now. Most of them have played in the NHL so I'm just trying to take in as much as I can off them and learn as much as I can."

Though now subject to the hectic travel schedule of a professional sportsman, Nathan keeps in touch with his roots. "Yeah every time I get back I usually get out and see all my old buddies. I practise with them when I'm back home as well."

Nathan is rather hopefully named as a reserve for the Australian senior men's team about to compete in the Division Two World Championships in Serbia, but for the foreseeable future he will be unable to play for the national team. The risk of injury, and his obligation to his employer, will limit his opportunities to wear the Mighty Roos jersey. The upcoming international exhibition series will be the only chance for local fans to see what an Australian NHL prospect looks like.

APRIL 2014

FRIDAY THE 4TH

Pat O'Kane now has a girlfriend. Stephanie is a teacher at the school where Pat works two days a week in Cranbourne. "She's got nothing to do with hockey. She saw her first ever game against the Ice Dogs," Pat says. Thankfully for all concerned, "she loved it". I ask, carefully, what it means to meet someone you care about when you are travelling. "I mean I wasn't looking for it," Pat says. "I wasn't planning it. I'm just trying to take it one step at a time. I'm only 24, so we have some time to work it out." It is easy to forget Pat is so young. He is more disciplined and focused than most twenty-somethings I have known.

He sounds weary. Work two days a week, four days at school, two late training sessions, hockey on the weekend, the gym ... "I just have to suck it up for the next year and a half," he says of the demands of his degree. "My weekend consisted of sitting at the kitchen table doing homework. If I did it part-time I wouldn't be able to have my student visa."

Pat is also now working in recruitment liaison for the Mustangs. He's already talked several times to Swedish import and former Nashville NHL draftee Viktor Gibbs-Sjodin, due in Melbourne soon, to assist in his transition. Mustangs hockey manager Andy McDowell told me the club aims to "undersell and over-deliver" to recruits. Pat knows he is the new benchmark, but doesn't mention himself. "If guys come out here expecting to be a big fighter or to get paid ... some of the expectations are just not possible. I think guys who have been to school are not looking to go to the NHL, whereas guys that have only played hockey their entire lives, that's all they have really. I don't mean to call anyone out because that's not my place. I just come from the school of thought that there's life after hockey."

SATURDAY THE 12TH
ROUND ONE

After four days of continuous rain, Melburnians congregate en masse under the re-emerged sun. Desperate Carlton AFL fans flock to the monolithic Melbourne Cricket Ground (MCG), hoping for an easy kill of bottom side Melbourne, a wish that will make their eventual humbling all the more shocking. At nearby Federation Square a crowd tiers itself to take in a stage of energetic dancers and each other. Cabin-fevered families descend upon the riverside aquarium. Trams are full to overflowing with citizens seeking company and distraction in the outdoors.

Harbourtown's outdoor mall hums with shopping, eating, observing hordes, that unfocused slack energy of people who need people. The Ice coaching panel, nattily clad in matching navy blue team jackets, march cheerily amongst them, past the cheap clothes and fast-food outlets, eager as kids on their first day of school. The people they move through are either completely oblivious to their upcoming mission, or jersey-clad Ice fans. The Harbourtown Hotel contains clumps of Ice diehards, laughing. Then, as one curves past the shuddering machines of the mini-amusement park and its unexplained model T-Rex, the tall, white Icehouse imposes itself, pleasingly lined by a queue of impatient hockey fans, an hour early for the first game of the season.

By this point, there is no escaping hockey fever. The day suddenly feels focused. I run into media polymath and hockey convert Nick Place and his son Will, who have bumped into two other ebullient fans, and soon we are in the member's line at the side entrance, amid old friends greeting each other, spirits high. Ice insider Ian Webster says an unprecedented five Ice folk greeted import defenceman Jeff Smith at the airport the night before. A great guy, Ian says, eyes a-glitter. Not much is new, the faces are familiar, Ice has done this all before. Memberships, merchandise, raffle tickets. Everyone knows their job, fans included.

Everyone except the unfamiliar folk representing Melbourne Ice on the rink. I refer constantly to the game book through the first period, trying to connect names and numbers. The longer the game goes, the more glaring the errors made by greenhorns, and even stars. It becomes obvious that Ice does not have the depth to cover its six missing national team representatives. In the second period, after an Ice Dog pushes his gloves in the faces of two Ice youngsters, precipitating a patch of four on four, Ice falls apart completely.

So often a lack of confidence leads to a team looking lazy. The better you are, the harder you try, and vice versa. You understand what effort is needed to succeed, if you have succeeded. If a confident opponent, well-drilled and hard-working, senses you are tentative, mistakes and turnovers abound and a rout ensues. More than once, a pair of Ice defenders are split by a swooping Ice Dogs forward after neither takes control of the puck. There are failed clearances; dangerous, hopeful passes; missed checks; and shorthanded goals against the top Ice line. There are two Matt Armstrong goals from Jason Baclig passes, at the beginning and end of the game, but even Matt doesn't seem as sharp as usual. New net-minder Gustaf Huth takes himself out of the game after conceding four goals.

The final score is 9-2, an accurate measure of the thrashing Ice endured despite matching the Dogs for shots. The champs looked everything Ice was not – cohesive, purposeful, direct and organised. On their bench stood coach Ron Kuprowsky, as solitary as a traffic cop. On the Ice bench I counted eight uniformed coaches, trainers and assistants of one kind or another. Ice's problems were not off the ice, however. They simply didn't have the players to counter a strong, well-drilled opponent. The impossible thing to measure is whether this debilitating loss can be put behind a group that will be one-third transformed a week later when facing local arch-rivals the Mustangs in the year's first derby.

MEDIA POLYMATH NICK PLACE WRITES ONE OF THE MOST UNIQUE HOCKEY CHRONICLES ON THE INTERNET: HIS *NICK DOES HOCKEY* BLOG HAS TRACED HIS PROGRESS AFTER TAKING UP THE SPORT AT THE AGE OF 45. HE FIRST WATCHED HOCKEY WHEN "SICK AS EIGHT DOGS", HE LUCKED INTO A TELECAST OF THE STANLEY CUP PLAYOFFS. HE FELL IN LOVE WITH THE SPORT, AS DID HIS SON WILL. THEY WENT TO MELBOURNE ICE GAMES, WILL STARTED LEARNING THE GAME ... "AND HAVING YET ANOTHER MID-LIFE CRISIS, I SAID 'I'M GOING TO LEARN TOO'." NICK IS BULLISH ABOUT THE POTENTIAL OF AUSTRALIAN HOCKEY TO GROW, BUT WORRIES THAT THE SPORT COULD WITHER BECAUSE THERE ARE NOT ENOUGH RINKS TO COPE WITH FAN AND PLAYER DEMAND. "I READ AN ARTICLE FROM THE 1950S ABOUT AUSTRALIAN ICE HOCKEY AND THE WRITER PREDICTED THEN THAT 3000-PEOPLE STADIUMS WERE NEEDED FOR THE SPORT TO THRIVE. NOTHING HAS CHANGED. IT COULD SUBSIDE AS QUICKLY AS IT HAS RISEN." HOWEVER, HE BELIEVES HOCKEY COULD BE A "TRAILBLAZER" IN THE NEW MEDIA LANDSCAPE. "AS YOU TUBE CHANNELS AND MORE NICHED VERTICAL MEDIA HAPPENS THANKS TO ONLINE STREAMING ETC, HOCKEY IS IN A PERFECT PLACE TO EXPLORE THOSE FIELDS."

SUNDAY THE 13TH

With the Dogs about to take on the Mustangs, the first hockey folk I run into are the Ice brains trust, exactly where I saw them yesterday. Today Brent Laver, Glenn Mayer and Johan Steenberg are in their civvies as they scout their upcoming opponents. They have watched the replay of the previous day's debacle twice, a luxury their forebears never had, thanks to the unpaid labours of ATC Productions. I offer that his team was grossly undermanned because of national team absentees, but Brent says "non-negotiables" were broached. Seventeen-year-old third-liner Sam Hodic, who still has to play in a full cage helmet, was good, and has earnt himself a position for the next game. Other fringe players have made selection easy with sub-par performances.

Mustangs president John Belic is on the ice before the Mustangs' first fixture, excitedly announcing a 100 per cent rise in membership and the introduction of livestreaming (ATC have further extended their always growing involvement in Australian ice hockey).

The Mustangs, less weakened than Ice, begin their season impressively, creating three early chances, Pat O'Kane scoring after four minutes with a cracking wrist shot. Joey Hughes says hello to his new fan base with a powerplay goal a minute later, combining with bull-like import Viktor Gibbs-Sjodin. The Dogs are rattled enough to call a timeout. It is halfway through the period and they have had only one shot on goal. But the tough visitors regroup, taking advantage of a defensive error to get within a goal, then scoring with only their fourth shot 30 seconds from the end of the first period. It is 2–2 after one period, despite the home team dominating.

The Mustangs continue to set the pace, their young team hurtling at the Dogs incessantly. And the Dogs keep holding on, then taking advantage of their rare opportunities to level the game. It is 3–2, then 3–3. Late in the second period, the Mustangs again lead, 4–3 after skipper Sean Jones tips in a wrist shot from the point. But the pattern is broken on the powerplay late in the period, when Jack Wolgemuth finishes a beautiful passing play with the one man advantage.

Leading 5–3 early in the final period, and once again all over the Dogs, the Mustangs rattle the ironwork and spurn chances to put the game away. It feels like they must score or make themselves vulnerable to the inevitable counter-attack from the reigning champs. That charge comes, but the Mustangs get some luck their way, the post saving them with ten minutes to play. Despite the best efforts of both teams, the puck is only prepared to visit the vicinity of the net, not enter

Odd couple: Pat O'Kane and Jamie Bourke are a lethal scoring partnership for the Mustangs.

its jurisdiction. It rolls across the crease and is swatted away from the slot in front with the net unguarded.

With less than two minutes to go, Pat's pace draws a penalty from the Dogs, and they cannot pull their goalie. With twelve seconds left, Mustang import Martin Kutek taps in a powerplay goal and the whippersnappers have overcome the champions 6–3 in their opener.

The Mustangs are exciting, all pace, exuberance and multiple scoring options. However, there are concerns. Forward Jamie Bourke is given a game misconduct over a tangle after the final whistle. Jamie polarises. Fans consider him a loveable provocateur. To foes, he is a trash-talking pest. On-ice, Jamie is always on the edge. Off the ice, he is friendly and charming. All that matters to his team is that he maintains his often shaky discipline and doesn't get sucked into costly and needless penalties, for there is no doubt he is an elite scoring threat, particularly in tandem with cleanskin Pat. Their chemistry is one of the more curious pairings in the league, rogue and saint undeniably simpatico. That dynamic duo will not be available for the first Melbourne derby of the year next Saturday, with Jamie now out suspended.

The league must be tempted to begin its season later, after national representatives have finished their overseas duties, and when most imports are free from northern hemisphere responsibilities, for most games in the first week or more are played without many of the key players who will shape the rest of the season.

It's hard to get a read on the first weekend results. On Saturday, CBR Brave began its existence at home, with a hard-fought 2–0 loss in a penalty-marred affair against the Newcastle North Stars. On Sunday, the North Stars are blanked 4–0 at home by last year's second-last placed Sydney Bears, whose primary recruit Sean Hamilton Steen grabs two goals and an assist. It pays to expect the unexpected early in the season.

WEDNESDAY THE 16TH

It is the elephant in the room, the room being the Medibank Icehouse. The Mustangs don't want to talk about it, and the men at the centre of it are publicity-shy. But now comes the test. What will happen when Joey and Vinnie Hughes play as Mustangs for the first time against their old club and arch-rivals Melbourne Ice this Saturday evening? It is understandable in a game so reliant on teamwork and cohesion that the Mustangs don't want the focus on two of their players at the expense of the rest. But stories like this are irresistible talking points. There is only a first time once.

Ice coach Brent Laver used to give the Hughes brothers rides home from junior training at Oakleigh. He is an unabashed fan, predicting that Joey, who helps run Next Level Hockey at Oakleigh, could become one of the best-ever Australian coaches if he chooses such a path. Brent's admiration for the Hughes brothers is typical of a rivalry in which everyone knows each other so well. The real heat in the relationship belongs to a handful of club figures. Put simply, some key Mustangs feel their club's existence was unfairly resisted, initially, by the established club, and some key Ice figures feel the Mustangs railroaded them in their haste to enter the competition. The natural competitiveness of players who were initially on the outer at Ice ensures intense games; every Mustangs player asked about which team he most wants to beat nominates Ice and the older rinkmate proudly guards its status as the pre-eminent Victorian club. It did the hard, cold yards at Oakleigh for years before the Icehouse opened and the Mustangs were created. The Mustangs always have something to prove to 'big brother' Ice, whose championships and crowds form a natural measuring stick. Fan numbers and passions increase by the game, making the derby a must-see local sporting experience.

One game and five months into their Mustangs careers the Hughes brothers have kept a low profile, but they have added hugely to the Mustangs' depth. Joey's virtuoso stick-handling and powerful skating was a major weapon last Sunday, and his renewed willingness to dish off promptly helped create gilt-edged chances for line-mates. Vinnie appeared rejuvenated, solid at the back but spritely enough to follow up a couple of good scoring opportunities. After round one, it appears Andy McDowell's interrogations have yielded two fine additions to a growing team. And it appears he was right to believe his club was a contender.

It is impossible to predict how Ice will fare this season, given their strongest team this season could field up to eight different players from their line-up in their opening round debacle. But there is no doubt that the Mustangs, confident, focused, and fast, should start favourites to beat Ice for just the second time in this Saturday's derby. Though much will change over the course of the season, and no team yet has its full complement on the ice, none of that will matter this Saturday at 5 pm when the puck drops.

Australia has completed its campaign at the Division Two, Group A World Championships content that they have held their ground despite a frustrating tournament. The Mighty Roos lost two of their games in overtime after leading late in the third period. They belted Belgium 7-1 to avoid relegation, then were frustrated again by a 1-0 loss to host Serbia. Former Gold Coast Blue Tongue and Sydney Ice Dog goalie Anthony Kimlin starred in the net, keeping the Australians in games when they were consistently shorthanded after incurring multiple penalties at the hands of strict referees, and facing an average of nearly 40 shots per game in recording a save percentage of .927. He was named the best Australian player by the tournament's coaches. Ice captain Lliam Webster, Adelaide Adrenaline defenceman Josh Harding, nineteen-year-old Sydney Bears forward Cameron Todd, Anthony Kimlin and young Ice forward Mitch Humphries were named best Australian players in their five games. Cameron led Australian scoring with five points, with Mustang Brendan McDowell, 22, amassing four and Ice captain Lliam Webster, Ice Dog Billy Cliff and CBR Brave captain Mark Rummukainen adding three points each. The Aussies finished fourth, with only Serbia (two wins) and the dominant, unbeaten Estonia (five wins) bettering their regular game win tally.

SATURDAY THE 19TH

I'm as flustered as Pat O'Kane is shattered. I was coming down to the rooms after this sensational derby to arrange a later chat, but because I have intruded upon the obligatory post-match interviews and I am "the journalist", I'm expected to address what just happened. The club cubs wait for the incisive questions from the paid professional which will fill up their game report, or provide a compelling website soundbite. I fumble to find words, my recorder remaining in my pocket. Pat is physically and emotionally spent, his eyes bleary. To leach words from him now, so soon after this 3–2 overtime loss, is cruel. It was a pulsating game which neither team deserved to lose, and the Mustangs thought they had won. They had scored the go-ahead goal with three minutes left. It was overturned after a major penalty was belatedly called on ex-Ice recruit Joey Hughes, in an ignominious end to an excellent first league game against his old club. The Stangs had out-shot Ice 38–29. The Stangs had led 1–0 in the shootout, but eventually lost 2–1, Matt Armstrong netting the fourth shot to claim the game for Ice.

It was an end-to-end thriller with few stops in play, constant drama, a disallowed goal per team, heroic penalty-killing and goalkeeping, and glorious passing goals; everything one could hope for in a highly-anticipated derby. Pat cannot snap out of game mode, standing there with just his jersey removed. He is in the first stage of sport-loss grief, and my interruption forces out the resentment of the competitor at an adverse outcome. No amount of thanks for a great game or congratulations for providing a great spectacle provide solace. Not yet.

But someone has to lose, and the losers must be questioned as well as the victors. Pat looks like he'd rather be undergoing a root canal than an interview, but ever the gentleman and the professional, he answers. He doesn't want to denigrate the officiating. He thinks the Mustangs played well, and the team is happy with their efforts, but ... The digital recorders gobble up the slim pickings. I ask Pat about the big, passionate crowd that spilled into usually inaccessible VIP corners of the rink. He says the players know they have great support, but the question seems as relevant to him right now as if I was asking about base rate neglect, or flower arrangement. This isn't the time for reflective observations. We're not chatting at our leisure on a sunny summer Saturday in Langwarrin. We are under an emptying grandstand minutes after a shoot-out loss to an arch-rival, in April, during the season proper.

A crestfallen Brad Vigon digests his post-match discussion with a referee. Mustangs media boss Myles Harris wrangles players for interviews, relieved like a funeral director to be busy, his countenance grave. Andy McDowell calms an enraged mascot, then shakes the hands of Ice officials. He is philosophical, gracious, classy. He even smiles, ruefully, his composure matching his substantial stature.

At their end of the corridor, Ice officials are respectful but exhilarated; a win in such an epic match a relief as much as a triumph a week after they were thrashed in their season-opener. Brent Laver is almost as ashen as Pat. "I went in and said: 'Pricks! You've given me the lowest low and the highest high in seven days!' " He admits to being spent. But he speaks most, unbidden, about the game's seemingly inevitable controversy. The crowd, the event, seemed to demand not just hurtling end-to-end rushes and sprawling saves, but a couple of big officiating moments.

First a Chris Wong snap from the low slot was correctly assessed as a no-goal, then Joey Hughes had his brain-snap. He had been tangled in an awkward scramble on the boards right in front of the Ice bench with prone opponent Marcus Wong. His attempts to extract himself were vigorous, and in the eyes of one official at least, constituted a kicking action, which meant a five-minute major, a game misconduct, and an automatic suspension. On video, later, his action is revealed as both innocuous and unmistakably an unnecessary kicking motion, and the call correct. That the Mustangs scored on the same passage of play before the officials could codify their response heightened the drama. The goal was ruled out, the game stayed tied and it went to the shoot-out.

In these moments so soon after the game, the heat of battle still steaming up the hallway between the locker rooms, what you think of Joey's act depends on which end of the hall you occupy. He was being held, he was just trying to extricate himself, say the Mustangs: how can you lose a goal after it has been scored? He lost it, say some Ice folk, it was dirty. Both teams believe video – now apparently permissible in AIHL hearings because enough games are livestreamed - will vindicate their view. "No penalty, we wuz robbed" versus "crude act, no goal, good call". Diametrically opposed viewpoints of the incident make the gap of a few metres between the two dressing rooms a yawning chasm. Brent believes Joey stepped over the line, but he hopes his friend and opponent finds clemency. "I hope they don't crucify him" he says. By his own admission, Brent played "on the edge" in both footy and hockey. He feels for Joey, and worries

Melbourne derbies pack out the Icehouse.

Jason Baclig and Viktor Gibbs-Sjodin, pros playing for free.

Joey Hughes gets reacquainted with his former team.

that priors may consign him to a long suspension. "I just hope they don't crucify him."

I leave the aftermath knowing that I have, after all, been in the right place. The standard post-match questions are the front necessary to get the real story, which hovers everywhere around the interview. Next time, it's out with the recorder and "How do you feel, Pat?"

Ice fans with the Yarra Cup, a trophy supplied by fans of Ice and the Mustangs for the winner of the Melbourne derby.

WEDNESDAY THE 23RD

I had been thinking about how a day didn't pass now without AIHL news of note. A few hours away from social media and what have I missed? The entire coaching panel of the reigning AIHL champions, the Sydney Ice Dogs, has resigned. Head coach Ron Kuprowsky and his assistants Colin Dowie and Brad Andrlon are the departed. Ron had led the Dogs since 2010 and guided them to their second Goodall Cup in 2013 after they made the semi-finals in 2011 and 2012. Born in Edmonton, Canada, Kuprowsky played for the Central Coast Rhinos and Ice Dogs from 2005 to 2007 before moving into the Sydney head coaching role in 2011. Dion Dunwoodie, father of star Ice Dog David, has been named as the interim replacement.

The club statement on the shock news thanked fans for their support and spruiked the club's first home game on May 10. "We would also like to ensure our fans that the club's goals still remain very high for the 2014 season and we look forward to another successful campaign."

Always a hard-checking team with a defiant attitude, the Dogs had their issues a few years back, when they were known as the roughest team in the league. An ugly off-ice incident was penalised by the club being restricted to playing three, not four imports. After their title win last season, President Shane Rose said vastly improved discipline had been vital to his club's success. "Two years ago there was no discipline at all, and there was a bit of a shadow over the club," he told Sydney's *Daily Telegraph*. "But we took the bull by the horns and made some dramatic changes to the culture. It's been a lot quicker turnaround than I thought – to change a culture going on for 10 years in just a few years is incredible." Last year's championship seemed to vindicate the club's approach, but a reputation for partying as hard as they play has followed the Dogs into 2014.

Elsewhere in Sydney, the Bears are using Facebook to seek jobs for their imports.

THURSDAY THE 24TH

Which is the world's most travelled amateur sport team? Perth Thunder general manager and former coach Stan Scott reckons his club is the most frequent flyer. He says Thunder's distance from all of its Australian Ice Hockey League opponents means it faces unique challenges. Higher travel costs, a lack of preseason match practice and more demanding final weeks of the season are among the issues facing the Western Australian hockey outpost. But the third-year club is also isolated in a more positive way. Stan is ebullient about his club's future because his team has so many promising young players, thanks to a good relationship with a committed and organised state administration.

"Jamie Woodman will be a starting player and he'll get plenty of ice time. He's six foot two [187 centimetres], a defenceman, and he's eighteen. I have two kids who are sixteen who are unreal and they'll probably get ice time this season. And I've got one kid – [Jamie Campbell] – I don't know what his mother feeds him, but I want her to start feeding the team! Seventeen years old, six foot three [190 centimetres], weighs 105 kilos and he's got no fat on him." Stan says he has a stockpile of the league's most scarce commodity – tall, skilful local defencemen. "Four defencemen under the age of nineteen and all over six foot two. There's a good future in that when you've got that coming through. You can buy a lot of things but skilful tall defencemen who are locals are very difficult to come by."

Stan started Perth Thunder because he saw a fine crop of young talent in junior ranks in Western Australia and imagined such players forming the backbone of a strong AIHL team. Those juniors are now core regulars aged 21 to 23 years-old, like Jordan Kyros and Simon Kudla. "I'm looking around now and I'm seeing the same thing. I'm seeing a whole bunch of really good talent that's seventeen and eighteen and I'm thinking in the next three years they are the kids who will be dominating," he says.

Stan believes "youth, speed and depth" will define this year's most successful AIHL teams. He admits his team possessed offensive firepower at the expense of defensive nous last year, and has recruited accordingly, aiming to assemble a more balanced list. It is a sobering thought for his rivals. Thunder finished third at the end of the regular season in 2013, just its second in the league, despite losing two imports halfway through the season and another – gun points machine Michael Forney – earlier than expected.

They also went with an import goalie mid-stream.

Like last year, two of Stan's ace recruits will not arrive until their North American playoff responsibilities are completed, and he expects his team to reach full momentum mid-season and prove an irresistible force on the run home. He has faith in what he believes will be the strongest imports yet to play in the AIHL, and the young local talent which will be the bedrock of the club.

Stan has an interesting take on the "pay to play" question. His players don't pay a fee to represent Thunder and their flights, insurance and gear are covered, but the club asks for them to bring in a $500 personal sponsor. "It doesn't bring in a lot of money, but it encourages them to get sponsors who will then come to some of our games and opens doors to other businesses, which helps us in the long run. And I also think the players have to commit something, they need to feel a part of the ownership of the club and they have got to realise the club can't keep forking out for everything." A player's sponsor may come to a few games, enjoy the sport and later become a major sponsor, or bring along friends and business associates. The same principle applies to imports. "Every person you bring in opens doors to other people. Every time you meet an import who is credible they open the door to three other people who are credible. It's a small world, somebody always knows somebody who knows somebody." This was how Stan ended up in possession of a Perth Thunder jersey signed by Wayne Gretzky and five other NHL Hall of Famers. A goalie he knew knew someone who knew ... The jersey will be raffled to raise money for a Gretzky-approved charity later in the season.

Stan came to Australia in 1984 from northern England, aged 20, following his parents, who had followed Stan's sister and brother to Western Australia. He was captain of the Flyers in Perth for 20 years, and became active in junior development over the past decade. Watching talented eighteen-year-olds playing alongside 52-year-olds in the local league, he concluded that such kids had to have something better to aspire to. He only decided to put together an AIHL team when he was convinced a "sustainable" amount of junior talent would continue to emerge from Perth's comparatively plentiful three rinks. To continue to encourage and develop "premium" talent, he invites selected youngsters to train with Thunder for free, which gives them a precious two hours extra of ice time per week, an offer popular with parents. This encouragement and development can only go so far – there have been those who have turned away after not getting opportunities – but those who have stuck it out have become strong players. Stan says it takes years to develop a leadership group that will set its own standards and mentor successors. He expects his team to fully come of age in two or three years when its core locals are 26, not 23.

Perth Thunder is Stan's passion, and he says he his involvement is "eternal". "I will always be involved in this team. I started the club and it was a passion of mine, I can't see me dropping out of it, not at the moment anyway, I can only see positives." However, being coach and general manager, a self-employed businessman and new parent took its toll by the end of last season, when he was "absolutely dead, wiped out". Consequently, he sought out a coach, Canadian Dylan Forsythe, to ease the load this year. "I can't do both roles anymore. It was too much. Over the three years that we have been around you can see the cracks and you can see what is and isn't working, but I never really had the time to go out and fix things and change things. But now there's more time, so all the issues we had can be fixed up."

It has also given Stan time to source volunteers with the right skills. "You get a hundred volunteers and out of them two turn up, and one of them turns out to be a 'gunna'. He was gunna do everything and then you end up doing it yourself." But now he has been able to hire "two capable people with excellent skill sets that I don't have", who have taken over some of the administration of the club.

Stan predicts the Mustangs, Ice Dogs and Thunder will make the finals, with Ice and Newcastle fighting out the final position. "I think this is going to be the best season ever ... I just really believe that picking the winner this season, I couldn't do it." He thinks some perennial finalists are starting to look too old or tired. However, he has not become one of the most admired figures in Australian hockey because he is partisan. "We all have one goal: that we want the league to succeed. We want the AIHL to become a prime product and an alternative sporting option for the Australian public. The only way we are going to achieve that is by working together, not just running our own little empires. We've got to help each other. And I think this year is incredible the way everybody has helped the Brave and they've got a competitive team now. When we all work together we'll end up with a really great league."

PERTH THUNDER'S IMPRESSIVE 19-YEAR-OLD DEFENCEMAN JAMIE WOODMAN SAYS THAT GOING OVERSEAS WILL NOT AUTOMATICALLY IMPROVE THE GAME OF YOUNG AUSTRALIANS. "I REMEMBER MY FIRST YEAR I WAS TERRIBLE. I THOUGHT I WAS AWESOME, BUT I WAS A LITTLE FISH IN A BIG SEA. YOU JUST NEED TO PUT IN THE WORK; YOU CAN'T GO OVER AND THINK 'OH I'M HERE, I'M GOING TO BE GREAT'," HE SAYS. JAMIE LEFT AT SIXTEEN, SPENDING THREE YEARS AT THE BANFF HOCKEY ACADEMY AND GRADUATING HIGH SCHOOL BEFORE PLAYING A SEASON IN FLORIDA. THE DEDICATED YOUNGSTER SAYS HIS NORTH AMERICAN SOJOURN WAS AN "AWESOME EXPERIENCE", BUT IT IS OVER. HE WAS ACCEPTED FOR ADMISSION INTO TWO COLLEGES, BUT THE SCHOLARSHIPS DIDN'T COVER ENOUGH OF THE "STUPID EXPENSIVE" COST OF TUITION. "MY PARENTS WANTED TO DO IT BUT IT WAS GOING TO BE TOO MUCH MONEY. I WOULDN'T FEEL COMFORTABLE PUTTING IT ON THEM." HE SAYS AWARENESS OF AUSTRALIAN HOCKEY HAS INCREASED IN NORTH AMERICA. AND HE'S UTTERLY CONVINCED OF THE GAME'S FUTURE HERE. "IT'S GROWING. IT'LL BE A BIG LEAGUE ONE DAY BUT IT'S STILL BUILDING."

Stan Scott, Perth Thunder founder, GM, and coach.

Jamie Woodman is one of the future stars of Aussie hockey.

FRIDAY THE 25TH

ROAD TRIP ONE:
PERTH THUNDER V MELBOURNE ICE
DAY ONE

I am apprehensive, sitting amid Melbourne Ice players on my first road trip, a four-hour plane ride to Perth for their two round three clashes with Perth Thunder. I wonder what the hell I'm doing there, an impostor among athletes. Then, five minutes into the flight, Ice recruit Sean Hamilton introduces himself, we chat, and he puts me completely at ease. Game on. Amiable Ontario native "Hammo", formerly a Thunder player, talks politely about adapting his feisty game to the AIHL. "You had to be physical where I came from," he says. I mention Chris Frank, the import defenceman who played for Ice last year. "He kept saying he was going to end my career," Sean says. "It must have been his line." He shrugs off the threat with a smirk: "He's going to end my career? This is not my career!" Sean makes his living selling windows.

Sean was with Perth from the start of their AIHL adventure, but suffered the cruel fate of being one of their "extra" two imports. He didn't play at all in year one, then played twelve games at the beginning and end of 2013, when the top-liners were late arriving and early to leave. He chose Perth for the weather, got naturalised while living there, then met his girlfriend in Melbourne on a road trip – really a sky trip for a Thunder player – and he admits she didn't want to live in Perth. He has only been in Melbourne a month, but is quick to point out he wanted to play with a "big, well-run" club like Ice at the end of his career. While he looks barely 30, he is actually 33.

Towering Ice import Jeff Smith once endured an eighteen hour bus trip – Trenton, New Jersey to Dayton, Ohio - but this is the longest plane trip he has taken for a hockey game. It's the same for Matt Armstrong. "This is a luxury!" Army said at the airport, still enjoying AIHL road trips after five years. The Perth trip is different to most, even in the AIHL. The logistical risks of travelling 2730 kilometres on game day are too great, so Ice leaves Melbourne and arrives in Perth on Friday night, meaning they wake up in a foreign clime on day one, and have plenty of time to kill before game time. The team meeting is not until 2 pm Saturday. On trips to Newcastle and Sydney, teams often travel straight to the rink from the plane, and I am told travelling teams sometimes fare better on day two of their journeys, having had time together and a more restful preparation.

Upon arrival, Swedish goalie coach Johan Steenberg only half-jokingly enquires about the opening hours of the pub adjacent to the beachside accommodation. After a day's work and a long flight (by domestic standards), most of the posse are content to head for bed. With the idea for a drink forgotten almost immediately, Johan says he was told the Ice Dogs were out until 5 am before losing to the Mustangs on their round one road trip. My first impression of Johan is that he is boyish, unguarded and keen to engage, overturning my stereotype of Scandinavians as reserved. Before the group disperses to turn in, he conveys that his countrymen are insular and he likes "more outgoing" Australians. Johan is more outgoing than anyone in this Ice travelling party.

In the dark, the warmth, the seawater odours and the salt stains on the hotel concrete offer hints, and the huge apartment's maritime theme stucco confirms it – the Indian Ocean is lurking just behind one of these buildings.

SATURDAY THE 26TH

ROAD TRIP ONE:
PERTH THUNDER V MELBOURNE ICE
DAY TWO

I can see why Sean Hamilton chose Perth after living in the snowy cold of Canada. Late April and it's still summer here; at 7.30 in the morning it is balmy and I shop for shorts. I run into Johan Steenberg, Ice coach Brent Laver and trainer James Meredith heading for breakfast and do the journalistic thing by joining them. Talkative Johan is wildly enthusiastic about something, then totally distracted by a new novelty, but one topic he returns to is goaltending. He was a goalie for a long time himself in Sweden and England. He tells of having coins thrown at him by opposing fans in Coventry. Having pointed it out to authorities – 'there must be twenty pounds out here' – they made an announcement over the PA. The crowd threw more coins.

Brent and James detail their pre-match routine. Review Tuesday; upcoming game plan Thursday; meeting of eight to ten minutes an hour and a half before the game; physical preparation; final address three minutes prior to puck drop. James feels he hasn't done his job if the team is not switched on in the first five minutes. Both have worked in Australian football and they use the local game as a yardstick for physical conditioning, but psychologically, nothing prepared anyone at the club for Ice's week-one hiding. Johan says the coaches were shattered by that loss. Brent says that as a player, if things were going a way he didn't like, he could and would intervene. As coach he can't affect anything until the game is completed.

Back at the apartments, Ice president Emma Poynton has a cold and is "totally zonked" after enduring a murderous travelling regime in the past six weeks. She says she just needs some sleep. Magically, talking about how she became so exhausted – a women's national team camp in China; the world championships in Italy; the Melbourne Ice pre-season camp; a rural running event; this trip – her sinus seems to clear. She talks of the hilarious travails of trying to get food and water in provincial China, and workaholism kicks in. Her duties here are varied: the hockey bag she has brought contains, among other things, muesli bars, extra jerseys, and goalie hockey pants she had to source from the mother of former Ice net-minder Dahlen Phillips. There's also a hair-straightener which she uses to iron letters on to jerseys and a charger gizmo to keep the social media coverage humming during the game.

HAVING WORKED FOR AN AMATEUR FOOTBALL ASSOCIATION'S REPRESENTATIVE TEAM AT THE AGE OF EIGHTEEN, EMMA POYNTON IS ACCUSTOMED TO MALE SPORTING REALMS, AND WHEN SHE TOOK ON THE ROLE AS ICE PRESIDENT, SHE SAID GENDER WAS NOT AN ISSUE AT MELBOURNE ICE.

Emma was the first female president in the AIHL, and possibly the hockey world when she took on the role last year. She was groomed for the role by predecessor Andy Lamrock, who at the time said "she's created everything in her life; it hasn't been handed to her on a platter. She has the right attitude – nothing's impossible." He also said she has "incredible energy and drive", is a "concise manager of time", and she "just gets stuff done". Having worked for an amateur football association's representative team at the age of eighteen, Emma is accustomed to male sporting realms, and when she took on the role, she said gender was not an issue at Melbourne Ice, a family-oriented club where half the committee are female. "I've managed athletes, I've managed teams, I've been an athlete myself, travelled as an athlete myself. I've got a pretty good understanding of both the administration side of things as well as the athlete's side of things."

Ironically for a podiatrist, it was a foot injury that brought her to hockey only four years ago, when she didn't know a puck from a powerplay. Seeking a form of exercise that was "flat-footed", she took learn-to-play hockey classes. Within no time, she wasn't just playing, she had organised a women's team, the Ice Wolves, despite hurdles like being asked to provide a fully-fledged constitution in 48 hours. Now her busy life is as packed with hockey as her overworked luggage. She calls Ice players "the kids", like an affectionate mum, though, being in her early thirties, she is younger than some Ice players. Having discussed her weariness, she seems revived, and she's off to eat and walk, the day under way despite no further sleep.

It feels like a holiday at this balmy beachfront. Surely only the Gold Coast tops Perth for hockey incongruity. Matt Armstrong says he and Sara always stopped off at picturesque Byron Bay after the annual trip to play the Gold Coast Blue Tongues and the Queensland trip was a big selling point of the league to many shivering northern hemisphere hockey players. As we returned from breakfast, presented with kilometres of fine white sand beach, Johan said "that's the picture which sells hockey here".

Much more of the Ice team is assembled for this road trip, but captain Lliam Webster and young forward Mitch Humphries have not travelled following their return from national representative duties, and assistant coach Glenn Mayer stayed at home with his young family. Brent Laver says he was a model husband yesterday, mopping and vacuuming for four hours in order to justify his interstate weekend. The players who have made it exude vitality as they spend their hours chiding, quipping and joking. You can hear the banter, the whoops, hollers and laughter as obscure, uproarious games are played, transforming the apartment enclave into a giggleplex. The sound of fit young men enjoying each other's company on a trip away is a tonic that should be used alongside music therapy in rehab and aged care. Just being around people having so much fun makes you feel healthier.

Matt Armstrong is chief mood enhancer, the loudest of the voices cheering and jeering, greeting teammates with a "Hey Boi!" (delivered Foghorn Leghorn–style). Matt says he is "not a serious guy" and as soon as hockey isn't fun, he will stop playing. But he is smart and he has established his priorities. Life is to be enjoyed. Don't take yourself too seriously. Give of yourself. In some ways, he resembles a model old-school Aussie, or at least how many of us like to think of ourselves – easygoing, outgoing, unpretentious, a stirrer. Fittingly, some of his schtick is mock-Aussie - "JAAAAAYCE!" he pronounces with all the nasal brutality of the widest down-under accent when addressing fellow Canuck Jason Baclig.

There are big statements made on this trip, however. The Ice brass set parameters that create a happy team environment. Their pre-season camp established the team's priorities, and standards are set by having the right imports, like Matt and Jason, and insisting on developing their "kids" with the right values. Patron and past president Josh Puls is on his first interstate trip in a couple of years. He took on the fledgling club when it was based at dingy Oakleigh nine years ago, after founder Mark Weber inevitably suffered burnout. Josh's "family" values guided Ice and his legal and administrative background gave him the tools to implement a structure which nurtured those values, helping the club evolve from private ownership. He is passionate about proper governance, the importance of transparency and democracy, and the need for vigilant self-regulation. Josh believes too much responsibility is in too few hands at some clubs, and many problems can be avoided with the right structures, guided by the right philosophy. "The sum of the human condition is not advanced by whether we win or lose," Josh says. "If you are a better version of yourself because you played hockey in the right environment and take that back to work, school, family, that does advance the sum of human happiness."

Ice fractured in 2013. Off-ice tensions and staleness followed three consecutive championships. There was indiscipline on the ice and instances of insularity and selfishness. It now appears that president Emma Poynton and road manager and off-ice veteran Ian Webster are at odds. But Emma and Ian put aside their differences publicly and Ice appears a happy team again ahead of game one in Perth. The new coaching panel, only two games in, are experienced in sport but fresh in their Ice roles. They are not interested in past enmities.

Johan Steenberg, like Brent Laver, brought on board as an assistant coach midway through 2013, gets much ribbing for his inability to pronounce the letter "g" or "j", but gives more than

Fans, players and even kiosk customers mingle on the concoursea at Perth Ice Arena.

Blue skies and beaches, Perth's recruiting advantage; the glass-bangers at ground-level.

he gets, again more "Aussie" than many of the locals. Johan is definitely one of Emma's "kids". He is so much fun that she makes it known that he is stern enough to have forced rising forward Austin McKenzie into onerous skating drills for being late to training. All of the off-ice staff enjoy the banter and a beer, but have strict lines they won't cross. The balance between being approachable and good company has to be achieved while maintaining authority and respect and keeping the message fresh.

The team meeting before game one is held in the coaches' living room. It is central to the apartments, and its two doors seem open all weekend. Josh Puls, Emma Poynton, Ian Webster, the coaches, new team manager Tom Harward and medico–physio James Meredith have all changed into team-issued embroidered dark blue. Brent stands and everyone else sits, close together, as he reiterates the line-up. Tommy Powell is captain in the absence of Lliam Webster. Import goalie Gustaf Huth is unwell and Jayden Pine-Murphy, the Kiwi-born goalie who recorded good numbers as back-up last season, will start today. This enables tall Swedish forward Tim Johansson to get a first start. Though the players know such information – Brent did the rounds after arriving late last night, informing the relevant individuals - the ritual announcement in this intimate setting feels necessary and is greeted with loud affirmation. Matt Armstrong, sitting on Brent's immediate left, is a kind of cheerleader, offering a translating echo of each announcement, in nicknames and other team parlance, raising cheers and laughs, getting the mood up. "CK!" he cries when Tim's debut is announced. (Tim infamously insisted on getting changed into fine clobber for a short trip: he is Calvin Klein.) "Drop the gloves!" Matt jokes about Sean Hamilton, known for his feisty style. It's Sean's first game against his old club.

When Brent asks if there are any questions, six foot six [198 centimetres] import defenceman Jeff Smith finds voice, however quietly. "We've come all this way boys, may as well win. May as well." The players save the real rev-up for the dressing rooms. To this end, Matt is carrying an odd looking octagonal box with protruding wires, some kind of multi-directional boombox. Waiting for the transport, several players hook into their hip-hop headphones. I'm informed that music is crucial to a build-up. Most players seem happy with the choices, a couple even busting a move.

Our car gets lost for a few minutes as we head away from the coast, but to find the Perth Ice Arena we would only have had to follow the trail of two-storey tilt-slab factory/warehouse/showrooms inland. Massive, ugly buildings, many identical

Perth Ice Arena, like most Australian rinks, features seating on only one side of the facility.

The MOTH (Monday Old Timer Hockey) bar houses the rowdiest Perth Thunder fans.

but for their signs: TILES; FORKLIFT SALES ... And at the final corner before the arena, the FLAMING BIBLE CHURCH, an inscrutably secular structure if ever there was one. On two sides, the blue-painted rink shed has no neighbours and red desert sands stretch away into the hinterland. The Perth Ice Arena is classically Australian – 25 minutes from the city centre on its northern industrial fringe. Stan Scott told me during the week that the greatest virtue of the Icehouse was its proximity to Melbourne's city centre. It is unique in that respect in Australian hockey.

Rain starts fitfully as Melbourne Ice enter the building, and continues for most of the night. "First rain in six months," Stan insists, giving us credit as Bleak City drought-breakers. We're early, and arena staff are rusty for the first game of the year, but soon enough, music pounds, the scoreboard lights up with zeroes, and fans, mostly in hockey jerseys, start filtering in.

The Arena feels like a converted factory. Above and behind the ocean end goals – or is it the desert end? – a slit is cut in the metal which enables the Thunder's most feral fans to make their voices heard from the MOTH (Monday Old Timers Hockey) bar. The emblem for that group is a wizened old skating moth using a Zimmer frame. The grandstand is clamped into one side of the rink on a mezzanine, and the walkway at ground level has to accommodate fans going upstairs and to the kiosk, and both teams. It is potentially problematic if teams are not getting along: with side-by-side dressing rooms, a common entrance to the ice surface and only one thoroughfare, fans, players and officials of both clubs are forced to mingle.

Goalie Jaden Pine-Murphy warms up in a couple of square metres between dressing-room door and kiosk entrance, headphones in, throwing a weirdly bouncing ball against the wall. Thunder players get their pre-match rub-downs outside the obviously cramped dressing room. The Ice dressing room is thumping thanks to Matt's speaker. The occasional exhortation can be heard, fiercer than before. Jeff Smith, who has played all over the world, is wide-eyed at the architecture, asking where to go when the game starts; the player's benches, and the cameraman's perch, are on the opposite side of the rink.

One other figure is limbering up. He has late-seventies punk hair, an enormous nose ring, a black leather kilt and singlet, tattoos – whatever else he needs to be "Badpiper", the pre-match entertainment. Badpiper traverses his red carpet (it is grey) on to the ice surface and starts playing, a hard-rock soundtrack kicking in as accompaniment. His gimmick? Flames intermittently spew out of the end of his customised pipes. It is the sort of act, a novel idea with few dimensions, that delights for a minute or two and

Perth Ice Arena is attracting strong crowds in Thunder's third year.

Badpiper struts his stuff on the red, er grey carpert.

There are no 'nosebleed' seats at AIHL games.

grates soon after. The generous crowd applauds Badpiper each time they are loudly instructed to do so by the announcer. But on he plays, through the team warm-ups either side of him. He is determined to deliver value for money.

I gaze up and down the lines of the two teams as they line up for the national anthem. Perth are young but have two years under their belts and their imports should be good, though two are still on their way. Ice look unfamiliar, lots of changes from 2013. National song completed, Metallica takes over the airwaves, the announcer roars 'Here we go Thunder, here we go!', and the crowd on the narrow ground-level walkway dutifully slam the glass to the simple rhythm. It won't be the last time the announcer cries here we go, in fact, he will utter little else all weekend. I take up position on a handy ledge along the rink-side walkway, the Ice inner ranks to my left, Josh yelling, 'Let's go, Melbourne!" We're away.

It turns out that Gustaf Huth's absence from goaltending due to illness opens up an entirely new set of dimensions for Ice. It takes less than two minutes for Tim Johansson, in his first game, to become a selector's headache. Tim is Ice's fifth or sixth import, so he is only meant to play when one of the other imports is out of the line-up, with only four non-Australians permitted to play in a single game. Playing second line with lanky up-and-comer Austin McKenzie and diminutive hustle merchant Chris Wong, the Swede's speed, balance and puck-handling skill are immediately influential and it is no surprise when he bangs in a rebound in from a tight angle on the powerplay after the first unit failed to get past resolute Thunder netminder Mathieu Dugas. 1–0 Ice.

Seven minutes in, a wicked deflection floors Thunder import defender Corey Toy, opening up a thick red crescent on his right cheekbone. He is helped off the ice. Nothing is going right for the home team. Down to one import, Mathieu Dugas in net, Thunder is facing a focused opponent. Ice is organised, disciplined, and controlling most of the game, only its third line experiencing any real pressure in the first period, and Jaden Pine-Murphy doing the rest in net when defences are breached. Brent has emphasised no-fuss clearances from Ice's zone, and no-frills attack. It is a small rink, the neutral zone is pinched, there is extra room behind the net; efficiency is called for.

Perth are dogged, but uninspired going forward. Import Stuart Stefan moves well, but most Thunder attacks fail at the blue line. However, the Thunder defence stands firm, led by eighteen-year-old debutante Jamie Woodman. Ice persists, and Jeff Smith taps in a second powerplay goal near the goal crease, giving them a 2–0 stranglehold near the end of the second

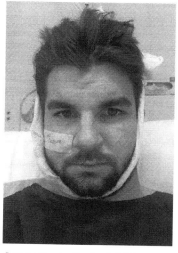

Corey Toy's first night in Australian Hockey

period. Thunder survives two more powerplays in the final period, but the weight of possession and quality rushes tells. Army intervenes brilliantly from a face-off in the defensive zone, setting Tommy Powell up mid-ice, and the interim skipper finishes the breakaway on the backhand.

All that remains is for Ice to get Jaden Pine-Murphy his shutout. He jeopardises it himself by getting lost in the ample behind-net space, his giveaway ending up with a point-blank shot from the slot. Which he makes an amazing glove save on, gliding back to his rightful position. Johan is going spare on the bench, but even the Perth crowd applaud that effort. 3–0 to Ice. Three games into the season, Ice are suddenly developing some momentum after their first win in regulation time. They have five points despite being smashed in round one.

Both teams proceed to dinner at Perth's sponsor, the Springs Tavern, somewhere nearby in the teeming darkness of Perth's outer suburbia. Inside that oversubscribed establishment, I notice Matt and Brent having a long chat alone at the side of the room. In the foreground, Johan has a whisky. At breakfast, he had revealed that pesky seagulls can be dissuaded from swooping one's outdoor meal by placing bread that has been dipped in whisky nearby. Never-deterred Stan Scott says Thunder will split the points by winning tomorrow. He has a natty suit on his slight frame and is never still, shifting on his feet from side to side as if skating, looking up from over his glasses. I find myself sitting next to Matt. I mention his role at the team meeting, his chat with the coach. He says he is aware of his impact, but he doesn't need a letter on his jersey; Emma won't need to get out the hair straightener. Matt is happy making his contribution unofficially, as one of the boys.

Perth players scatter to their homes. After a delayed meal, Ice players return to home base by the beach and spread through their various rooms. Some players get post-match treatment on a table set up at the back of the coaches' room. And that nerve centre becomes a post-win drop-in centre. Brent, Johan, Emma, Ian, myself and Josh are joined by a revolving crew of players, all relaxed by victory, exertion and a couple of beers. We talk hockey. Youngster Austin McKenzie

LONG-TIME REFEREE MARK WEBER SAYS HE HAD HIS OWN MONEY TO PUMP INTO FOUNDING MELBOURNE ICE BECAUSE HE HAD "NO OTHER REAL BAD HABITS". A GEOLOGIST IN THE OIL TRADE, HE MOVED TO ADELAIDE FROM CALGARY IN 1982, AND TO MELBOURNE IN 1985, WHERE HE WAS A LOCAL ADMINISTRATOR, AND IN 2002, STARTED MELBOURNE'S FIRST AIHL CLUB. MARK ALSO HELPED RUN THE AIHL FOR A YEAR BEFORE HE "BURNT OUT" IN 2005, EXHAUSTED BY "POLITICS AND CRAP". THE CHALLENGES INCLUDED DEALING WITH SHORT-SIGHTEDNESS, TALL POPPY SYNDROME, AND "GUNNAS"; VOLUNTEERS WHO NEVER DELIVERED WHAT THEY PROMISED. HIS SOLUTION? "IT'S ALL ABOUT COMMUNICATION," HE SAYS. HIS MISSION, ACCOMPLISHED, WAS TO "IMPROVE THE STANDARD OF LOCAL HOCKEY PLAYERS AND IMPROVE THE EXPOSURE OF THE SPORT". HE'S PROUD THAT AUSTRALIA ROSE IN THE WORLD RANKINGS DURING HIS TENURE. PART OF HIS METHOD WAS TO ATTRACT THE "RIGHT KIND" OF IMPORTS, SOME OF WHOM GOT MARRIED TO LOCALS AND BECAME KEY PARTS OF AUSTRALIA'S HOCKEY INFRASTRUCTURE. NOW RETIRED, MARK RUNS AUSSIE PUCK, THE ONLY LOCAL PUCK MANUFACTURER. HE ALSO HELPS PROMOTE JUNIOR EVENTS AND REMAINS A FIXTURE AT LOCAL HOCKEY EVENTS.

says that he sledged ex-teammate Joey Hughes during the Melbourne derby by saying "You know we're getting paid at Ice now, don't you?" And he goaded a Canadian defenceman with a peculiar accent purely to hear him ask: "Do you woont to goo?"

The afternoon's game, the recent world championships, league gossip – including the coaching exodus at the Ice Dogs – all get an airing. On the second glass of shiraz, I realise there is a common theme here, whether the chat consists of jokes or analysis: character. The players are talking about who they do and don't admire with their tales, and the coaches and administrators are explicit about culture, honesty, responsibility and generosity. The talk from the Ice leadership is of creating a culture that becomes self-policing among the players. They believe they are two years away, which intrigues me, since the group they guide hardly seem a bunch of bad eggs now.

The banter is effortlessly, endlessly amusing. I remember now that team sports can be uniquely stimulating fun when the art of companionship is expedited by wordplay. Clubs are great incubators of language: in-jokes arising from shared moments become a verbal shorthand inaccessible to an outsider, and a protective, reinforcing shield to those within the group. Nicknames, specialised tropes of abuse – they build a sense of otherness that fosters togetherness. The lexicon is always evolving, as stories get told and weighed for their amusement level and their worthiness as staples. The team and club's ethos emerges from these storytelling sessions. It is a most productive idleness, and the player who retreats to his room too quickly is missing out. Typical of the exchanges: Emma says to Johan: "I've told you, it's not all about you!" Johan replies: "It's 90 per cent about me!" I am usually a little slow to form connections, but by day two of this trip, I have dubbed Johan "Supercoach". It is revealed that Joey Hughes gave Josh his "Big Money" nickname. Josh's team-issued backpack is embroidered with dollar signs instead of his name. (He is not excessively wealthy.)

Person by person, the road trip gives each player time to get to know the team and their role within it. Joker, dependable rock, ladies man ... characteristics are tried on for size, by individual and group. The slightly older off-ice team gets the best view of these shifting and settling identities. And they find their own roles as oddbodies, gofers, pseudo-guardians and teachers.

Road manager and club-shaper Ian Webster, big and white of hair and beard, always wears shorts, even in the coldest rink. An outdoors education specialist, he is the arch-organiser, perfectly suited to shunting distracted young men from place to place on time. Ian never backs down from defending his own; he is opinionated, has strict convictions, and speaks his mind, so he has his conflicts. But he is also a thoughtful and generous volunteer and a personable conversationalist with friends all around the league, one of the essential "heart and soul" hockey people Andy McDowell referred to.

Trainer James Meredith is an ex-soccer goalie who spent time with English club West Ham as a junior. He worked at the AFL's Richmond Football Club, but was seeking a more active involvement with sport again. Getting his physiotherapy business Fluid involved with Ice as a service provider as well as a sponsor was a big investment. Quietly spoken, thoughtful, wry, he is always monitoring his players, always switched on. Like Josh, he was brought into the Ice fold by Ian Webster. Josh sums up the feelings of the off-ice crew about this year's team: "There's not one guy here I wouldn't want to chat with".

SUNDAY THE 27TH

ROAD TRIP ONE:
PERTH THUNDER V MELBOURNE ICE
DAY THREE

The team's enemy on the Perth trip is too much time. Meals are a good way to use up some of it, and these energy-burning players will not miss out on their protein. A barbeque breakfast at the hotel offers lashings of bacon and eggs, simple to cook and well-subscribed. Breakfast leftovers are gathered by young fringe forward Daniel Szalinski, who did much of the cooking, an impoverished student. Fellow third-liner Robbie Clarke also scored. He noticed a toothbrush in a package left behind at the breakfast table and asked the breakfast stragglers if it was theirs. When no-one said yes, he grabbed it, having forgotten his own brush. It turned out that the utensil was the property of the coach. Robbie will not live this down for the rest of the trip, Josh Puls quizzing him about his "criminal tendencies" on the way back from the rink ten hours later.

Emma Poynton's hockey-loving mate Nigel Tearle is catching up with her, and he gets involved with the team, helping transport some gear in his van to ease bus congestion, and donning a Maple Leafs jumper to the approval of Sean Hamilton and the chagrin of Jeff Smith, who says Nigel will have to take the offending garment off.

"Where is the Hockey Hall Of Fame?" Nigel asks.

Toronto, comes the answer.

"Where is the NHL War Room?" he inquires.

Toronto.

"Where is the centre of the hockey universe," he asks.

"Melbourne!" Tommy Powell interjects.

Taciturn team manager Tom Harward quietly gathers stray players after lunch. Despite being economic with the chatter, he is a social guy. He just won't be hurried to do or say anything. Tom reminds me of the staunchest mates I had when playing sport, who only spoke when there was something important or amusing to impart. His only words to me this trip? "It's good we [the coaching team] are all fresh. No baggage. If everyone leaves us alone ..."

The best player from each game has to wear an ugly helmet, the incumbent choosing who takes it on next. Emma was sent on a wild goose chase to find a suitably disgraceful "bucket" for 2014, ending up with a beaten-up old white Cooper from the back of a Perth Ice Arena cupboard. Goalie Jaden Pine-Murphy was the original recipient of the headwear for his shutout yesterday. But today, a new road trip ritual is born. A rookie on the road now has to wear a gloriously indecorous koala hat, purchased at a Japanese souvenir shop. Swedish forward Tim Johansson has had this honour all afternoon and professes to love this grey monstrosity, which covers the top of the head and his ears and has two tails which flow down like a Peruvian toque. He spends much of the wait for buses strumming a ukulele while wearing a koala on his head, for all the world a hungover bucks' night victim, not an elegant athlete preparing for battle. "CK" the fussy dresser has embraced the grossest excess of Australian souvenir merchandising; there is no doubt he is making an impression on his teammates, on and off the ice. Tim, 22, who has played high-level Swedish hockey, was on a holiday with his girlfriend when he caught wind of the existence of the Icehouse. Ice forward Jason Baclig, managing the Pro Shop, overheard him and introduced himself. Ice had already signed its main imports, but granted him a tryout. In James Meredith's words, Tim "completely destroyed everything" in such sessions, using gear borrowed from Emma.

The trip to the rink on day two feels like a jaunt to the corner shop after the odyssey of the previous day. The players don't seem complacent or distracted despite having killed so many hours with frivolous chatter and improvised soccer games. They know Perth will come at them harder. The Thunder will improve with a game under their belt, even with their import defender out.

Pre-game, Stan Scott says of Thunder "the boys look confident". It's hard to tell whether the eternally positive coach is indulging in wishful thinking, but for most of the first period his statement appears well founded. Thunder press deeper than Ice, and shut down the visitors more aggressively. Ice incur four penalties to one in the first period, but hold firm. Sean Hamilton provides the best chance for Paul Lazarotto, with a deft pass, but there's no way past Thunder goalie Mathieu Dugas until Jeff Smith stuffs the puck in from close range at the end of Ice's only powerplay of the period. This role, playing as massive obstructer just outside the goal crease on the powerplay, has now yielded Jeff three goals. He says the last time he played as a forward he was six. On Saturday, it was evident he was feeling at home with Ice, his composure at the back exerting order over his shifts. After a rusty first game when fresh off the plane, he is proving every bit the recruit hoped for, on and off the ice.

Between periods, I chat to Perth import Corey Toy, who is signing autographs from behind the merchandise table. His cheekbone was fractured in three places by the ricochet in the opening minutes on Saturday. Working for a church in Perth, he has four SPHL teammates playing in the AIHL this year. He has had four surgeries recently and it is taking a toll, but he hopes to play again in two or three weeks. Thunder defenceman Jamie Woodman told me yesterday that Corey is a "brilliant guy and an excellent motivator" who has been taking him to the gym and "wrecking him" as part of his off-ice conditioning program.

There are no goals or penalties in a tense second period, Ice leading 1-0, and only seven shots each in the fifteen minutes. You can sense something will break. Thunder is much more tenacious than during Saturday's game. Eventually, it is a five-minute major for checking to the head, considered contentious by Thunder and its fans, which looks the game-breaker. But even then, Ice cannot score.

Both goalies are exceeding themselves, Jayden Pine-Murphy playing better than on Saturday, Mathieu Dugas denying several close range chances. Ice finally break through with eight minutes left, stand-in skipper Tommy Powell receiving the pass in the high slot, then using a toe-drag to force the moment's hesitation which helps him finally get the puck past Mathieu Dugas. Ice have fought long and hard for safety at 2–0, but a minute later their weekend gets its cherry on top, Matt Armstrong out-skating an opponent in his own zone, pushing deep down the left, then sending a peach back to Jason Baclig, who ladles it past Mathieu with a one-timer. Ice's second 3-0 win has been much more difficult to achieve than the first, Jayden Pine-Murphy's heroics in net featuring 33 stops instead of 22, but tradition makes him the judge of best player, and Jeff Smith happily dons the white helmet.

Emma doesn't like that some players wore non-club issued shorts into the rink; it looked 'unprofessional'. James Meredith says he hated uniforms at school, but he now appreciates their worth to a team. A different sort of uniform provides the lasting image from the rink. Josh Puls tells me that as he stood guard on a dressing room door that would not close properly, intending to protect his players' modesty, it became evident that Tim was holding up his end of the new rookie headwear tradition. When the door was flung most wide open to the departing public, Josh said the Swede could be seen, naked as the day he was born, but for the ridiculous koala hat on top of his head.

MONDAY THE 28TH

Perth has a strong and growing hockey culture.

While I was enjoying my first road trip, the league's confounding opening continued. Adelaide opened their season by delivering 2013 runner-up Newcastle their second 4–0 loss at home. But Canberra Brave were the big news, welcoming recruits Mathieu Ouellette (two goals) and Stephen Blunden (two assists) by stunning the Ice Dogs 6–2 to thrill their fans old and new. They scored four unanswered goals in the final period to deliver the first win of the new franchise in its second outing, against the reigning champions. On Sunday, it took a shootout for Adelaide to overcome the Bears 6–5, also starting the season with strong form.

The Mustangs have had an untimely hiatus, with no game scheduled between their overtime loss to Ice on 19 April and their second Ice Dogs home fixture on 3 May. Pat tells me the players used the week off to "catch up on the rest of our lives" and to bond. "We made the most of it, the whole team got together and we had some fun. We got to know the new guys." He feels this event – "a few drinks, some laughs" – was necessary because the team has not yet had a road trip. "There's nothing like road trips to Perth, they're so much fun. You're just with the team, you have two whole days with the guys and it's definitely a huge advantage to have it early in the season. It's important to build chemistry as soon as possible. Any time you get to spend quality time together is important." The weekend Mustangs gathering introduced the group to late-arriving import Jeff Grant, a Burlington, Massachusetts-born SPHL stalwart and former teammate of Jack Wolgemuth, who had just finished his first season with the Louisiana Ice Gators after four years with Mississippi Surge. Pat says it will be strange playing the coach-less Ice Dogs, but the Mustangs have to concentrate on their own game. "It doesn't mean they're not talented players and they can't kick your ass any given night."

The Mustangs are as interested in the dazzling start from CBR Brave as any other AIHL watchers. "I think it's important that the league is tougher because you're only as good as your weakest team," Pat says. He admits it was "tough to show up" when the Mustangs took on the ailing Knights last year.

Pat has just hosted his brother for a week. He says his sibling is different to him, and he wanted to make sure they were doing things his brother enjoyed in Melbourne. I'm interested to hear what an American living in Langwarrin decides to showcase of Victoria. There are some solid choices – the Great Ocean Road and Mount Dandenong – but I like his description of Melbourne's vaunted laneway and alley culture best. In Melbourne's CBD Pat and his brother went to "a lot of corny bars", the frank Yank says.

MAY 2014

SATURDAY THE 3RD

At my next hockey assignation after the Ice road-trip, the Mustangs' home game against the Ice Dogs, I find myself sat beside Brent Laver, Johan Steenberg and James Meredith. Johan likes me greeting him "Supercoach", but I am corrected by the other two Ice luminaries: after the Perth trip, he is officially known as the "yolie coach", Josh Puls's interpretation of Johan's Swedish accent having stuck. His student and housemate, Ice import goalie Gustaf Huth, is also quietly ensconced. I tell the Ice staff how much I enjoyed the road trip, and how much their players seemed to bond away from home. James admits that he would prefer that Ice played a full road trip around the nation before having a "homecoming" game. "They get more nervous playing at home," he says.

Johan says the Dogs are very well organised for a team that has been without a coach for ten days. There is mention made of some Dogs players being asked to pay more than others to play. The Dogs, despite winning last year's championship, are not one of the more financially powerful AIHL clubs, and their players have to fork out for costs to keep the team on the ice.

For the first period, it appears the Mustangs are being careful after their week off, their usual up-tempo style compromised in order to ensure lethal Dogs stretch passes don't breach their neutral zone defence. The Mustangs depend on the passing game themselves, however, and when they take more risks at higher pace in the second period, the puck starts hitting the tape. Pat hits the crossbar when left alone in the slot, but fellow imports Viktor Gibbs Sjodin, and Jeff Grant, a defenceman fresh off the plane, find the net. Grant's two powerplay goals give the Mustangs a 3–0 lead after a dominant second period. Fox commentator and former Ice championship-winning coach Paul "Jaffa" Watson says "The Dogs look like they don't want to be out there ... effort is the key."

The Mustangs are in total command at the beginning of the third period, but they linger too long over good chances, and make one too many passes. It is what coach Brad Vigon later calls "too pretty" hockey. The hockey gods punish such largesse. Early season scoring-machine Simon Barg gets a wraparound past Fraser Carson to make it 3–1. Then the Mustangs spurn a four-minute powerplay. Suddenly, the limp Dog rushes have pace and purpose, and the remainder of the game is tense. Simon Barg adds the seemingly inevitable second goal thanks to a canny stretch pass with just over three minutes remaining, and it seems the Mustangs may throw away a game they owned. But they are not kids any more. The home team holds their composure and Jamie Bourke adds the empty-netter with twelve seconds left for a 4–2 win over the reigning champs. The loud Mustangs fans rejoice. Their first-choice goalie Fraser Carson has fought through his first game of the season with 20 saves on 22 shots.

I chat to Brad Vigon outside the rooms after the game, in what is now a very active post-match scene. Mustangs volunteer reporters conduct video interviews; family and friends mingle at the dressing room doors; and Brad's kids are pulling at his suit, asking if they are allowed to kick their soccer ball. Yes is the answer, because that allows Dad to tell us that the week off came at a bad time for his team. "We hadn't played in two weeks and that definitely told in our play in the first period." After the increased pace delivered a three-goal lead, the players "started getting a little bit fancy". "We stopped doing the things which got us to a three-goal lead in the first place, trying to score too pretty a goal instead of taking a shot. We're making an extra pass, it's not coming off ... they get one goal, they get a sniff." I ask if this reluctance to shoot is unselfishness gone too far, but the Mustangs coach will have none of it. "I don't know if it's unselfish if they want to score a goal that's pretty. Put the puck on the net and clean up the rebounds, it doesn't have to look like the Russians."

Brad is impressed with recruit Jeff Grant, who has scored twice in his first Mustangs outing. The scouting report, which said he could play defence but remain a scoring threat, appears vindicated. The Mustangs coach is less sanguine about the fixture, though he searches for a silver lining. After two games that are way more intense than any amount of training could offer, some players have a couple of niggles. But he admits that he didn't want a break. "We had that little bit of momentum, we were playing well, we wanted to keep rolling into it but now we can move on."

Sydney's fixture anomaly is that they travel to Melbourne twice in the opening four rounds. Though Melbourne is the most comfortable trip for most teams – the rink is relatively close to the airport, and accommodation is near the venue and the rest of the city – facing the Mustangs and Ice on consecutive days is not shaping as an easy ask in 2014.

SUNDAY THE 4TH

The Dogs back-up on Sunday against Ice knowing that a loss will leave them with one win from five games, a major head start to give their rivals in a 28-game season. The pre-game ceremony celebrates Mother's Day with Ice players admonishing Marcus Wong for not kissing his mum, who presides at the ceremonial puck drop. It is a gentle, affectionate way for a combative game to begin, but Ice like it that way this year. Ice start with Gustaf Huth in goal, so their extra import skater Swede Tim Johansson sits out. The Swedish goalie is extended early, the defence in front of him looking more vulnerable to rebounds than the Mustangs. But Ice hold on, and when they get powerplays, they make the Dogs pay.

Yesterday Brent said "this is a special teams league". As if to demonstrate, Ice pound three powerplay goals past Dogs goalie Tim Noting. Jeff Smith gets an assist on the first, which Lliam Webster powers past the glove with a rocket from a heavily screened slot. Jeff says he is enjoying the chance to "just play hockey". In many leagues, at his size, he is the designated fighter–protector; he arrived with puffy eyes from taking blows in Britain's Elite Ice Hockey League with the Hull Stingrays. But in the AIHL he's resisting every entreaty to "dance", and they are coming thick and fast. Jeff is a vigorous, timely defensive presence, and a surprisingly potent attacker on the powerplay. It's clear that he hasn't lost his aggression, his on-ice chirping disturbing opponents. The fiery Tim Noting in particular is aggrieved throughout this encounter, ending up with two penalties and two misconducts.

Despite conceding many more scoring chances than their rinkmates did the day before, and relying on Gustaf's work in net, Ice hold a 3–0 lead with half the second period to play. The Dogs are frustrated and losing their cool collectively. The Ice fans have started yelling "HUUUUUUTH" every time Gus blocks a shot. The festive atmosphere goes up a notch when Austin McKenzie makes it 4–0 late in the second period. Austin, just 21, looks faster, stronger and more assured this season.

Mitch Humphries, 21, and Sam Hodic, seventeen, create two huge chances early in the final period, and it's a poor shift by Ice's first line that concedes the first Dogs goal. Once again, the reigning champion are finding their best hockey under the most duress, when well behind. Aussie young gun Billy Cliff's shot is not cleared and Chris Sekura fires home the rebound to make it 4–2 with nine minutes to play. The Dogs press and Ice cannot put together any meaningful attacks to ease the pressure. But from a face-off, Lliam Webster's strength creates a chance and Austin Mckenzie buries a backhand to record a hat-trick and end the game with five minutes to play. 5–2.

Cue yet more Dogs penalties. They end up killing off a five on three, looking an unhappy team, Tim Noting being penalised a game misconduct after the final whistle in his final tangle with Jeff Smith. They are 1–4 without a coaching replacement and their ace goalie is out of their next game. The title defence is not proceeding as planned in western Sydney.

For Ice, their 9–2 loss at the same venue to the same team just three weeks earlier is now forgotten. No matter what the coaches say, no team in this league can miss half a dozen top-liners and remain competitive. It wasn't just classy veterans Lliam Webster and Tommy Powell who were missing. It turns out Ice are now highly reliant on the likes of new Australian representatives Austin McKenzie and Mitch Humphries. Austin scored fourteen points in 26 games last year. He has five in three games so far in 2014.

Newcastle is the other superpower in trouble at the outset of the season, after losing 3–1 to the Sydney Bears on Saturday. That makes one goal in three games for the 2013 runners-up, and a 1–3 record. The Bears could not be much happier – two wins and a shootout loss making their opening brighter than many would have predicted. Perth Thunder's tough start ended with a heartbreaking road double against Adelaide – a shootout win on Saturday, when they conceded the lead with 1.30 left in the final period, and a 1–0 loss on Sunday. They cannot fault their choice of import goalie so far: Mathieu Dugas stopped 104 of 108 shots he faced over the weekend. The irresistible compulsion now is to write that he "really earnt his money" with that effort. In lieu of payment, let's hope he was proffered a refreshing beverage by team brass after that effort. Thunder at least now have two points after four games, and seem to be hitting their straps despite still missing key imports.

THURSDAY THE 8TH

I have only one team shot, from 1981, which Glenn Grandy provided me, that contains a picture of Andrew Petrie, our junior teammate. But I remember him. He was a consistent scoring threat, despite not having great pace. He read the game well, got where the puck was, or was going. He was a little tubby, self-confident, pugnacious. I liked him.

Andrew Petrie takes on a troubled club.

Thirty-three years later, Andrew Petrie has just been appointed coach of the Sydney Ice Dogs, and this is his estimation of his playing abilities: "I was never the most skilled player, but I've always felt I knew how the game flowed, how its structures and systems work and what you need to do to be successful." Ice coach Brent Laver said this of Andrew: "He was a great hockey player, I learnt a lot from him. He was a student of the game, just one of those guys who saw the whole ice and could really sort of dissect it for you."

Those who played with Andrew longer than me, or were coached by him, know him as "Frij". Ian Webster described him as a "classic mesomorph". Perhaps as a result, Andrew became a gym junkie. He met his wife in a North Sydney gym after leaving Melbourne to run an inline shop on Manly beach, and he never returned south. Though Andrew says he stopped playing at the highest level when he became "too old, slow and fat", he is hardly a couch potato, still playing every week, and participating in over-35s hockey trips to Thailand and Hong Kong.

Despite representing his country and playing hockey in Canada, Andrew is respectful of the "very highly skilled group" he has inherited, and admits he is "like a fan" watching them at training. He has to remind himself that he is not a teammate but a boss of the players on the Ice Dogs bench. However, coaching has been an ambition. "I've always had a real desire to do it (coach). I probably lacked the grounding and structure in life to commit to do it for a season until now, and I was always playing." Andrew has definite ideas on how to mould his talented Ice Dogs. "I'm trying to work more on very basic structures from a hockey perspective. I don't want to teach these guys fancy plays; I just want them to adopt fairly basic offensive and defensive structures. We do quite a bit of work on special teams – powerplay and penalty kill – but what I want to achieve is more to do with their collective attitude to the game and each other rather than teach them in terms of skills. What I am really interested is group dynamics. What you can always do with a group is get them to come together and play for each other and just learn to dig deep when the going gets tough."

Andrew has a positive attitude to poor form. "Sometimes when you've got a really highly skilled group of guys, adversity throws them a bit because they're so used to doing well. So what I'd like to do is draw that collective discipline together and help put mechanisms in place to deal with adversity when they encounter it." On a small scale, the Ice Dogs have already faced adversity this season. Coaching and administrative "turmoil" were followed by multiple losses.

Andrew is the most diplomatically astute AIHL personality I have met. I ask him about his club's reputation as party animals, and the departure of his coaching predecessors. He says there is "no misunderstanding" about what is expected from the players and he would be "extremely disappointed" if any player stepped out of line. He says the club is in the process of instituting a proper administrative structure, but for now his position is subject to a very informal arrangement. "There was a lot of angst involved at the time I came on board. Thankfully I wasn't a party to it, so I came on with a clear understanding of what was required to rectify the situation. It was a fairly interesting environment. I needed to come to an understanding with the club leadership about what they wanted to achieve. Then I needed to win the trust of the playing group and galvanise them as a group of men."

Despite the Dogs being the reigning champions, Andrew says he doesn't think the group "recognises collectively just how talented they are". "Within this group, despite reputation and rumour, there's a really strong leadership group. There's a lot of maturity and a couple of senior guys have played very good hockey in very good leagues and that is filtering down through the group. It's just a really good bunch of guys. It's not difficult to work with them."

Having played with the Blackhawks and the Demons in Victoria, Andrew moved to Sydney in the mid-nineties, where he played with the Blacktown Bullets, who became the AIHL's Sydney Ice Dogs, where he played in 2002–03. He also suited up for the short-lived AIHL team the Central Coast Rhinos (much closer to where he lives) in 2005, playing eleven games for seventeen points. When he heard about the vacancy at the Dogs, Andrew contacted Ice Dogs president Shane Rose. "I had a connection to the club, I still knew some people here and I have a lot of affection for the organisation and was more than happy to put my hand up and help out."

As a replacement coach taking over a troubled club, he is not ideally positioned to think big, but he has opinions about what the AIHL needs. "We're not completely professional nor are we completely amateur. If all the teams were self-sustaining financially then we could look at a collective effort to push the sport up the market ladder a bit. I'd just love for the sport to succeed. I'd love to see it become mainstream. If I had ten years I'd love to nurture an environment where four or five years from now we had two lines of purely Australian players that skated all the time. As a coach you've got to try and find the balance between development and exposure of your fringe players and winning games of hockey. It is the biggest challenge, even more so than discipline."

Discipline. It is the word that everyone mentions in relation to the Ice Dogs. But there are more tangible realities governing the future of the Ice Dogs, who operate on a shoestring. "Financial challenges abound," Andrew admits. "I can't speak for other clubs, but they're very real for us and there's a lot of people putting their heads together to find a solution to that." He says it would be "unfair on a number of parties" to discuss the rumoured disparities in player payments in his group. In the AIHL, that means how much the players pay, not envy over income.

Andrew says that there are challenges particular to teams playing in Sydney, "an incredibly competitive market". "We've seen organisations with millions and millions of dollars struggle to get market share so we're clearly up against it. It's a niche sport, so we look for niche fans. The fans that we do have at the Ice Dogs are incredibly motivated and loyal. There's a particular group that makes more noise than a hundred people could, they're at every game, they're committed, and they're very, very involved. But from a business perspective I'd hate to have to launch [ice hockey in Sydney] with my own money on the line, it's very difficult. Liverpool [home of the Ice Dogs rink] is a heavily populated area but how do you get it out there that there's this entertainment that people can come along and watch?"

Andrew was bullish after his first training session, despite all the challenges he had just taken on, saying contemporary AIHL hockey is "the most exciting I've seen in my 35 years." Hockey has been the "one consistent passion" in his life over those three and a half decades. "There are two things I need in my life. I need to make enough money to support my family and I need a passion to identify myself with. If I could ever find a way to kill two birds with one stone, that's when I would be truly happy. If I could make what I would need to make to support my family by coaching kids and running the Ice Dogs I'd be ecstatic. But at least in my lifetime it's not going to be."

FRIDAY THE 9TH

Sydney Ice Dogs president Shane Rose doesn't sound overly concerned that his entire coaching panel has departed and his team is five games into the season with only one win. He believes in his coaching appointee Andrew Petrie. "I think he will be a perfect fit for what I want." He says he and Andrew are "culturally aligned". That statement gives a clue to his real preoccupation – not wins and losses, but culture change. A non-drinker, Shane Rose presided over the makeover that helped deliver a title last year, but his work is far from done. It's all about that 'D' word. "Last year we had quite good discipline but still not really where we need to be and I think we've just had a relapse. We need to be more disciplined on the ice, people need to be accountable for their actions. The club has a responsibility to provide the right image for juniors to aspire to. I think a lot of AIHL teams have to look at how Melbourne are going, they're leading the pack here ... Drinking, or any other sort of partying antics that go on ... that's all going to be curbed."

Shane is trying to build a club that will contend into the future. "It's not about winning another title. It's about making sure you're winning titles that are built on the right foundations. So that for the future you can build, you've got juniors coming through the ranks and you can continue to win championships. If we have our foundations set right, the rest will follow." These words don't sound like platitudes, given what Rose says next. "I look at it from my own point of view, I have seven kids. Would I want to send my sixteen-year-old son to be training with a team without a solid character?"

In amateur clubs without a large number of people involved, such culture change can mean it gets personal. Shane's sympathy for former Canberra boss John Raut is telling. He says the Brave story is great and emphasises that he doesn't know all the details of what went down in Canberra. But ... "We just need to be mindful that we don't have players holding clubs to ransom. Players say 'well I'm not going to play' and basically clubs can't operate. I'm not saying that's what happened but ... We've just got to be careful. If you put on too much discipline players don't like ... next thing you know they ... come up with a new club? We've just got to be careful that doesn't happen."

For all that, Shane, like most club-runners, believes in his charges. "The quality in the players is there. I have faith in the players, it's the discipline that's killing us." He believes that had the Dogs stayed out of the penalty box, they would have beaten Ice in Melbourne recently. And he believes the players are embracing his vision for the Sydney Ice Dogs. "The feedback that Andrew has got, it's all been very positive. They're happy that there's more structure and more discipline, maybe they were screaming out for this."

He says more volunteers are on board and more season tickets are being sold. But the reformation of a club with a rebellious attitude in its DNA sounds like it has been trying. "When I took over it was like a fifteen year-old boy that had never been disciplined and it was my job to lay down the law and try to put down processes and procedures to make this a professional outfit. It's not going to happen overnight and there's going to be lots and lots of challenges. The previous coach did a great job. It's the next phase in our journey and Andrew is the right guy to take us on this journey."

FRIDAY THE 9TH (2)

Every team runner I talk to emphasises the importance of the league being even, with the title winner unpredictable, and every team competitive. So far, the 2014 season fulfils this ambition. On Saturday 10 May, the grand finalists of 2013, Newcastle and the Sydney Ice Dogs, clash at Liverpool in Sydney, both more desperate than they've been for years to win because they are second last and third last in the standings. There is not a team that believes they cannot make the playoffs.

Sydney Ice Dogs general manager Shane Rose reiterated the importance of parity as I spoke to him about his new coaching appointment. "We need every team to be competitive ... and we need to make allowances for the teams that aren't competitive. We don't want our league to become like the English Premier League [soccer], where only a couple of teams can win the title and the rest are just there to make up the numbers. We want fans to be asking 'who's going to win this year?' " Early season bolters may yet come back to the field as teams bed down their full line-ups, but the question at the moment is not which team will win the championship, it is "Who is going to win this week?"

Perth Thunder, placed last, took points out of their road trip to Adelaide and have played with their import forwards for only two games. They must be the strongest last-placed team in recent memory and now have a home double-header against the Bears. Their ace scoring threat Justin Fox is yet to arrive.

Newcastle has defended well enough, with import goalie Harrison May making a solid start, but they have scored only three goals in four games. If their well-credentialed import forwards start finding the net, they will be in every game. And later in the year, their gun local youngster Beau Taylor returns to further bolster their firepower.

The Sydney Ice Dogs, reigning AIHL champions, pummelled an under-strength Ice in the season's first game, but that has been their only win. The talent level is still high, but the off-ice ructions have clearly had an effect. But if they are galvanised by the impressive Andrew Petrie, they remain one of the league's most potent combinations.

Canberra's CBR Brave have played just two games, a "respectable" defeat first up to the North Stars, and a barnstorming win over the Dogs, in which they scored four third-period goals. They look obviously improved, but their real standing will be determined when they leave the embrace of their adoring fans and hit the road. Their clash with the North Stars in Newcastle on Sunday should say a lot about both clubs.

The Mustangs lack for little. Their attack, with Pat O'Kane buttressed by talented locals Jamie Bourke, Joey Hughes and Brendan McDowell, has allowed them to shore up the defence with imports Jack Wolgemuth and Jeff Grant. But both of those defencemen are huge scoring threats, playmakers as much as stoppers. On top of that, the Stangs have a solid core of young, fast locals, meaning they play a genuine three lines. Little wonder the club felt it could back local goalies. If that risk comes off they are a title threat. If they continue to play up-tempo hockey, their continual pressure will wear down a lot of teams.

The Sydney Bears would be the feel-good story of the year but for the Canberra resurrection. They were more mediocre than terrible last year, but never seriously threatened to be a finalist. At the outset of 2014, however, they are hard to score against and are yet to be beaten in regulation time. Their import forwards are scoring, but so is their 20-year-old national team ace, Cameron Todd. Their clashes on the road to Perth could define the trajectory of both club's seasons.

Adelaide, the most low-key team of the pre-season, have been outstanding, overpowering the North Stars then fighting back from a three goal deficit in the last period against the Bears, and holding the improving Thunder at bay at home.

Ice will continue to gain playing strength as the season progresses. By the time promising youngster Jeremy Brown and stalwart defenceman Todd Graham join the squad they will be almost unrecognisable from the team that leaked nine goals in a home ice loss to the Dogs on the opening day. They may look back at the second round road trip to Perth as a godsend. The squad re-grouped superbly out west, and the bonding momentum gained from those two 3–0 wins has been significant.

SATURDAY THE 10TH

Why do goalies ever leave their crease? There seems too much risk for too little reward in a net-minder leaving his net. In the NHL it is necessary for goalies to be more interventionist in search of a one-percenter that prises open an advantage, but in the sudden-death AIHL?

In the second Melbourne derby, Melbourne Ice defeated Melbourne Mustangs 5–3. Four of Ice's goals were as a result of catastrophic mistakes from the Mustangs. Two of them were errors from goalies straying too far from home. In another dramatic, pulsating game between the increasingly heated rivals, these giveaways muddy assessment of the true standing of the teams. And they inevitably bring scrutiny upon the Mustangs' bold call to back their local goalies instead of an import.

In keeping with the aura now surrounding these Melbourne stoushes, there was some intrigue when the teams lined up. Michael James, not Fraser Carson, was in net for the Mustangs. Jaden Pine-Murphy, not import Gustaf Huth, the fans' new cult hero, was in for Ice. That meant flying forward Tim Johansson was back in the Ice line-up. So exciting is the unexpected Swede that it was suggested after the game that one of the other ice imports, Jason Baclig or Matt Armstrong, might have to sit out at some stage to enable the flying Swede to get more game time. This would have been considered sacrilegious prior to this season.

Michael James' stint in net was brief and agonising. A couple of minutes in, the shorthanded Ice dumped the puck in along the boards and behind the net. Imposing skipper Lliam Webster was there on the opposite wing when the puck completed its journey. He later told his dad Ian that he decided to just get a shot on net. He did that. But when he fired and looked up, he was shocked, as were the 1500 others watching, to see an empty net. Michael had left his stick behind, and while retrieving it from behind the net, Lliam's speculative shot went in unimpeded. 1–0 for Ice.

Ice had to conjure their second goal themselves, a superb look-away backhand pass from Lliam setting up Tim Johansson for a backhand score from close range. 2–0 to Ice.

Michael James did not return as Mustangs goalie after the first period, nineteen-year-old Fraser Carson his replacement. Fraser's opening minutes were promising, but five minutes in, in-form Ice ace Austin McKenzie fired a shot wide of the net, and kept skating hard at the crease, picking up the rebound off

Mustangs goalies Fraser Carson and Michael James.

Melbourne derbies are never short of drama.

the backboard, and slotting it past the hapless goalie, who had drifted too far out and left a big gap behind him.

The contest did not feel like a 3-0 game, despite the habitual slow start from the Mustangs. They had been unable to convert six minutes of powerplays in the first period. It was almost as if the one-man advantage rendered them impotent, as they fussed over too many options, refusing to get shots away. Once the game opened up, with fewer stoppages, they found their rhythm, Jamie Bourke and Jack Wolgemuth combining superbly for a shorthanded goal to cut the deficit to two goals. But it seemed the Mustangs were destined to set themselves a big task. Matt Anderson started out of his zone seemingly oblivious to the rather large presence of Lliam Webster in the slot. Steal, powerful wrister, goal. 4–1.

It wasn't the destiny of this game to be one-sided, however. Mustangs skipper Sean Jones, Jamie Bourke and Pat O'Kane combined beautifully just over a minute later, Pat making sure of the tic-tac-toe goal by getting down on his knee. 4-2. From then on, the Mustangs just kept coming, and Ice kept resisting. Viktor Gibbs-Sjodin repeatedly rushed the length of the ice, Jack Wolgemuth became a damaging creative presence at the back, and the game reached the frenzied tempo now expected in these encounters.

With the pace of the game accelerating, time seemed to be on the side of the Mustangs in the final period. With 12.10 remaining, Vinnie Hughes took advantage of a bad Ice line change to split the defenders with a perfect pass to the late-arriving Andrew Fitzgerald. 4–3. The tension and crowd involvement rose yet again.

Ice kill more penalties. Jaden Pine-Murphy pulls off more big saves. The end of regulation time seems to be a magnet pulling an inevitable Mustangs equalising goal. Their pressure becomes more and more relentless. They rattle the iron twice … It's end-to-end hockey. There's incident upon incident, no time to digest one before the next cascades upon us. A big save from Fraser Carson; then Jamie Bourke fans on a breakaway; then Pat O'Kane out-skates the defence and is just stopped; and Jack Wolgemuth's huge shot off the rebound is saved. Finally, with just under two minutes left, there is some respite as the puck is dumped into the Mustangs zone. But Stangs goalie Fraser Carson drifts out to gather the puck … and his 'pass' across ice goes straight to the stick of Ice forward Chris Wong, gliding into the slot. He dumps the puck into the empty net gleefully. 5–3. Game over.

Mustangs coach Brad Vigon, red-faced and crushed after the loss, is not about to allow anyone to "call out" young Fraser, whom he said would be able to overcome the defining act of the game, which commentators described as "lunacy", "insane" and a "howler". But he confirms that he wants "no wandering" from his goalies. "Nothing bad is going to happen if you stay in the net. I don't want them to ever leave the net." Even with the loss so raw, Brad is even-handed. Both goalies will escape censure. They know what they have done wrong. Their errors bookmarked another classic derby. "There's only one way to learn."

Mustangs hockey director Andy McDowell's habitual smile is now a philosophical grimace, which he admits is masking pain. He muses on the nature of experience, how you need mistakes to learn. His verdict on a game the Mustangs threw away, and the goalie mistakes? "They won't be doing that again."

Ice boss Brent Laver is more than happy with his goalie Jaden Pine-Murphy. The Kiwi had his shutout streak ended at 142 minutes during the derby, but again performed strongly. Brent praises the "fantastic" work of "yolie coach" Johan Steenberg. "Our goals-against reads really well, it's just comes down to the work that he's done."

Brent wasn't surprised by the fever pitch nature of the derby. "You know that they're going to bring the intensity, because that's what Brad's got them doing, playing with that spirit and that energy and you know straight away that you've got to try to match it," he said. "You look at the stands and just the energy coming down to the bench is incredible. It's awesome for Australian hockey."

Oh, oh ... Fraser Carson's fateful pass.

SUNDAY THE 11TH

There was plenty going on around the league while the dramatic derby entranced Melbourne fans. On Saturday, NHL prospect Nathan Walker dropped the puck at the Sydney Ice Dogs versus Newcastle clash at Liverpool. Missing their suspended goalie Tom Noting, the Dogs conceded the three goals scored in the final period to lose 5–3 and plummet to the bottom of the standings. North Star import Chris Wilson found his range with a goal and four assists. The North Stars scored three of their goals on the powerplay.

Adelaide halted Brave's fairytale start to the season with a 6–2 win in Canberra. Adelaide Adrenaline captain Greg Oddy says his team is playing to erase the disappointment of missing last year's playoffs. "We know what we are capable of. We've got the guys that have been there before and done it and we know what we can do if we are playing at our best," he said about his team's strong start to the year.

The Sydney Bears had a laudable 4-3 shootout win in Perth, further consolidating their encouraging season start, import Sean Hamilton-Steen scoring twice. He has two further claims to fame: a brother, Alexander, in the NHL, and his cameo role in the hockey feature film *Goon*.

Sunday's results could prove even more telling. The Bears beat Thunder 3–2 in regulation, to take a remarkable five points out of six from their road trip west. Hamilton-Steen again netted twice, and obviously gifted goalie Bears Daniel Palmkvist stopped 40 of 42 shots faced.

Brave bounced back from their home rink loss to win in Newcastle, 4–2. Brave have now matched their two wins tally from the 2013 season in just four games. The North Stars have lost all three home games, in which they have scored just twice.

And in Liverpool, with goalie Tim Noting back, the Ice Dogs stunned the in-form Adelaide with a 10–4 thrashing, local David Dunwoodie tallying seven points and import John Clewlow four goals. "I've learned some lessons and had a chance to learn about the boys," Andrew Petrie said after his first win as coach. "I've only had one practice session on Thursday where I watched them before setting up the roster to play." Adelaide Adrenaline coach Ryan O'Handley says a tough game against CBR Brave had left his team a little "flat" for the clash at Liverpool. "CBR Brave are a good team and it was a hard physical hockey game on Saturday," O'Handley says. "We had some penalties in that game where we were down to three on D and that showed today. There was a bit of carry-over from that where we were making mental mistakes that we don't normally make. But that's hockey."

The Ice Dogs, off the bottom of the table after their second win, host the Melbourne Ice next Saturday and the Melbourne Mustangs on Sunday. The clashes will have a personal dimension for Andrew, who played against both coaches. "Brent Laver is a good friend of mine from my Melbourne days," Petrie says. "I wish him all the luck in the world against every team in the league except for us. The Mustangs are a well-oiled, well-drilled, enthusiastic and well-structured team. Any teams that don't have a great deal of disparity between their best player and worst player are the teams that are going to succeed in this competition, and I see them as one of those teams."

It's early in the season, but the standings are fascinating. Perennial finalist Melbourne Ice leads with fourteen points, but the top four is rounded out by Adelaide Adrenaline, the Sydney Bears and the Melbourne Mustangs, none of which made the finals in 2013.

SATURDAY THE 17TH

The Sydney Bears, off to their best start in years, are supported by a small crew of hardy survivors, train once a week at a rink they don't play at, and operate under the smallest budget in the league. And the potentially excellent rink they play at, the Sydney Ice Arena, just twelve years old, is slated for demolition. Its owner, the Hillsong Church, has received council approval for a massive double-tower housing development on the rink site. The imminent redevelopment includes a swimming pool, a tennis court and some trees - but no ice rink.

Vlad Rubes, the Czech-born and raised Australian national team stalwart and Bears coach, is affable, philosophical and diplomatic. He's seen it all before. "SIA is a fantastic facility but ... It is out of our hands. This is the way it is ... You try to get in the best position you possibly can."

Vlad was there when the Sydney Ice Arena, then named the Glaciarium, opened twelve years ago. He played with the Bears in the halcyon days of the 1990s, when the club packed out the Macquarie rink in North Ryde, 20 minutes from the Sydney CBD. He has seen boom and bust, staunch and fickle sponsors, generous and unreliable benefactors and a move of venue westward, initially to Penrith, even further from the coast. He saw the club enter the AIHL as a power, and struggle for wins and fans in recent years. Vlad's career dream was to be a professional hockey coach. "It's totally different here [in Australia] with hockey not being professional. I would like to be a professional coach but I would have to go back home. It's not to be."

Vlad was until recently coach of the Australian national team. His charges won Division Two gold in Melbourne in 2011. Prior to that, he had overseen the rise through the ranks of national junior teams. He wishes he still had the national team job, but refuses to be negative about even that. "Not being away with the national team definitely gave me time to focus on the Bears," he says. More time spent on off-ice sessions, which have been embraced by his players; more time looking for the right imports.

Vlad measures the health of the team by its enthusiasm for training. "We went through some tough years where going to training was hard for everybody, for coaching staff and definitely for players. Sometimes you are looking for excuses for why this happened or why you can't come, but when everybody plays better and the team is doing better everybody seems to find ways to be at training and come to the games. At 9 pm the last two weeks, watching guys getting ready for training, laughing around and warming up, it was a great feeling."

Queried about the club's lack of major sponsorship, he says only that if the club plays better, it will attract more support. It sounds simple, but that's the reality of Sydney, one of the most competitive leisure and entertainment markets in the world.

Vlad is reluctant, ahead of a double-header against the well-performed Melbourne teams, to talk up his team too much, saying they have been "lucky". But he can't hide his pleasure at the early-season efforts of his tight-knit group. "The goaltending is very strong, imports are playing well. The first game we were missing Cam Todd and Michael Schlamp who were away with the national team ... but the locals are all playing well. So now we have imports, the guys from national team and the local guys who are able to step up and play really well. If we add another import or a guy who played on the national team who plays D [defence], we would be even better. We don't have that experience on defence, but we have pretty strong offence and strong goaltending so that's why we're doing well in games with one goal differences. If you come back ... It happened in Perth last week, it gives you confidence."

Vlad says the Bears are a "humble and hardworking team." He could be describing himself. He is the product of a rink-heavy landscape, having played hockey in the Czech Republic from the age of five. "There's no competition; soccer is a summer sport," he says. "In winter time you play hockey. It's a big sport there." A friend who played in Sydney alerted Vlad to Australian hockey. "He came here to improve his English and got involved with Canterbury Eagles in 1996. And he sent me a letter which interested me in coming. I came in 1996 for two and a half years and played with Sydney Bears in the second year. I had to go back to Czech to finish uni." He returned in January 2000, the chance to play for Australia a major attraction. Unable to make a living as a coach, he works as a production manager in a chemical company.

It took a back injury to finally curtail Vlad's playing career at the end of last season at the age of 43. He had played 235 games for the Bears, a total attained by very few in Australia. Two years ago, he was still putting up stellar numbers, averaging 1.8 points a game. "Maybe it's a good thing in some way because otherwise I would still try to be out there. I was ready to stop playing three, four years ago, but they persuaded me to come back when there were no players."

He sounds grateful the decision to stop playing was taken out of his hands, and says he is having more fun coaching the Bears without national duties on his plate. He says he always had a bench coach running games while he played, but having his undivided attention on gameday is working well for the team. It might be part of the reason the Bears have made such a great start to the season. Picking up some talented recruits hasn't hurt either. Alec Stephenson came across from the Ice Dogs, and the imports are firing. Vlad says a lot of research and hard work behind the scenes goes into their choice of internationals.

Vlad says the culture of a team depends on leadership. If that is strong, you don't need rules. "It's hard to control, they are not kids. You don't want to be policing them. If they were professionals, you could tell them exactly what to do."

For a man who will never be able to make a living at the job he loves, Vlad is very well-adjusted. It might explain why he is so well-liked around the league. "As a coach you can't have a better feeling than if you see the people going on the ice and working hard."

SATURDAY THE 17TH

ROAD TRIP TWO:
SYDNEY BEARS V MELBOURNE MUSTANGS
DAY ONE

"When you think of Australia, you think of Sydney," says Mustangs' American import Jeff Grant. It's a reason why the Sydney teams, based in the boondocks and possessing small support bases, continue to attract high-quality internationals to their clubs. Beaches, cliffs, inlets, brash big-city energy … Sydney's image screams 'fun!' It may lack some of the subtle pleasures of Melbourne, the nooks and precinct-based sub-cultures, but its coast is so gosh-durned pretty. Think Sydney, and you think of barefoot walks on crowded beaches in sunshine. You think 'party!' But that attitude is the tourist's prerogative. The reality is that Sydney is more expensive and more highly pressured than anywhere else in Australia. Many Australians who don't live in Sydney say, "It's a great place to visit, but I wouldn't like to live there."

And Sydney isn't all about the Bridge, the Opera House, the Harbour or Bondi Beach. The bulk of the populace live far from such attractions, many stations west along railway lines, many kilometres west down motorways that use tunnels to escape the bountiful coast. As in Melbourne, the sprawling west is mythologised as working-class, ethnically diverse, and fraught with crime and fear. It is also vibrant and down to earth, being invented and reimagined before one's eyes by people who couldn't care less about such judgements. More supposedly secure and beautiful inner city realms are long completed, their towers built, their fences up, every square inch of useable real estate exploited and valued. But the urban sprawl towards the Blue Mountains remains a work-in-progress, growing rudely, superseding stereotypes by the minute, anomalous and surprising.

A disclosure: A few years back, I wrote a novel *Suburban Tours* in which the protagonist conducts minibus tours of everyday urban areas which are considered boring or ugly, and through his commentary, tries to evoke a sense of wonder at the quotidian suburbs on the metropolitan fringe. The quixotic main character doesn't succeed in enrapturing his fellow citizens with his re-presentations of their surrounds – tours of gangland murder sites fare better – and his fascination is that of an inner-city kid who doesn't have to put up with the limited services and boring realities of life in the sprawl. Like that character, I'm an inner-city type, though I spent formative years living on the rural-suburban fringe, far enough out of town that

The Hillsong Church dominates the Ice Arena's precinct.

An ice rink was part of the initial Norwest vision splendid.

Miniature remote controlled sailboats on Norwest Lake.

IN A CITY SPOILT FOR CHOICE, HOCKEY HAS TO GRAB THE ATTENTION OF MINIATURE REMOTE-CONTROLLED SAILING BOAT ENTHUSIASTS.

I played my hockey at Dandenong's "Coliseum", 35 kilometres from the Melbourne CBD. I say this so you can understand how I found my weekend voyage through the deep west of Sydney so stimulating.

The thrilling vistas of the inner city - glimpses of glinting water; exotic structures craning to get an eyeful of the vista they collectively create; jumbled, stacked vantage points – give way to transport hubs, silos, mosques, high-rise shopping centres, apartment blocks, warehouses, market depots, factories, playing fields, seas of netball courts, and I'm transfixed. The bright sun and the novelty of travel have opened my eyes wider. The railway stations here still have conductors who use whistles and flags as well as their modern nanny-state hi-vis vests. At Blacktown, my stop, I am the only person with an Anglo heritage. Asian, African and Middle-Eastern Aussies crowd into a burgeoning shopping centre which offers deep fried fast food, cheap clothes oveflowing from cardboard boxes and loud beauty parlours. My Indian cab driver takes me past a bland Anglican property that looks like a military establishment and a huge hilltop building with mustard-hued toadstool towers announced by a huge drooping banner to be "Sikh Centre".

Thirty dollars and a few crossings of major motorways later, we are entering the Norwest Marketown shopping centre. This is the home of the Hillsong Church, the most famous of Australian showbiz evangelist centres. Any notion of Australians as irreligious is already overturned by this voyage, but it has to be admitted we are nowhere near as devout as North Americans, less than 17 per cent of the Australian population attending church regularly. But out here, the white church arena commands the manicured rise. Hilltop became famous enough five years ago to feature on the Australian version of *Sixty Minutes*. Everything here feels five years ago, the shine barely off.

There's a second chapel that looks like a huge sail, narrow and concave. Below it a modest young retail sector nestles around a supermarket and an artificial lake is ringed by ten-storey corporate headquarters. The entire precinct is landscaped like a designer's version of itself, down to the pretty green ferns sketched in beneath the waterside restaurant decking, a vision splendid of profiteer chutzpah. To the north side of the lake a "luxury resort" accommodation development is underway, new roads half unwrapped. Between those nascent dream homes and the sail church? The Sydney Ice Arena.

Back on Norwest Lake, metres from the front steps of the rink, drift stately miniature sailing boats. How progressive, I muse, to provide these pretty, pirouetting vessels for the edification of random dog-walkers and pausing shoppers. Then I notice that the boats turn a little too sharply to be operated just by the gentle breeze. And there are middle-aged men on the tastefully landscaped shore opposite, operating the boats by remote control. Hockey in Sydney is another potential leisure/entertainment option that many locals do not know exists. It competes not just with having a barbie on the balcony of your harbour view watching sport on TV, but with activities such as CrossFit training, rollerblading, surfing, boating, four codes of football, horse-racing, netball, basketball, bocce, petty crime, dog trials, highland-dancing, drag-racing, dragon boat racing, hanging in a gang, fixing up the car, and wasting one's life in a soul-sucking

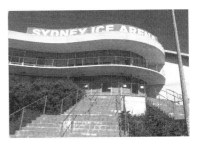

pokie facility. In a city spoilt for choice, hockey has to grab the attention of miniature remote-controlled sailing boat enthusiasts.

Sydney Ice Arena (SIA) is a high-ceilinged, modern structure which seats hundreds in comfort. It has a big ice surface, upstairs spaces suitable for a café, a bar and a large function room, and it provides proper dressing rooms, a luxury in Australian rinks. It even possesses design flourishes, most notably its impressive inclined wall of windows behind the grandstand wing. Though 45 minutes west of the Sydney CBD, it is at the centre of a precinct targeted for major growth in jobs and population, and a railway station is planned to go in 260 metres from the front door. It's way more salubrious than other Australian rinks I have seen apart from the Icehouse. I am frustrated standing in its mostly unoccupied spaces, contemplating its immense potential and the fact that it may not be here in a couple of years. Just before the Mustangs take on the Bears, the excited cries of a handful of skating children echo around the hangar-like arena. As the afternoon darkens, the sky through the grandstand window merges with the reflection of skaters. For a few twilight minutes, kids skate in the sky above Western Sydney and anything feels possible. Then the windows are dark, and all you can see are empty seats.

The rink is well appointed, but it does not have plexiglas. Great swathes of heavy netting are draped around the perimeter, overlapping at the corners, where the scene resembles fishing reality show *Deadliest Catch* and I expect to see fat, flapping salmon. When the puck hits the nets, it is flung back in a strange slow motion that sometimes short-circuits the players, who must feel a whistle will be blown. There is a globe out in one of the high lamps at the church end. I don't see many of the shots at that goal.

The home of the Bears, at least in 2014.

SIA: clean, spacious, modern and haunting.

Yet it's a goalie's game. Fraser Carson, fresh off his derby ignominy, keeps the Mustangs in the game after they start brightly, then stagnate. The Bears become more aggressive in the second period, and it becomes a game of neutral-zone turnovers, neither team able to convert the opportunities their pressure creates. The Mustangs lead 2–0 until near the end of the second period, when the Bears get one back on the powerplay from their indefatigable Regina-born captain Thomas Schlamp.

I roamed the spacious arena early in the game, but when I stray near the Mustangs bench during intermission, Brad is keen to talk, with team manager Mick Burslem and trainer Andrea Heywood busy with oranges, towels, nicks and strains. Fan Jesseca Kirwan is also there, in Mustangs clobber. I try not to say too much, but astute, forthright Jess isn't scared to contradict the coach, or point out something she considers more important than his worries about puck control and driving the net. "We're getting too fancy," Brad says. "We need to get back to basics. We were doing it in the first period but … these guys think they are better than they are."

It's becoming a familiar refrain with this team, the tendency to get too fussy when attacking. But I'm surprised to hear the coach say he thinks they overestimate themselves. They have always seemed an honest, feisty lot, effort no problem. The more I watch them, the more it feels to me that they prefer a wide-open, flowing game. Brad talks about getting 'dirty' goals, and scrapping in corners and in front of the net.

In the third period, the Mustangs suffer through shifts where they are unable to clear their zone but they somehow hang on. It makes for a tense final ten minutes as the Bears force the Mustangs back in search of the equaliser. Fraser leaves the net twice, to simply stop pucks for defencemen. No mistakes. He hasn't shown the slightest apprehension following his horror game the week before. "He's 19," I hear more than once as older men explain how he's coping after his disastrous derby. Later he tells me: "You've got to just put it behind you. The toughest part is just forgetting about it, so you cry about it for a day or two and then move on as quickly as you can." Fraser has moved on.

Lucky he has. Forward Jamie Bourke's appraisal of the 2–1 win sums up the general attitude of the Mustangs: "Our only good player was Fraser." Brad Vigon says "It was an ugly, ugly win." He's worried by the last two periods, the lack of penetration on Bears goalie Daniel Palmkvist, and the inability to clear the puck. Brad is confused at how they looked *tired*. The flight got them in at 1.30 pm; they had a bus ride of an hour to the accommodation, then a fifteen-minute trip to the rink. You can see him working through why they were lacklustre, and trying not to be downbeat after winning.

Way out west:
Sydney Ice Arena.

Imports are often amazed that Australian rinks feature nets.

Bears boss Vlad Rubes wears the same good-natured smile after the loss that he wore before the game when discussing his club's challenges. He shrugs his shoulders. We didn't start well, we didn't take our chances ... There's nothing to be done about it. The effort was there.

Outside in the warm evening, Mustangs players scoff down pizza, reclining on the lakeside next to their waiting buses. This is a new trip and there is a little trial-by-error going on with the arrangements. It is deemed more important for the players to get some sort of nourishment as quickly as possible at this late hour. And the budget is not stretching to five-star nosheries.

I feel a little self-conscious about assuming a seat in one of the two cramped minibuses. Driver Mick Burslem has a licence for a full-sized vehicle, but no such vehicle could be located nearby. One's initial bus perch is theirs for the entire trip, according to hockey tradition. I take up residence with Fraser Carson to my right, Andrew McDowell's son Brendan to my left. No need for self-consciousness around these upbeat young guys. Fraser is giving Mick backseat passenger advice, and Mick is giving it back with interest, in a panto of abuse that makes up in mock anger for what it lacks in elegance. At first glance, Mick doesn't appear to be the sort of person one should tell to shut up; he looks like he can handle himself, and has had to in the past. But he's been driving Fraser and many of these boys for years, the relationships are well-entrenched, and it quickly becomes obvious that he loves these kids – and the affection is reciprocated via the traditional Australian means – ribald abuse.

When introduced to Fraser by Pat, I took away a first impression of a polite young man, but I am now learning that Fraser is also mischievous, he likes to sing (and knows the words to a lot of songs) and he gives as good as he gets. On Sunday he will call his beloved grandparents to arrange a visit. Now, after a win, on the team bus, it is the time to tell Mick to shut up. "Embedded" like this in a group of strangers, you learn things incessantly; no notebook can keep up with all the new information. A surprising number of young hockey players are partial to country music; only senior players get to play DJ; Fraser's pre-match routine is to drink a coke in the shower.

My other bus-mates are import Granty (Jeff Grant), 28, a forward playing defence for the Stangs; Brendan's older brother, defenceman Mikey McDowell, 25; his mate, forward Andrew 'Fitzy' Fitzgerald, 24; coiffed goalie Michael James, 24; and imports Viktor Gibbs-Sjodin, a 26-year-old forward from Uppsala, Sweden who possesses even more impressive hair, a ginger afro; and gun Alaskan defenceman Jack 'Wolfman' Wolgemuth, 29.

As with Ice, the Mustangs banter in the sharp but laid-back manner that denotes young men at ease with each other. It puts me at ease. After traversing motorways for a few minutes and stopping at a drive-through bottle shop, we crib along a curb-less road in dark semi-rural night, and then disembark at the Avina Van Village. Locals and the owners are having Saturday night beers outside a huge on-site bistro, alongside a massive swimming pool, vans and cabins and houses stretching up driveways into the unlit distance.

The Mustangs are housed in a rectangular dormitory which features a large central space flanked by bunk rooms. It reminds me of a school camp: basic but made cosy by company. Its only luxury is a TV, which has been turned to the footy, sound off. Long tables give it the feeling of a Viking hall, players sitting either side like resting warriors, surrounded by their drying hockey gear and strewn bags. The entire group plays an iPad version of Celebrity Heads. The contestant sits on a chair facing the room holding the iPad above his head. Those watching can see the word or phrase on the screen and the crowd has to offer clues to help the iPad holder guess the word or phrase he cannot see. Brad Vigon is a particularly enthusiastic mimer of actions. Most players are raucously involved.

Alex Hall, as the contestant, provides the biggest laugh:

iPad answer: HUMAN BEING.

Loudest clue? "It's what you are!"

Alex Hall's response?

"Mustang?"

Yes, everyone is a Mustang in the room, even me, in a sense – I have bought a membership for both Melbourne clubs – and they are happily so. It is a family club enjoying itself, and there are actual family members along to underline the vibe. One of the better performers at Celebrity Heads is ten-year-old Paddy, son of sponsor Bryan Jeffrey. He wears a Mustangs jumper all weekend and is surely having the time of his life. The partners and babies of defenceman Troy Robertson, veteran Vinnie Hughes and forward Jamie Bourke are all in the room, and there is no need for beg pardons. No one pulls punches, but this is not a vulgar or disrespectful group. Pat plays with one of the babies. He has his computer and iPad out, trying to get the final thousand words of an assignment done. It is due Tuesday, and he has hockey tomorrow, and work and school Monday. He struggles through his one beer, picking at its label, and scrapes out 150 words.

There is some mention of a two-beer limit for players. It has more strength as a rumour than an edict; no-one seems to want to test it. Older players Vinnie Hughes and Viktor Gibbs-Sjodin share a couple of glasses of red, as does your author with the older brains trust. The players are so early to bed that Brad Vigon, assistant coach Mark "Chuck" Connolly, Mick Burslem and myself are forced to whisper as we talk hockey into the night. Some of the stories are about the shenanigans AIHL players got up to seven or eight years ago, when Brad was a Melbourne Ice star. I am back writing in my cabin before 1 am.

SUNDAY THE 18TH

ROAD TRIP TWO:
SYDNEY ICE DOGS V MELBOURNE MUSTANGS
DAY TWO

There are no tales of hangover woes or outrageous exploits the next morning; the stories being told over breakfast are about a previous import who managed a perfect backhand saucer pass early in a game despite being highly intoxicated. Mick Burslem, up since 6 am, has found a huge barbecue perfect for the task of cooking the apparently mandatory carbo-loading breakfast. As with Melbourne Ice, it's the meal the management is most comfortable with. Lashings of bacon, dozens of eggs, toast. Cheap controllables that they know will be consumed. Mick says the thanks of the players are all the reward he needs for all of this work. He is the sort of capable, down-to-earth volunteer indispensable to amateur teams. Well-versed in Australian Rules football, which he played and coached, he knows the mysteries of team dynamics. Despite being busy, he is taking in more than some might imagine. He will get an hour and a half's rest after this trip before starting his night-shift job at Melbourne's vegetable market.

Leaving Avina at 10 am, the Mustangs now have seven hours to kill. This is Sydney, so that means the beach, 50 minutes away. Jeff Grant hooks up the music, everyone resumes their now customary berths in the buses, and we're on the road again. After a couple of coastal wrong turns, we find Cronulla's main beach. It is classic Sydney, a sandstone cliff, a sandy beach and a nook of cafés wedged between the two, people everywhere. I ascend the cliff, desperate for some exercise; the recovering hockey players take to the water. When we arrived, Fraser said that Pat is scared of any water over four feet deep. "You would be too, if you were only four feet high!" someone joked. It is determined that the small forward will need some assistance getting into the Pacific Ocean. He is therefore manhandled and dumped into it, headfirst. Hockey players look out for their mates.

Brad tells me he was worried about the team's state of mind after the prolonged bus trip, but the swim and pleasant park and beach surrounds have settled them down. He speaks of the players, as did Ice management, as if they are children, or young horses – flighty, temperamental thoroughbreds capable of great feats if they have grazed happily and don't have colic. Lunch is improvised on a park bench. It is healthy enough – wholemeal rolls with a choice of cheese, lettuce and chicken. But I'm with the French about eating: you have to do it sitting down at a table. A few players were expecting a cafe or restaurant.

The small crowd is close to the ice surface at Liverpool.

Small rinks make for fierce hockey.

The Ice Dogs are convinced they can win another title.

That's the budget, fellas. Then it's another long bus trip back out west for the Dogs game.

Alex Hall commits his second infamous act of the weekend by decamping in the wrong bus, forcing Jack Wolgemuth to drag his six foot four frame to the back, cursing Hall all the while. The bus revels in the sport of having a scapegoat, grinning Alex included. Fierce imprecations.

It gets really hot at the back of the bus. Jack asks for air-conditioning. He gets it but it remains stifling. Soon everyone is asleep, as surely as if we have all been gassed. The last thing I see before nodding off is a huge sign on a factory pronouncing "JESUS: COMING SOON". By the time all awaken, rink beckoning, I'm trying to convince myself that three hours of cramped bus travel won't matter, and it's good for players to be relaxed enough to nap, conserving crucial energy ahead of a game. There's something informal about the disembarkation. Some Mustangs wander inside, some warm-up on the rugby field out the front of the Liverpool Catholic Club (LCC) complex. We're early, so I go off exploring, marvelling at an even stranger sporting precinct than Norwest business park. The LCC – a large building hosting a gym, indoor mini-golf range and small ice rink – is flanked by two rugby pitches and netball courts. Alongside it sprawls a massive pokies/club venue and a ten-storey Mercure hotel. New South Wales pioneered the fleecing of its citizens by pokie machine gambling. Particularly in working-class communities, clubs squeeze out cash from patrons and provide gaudily lavish venues, and in this case one of the state's handful of rinks. Again, Sydney money-making largesse is writ large on the landscape, this oasis of faux glamour situated in the middle of an industrial area dominated by grey tilt-slab concrete warehouses, factories and powerlines.

There are two other elements that make this a Suburban Tour for me. On the other side of the LCC rugby field is a circus, a real-life, in-session Australian circus, which means a faded, down-at-heel family concern that has to set up shop in outer suburban easements. The techno music throbs, and honest-to-goodness gasps are heard from within the blue-and-red striped tent, so perhaps I shouldn't judge the quality of the venture from its poignantly bedraggled behind-the-scenes appearance. I see two camels, a Shetland pony, and a sign about African lions.

On the gambling Mecca side of the rink building, there is a large brown caravan parked against the fence. Upon closer inspection, it is revealed to be a life-sized portable nativity scene, complete with farm animal sculptures and a tall Christ, its glass front parked away from the intrusive gaze of the car park. Perhaps we are only meant to see this stable panorama at the right time of year. In a form of miraculous concealment, the sun shines so directly at this apparition that I can't take a photo which adequately conveys its incongruity. Like a Mayan calendar-aligned icon, its perfect positioning defies modern technology. You will have to take my word for it – this was the oddest object ever parked outside a sporting arena. This Sydney trip has been the most religious experience of my sporting life.

The rink, once they let us in, belatedly, is small; the viewing is from seats that extend only three deep along the white interior walls, and it is another matchbox-sized ice surface, guaranteeing an intensely physical game. A small balcony opposite the seating houses the announcer and a couple of officials, perched like Roman emperors over the benches. A proud, vividly red digital sign graces the wall behind the southern goals, proclaiming the temperature, alternating between Celsius and Fahrenheit. It is four degrees at the start of the game. Finally the jacket I have carried all weekend is indispensable. It is damned cold to an Australian, and the LCC seems proud of the fact. It was 25 degrees Celsius in the bright sunshine outside. The rink, entered from well within the complex, is windowless, completely removed from the sunny Sydney outside, and the few voices inside echo loudly. As at Baulkham Hills, there is no beer on offer. Lord knows the refrigeration costs would not be high in such an environment.

Mustangs sponsor and road-trip regular Bryan Jeffrey, replete in jersey, drops the puck for the pre-game ceremony. A Scottish hockey-lover and former psychiatric nurse, he now runs MOAT mental health services, and has just become naming rights sponsor of the club. He is another Melbourne hockey person who had dealings with Ice before finding his home with the newer club. He is also Pat's personal sponsor, and holds the American in high regard.

Early on, the main scoreboard doesn't read too badly for the Mustangs, who seem to shake off whatever stiffness and sleepiness remained from the bus trips with another bright start, scoring first. But the longer the game goes the more listless and overpowered the Mustangs appear. The Dogs, egged on by a small group of fanatics, voices amplified in the cold whiteness, are fiercely physical. The atmosphere is hostile. Manager Deb, who took our money at the front counter, periodically hammers a locker with her fists. There may be even fewer fans here than yesterday at the Sydney Ice Arena, but the intimate surrounds and the aggression make it a more compelling experience.

The score is 1–1 after one period, but by late in the second period, when Ice Dog Simon Barg scores a typically opportunistic short-handed goal, the hosts lead 4-1. Andrew Belic scores seconds later to give the Mustangs some hope going into the final period.

At the breaks, fans flood out of the rink freezer, reaching for their phones, desperate for some warmth. When they return, there is a delay as volunteers struggle to re-fasten the nets where they were parted to allow the Mustangs players back on to the ice.

In the final period, the Mustangs look like a young, small

team intimidated by a bigger, older, meaner opponent. The Dogs pour on three more goals, and it could have been more. Beaten 6–3 the day before by Melbourne Ice, the Ice Dogs are fighting to keep their season alive, a proud team stung to find their best form, physical and skilful. This 7–2 win revives them, and must have some ramifications for the Mustangs, suddenly vulnerable after a strong start to the season.

There is little time for post-mortems after the game, the late start at Liverpool making it a rush to the airport. I get to shake hands with Andrew Petrie, and little more. He has a singing team to greet, I have another state to be in, and the bus waits. The post-drubbing journey is understandably the quietest of the weekend. Players half-heartedly check other results – Ice has beaten the Sydney Bears 4–2 and caught an earlier flight home from New South Wales with two more road trip wins under their belt; Adrenaline have beaten the North Stars in a shootout in Adelaide; and Brave have continued their great start with a home rink shootout win over Thunder, who seem to be continually on the end of narrow losses.

Gradually, the usual banter returns – girls, hockey jibes, fashion critiques. No-one has died, it is no good remaining morose … But the exchanges lack conviction. I see Pat boarding the other bus, looking as angry as I have ever seen him. He had as many as fifteen scoring chances, but couldn't find the net – is that it?

Jack Wolgemuth, who incurred three penalties, says he hates losing to the Dogs as much as to Melbourne Ice. He will be working for president and landscape gardener John Belic, 900 kilometres away, in a few hours. The Alaskan is a mixture of wide-eyed innocent and worldly traveller, always curious. He seems to take more pleasure in Mick's statements than anyone else, imitating the driver's broadest Australianisms as if trying to distil their occult significance. Like most smart imports, he is a little more awake than his teammates, with time ticking away on his Australian adventure. When we were lost on Captain Cook Drive on the way to Cronulla, he marvelled, "That's the same guy who named places in Alaska!" He is taking in and participating in as much as he can.

Brendan McDowell muses over an architecture assignment. He will have to do five or six hours on it when he gets home, near midnight. It is due at 1 pm tomorrow.

At the airport, Brad thinks aloud. The Dogs were desperate, they were hungry. His team hasn't "caught the disease of winning". He worries whether such losses are hurting his group enough. Are they content playing together? Do they have the drive to step up a level? Brad talks briefly on the phone with Andy McDowell in Melbourne. The vice-president is keeping positive. Get home, regroup. But Brad is searching himself and anyone whose counsel he values for insights. He is not so much angry as shaken.

THURSDAY THE 22ND

The turmoil is not over at the Sydney Ice Dogs. There was an announcement today that president Shane Rose had stepped down due to time constraints. It was later updated thus: "After discussions with the board Shane Rose has taken an absence of leave for one month. The club is hopeful of retaining Shane's services, as he has given so much to the club in the past few seasons. The club board was happy with the outcome and look forward to meeting again with Shane in one month." Andrew Petrie has not taken on an easy task.

Trouble is not limited to the east coast and the Ice Dogs. Perth Thunder has parted ways with coach Dylan Forsythe, eight games into its season. Though general manager Stan Scott accepts that Thunder will always start its seasons slowly, its current record leaves it in danger of finishing at the bottom of the standings the year after it finished third. Perth has only four points – derived from two overtime losses and one overtime win – and is yet to win a game in regulation time despite being involved in a succession of thrillers. Co-owner Rob Cox made the call to reinstate Stan as coach. Stan is concerned about team discipline on road trips. "You're not going to please everybody when you take away the party," he says, but news that the team had gone "from the nightclub to the bus" on an interstate trip did not sit well with the club pioneer, who says it is harder to reinstate than create the right culture.

FRIDAY THE 23RD

Attending my first training sessions at the Icehouse in weeks, I hope for some news or an insight. I tell myself that there is always something to be gained, someone to talk to when at the Icehouse. But Mustangs president John Belic has company. Ice president Emma Poynton and various Ice players are also occupied.

On my way out, I run into Mick Burslem. After he debriefed with Andy McDowell on Monday morning after the Sydney road trip, it was agreed that he should address the group. "I don't usually come to training, but I'm going to say a few things to the boys … I can't skate to save myself, but I know a thing or two about sport …" Mick says the team's "attention to detail" was lacking in Sydney. Its preparation was not up to scratch. He says Pat O'Kane wasn't happy with what he saw either. The pre-game on Sunday was haphazard. One player was still taping his stick when the team began its warm-up. "They're a little comfortable with themselves," Mick says. "They're not the best team in this league. They're not even the best team in this building." The players have to realise that they will never have this particular group together again. They have only fourteen-and-a-half weeks more together.

He is about to give the players a rocket, a reality check. "They've got to buy-in," he says. "It won't matter if they're just nodding at what I say. I'm going to tell them something I told footy teams … If you want to play a game, go buy a monopoly board. This is sport. This is brutal. We all want to feel the hair go up on the back of our necks. They have to get the togetherness back that they had last year."

Mustangs equipment manager Mick Burslem packs up after the loss in Liverpool, with time tight for the trip to the airport.

IF YOU WANT TO PLAY A GAME, GO BUY A MONOPOLY BOARD. THIS IS SPORT. THIS IS BRUTAL.

SATURDAY THE 24TH

It turns out Pat O'Kane - aka "Simon The Likeable" - had not been frowning of late because of study pressure, or a lack of goals. There were issues within the Mustangs ranks, he tells me when I call this morning. "There's the haves and the have-nots. Guys that aren't playing so much are kind of bringing some negative attitude into the locker room and I think it's wearing on other guys, it's wearing on the coaches, and it's wearing on the volunteers like Mick. I think they're doing a hell of a job to correct that. That's the way it goes on any team you put together. You're going to have guys who play and guys who don't play. I think a lot of these guys aren't used to that, they have always been the top players on the team, so it's just growing pains."

Pat is sure his team will "right the ship", but he fully endorses Mick's direct words at training. "I think we needed that so much. There was a strange feeling after the road trip in the locker room. We didn't really play all that great and there was a division in the team. But Mick coming in and talking to us I think addressed that. The people I talked to after that agreed that everyone was re-energised."

I tell Pat I am surprised by his frankness, criticism of teammates being so rare to hear from a sportsman. "I'm not going to hide anything. I think our team is so close with fans and media that it's important for them to know what's going on."

SATURDAY THE 24TH (2)

After their 9-2 loss in week one, not much has gone wrong for Melbourne Ice. They uncovered a gun fifth import in Tim Johansson, and their back-up goalie Jayden Pine-Murphy was so good that they now say they have two "number one" goalies. Their younger players are flourishing and Jeff Smith has been a boon at the back and on the powerplay. Ice are six points clear atop the standings, but the team seem as enthused by once again being a harmonious group, enjoying each other's company. Every team, every year, is different. The coach is getting to know, and enjoy, this iteration of Melbourne Ice. Their bonhomie is proved by their love of travel; Ice are four from four on the road.

While the Mustangs were splitting their Sydney road trip, Ice maintained their perfect road record by racking up another two wins, covering an undisciplined Ice Dogs team on Saturday and hanging on against the tenacious Bears on Sunday. But Brent expects to confront the difficulties Brad is now facing. "You wait as a coach for the real challenge. And only adversity brings that which challenges your ethos and your cultural drivers. So it's very easy to think you are doing the right things on that sort of spiritual level when you're winning. It's like having a German Shepherd and knowing that sooner or later they're going to have a go at you. And if you get them at that point you will have them for life. You don't want it, it's the last thing you want, but you know you really need it to know where the group's really at."

There's no adversity right now for Ice. This week's bye is welcome, though there are some players who prefer to stay in the groove of playing, and it presents a dilemma for coaches – go hard or lighten off at training? Ice chose to do the latter. This week there was no talk of systems, and training sessions featured skills battles. Brent says that helped freshen up the coaches as well as the players. "We're only eight or nine games in, but we've been going since November, it's been full-on."

Brent's mission is development, and he is most enthused about the form and maturation of his younger players. Brent says he is being "enormously challenged" by the role in which there is "not a minute's reprieve". He admits he has to learn not to be drawn into every pass, every hit, but says the busier he is, the better he feels. Brent may be challenged, but outwardly, he never looks ruffled. He is not a ranter and raver on the bench, and with glasses on and his Ice cap on, he usually appears implacable during games. Johan Steenberg, who supplies the histrionics on the Ice bench, tells Brent to loosen up. But the head coach takes everything in and picks his moments to make a comment or issue an instruction. Though he often says his team gives him heart attacks or high blood pressure, he invariably exudes a thoughtful calm.

He still chats with the coach of the arch-rival Mustangs, Brad Vigon. "We touch base, ask how the other is going … it's nice to chat with someone who knows exactly what you're going through."

In today's game at the Icehouse, the Mustangs answered an early Adelaide Adrenaline powerplay goal with two of their own to lead 2–1 after one period, and they added four goals to one in the final period in a more typical Mustangs performance. 6–2 with the name Pat O'Kane all over the scoresheet - two goals and an assist. First indications are that the club has re-set following its humbling loss to the Ice Dogs.

I ask blunt youngster Fraser Carson what the message was from his coaches following his costly game against Melbourne. "Do better," he replies. It's funny, but it's not a throwaway line.

The form of Brave and the Bears are two of the surprises early in an unpredictable season.

You can't dwell on stuff-ups, or your confidence and performance suffer, and you can't hide from them, so you address them and don't let it get you down. As a goalie, if you make mistakes, they are more costly than anyone else's errors, but you can't do anything about it until the next game. Fraser knows what to do and not to do. He knows the score, accepts the deal. Most of us know what we have to do, and we are trying to get better at doing it. Good coaches are there either to teach us how to do it, to remind us to do it, or when our confidence is down, confirm to us we can do it. But Fraser is "coachable" because he takes responsibility for his actions. He doesn't really need to be told.

Fraser tells me Jack Wolgemuth broke his jaw at training, but the defenceman is insisting he will be back in three weeks, not the seven weeks recommended by doctors. "He doesn't have time to not be playing," says Fraser of the Alaskan, who is possibly playing his final season.

The Sydney Ice Dogs have suffered a shaky start to their title defence.

The Mustangs must rediscover the togetherness which propelled them up the standings in 2013.

Today, once more, the most intriguing results occur outside Melbourne. Canberra, fresh off beating Thunder 5–1 and 5–4 (shootout) at home, have beaten Newcastle away 5–2. They are becoming not just a feelgood story, but a bona fide contender. Andrew Petrie's Ice Dogs, sans president, have added a 6-2 'Battle of Sydney' win over the Bears to their 7-2 Mustangs mauling.

SUNDAY THE 25TH

A brief note on Facebook states that the North Stars bus has broken down halfway to Liverpool and their game against the Dogs has been postponed. Simple as that. The pivotal fixture will have to be rescheduled.

The Mustangs players march out for the second game of their Icehouse double-header against Adrenaline, and sixteen-year-old Ethan Cornford skates on first, then alone, as he is announced as playing his first AIHL game. He will later be credited with a point for an assist in his debut. Captain Sean Jones and yesterday's goalie Michael James are out, on their way to the world inline championships. And Jack Wolgemuth is a massive loss. He can be seen on social media doing a muscleman pose in a hospital gown after undergoing surgery for his broken jaw. So some of the Mustangs fringe players previously frustrated by lack of ice time will have big jobs today. And Pat is captain. Win this, and the Mustangs' weekend will have vaulted them above Adelaide into the top four and as high as second.

It's no scoring fest today. Joey Hughes opens it up at the start of the second period, and there isn't another goal until Adelaide's equaliser, halfway through the final period. The home team goes ahead again, but the visitors level up with three minutes to play. It ends 2–2 and Adrenaline take the shootout.

My regular hockey-watching mate Kristian Schafer, still new to the game, says hockey players remind him of birds, head on a swivel, having to take in many things at once. It is particularly relevant to this game, which went up and back ceaselessly, interrupted by only two penalties.

The Mustangs end the weekend fourth, Adrenaline second. The Mustangs have two games in hand on their vanquishers, but Adelaide have a slew of home games to come, having played six of ten on the road. Remarkably, the teams have now gone to overtime in five of their past six contests. Both played pacy, clean hockey and looked to have depth across the lines. A third of the way through the season, they both look like worthy finalists, but then so do most AIHL teams so far this year.

TUESDAY THE 27TH

In a distracted moment at work, I suggested Australian hockey as a subject to the new multimedia editor at *The Age*, who shocked me by embracing my proposal. So here I am visiting the Icehouse with a cameraman and art designer, after my emails managed to deliver three Ice women, three Ice men and two Mustangs, one of whom is Jeff Grant. The other appears to be Pat O'Kane, carrying on like a clown. He is falling on the ice, pretending to miss face-offs by a metre. Fake slashing; taking shots at the puck bucket from his knees; and staging play-fights with Ice's Tommy Powell.

Except that it's not Pat O'Kane. Pat is working hard, or studying. It's his best mate, goalie Fraser Carson, who has borrowed Pat's No. 89 kit, taped captain's "C" and all, and is doing his best to trash the O'Kane brand in Pat's absence. While video colleague Tim Young, a Chicago Blackhawks fan born in Halifax, Nova Scotia, sets up his gear, Fraser Carson, Tommy Powell and ice captain Lliam Webster horse around. "Bitter rivals!" Lliam jokes at one stage during their tomfoolery. To help clean up the pucks used in Tim's shoot, Fraser and Tommy somehow contrive an impromptu game of tip-in baseball, on their knees. Fraser spends more time spread-eagled on his back than on his skates, revelling in pratfalls and chiacking dives. Little wonder he doesn't mind throwing his torso around the crease as a goalie.

Jeff Grant chats while awaiting his call-up, discussing life in minor pro hockey. His Southern Professional Hockey League team the Louisiana Ice Gators played to packed houses in a fourteen thousand seat stadium for four years and won championships. Two years later they were out of the league. When they returned, crowds were down to four thousand. Some minor pro clubs fold purely because a nearby rival has gone under and more frequent travel to farther flung centres is too costly. Jeff has done his share of hours on buses. For leagues with 40-game plus seasons, air travel is prohibitive. The most exotic venue he played in was a former rodeo barn, which duly retained the odour of a building used to house farm animals. Many minor-pro clubs are limited liability companies, which means they can leave town rapidly, without much responsibility for what they leave behind. In the competitive US sports market, clubs uses all manner of gimmick to retain fans and forge links with their communities. Jeff has seen sumo-wrestling in bubble balls on the ice, and he is accustomed to making three visits a week to community events. He is familiar with today's activities, and may be surprised when few other such obligations follow this season. Jeff says the situation for many SPHL teams is similar to Australian hockey – there is a core of people who love the sport and a mass that doesn't know it exists.

Fraser and Jeff discuss the prospect of snaring a rich Canadian as a team owner in Australia.

Maybe this would-be sugar daddy should take on the whole league; for comparative chicken feed, he could have dominion over eight or nine teams, not just one. Any sponsorship or ownership of professional sports stature would completely transform the AIHL.

FRIDAY THE 30TH

Mark Rummukainen, club-saver, has helped create a monster. The Canberra Brave captain helped mobilise a player-led fightback when Canberra Knights owner John Raut wound up that club six weeks from the start of the 2014 season. With so little time to put together supporters and a plan for the new team, the birth of the CBR Brave was miraculous. But amid all the discussions about everything from logos and memberships to the price of road trips, it was determined that a new training regime was necessary. And it's a killer. "The group of guys that were involved with the Knights and now the Brave needed a culture change, to get a bit of a shock to the system, and if you can train four days a week to get your arse into gear, then that's what we were going to do," Mark says. "Some guys complained about it – I do personally at times. If I'm tired, I think 'I don't want to go to training today' – but you go there and there's 20 guys there all doing it together ... the culture is changing."

Training four days a week, on top of weekend games, and often travel, is a major impost on amateur players, but Mark says the club was determined to "hit the ground running". Mark is unsure if the extra sessions will continue all season, and if they do, whether he will be able to fully commit to such a regime next year. Club runners Peter Chamberlain and Jamie Wilson, hands-on presences on gamedays, are swamped, and team leaders such as Mark aren't looking too far ahead.

"I haven't really sat down and thought about what we've achieved ... I've sort of drifted into the player role, getting into the season. I want to just keep rolling with the winning streak we've got going." He was forced to reflect on the bus back from Newcastle last week when veteran goalie Brad Hunt said, "You did it, we've done it!" "It's a great feeling to have gotten the thing up and running and get it to the point it is at now ... Once the season is done I'll sit down and see everything. It fell apart and we sort of picked it up and ran with it. Off the ice I think we've been more than successful and I think we can continue with that."

Mark admits the club is "riding an emotional high" after excelling early in its first season, and he expects a test of the fledgling Brave's mettle. "At one point last weekend I was thinking this team needs to have a tough period to see where we're at. It's all good and well and everyone's happy and loving and we've won four games in a row. What happens if we lose four games in a row? Is everyone still going to be pitching in together and practising and getting behind each other?"

Mud and sweat are behind Brave's impressive debut.

He thinks yes, because of personnel such as fitness and motivational guru Lee Campbell. "He's helping us out with our training off-ice and our camaraderie. He can pull us into line and make sure we're pulling in the right direction. There will be a letdown at some point but I think we have the people and the experience within the club to push through it."

The 32-year-old, 223-game veteran admits that the players needed some convincing when he proposed reviving the Knights. "When everything fell apart with the Knights guys were asking 'what's going to change? It's going to be the same guys playing together against the same teams at the same rink. What makes you think it's going to be any different?' " But Mark, despite playing on a losing team for so many years, believed. "I've always felt that this group of guys in Canberra was 90 per cent of the way there. It's that final 10 per cent, that last hurdle to get everyone on board. In a hockey sense the right people were here all along. We got them involved. I'm not saying we're 100 per cent way there and we're going to win the championship, but that last little bit everybody's seeing now."

Self-sacrifice is driving the Brave juggernaut.

Mark says this season has proven to him that "we can still dig deeper and perhaps be successful for a while". Brave's imports, Mathieu Ouellette, Anton Kokkonen and Stephen Blunden have formed a lethal first attacking line; returning local veterans have added depth; and the recruitment of the Harvey brothers, Canadians with New Zealand heritage, was a master stroke. Kiwis are classified as locals, so Brave effectively suit up six import-quality players. "By getting guys back and getting permanent residents involved in the team, it has raised the competition for spots, so it's pushing everyone to improve and basically earn their spot rather than just have it given to them. It's given guys an appreciation that it's a privilege to play in this league; it's not just a right. You can't just show up and be lacklustre about it, you need to prove yourself at practice, prove yourself with your dedication." The rise in "internal competitiveness" at training is pushing Brave players to be "as good as they can", a collective rise in expectations having an impact on gameday.

Canberra, like Adelaide and Perth, face some unique travelling challenges. Many of the Sunday games finish too late for the team to catch the final flights into Canberra, which has a more limited air service than other Australian cities. "The toughest thing for the Canberra team is four of our trips are flying trips. All four are basically within six weeks and the return trips on those ones are usually on Mondays, when you get back at lunchtime. A lot of guys can't really turn around to their school or their job and say 'I need four Mondays off in the

BEAR MCPHAIL HAS A UNIQUE PERSPECTIVE ON THE TRANSFORMATION OF CANBERRA. A FORMER KNIGHTS COACH AND FATHER OF CURRENT PLAYER CHRIS MCPHAIL, HE HAS EXPERIENCED THE OLD AND THE NEW. "IT IS VERY DIFFERENT NOW BECAUSE PREVIOUSLY IT WAS REALLY JUST ONE OWNER WHO RAN THE TEAM AS MUCH AS HE COULD, APART FROM THE COACHING. BECAUSE OF THE LEVEL THIS LEAGUE PERFORMS AT NOW, I THINK IT WAS NECESSARY TO HAVE THE WELL DEVELOPED TEAM STRUCTURE OF BRAVE." BEAR SAYS THE NEW REGIME "FREED UP FAN SUPPORT". "IT WAS ALREADY REALLY GOOD BEFOREHAND, BUT THEY'VE REALLY SHOWED THEIR COLOURS BY INVESTING THEIR OWN MONEY. BRAVE REALLY IS A CINDERELLA STORY."

next six weeks', so you get guys not able to show up because of that. Clubs like Brave need games scheduled earlier on Sundays so players can fulfil their actual responsibilities in real life".

Mark says his team is not "overly physical and aggressive" despite the intimate confines of their home rink, which guarantees body contact. "We've got big bodies that can handle physical play but we're not out there trying to run people into the boards. We've got good imports, a great goaltender and we're trying to be a bit more balanced team that plays structures and systems." He says the Knights were "never the prettiest team". "We're basically your hardworking team that sticks to a system and scores timely goals. We're pretty lucky to be firing on all cylinders."

Mark's Finnish father played hockey on outdoor rinks in his homeland, but Mark came through the ranks in Canberra after a friend of his father got the young Rummukainen involved at the age of nine. He "grabbed his chance" with the Knights at sixteen, and has played at the highest level for club and country for sixteen years since. Lean, ginger-haired and lanky, Mark looks like the sort of defenceman who could go on for another decade. Though he briefly contemplated retirement when the Knights were wound up, Mark sounds excited by the modern AIHL, and it's hard to imagine he would turn away too soon. "The changes that have happened over 16 years are incredible. The league's going from strength to strength, the class of players coming out from overseas has gone up and up and up and the local guys are getting better and better. It's been a fantastic trip so far and I'm still enjoying it."

He agrees that improved facilities are essential to the continued growth of the league – and not just in Canberra. "If you can get more seats into a rink you can expose the game to a lot more people, and better facilities make players feel happier. They want to come out and do more, I guess."

About to visit the famed Phillip rink for the first time, I ask Mark what to expect. He says his home ice may not be the most aesthetically pleasing arena to visit, especially for fans used to the Icehouse, and it hasn't changed much in 35 years, but a Brave game there is an experience worth the visit. "The fans, they're rowdy, they're crazy, and they're fun. We love playing here, it's the best rink in terms of atmosphere."

CBR Brave, created to survive, are surprising even themselves with their progress so far in 2014.

Canberra hockey fans made their own fun when their team was mediocre. Suddenly they have a title contender.

SATURDAY THE 31ST

ROAD TRIP THREE:
CBR BRAVE V MELBOURNE ICE
DAY ONE

Brent Laver might appear outwardly calm, but the Melbourne Ice coach is disquieted by the small propeller-driven plane his team is catching to Canberra. There are several others among Ice's travelling squad who also prefer their air transport bigger and jet-powered, but Ian Webster, the most experienced traveller in the gang, is unperturbed. As we take off, he begins telling me stories of players, coaches and venues long gone; an import from Saskatchewan who turned up wearing a ten gallon hat; an import who after being told there were no sharks in Melbourne's Port Phillip Bay had to be evacuated from those waters due to the first shark warning at that beach in living memory … I'm not sure how we get to the topic, but Ian also says the Mustangs want to beat Ice more than they want to lift the cup. But not too long after, he asks about Jack Wolgemuth's jaw – Ice are thinking about next Thursday's third derby as well. The two Melbourne teams are drawn to each other.

Nineteen-year-old forward Jeremy Brown is on his first Ice trip, fresh off a bigger plane from Canada after his team there lost game seven of its playoffs. He went back to Canada on his own aged fourteen to further his hockey career after his family moved to Australia when he was twelve. He did so without telling his mum, who would not have allowed it. Given the travails he matter-of-factly lists, I think I'm with Mrs Brown. He has been the victim of a last-minute selection broken promise which destroyed his hopes of higher honours, and a few years back, a bad check broke his back. That's a broken back we're talking about, not a hamstring tweak. Jeremy says all of this almost shyly, without sentiment, every pore of him dedicated to playing professional hockey. It's hard to doubt such a determined kid, and I haven't seen him skate yet. I notice that he has the subtly altered accent of a regular French speaker. His team is in Quebec.

Jeff Smith is fresh off four days in sunny Queensland, which lacks a respectable winter. It is cloudy and cool in Melbourne as we head to notoriously cold Canberra. The Canadians in the team, and those who have played there, discuss real cold – minus 57 in Winnipeg – and how snow made a ten-minute drive to 7 am training an hour-long odyssey, but even Ottawa native Matt Armstrong concedes Canberra is on the cool side.

After surviving an uneventful flight, we're seated in the lunch lounge of our accommodation, a sprawling hotel/function

A SUCCESSFUL TEAM IN OTHER COMPETITIONS PRIOR TO THE ONSET OF THE AIHL, THE CANBERRA KNIGHTS NEVER MADE THE AIHL PLAYOFFS. THEIR BEST RESULT WERE FIFTH PLACE FINISHES IN 2005 (11 WINS, 13 LOSSES) AND 2008 (10-15).

room complex on the outskirts of the nation's capital. Upon a previously organised cue, the entire contingent of Ice players, apart from seventeen-year-old Sam Hodic, cries "shoe check!" Chief inspector Matt Armstrong makes a great show of checking everyone's footwear then stops at Sam's table, bent over, brow furrowed. He has found the dollop of spaghetti sauce on Sam's foot that he put there moments before. Sam, wearing the ludicrous rookie's koala hat, has been officially welcomed on to his first road trip.

Team manager Tom Harward has organised a guest speaker, Paralympic silver medallist and former world championship water-skier Scott Reardon, whose right leg was amputated following a farming accident when he was twelve. He speaks about taking positives from negatives, but also the necessity of being brutally honest with yourself when setting goals and evaluating performance, and the necessity of training like you are the second best team when you are the best. The final point might be most salient to Ice, who lead the standings. Canberra are desperate to test themselves against the top team over the next two days.

"It's a shit rink, but it's a fun place to play," says Brave captain Mark Rummukainen about Brave's home the Phillip Swimming and Ice Skating Centre. Fans love the earthy delights of the league's oldest and most infamous venue, a relic, an un-renovated theme park of 1975. Only the modern designs of the team uniforms provide a clue to the era as league leaders Ice take on the Brave. Social media may have helped organise the resurrection of the Canberra AIHL presence, but in this dim, cold, congested museum, the Berlin Wall still stands, phones are located on street corners and with blokes in beards wearing turtlenecks and many women dressed in tight jeans and long boots, it feels like the hockey folk of my childhood have been reanimated.

Once past the formidable turnstiles you are in the midst of a faded aqua blue pool complex, and to the left, a low-roofed rink, its feature window showcasing dusty Canberra Knights merchandise and that team's MVP award, a handsome detailed to-scale knight in full armour. The entrance features a cursive seventies font now only used ironically.

Brent Laver says playing here provides "raw hockey", and he loves it. Johan Steenberg says the rink has "the smell of pure hockey". The Swedish assistant coach is putting on his usual bravura off-ice performance. His stock jokes and targets of abuse, the Mustangs and Finns, have been joined by Tom, who tells him to shut up several times, to no avail. From airport to airport to bus to hotel to rink, Ice personnel are either returning Johan's verbal volleys or laughing because of him. The Swede's boyish, irrepressible, endless yapping and leg-pulling lets off the management's collective steam. He makes mock claims of "racism!" in response to any direct hit retorts. "I'm a proper yolie coach and this is how they treat me!" he cries in mock indignation. Brent recalls, with enjoyment, a Steenberg outburst on the bench after a bad goal, which was delivered entirely in Swedish. Later, Johan admits that there are times he loses perspective during a game, and he has to improve his body language. Captain Lliam Webster backs that up, saying Johan "goes crazy" on the bench and it can be a distraction. Coaches have things to work on as well as players.

The Swede tells me that he was initially coming to the Mustangs but they did not call as soon as expected after he landed in Melbourne. He met Emma Poynton, agreed to work for Ice and five minutes later Mustangs president John Belic called. The Mustangs are the scapegoat in many of his stream of consciousness rants and absurd interjections, but when he gets me alone he makes sure I understand that it is all in jest, and he holds most of his rivals in high regard. "But I hate them!" he adds. He enjoys the rivalry too much not to finish with that. Johan loves "relaxed" Australia. He is glad his kids are "already Aussies" and that he married a local he met in Chelsea, London. He tells me that his two-year-old daughter recently made a solemn announcement: "Daddy I'm not going to be an ice hockey player. I'm going to be an ice hockey ballerina."

Tom Harward is now established as Johan's verbal sparring partner. He complains constantly about being put in the same car as the Swede, but somehow they always end up together, bickering like a cartoon couple. "Twenty years away from

Ice staff watch the NHL playoffs at Canberra airport.

Timewarp: Canberra's ice rink/swimming pool complex is a 1970s throwback.

The home team uses the pool's women's toilets ...

... and follows a grey carpet trail to the rink.

Visitors access their dressing room via the men's toilet.

Mind your skates, fellas. CBR Brave enter the arena.

hockey and as soon as you're back … I love it, it's in my blood," he says.

Brave enter from outside the rink, their dressing room being the dormant swimming pool's female toilets. They parade in single file along a narrow line of battered carpet placed over the concrete that leads them to the rink entrance, where they walk up the steps and through the crowd, past the merchandise table and wooden bench grandstand, and through the parted netting – no plexiglas here – to the ice.

Ice have been assigned the male swimming pool toilets as their dressing rooms. They enter the arena via a "secret" door in the rink's men's toilets, which Ian Webster and James Meredith later spend many minutes trying to lock in order to secure their team's gear during play. The potential for trouble with hockey players mingling shoulder to shoulder with crowd members is real, but players and crowd interact with good humour this night.

At the end of the first period, waiting outside while the toilet/dressing room door is un-locked and re-opened, towering Ice defender Jeff Smith engages with a bearded guy almost as big as himself who has pulled back the face-covering head of his full size tiger suit. "Man, I thought you were a real tiger! Now you're messing with my head!"

Canberra's raucous self-named Hecklers stand at the corner of the rink, and upstairs at the end of its no-frills bar, aiming to rile opponents and entertain themselves and those in the vicinity. At the moment, there is a perfect balance of abuse and laughter. The language is fruity, but all the yelling,

drumming and bell-ringing is amusing as much as intimidating, and it means the game is never dull. Lliam Webster will later say that this weekend was his best Canberra experience. In earlier times, playing there sometimes showcased "bogan ferals after blood" in the stands and "psychopaths" and "maniacs" on the ice. There was a dark side to the crowd being so involved when Saturday nights at Phillip meant beer and fights and hockey, often in that order. Now, Brave have reversed the order, and subtracted the brawling. They are a clean but physical team out to win, and they don't resort to minor-pro fisticuffs to get the mob roaring.

It's true that many of Canberra's hockey tragics turned up when the Knights languished year after year at the bottom of the standings. But the CBR Brave revitalisation has sparked the crowd, who cheer loudly, loving the efforts of their new unit, keen to measure themselves against the standings leader, convinced that Brave is up to the challenge. You can sense the self-belief gain momentum by the minute, as each cheer resounds throughout the old Phillips shed. New volunteers abound, flogging keenly sought windcheaters and caps bearing the expertly designed Brave logo. This club is going places, and needs to go places other than this rink, long-term. But for now it's all about beating Ice at its dingy fortress, and being outrageous and witty while doing so. League commissioner Robert Bannerman sidles up to the corner to hear the hecklers, and tells stories about their more outlandish exploits, like holding up posters of an opposing players' swimsuit model girlfriend with their own faces superimposed. Sample abuse from the first

VETERAN CANBERRA GOALIE BRAD HUNT REVEALED THE EXTENT OF THE CBR BRAVE "MIRACLE" WHEN HE SPOKE TO CANBERRA SPORTS MAGAZINE *PLAY*. HE SAYS THAT HIS INITIAL REACTION WAS TO FAREWELL THE KNIGHTS. "ALL I WANTED TO DO WITH RUMMO WAS SET UP A CHARITY GAME, SAY GOODBYE TO THE FANS ..." IT'S HISTORY NOW THAT THIS INITIAL MEETING LED TO THE ESTABLISHMENT OF CBR BRAVE. "NOW WE ARE PLAYING FOR US. WE ARE NOT PLAYING FOR THE RINK, WE ARE NOT PLAYING FOR AN OWNER, WE'RE PLAYING FOR EACH OTHER. WE ARE DOING THIS FOR US ... AND FOR EVERY ONE OF THE FANS THAT COME OUT ... WE ARE HERE BECAUSE WE LOVE HOCKEY." BRAD, LIKE MARK RUMMUKAINEN, FOUND THE FITNESS REGIME OF THE NEW CLUB TAXING, BUT REWARDING. "THAT FIVE-WEEK PRE-SEASON WAS THE HARDEST THING I'VE EVER DONE IN MY LIFE. THE WHOLE TEAM HAD TO DO IT AND THEY DID. LAST YEAR THAT WOULDN'T HAVE HAPPENED. THIS YEAR YOU ARE ACCOUNTABLE TO THE GUY NEXT TO YOU ..."

period: "I had sex with your spouse and or significant other!"

On this occasion, the hockey is good enough that the crowd enhances the experience rather than dominating it. Ice score first, 45 seconds from the first intermission, via Todd Graham, who in his first AIHL game of the season puts away a rebound from an Austin McKenzie drive and shot. They have possession with good chances on nearly every shift in the second period, but Brave net-minder Petri Pitkanen – crowd-issued nickname 'Pitstop' – is a wall, economical in his movements, always in position. Ice's Jayden Pine-Murphy is increasingly stretched as well, but continues his outstanding season.

Brave step up their intensity in the final stanza, and after an especially persistent shift, hack the puck past Jaden after he has made several good saves. 1–1. Brave increase the tempo with ten minutes to play and the tension continues to rise, the crowd becoming hysterical as the teams swap blistering rushes. On the tiny rink, every deflection can put a player in position to shoot. It is not the place for stretch passes and considered geometrics. It is brutal pinball, puck and bodies bouncing off each other endlessly. Get hit, get it in, chase, and get it to the net. Raw hockey.

Funny abuse: upstairs at Heckler's Corner.

The excellent refereeing maintains the pace, and there are only three penalties all game, one against Jeff Smith for delay of game after he bats the puck into the low, dripping roof to get a face-off, surely a first for his globetrotting scrapbook. With six minutes to play, veteran Ice defenceman Ross Howell goes to the box. The scoreboard, equipped with space to record the progress of four penalties, shows none. The 'penalty box' is merely another section of the timber bench grandstand, another unique low-tech feature of the old rink. Players get plenty of free advice sitting among patrons. Some have grapes thrown on them. It is a volatile, amusing sight, but not much fun for the players and potentially dangerous; one hothead reacting to an abusive fan and the league has an ugly situation on their hands. The un-semaphored powerplay is killed and a volunteer hoists the side netting with a pulley to allow Ross access back to the ice.

There's no separation between fans and players in Canberra.

Ice forward Jason Baclig sums up the positive attitude of both teams to the unique surrounds. Finding a crushed beer can on the ice, he feigns trying to get a sip out of it before handing it to a ref for removal.

Matt Armstrong's assiduous forechecking draws Canberra's only penalty with three minutes left, just after Jaden has pulled off a big save to keep the scores level. Canberra have the momentum, and rush back after killing the penalty. They push hard, and the pulsating game ends deadlocked at 1–1. After the

Absolutely no separation.

first two shots of the shootout are saved, Matt Armstrong and then Tim Johansson score, and Ice have survived a mini-classic to nab a valuable two road points. They are still yet to lose on the road in 2014.

The coaches ask the watchers what we thought of the game, electrified by the battle. It was a ripping contest, we answer, great atmosphere, tough, exciting. Both teams looked like finalists …

Canberra are confident they will win on Sunday. "They're not so good. I expected more. They weren't that fast," I hear from the Brave fans. They misunderstand why Ice is on top. It is not because of superior individual talents, though Ice have plenty of fine players. It is because they are a happy group playing for each other, working hard on every play and running three lines. If their teamwork or work-rate drop, they're back in the pack. Several teams have individual players who are faster, stronger and greater scoring threats.

Post-game, there is a signature AIHL 2014 image. Tim Johansson, again winner of the battered Cooper helmet award as best Ice player, walks through the post-match crowd outside the rink wearing only a pair of shorts and the helmet, and grasping a towel. But he isn't a serial exhibitionist: Ice is taking advantage of the rink's flanking outdoor pools to perform an aquatic recovery session immediately after their game. The rink won't or can't turn on the lights, so the pale bodies of players – the rest of them without headgear – pad gingerly into the cold darkness.

Outside Andrew Deans chats with old acquaintance Ian Webster. He is a fifteen-year stalwart as Canberra road manager, after originally getting involved when his son played. It's four years since his son retired, but he has stayed on. His son-in-law is assistant coach Dave Rogina. Unique friendships are forged in these post-game minutes, a few times a year, over the years. Andrew says the Knights had "fizzled out". Like governments, the leadership of sports clubs need to be refreshed every ten years. He says there is a "great new enthusiasm" about the new club.

At the post-match dinner at the Tradies venue just across the street, Mark Rummukainen, busy wrestling crying infants, says Brave's rapport with their fans is based on their humble and engaging attitude, which creates a strong connection. As if to prove this, players wait in line to order their dinner with fans and coaches, no-one pulling rank. This is where I encounter Matt and Jordan, two Brave fans in their late twenties. "We don't care what the team is called as long as there is hockey in Canberra", Matt tells me. "I was so close I could be bled on," Jordan says of his first game at the Phillip rink. He says he was *checked* at his last game, while standing with the Hecklers. Matt and Jordan agree that it is best the league remains amateur. Professional sportsmen in Canberra often think they're above the fans, they say. Not so the Brave, several of whom asked Jordan and Matt's their thoughts on the game in the meal queue. They admit that they don't really hate most opponents. They want their rink to be hostile but they don't want anything really bad to happen to anyone. They respect any of these players who sacrifice their time and bodies for the game they love. Fan and player enjoy the show each puts on.

Canberra the city is derided by other Australians as boring. Matt and Jordan don't exactly denounce this stereotype. "The only things to do in Canberra are play sport, watch sport or go out on the town." These boys do all three, as do most of the Hecklers, who have formed their own teams to play rec. hockey. I ask why Canberra's hockey teams have had such a strong following. Canberra's cold winters and proximity to good ski slopes may be an influence, they say. Some diplomats in town from hockey nations add their love of the game and the people of the Australian Capital Territory always support teams in national leagues. (Hence the chant: "AC … AC what? ACT!").

But Matt and Jordan's key message is that hockey at Phillip filled a niche for fans left behind by more expensive, impersonal and "arrogant" professional sports, which sought mass-market income and audiences. Those who prefer simpler pleasures stuck with the Knights, regardless of results, and made their own fun when the team struggled. They have forged a self-perpetuating culture of parochialism leavened by humour. If bigger but more sterile stadiums were available, advocates of growth would have to account for these fans, a loyal core force many sports would adore.

After Ice has finished its communal meal, it's off to the bottle shop, players agonising over their choice of booze for their Saturday night chats, and movie-watching, card-playing or story-telling sessions. Waiting at the cash register – a wide-eyed cashier clearly busier than he has been for months at 9 pm Saturday night – I chat with Jeff Smith. He says he had been saving for a few years to be able to afford this experience, the vagaries of Australia's visa system meaning he is living off savings on this trip. It has got something to do with being 33, not 30. Many other players, including Jason Baclig, had told him "you have to do it" of the Australian hockey experience. France and Dubai remain on Jeff's hockey bucket list. His partner is coming out from Holland with the second part of his funds in July, so he chooses his wine economically.

The hotel is situated alongside kangaroo-laden paddocks, and Ice's Aussies have been taunting first-year imports Jeff and Gustaf Huth about their fascination with the famous marsupials. "Should we go Kangaroo-pushing?" one asks. "Look, here's an Australian magpie," one exclaims in mock wonder. It sounds like a familiar routine, honed on each year's intake. Jeff is not perturbed by such ribbing. In Perth, he took meticulous photos of daffodils. He is clearly not your garden-variety sportsman.

Ice players wait for their dressing room to be unlocked.

Brave administrator Jamie Wilson behind the nets.

The tiger-head fan is a Brave fixture.

JUNE 2014

SUNDAY THE 1ST

ROAD TRIP THREE:
CBR BRAVE V MELBOURNE ICE
DAY TWO

Ice's morning team meeting has an edge to it. Well, it is supposed to. The team crowds into a single hotel room, awaited by a grim-faced Brent Laver. Parties unknown tied his door shut during the night, and when heating made the room stifling, Brent and room-mate Johan Steenberg found they couldn't escape. Brent tries to deliver an outraged speech about the lack of respect shown the coaching staff by the callous overnight prank, but he breaks down laughing before he has finished his first sentence. Jeff Smith is considered the likely perpetrator. "I don't know who did it," he says, wide-eyed, a better actor than his coach. "But I can find out."

Apart from tips about adapting to the small rink, most instructions have been given to players throughout the week, so the coaches are surprisingly approachable in the hour before game time back at the rink. Assistant coach and Ice ex-player Glen Mayer says that he makes it to Tuesday's 8 pm training sessions at 7.55 pm, due to responsibilities with his young family at home. He leans much more to the calm style of Brent Laver than the excitable Johan. Our chat, and Ice's pre-game preparation, is interrupted by effluent overflowing in their dressing room/toilet. The "shit rink" call becomes literal.

In game two, Canberra starts fiercely, and it's no surprise when they score first. They look set to uphold their fans' expectations. Ice matches the challenge and the score is locked at 1–1 for all of the second period. At final intermission, I check out the upstairs bar, source of so much income, which looks like its fit-out was interrupted before the decorators finished. It feels like a conceptual art piece based on underlay. I meet Roger, an American who has lived in Canberra for 28 years. Brave has captivated him. "I don't really know the game, but I love it here," he says. He also enjoyed being sledged by Jeff Smith for his gaudy home-knit USA beanie/toque, which he says he wears to annoy his grandchildren. "I'm very impressed. He overturned the stereotype of a hockey player."

Ice leads 2–1 briefly in the final period, but when Brave fight back, their momentum surpasses the visitors, their imports

There are no corporate boxes at Phillip.

Brave fans cram every vantage point.

Brave players get amongst their people.

pouring in three final period goals to ensure an impressive 4–2 victory. Their star first line Mathieu Ouellette, Anton Kokkonen and Stephen Blunden have tallied eleven of the home team's twelve points over the weekend. Ice's nominal first line stars Matt Armstrong and Jason Baclig have not troubled the scoresheet, youngster Austin McKenzie and defenceman Todd Armstrong their goalscorers. Matt never has a good time in Canberra. This is the third time he has received a ten-minute misconduct in the rink. He says he was adjudged to have checked from behind when making a poke check, during which his opponent fell over. It changed the game's momentum, but he says Brave was too good regardless.

For CBR Brave's Peter Chamberlain there is nothing but wonder and pride. This win over the standings leader is another endorsement of his fledgling club, with the next step a major scalp on the road. He is yet to experience another AIHL rink but he already has a list of questions for the league AGM, and he is assessing rink options for the next two years. Despite his brief experience with the league, he believes the next step for the AIHL is a "true major sponsor" and more TV coverage. He would like the capacity to project messages and video on to his rink surface to ramp up the non-hockey entertainment. Peter is full of energy and plans and speaks with certainty, giving him the aura of someone who knows what he is talking about, someone worth following, a leader who gets things done. The ex-footy umpire is still learning hockey. But his regime is vindicated by Brave's position in the standings, their membership and Facebook numbers, and these crammed-in, ecstatic crowds.

> WHEN WE'RE ALL LEAVING EACH OTHER ON A SUNDAY NIGHT, THERE'S A REAL MELANCHOLY ABOUT IT. 'OH, BACK TO THE NORMAL ...' - BRENT LAVER

SUNDAY THE 1ST (9.15 PM)

It is Sunday night at an almost empty Canberra airport and Brent Laver, usually upbeat, is flat. His ladder-leading team just had its eight-game winning streak broken, and the Ice brains trust are disappointed that a couple of instructions were not followed by their players. However, their post-mortem acknowledges that their team's effort was unstinting and their opponent Canberra Brave was formidable. In any case, Brent is not downcast because of the result. He is afflicted by this malaise at the end of every road trip, regardless of results. Brent, and many of the travelling Ice crew, suffer from a syndrome unique to the AIHL. Sunday Night Sadness. This condition affects many amateur players and coaches when they realise the bonding road trip is about to come to an end and the plane they're about to board will transport them back to the "real" world, where they have to work at something other than hockey. "When we're all leaving each other on a Sunday night, there's a real melancholy about it. 'Oh, back to the normal' ..." Brent says.

Many coaches and administrators have the love of parents for the individuals they guide, advise and occasionally upbraid. Such a bond is a difficult thing to break because jobs, courses and traffic beckon. A self-confessed "man manager" as a coach, Brent uses visits to Perth, Adelaide, Newcastle, Sydney and Canberra to work on relationships with players as much as tactics. He enjoys the chance to get his players "out of their comfort zones". On road trips he can "get in the head of players a bit and try to get their story". "You get guys not necessarily sitting where they sit every week, guys sitting next to different guys having conversations."

For the past two days, Ice players and staff have eaten together, laughed at each other's idiosyncrasies, put silly hats on their rookies and best player, and utilised a customised dialect. They've sat in the same seats on their numerous bus trips, shared war stories from overseas leagues of groupies, maniacs, goons, injuries, bad luck, good wins, romantic misadventures, and odd teammates and opponents. They've crunched into and over old boards and into old nets and chicken wire. They've taken shots and dealt out and received hits, and sprinted up and back in search of an opening on a tiny ice surface. They've undertaken a recovery session in cold darkness in the pool outside the rink. They've been kneaded into game-readiness by physio (and sponsor) James Meredith. Their teammate Chris Wong has been taken to hospital with a damaged shoulder. They've frequented food courts and a mall cinema to kill time and relax, then played soccer to re-energise. They've played their hearts out against a team just as committed. They've scored and been scored against. They've triumphed and been vanquished.

For two days, Melbourne Ice have lived like the professional sportsmen and coaches many of them would love to be, and now the plane is boarding, and the illusion cannot be sustained. Now it's back to the factory floor, warehouse, classroom, or office, nursing bruises.

I mention my Sunday Night Sadness theory to Johan. "I am sad too. Have a drink," he says, interrupting my reverie with the coach and bringing up silly pictures on his phone meant to represent the sorry state of the Mustangs. "At the end of the first period, 6–0, we'll ask Brad to call it off!" he says of the upcoming derby, refusing to give melancholy any respect.

TEAM	GP	W	L	D	SOW	SOL	PTS
ICE	10	6	2	0	2	0	22
ADRENALINE	12	4	4	0	3	1	19
BRAVE	9	5	2	0	1	1	18
MUSTANGS	10	5	3	0	0	2	17
ICE DOGS	12	5	7	0	0	0	15
NORTH STARS	10	4	5	0	0	1	13
BEARS	9	3	4	0	1	1	12
THUNDER	10	1	6	0	1	2	7

THURSDAY THE 5TH

It's the third Melbourne derby, and the Mustangs have moved Jeff Grant from defence to join Joey Hughes and Viktor Gibbs-Sjodin as a forward, risking weakness at the back to pit their most potent attacking force possible against Ice's best players. The ploy works. Ice's top line is kept off the scoresheet, and the attacking, focused Mustangs finally come of age. After three seasons and 91 games, here it is – pace and quick transitions, yes, but also relentless, consistent pressure, a redoubled resolve once their nemesis arch-rival begins its inevitable fightback, and an absence of ridiculous errors.

Jeff Grant's line combines sublimely in the first minute of the second period to make it 2–0, and a white-hot Jamie Bourke scores what Mustangs hockey director Andy McDowell will later describe as an "NHL quality" shorthanded goal to make it 3–0 halfway through the period. Ice responds with its best hockey of the match, second-line stars Lliam Webster and Austin McKenzie capitalising on powerplays. With the Stangs leading 3–2 at the start of the final period, the packed house, and presumably Ice, are expecting another derby thriller.

But the Mustangs maintain and increase their pressure and tempo. Their match effort is an ever-steepening graph, precipitous in the third period. Ice rise to the challenge for a time, and spurn several big chances with the score 5-3, but then Viktor Gibbs-Sjodin holds them off with one of the goals of the season off his backhand, and the little brother of Melbourne hockey is revealed as fully grown. The Stangs push Ice over the edge with a pair of goals to Pat O'Kane, the last of which is utterly predictable and foreseeable – a two-on-one – but so perfectly executed that a stranded Gustaf Huth has no chance in the Ice net. He slams his stick on the ice in frustration. The Mustangs have ploughed in five goals to one in the final 20 minutes to win 8–3. It is the most comprehensive Melbourne derby win in recent memory. Though not the seemingly ordained derby cliff-hanger, this performance from the upstarts is thrilling. Gorgeous passing plays, canny interceptions, self-discipline and clinical finishing – the Mustangs are great to watch this night.

Fraser Carson is the right person for the Mustangs press corps to speak to afterwards. "It always feels good to beat them," he says. "It doesn't happen too often so we've got to take advantage of it. The team finally came together and showed the skill we do have and the power that we can generate. It's what we've been waiting for all season."

Have the Mustangs cared too much about beating Melbourne

Jeremy Brown and Jamie Bourke battle for the puck.

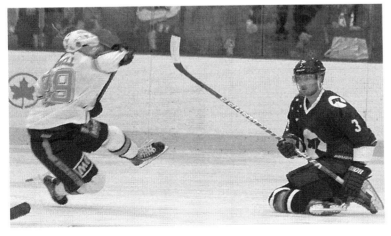

Pat O'Kane and Todd Graham sit down on the job.

Ice? Coach Brad Vigon does not shy away from the accusation the following day. "It's such a big game that you can't help it, even if you tried to treat it as any other game, you realistically can't do it. You want to win it so bad."

The Mustangs felt they had the better of Ice for much of their two losses to their rinkmates this year. "That's why last night was so important, because we almost felt like we had a bit of some bad juju or something with Melbourne Ice," says Brad. "We're ahead three-nothing and they score two goals and we start thinking to ourselves, 'Are we somehow going to have a puck go off a skate or a crazy penalty or a bad bounce and all of sudden they're going to take it to a shootout and we're going to lose this game? We can't beat these guys?' Believe me that was going through our minds." The win and its scope banish such superstitious self-questioning. "I think we might have found our heart last night."

The game is one of two Thursday night derbies scheduled this year. The final one, in August, is bound to count for something in such a tight season. But the timing

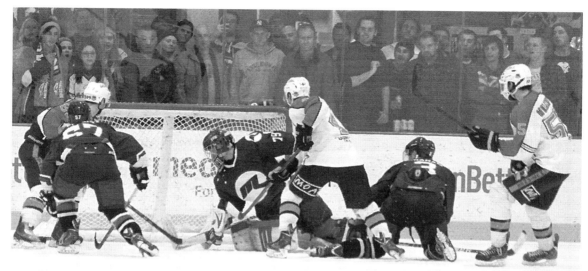

Eyes on the goal at the Icehouse.

of this one does neither club many favours. The Mustangs had a double-header the previous weekend, go to work Friday and then fly to play the improving Newcastle North Stars on Saturday before a bus ride to western Sydney to take on the Bears on Sunday. That's a professional schedule for an amateur team.

Ice, flying high a week earlier, are left to stew over consecutive losses for nine days. Star forward Matt Armstrong admits that the extent of the loss was a shock. "No one said it was going to be easy," he says. "We have to be better defensively. I guess the wait continues before we get redemption."

Brad Vigon faces the challenge of three games in four days squarely. "Guys don't want to practice, they want to play. It's maybe slightly harder on the body but it's better on the mind." He was not happy with his team earlier in the season. "We were doing pretty well but probably not as well as we were expecting of ourselves. But our expectations were built on last year and the league wasn't as good last year," he says. "If you don't bring your A-game in any game, you're going to lose. There's no easybeats."

Like most teams this year, the Mustangs have had games where they have been stymied by brilliant goaltending, and the depth of the AIHL means no team is dominating. Brad uses Perth Thunder as his example. Thunder started the weekend bottom of the standings, but ended it within striking distance of the four after two resounding home wins over an injury-hit Adelaide Adrenaline. They are on a three-game winning streak and Brad feels they will be hard to beat for the rest of the season.

The Mustangs will also be hard to beat. His team now has a benchmark for what it can achieve when it plays its best hockey. "If we can keep this kind of energy ... look out, we could be dangerous."

Those words reflect possibly the high point to date of Brad's coaching career. What he says next exposes the dark side of his job.

"This year there's guys aren't playing on a regular basis or when they do dress they're not playing that much. It's by far the most difficult thing I have to do as coach, to try to keep everyone happy. You're always going to have guys who are not having a run and they're not happy about it, but it's a little bit different in Australia because most of the guys that are playing at this level have been the best all their lives growing up and they have never been used to sitting on the bench. When you talk to them they say they understand but then they don't get chosen and its 'why, what have I done wrong?' And it's not so much that you've done something wrong, it's that other people are doing better than you. I'm trying to make sure that I've got the right team that's going to have the best opportunity to win games. It's not about being fair anymore."

Brad says such a dilemma is understood implicitly overseas, in more populous hockey climes. His subsequent admission is not something you expect to hear from a coach. "I want everybody to be happy, I want to be happy. I want to be liked. I don't want people to think that I'm a jerk or I'm not fair. You piss guys off, the first thing they're going to do is say 'Oh, I quit, why should I bother?' It's not like in Canada or America where most guys are going to say 'I'm going to work harder, I'm going to show him that I deserve to be in that spot'."

Dealing with such "angst", Brad admits coaching is a year-by-year proposition, which will be discussed at season's end with his family. "Especially when you're going through a bad spot and you're not going well and you're not enjoying it, you ask yourself 'what the hell am I doing this for?' It's not as if you're making a living doing it."

⊜⊜⊜⊜⊜⊜⊜⊜

The postponed Ice Dogs/Newcastle game has been rescheduled for Sunday June 22 in Newcastle. Ice Dogs members will get in free and the club is hiring a bus for fans. It is a measure of the difficulties facing teams getting ice time that the blameless Dogs, inconvenienced by the North Stars' bus breakdown, have agreed to play a home game in Newcastle.

WHEN YOU'RE GOING THROUGH A BAD SPOT AND YOU'RE NOT GOING WELL AND YOU'RE NOT ENJOYING IT, YOU ASK YOURSELF 'WHAT THE HELL AM I DOING THIS FOR?' IT'S NOT AS IF YOU'RE MAKING A LIVING DOING IT. - BRAD VIGON

SATURDAY THE 7TH

Rick Keyzer thrived on speed, danger and excitement. That was the obvious thing about him, and the reason he made a good hockey player, one who got in his share of scrapes. He was also creatively skilled and singular, hence his career as a sign-writer and his love of surfing. He understands the uncontrollable passions. It's why he hasn't watched a hockey game in fourteen years. "I know if I watch a game, I will want to play," he tells me.

We are at the reunion of the 1984 Blackhawks Senior A premiership team at the Icehouse, which coincides with the twenty-sixth annual national Old-Timers' tournament. Sure enough, Rick's most respected mentor, Charlie Grandy is pressing him for when he will play again. Charlie, in his seventies, is still playing at this tournament, and has flown from Queensland to be part of it. Two people tell me stories about Charlie's final days in A-grade, well into his 40s, when he warned forwards going into corners to "keep their head up". Those who did not take his advice felt the pain. Charlie says "any team sport is good" for developing character. His lifelong commitment as a hockey player and administrator in Canada and Australia is evidence of which team sport he favoured. The Grandys have lived by Charlie's ethos – his son, my mate Glenn, is a sports nut who played good level Australian Rules Football, inline hockey and club cricket as well as hockey. Glenn's boys were given an ultimatum by their mum Sharyn – one winter sport at a time, and they have chosen footy "because their mates were playing". Glenn is hopeful they will return to hockey. The closest ice rink to Glenn's outer suburban house is Oakleigh or the Icehouse, both at least half an hour away.

"When will you play again?" is the standard question asked of ex-hockey players. Rick explains why. "It's the most addictive sport. You can't get it out of your blood. I love surfing, but there's nothing like hockey. The sensation ..." Rick only stopped playing at 38 when he was injured in a bad hit, lifted by one opponent and smashed by another. He wears an inaugural Melbourne Ice jacket, a lighter blue than the modern model. He played their first two seasons at the end of his career. Searching for what had been missing in his life recently, he realised it was hockey, and this gathering is confirming it.

The game occurring beneath us, the top division of the over-35s, is deft and entertaining, and all the ballyhoo from ex-opponents and teammates fills the Icehouse's St Moritz bar with bonhomie. Most of the stories are of reckless acts and youthful misbehaviour: big hits, delinquency on interstate representative trips. So many here never stopped playing, or only gave up when their bodies or jobs demanded that they take a break. They are hooked for life, and though glad the Icehouse exists – with its warmed floors in the dressing room - they probably don't care that much that the AIHL is taking the sport to unprecedented numbers of Australians. Mostly, they care about each other, their mates who would play in a decrepit shed, and have done so, at crappy hours, all their hockey lives.

Andrew Petrie is here, having just played, and we speak briefly about the Ice Dogs. He has stood down an import for breaking curfew, and put the captain on defence, and his players have reacted well to both moves. He says he runs two systems, but he will never tell anyone what they are. Outside that, he gives his talented players freedom to express themselves. Andrew likes dangling in front of you what he won't tell you. He does it with a glint in his eye, hoping you are intrigued, then tries to give you something else you will be just as interested in. A salesman's habit, perhaps? He is enthusiastic and wholehearted. We vow once again to have a long chat about all things AIHL, but he has been a friend and opponent of too many present not to be in high demand; he is pulled back into squabbles of reminiscence.

Glenn talks about how the standards of local coaching have lifted because kids emulate the deeds of ever-improving senior players. He values the incremental trickle-down improvements that a first-class national league provides. Maverick Rick says that coaching juniors taught him more than any kid has learnt from him.

Blackhawks diehards Charlie Grandy and Andy McDowell.

John Sutton, Glenn Grandy and Rick Keyzer at the Icehouse.

TUESDAY THE 10TH

The Mustangs are unsurprisingly flat on Saturday in Newcastle, playing two days after the derby. They fight back to level twice before losing 5–2 against the ever-improving North Stars. Amazingly, its Newcastle's first home win of the season. Previously their rink has been almost impregnable. North Stars coach Garry Doré is understandably delighted. "The Mustangs are a great team this year," Dore tells the AIHL site. "They've got a lot more strengths than weaknesses, and we knew we'd have to play hard against these guys."

A day later, a come-from-behind win against the Bears puts the Mustangs on top of the standings for the first time in their history. Playing their third game in four days, they clinch victory with three goals in the final period. The Mustangs pummel Bears net-minder Daniel Palmkvist with a season-high tally of 51 shots. After surviving with two men in the penalty box early in the last stanza, Brad Vigon calls a time-out with ten minutes left in the game. "At the time, it seemed like we were just letting the game happen instead of enforcing our will on the play," he says later. "I'm not the kind of coach who likes to yell and scream at his guys but I had some choice words to get them fired up." It was the spark the Mustangs needed. With 4.22 to play, Joey Hughes scored his second goal of the night with a wrist shot from the top of slot that beat Palmkvist high glove-side and gave the visitors a 4–3 lead.

"It was a tough loss," said Bears coach Vlad Rubes. "It's tough when you have guys battling hard for pucks and it seemed when our guys lifted the stick or played the body, we got the penalty called against us. That was a momentum killer. They are a good team. We've got some experienced guys to come back into the line-up and that will give us a boost".

Newcastle hockey all-rounder Garry Dore.

HALF OF THE LEAGUE'S TEAMS **FACE** DIFFICULTIES WITH FLIGHT SCHEDULES THAT CAN DEPRIVE THEM OF THEIR BEST PLAYERS.

WEDNESDAY THE 11TH

Adelaide are second in the standings, but they are doing it hard. Coach Ryan O'Handley tells me that of his team's six injuries, two are fractures that will keep players out for six to eight weeks, and two are long-term concussions to their best import and best defenceman. The other is a strain, which thankfully is a day-to-day proposition. I mention Canberra's issue with losing Mondays to travel. Ryan faces similar problems. "Flights are a major issue. When we play against the Ice Dogs in Liverpool, we have to stay over Sunday night as we can't make the last flight out. We requested that the Ice Dogs move the game to 3.30 pm, like we do for visiting teams on Sunday, but the rink will not allow them to. As a result we lose four to five players after the first period because they can't miss work on Monday." Adrenaline also stay over Sunday night in Perth. Luckily this year, their game is followed by a public holiday, but usually the extra night's accommodation and meals costs his club a "considerable amount".

SATURDAY THE 14TH

Newcastle's livestream is a one-camera, slightly dim affair, but it misses nothing and the commentary is knowledgeable, thanks to AIHL stalwart Peter Lambert. He notes that Ice's diminutive defenceman Marcus Wong "plays bigger" than his size. Peter's North Stars score early and have a powerplay soon after. About the only game Ice has won at Hunter Ice Skating Stadium in recent times was the 2012 grand final. They just never get it together there, and the North Stars always rise to the occasion. It is 3-0 after a period, and 5-0 in Newcastle's favour after two. Shots are even, but Ice are committing all sorts of defensive sins, including conceding a shorthanded goal. Ice has a brittle element this season, despite their good record. When they lose, they lose big. This night, they fight back in the final period, Matt Armstrong scoring their first goal halfway through the last period. They end up losing 7-4, with Army having a hand in three of the four goals. Has the Mustangs loss taken the wind out of their sails?

Peter avoids all possible accusation of bias by understating. "Ice's defensive game tonight hasn't been strong enough to support their goalie." By the end of the game, that is plural – Jaden Pine-Murphy has conceded two in his half of the game, Gustaf Huth five in his. Ice have conceded fifteen goals in two games. There's no Tim Johansson or Jason Baclig, but it's still a mystifyingly poor effort from Ice.

The North Stars, with their scoring mojo restored, and their strongest line-up in place, are looking like barging back into finals contention. Pete's plain-speaking verdict: "The Newcastle North Stars were pretty ordinary early on, but they're coming good now".

PETER LAMBERT HAS BEEN A HOCKEY FAN, PLAYER, WRITER, WEBMASTER, MEDIA MANAGER, CAMERAMAN, COMMENTATOR AND AUSTRALIAN ICE HOCKEY LEAGUE COMMISSIONER, AND HE STILL DEVOTES HIS SPARE TIME TO THE NEWCASTLE NORTH STARS AND THE HOCKEYWISE WEBSITE. HOWEVER HE BELIEVES HIS GREATEST CONTRIBUTION IN CLUBLAND IS RECRUITING SKILLED VOLUNTEERS, WHO HE DESCRIBES AS THE AIHL'S "PRECIOUS COMMODITIES". "THAT'S THE THING I'M PROBABLY PROUDEST OF - THE PEOPLE I HAVE IDENTIFIED AND THEY LOVE IT NOW TOO." BEGINNING AS TEAM MANAGER FOR THE FLEDGLING NORTH STARS, LAMBERT WROTE ARTICLES "BECAUSE THERE WAS NO-ONE ELSE TO DO IT", BEFORE ESTABLISHING LINKS WITH NEWCASTLE'S PRESS AND TV NETWORKS. AS AN AIHL COMMISSIONER, HE HELPED RAMP UP THE LEAGUE'S WEBSITE, SOCIAL MEDIA AND LIVE BROADCASTING, AND HELPED ESTABLISH A LICENCEE MODEL FOR CLUBS, IN SEARCH OF STABILITY. THESE DAYS, HIS OCCASIONAL CORRECTIVES ON SOCIAL MEDIA PROVE ESSENTIAL READING, EDUCATING EAGER BUT IGNORANT NEW FANS. EXAMPLE: "THE SORT OF MONEY THE LEAGUE HAS WON'T BUILD YOU A RINK OR EVEN RUN A SHORT TV ADVERTISING CAMPAIGN IN CAPITAL CITIES. THE MARKET IS COMPLEX AND THE RESOURCES THE AIHL HAS MUST BE USED VERY CAREFULLY. EVERY TIME THEY SPEND A DOLLAR, THEY HAVE TO MAKE A DOLLAR BACK AT LEAST."

SUNDAY THE 15TH

Today, a couple of patterns repeat across the league. The Bears are hard to beat, but lose narrowly to Ice 6-4 after a tough struggle. Like nearly every Bears game, their opponent sets the pace, but they fight back, levelling the scores twice, then making it a one-goal game halfway through the final period. Jeff Smith's powerplay goal with eight minutes left is the final score of the game. The Bears, yet to be beaten as badly as Ice have been a couple of times, have now lost eight straight games. They lost 8-6 to Canberra the day before, as always in the game throughout. Ice has kept its finals campaign afloat by breaking a three-game losing streak.

The Ice Dogs, at home, again finish too strongly for a visitor, beating Canberra Brave 6-3, after trailing 2-3, and scoring three unanswered goals in the final stanza.

WEDNESDAY THE 18TH

Greg Oddy this year becomes the first player to log 300 games in the AIHL. It is a mighty number considering the league started with 15-game seasons. To northern hemisphere players, it represents maybe five years' service, but the evergreen Adelaide Adrenaline captain has been at it since 2000 to build his tally. Given his heritage, he was destined to be an Australian hockey icon. "My grandparents started the first rink in Adelaide in Hindley Street and that's where mum met Dad, who was playing hockey. And they got us kids involved at a young age; I have been playing since I was five."

Greg's father Steve and a business partner started the Adelaide Avalanche, one of the three original AIHL teams, and its first champion, in 2001. Greg admits he had doubts about the AIHL. "I didn't think it would survive as long as this just because others had tried it before and they hadn't succeeded. We all understand the costs involved in it. I wouldn't have bet that the league would be around now back when it started." He credits the "committed group", including his father, Canberra Knights boss John Raut, and Sydney Bears leaders Tyler Lovering and Wayne Hellyer, who "invested a lot of money and time" to make the league work. "They had a vision and they weren't going to let it fail. They had their challenges early on, the easy thing would have been to walk away, but they really stuck at it."

In 2005, Steve Oddy said of Adelaide, "the attendance rate is up, the standard is really improving and the sport is growing at an alarming rate. But it really needs an injection of money and someone with extra resources to take the club to the next level." Nearly a decade later, those words still apply. New owners have taken over Adrenaline's rink, the only one in South Australia, and have assured Adrenaline their future is secure, but Greg says "moving forward, we need a new rink". He's another Aussie hockey veteran who isn't easily impressed by endless talk about a new facility. "You've got two or three parties that are talking to different people and they all have their different agendas. Until that slab goes down, you don't want to get too excited."

Greg says players are treated well in Adelaide, they do not pay to play, most have long-serving player sponsors, and the relationship between the club and its rink is sound. He is excited by the prospects of the comparatively long-lived AIHL, but he remains concerned by the disparity between the successful and struggling clubs. "At Adelaide ... we can't fit any more people in our rink, so for us to grow we need sponsorship dollars and for that we need facilities, you need something more attractive. Getting all teams financially viable is the big thing and I think [the lack of] rinks are holding them back."

An account director at the Australian Radio Network, Greg says his lifestyle is "pretty full on". He travels for work as well as hockey and has two daughters under the age of three, but he believes he finds "balance" amidst his myriad responsibilities, and his wife encourages him to continue playing. He looks super-fit, but he is 34, and the commitment is much bigger these days, with seven road trips instead of five, and 28 games instead of 22, or that original fifteen. "I want to be able to play at this elite level. I don't want to play just for the sake of playing. I'll know if I'm not having fun. Right now I've still got the hunger, I enjoy playing and the team is in a good place; we have some really good young kids coming through, so I'm happy to keep playing."

Greg plays to win championships. But he finds it rewarding "just being around the boys and being able to play hockey at the highest level in the country". "That's what the AIHL has provided

Adelaide icon Greg Oddy.

us with: a great league to play in, so we've got more players staying here, not going elsewhere." That said, Greg believes elite Australian juniors owe it to themselves to test their talents overseas. He spent eight seasons in Europe and Canada. "You learn a lot over there, it's totally different, you learn a lot about yourself. It puts things into perspective, it's a bit of a reality check. There's someone at practice every day who wants your spot, you would never have that here. You're on the ice every day; some guys here are only on the ice three times a week. You just live and breathe hockey and you quickly realise there's so many good players out there. You quickly find out that you're not that good! A lot of guys who have a bit of success through the junior ranks in Australia find themselves over there and all of a sudden they're in the bottom six players and they've got defensive responsibilities. That can be a massive change, but it develops you, it makes you a better hockey player."

> **AT ADELAIDE ... WE CAN'T FIT ANY MORE PEOPLE IN OUR RINK, SO FOR US TO GROW WE NEED SPONSORSHIP DOLLARS AND FOR THAT WE NEED FACILITIES, YOU NEED SOMETHING MORE ATTRACTIVE.**
> **- GREG ODDY**

Bench left, dressing room right.

Behind the goals.

So close you can tap a helmet.

FRIDAY THE 20TH

It is a tradition of Australian ice hockey that players, no matter how talented, train at ungodly hours. Ice time at antipodean rinks is always at a premium. In my time, local clubs were granted the salubrious hour of 6 am Sunday morning to practice, a bracing prospect for Saturday night socialisers. The usual outcome these days for AIHL teams are late night midweek practice sessions. Melbourne Ice and The Mustangs swap rink time on Thursdays, with the second team not hitting the ice until 9.30 pm. It's easy for them to remember they are unpaid at times like that.

Adelaide Adrenaline coach Ryan O'Handley.

Adelaide Adrenaline goes to another extreme. Their main training session is Tuesday night, but their second session is Thursday at 6 am. Coach Ryan O'Handley, a senior lecturer in veterinary parasitology at the University of Adelaide, says the early hour is the choice of his team, which consists mainly of tradesmen. "They're used to getting up at 5am! These are plumbers, electricians and carpenters and those are the hours they prefer." He says if prime time was available, he'd take it, but he understands the competing needs of other ice sports stakeholders sharing the Thebarton Ice Arena. The rink is owned and run by the South Australian Ice Sports Federation, formed by the figure-skating, broomball and ice hockey communities in 2004, when the rink was threatened with closure.

Like Canberra Brave this year, Adelaide Adrenaline was forged amid crisis. In 2008, when the Adelaide Avalanche club folded after being unable to meet the cost of playing on the road, an interim club, the As, played out the season, and the Adrenaline were born in 2009. Despite the upheaval, the new club won the Goodall Cup in their first year. Whatever its name, the Adelaide team, there when the league faced off in 2000, has always been competitive, winning the title three times and topping the regular season standings five times.

But the cost of travel remains a major challenge for the only South Australian team in the AIHL, and the club is looking to spread the administrative load and lessen costs. Adrenaline is currently becoming an incorporated entity, making it responsible for its own budgets. "The Ice Sports Federation supports us financially, which is great, but to have an incorporated structure that has a little more independence, it allows us to operate more efficiently," Ryan O'Handley says. "In our sport with the amount of travel we have, if you don't have efficiencies in place it ends up costing you a whole lot of money.

If you're late booking flights it's not a trivial amount ... especially for us where we have to fly to every away game."

As Adelaide looks to follow the lead of other clubs in delegating tasks involved in its administration and its promotion via social media, Ryan is looking for volunteers with expertise. But he is choosy. "We've had a good start, there's a bit of a buzz around the club, that's always good, that's a good way to get people involved. But you want to make sure you get the right people too, because in the AIHL, things can go south pretty quickly! You need to have those motivated people who will get you through the tough times, not just the good times."

Such a measured outlook is not surprising for a man from the tiny Saskatchewan town of Kenaston, where hockey is a "religion" and played at a good level. Early in life, Ryan had to decide between pursuing the sport he loved and following his mother's advice to capitalise on his academic abilities. Choosing the latter took him to the University of Calgary; a six-month stint in Perth, Western Australia, where he met his future wife; Maryland in the United States; and Canada's easterly Prince Edward Island province. He subsequently lived and coached in Perth for six years, working with Stan Scott prior to the establishment of Perth Thunder, before a new veterinary school brought him to Adelaide, and an opening as an assistant coach brought him to Adelaide Adrenaline.

Ryan says that when he arrived in Adelaide in 2010, his wife told him: "Find a team to coach or you're going to drive me nuts!" It seems the affable Canadian has been able to balance sport and study, then work, everywhere he has travelled. However, he admits there is a time not too far off when he will have to step back. "Someday I probably wouldn't mind moving into more of an administrative role. Obviously you want as a coach to have that contact with the players and the teaching - that's something that really drives me in sport. But with the amount of travel, there will be a time when I have to say 'that's enough' and get someone else to take the coaching reins."

In 2014, Adrenaline started in the sort of form that can result in a championship. Ryan is confident about his team's prospects, but respectful of the competition this year in the AIHL. "If any team looks past another team, it will get the short end of the stick ... Anybody can beat anybody on a given day, it's exactly what we want as a league. The teams that are not prepared to work, they're not going to have success. It's going to make for a higher pace, a higher tempo hockey and I think the fans are going to be the big winner."

Considering the AIHL's bigger picture, Ryan says the limit to further growth is the dearth of good enough facilities. "If everybody had a rink that seated 1000 to 1500, who knows, you might be talking about professionalization. But we can't do that unless everyone can bring in that revenue. I think the level of play will continue to grow, we have some very good young players coming through and we seem to be getting a higher and higher level of import coming every year now." Ryan believes the example of the Icehouse in Melbourne shows that there is also "huge room for growth" in Australian hockey.

The simplest reason he has faith in the AIHL? "Hockey is the most exciting sport that humans have created". That's enough to get a white collar guy out of bed at 5am every Thursday.

ADELAIDE WON THE FIRST AIHL TITLE, THE 2009 GOODALL CUP AND HAS MISSED THE PLAYOFFS ONLY TWICE.

SATURDAY THE 21ST

ROAD TRIP FOUR:
ADELAIDE ADRENALINE V MELBOURNE MUSTANGS
DAY ONE

It's a privilege and a test being afforded the run of these teams on the road. Trying to capture the essence of the experience heightens it. The coaches, more my age than the players, enjoy the extra company in downtime before games, between periods and after games. They want to be questioned, and it's fun for them to tell someone else the war stories they have all told each other. People not used to talking to a writer are so much more eloquent than those accustomed to it; their honesty is unpackaged, their insights undecorated.

One of the temptations and necessities of such story-gathering is finding the theme of the story. You can't hunt it, or force it into being, but you have to know it when it presents itself. The theme whacks me on the head on this Mustangs trip of Adelaide.

At the end of the second period of Saturday's first game at the Adelaide Ice Arena, the injury-hit Adrenaline up 2–0 over the Mustangs, I linger near the rabbit warren beneath the grandstand. It has been made off-limits during play by the kindly looking security guard. He is absent from his post in the break, perhaps seeking a warming beverage, so I tentatively take a couple of photos of the narrow space. It brings to mind some sort of war zone trench, a cramped, narrow realm expected to be temporary, some metal here, some log cabin poles there ... The conflict has continued longer than expected and the improvised structure has become the permanent operational headquarters.

Adelaide coach Ryan O'Handley beckons me into that corridor, outside his team's well-hidden dressing room. He possesses the now familiar energy of the hockey-lover beneath a laid-back disposition and wears the uniform expected of a 41-year-old academic and hockey lover – a plain suit, no tie, slightly thinning hair. Ryan gleefully offers to show me the player's bench, and the journey doesn't take long – it opens off the corridor, which is all of two metres from the ice surface. It's a shallow notch more than a bench, with an extremely low ceiling. It's claustrophobic. Tiny. A bit on the small side. Now I know why tall six foot two Ryan has a slight stoop. Anyone of average height or above would hit their noggin on the roof in these Lilliputian confines. Hence most players choose to lean over the boards, which just elude the plunging underside of the grandstand. This leaning-out-over-the-rink surface method is

Mustangs fans turned out in force for
the road trip to Adelaide.

Joey Hughes' gear-drying
hanger.

The Adelaide "penalty box".

Mind your head: team benches in Adelaide.

fine except when play strays nearby. Then one has to quickly squat and take a step back. If not, you either hit the top of your head on the underside of the grandstand, or, as had happened to Ryan and many other Adelaide veterans, you get an unintended thwack from a player or his stick. Ryan shows me an angry horizontal red zip across his forehead. After playing hockey for three decades in three countries, his most visible scar came not as a player on the ice, but as a coach trying to watch from the bench at Adelaide Ice Arena. *Mind your head* ... Talk about being intimately involved in the game.

Why is it so? Ryan has only been in Adelaide for five years, but his understanding is that the rink was originally a decent size. But an owner going bust eradicated a bar behind the goals - one of the things the current rink needs – putting in a wall which truncates the rink's length. Then an ill-fated and highly expensive indoor ski run forced the rink to relocate and contract sideways, hence the cramped headroom issues on the bench. The elaborate sign tower outside the venue traces the venue's evolution. Its highest element announces the venue to be the Snow Dome. It mentions the Adelaide Avalanche – the AIHL team that died in 2008 – and it advertises tobogganing, long since ceased. The eccentric slide of roof opposite the main grandstand references the magnificently quixotic ski run. The meddling with a large building has conspired to create a weird and squashed little rink.

The ski-slope building now houses mobile telephone towers on each corner. And the venue beneath, home to all of South Australia's tenacious ice sports, exists in cramped, scuffed squalor. There is a baby rink sharing the boards of part of the main rink. An ingenious folding grandstand is opened up and released over this surface on AIHL gamedays, ensuring the most efficiently air-conditioned seating in hockey. Volunteers push the stands back flat at the end of the game like a group slowly playing a massive timber piano accordion.

A stark fluoro-lit 'corporate area' occupies one corner, completely sealed off by glass, but there is nowhere else to stand and watch – both ends of the rink, hard up against the walls, feature white painted boards four metres high, forming a corridor two people wide. Patrons visiting the main stand walk through this narrow, wet, slippery space. The stand itself, a six-deep terrace covered with fuzzy blue carpet underlay, is so low and close to the ice surface that crowd members feel like they could lean down and pat a player on the top of his helmet.

The less said about the amenities the better. Australian rinks specialise in unappealing loos. When I talked to Viktor Gibbs-Sjodin at the airport on the way in, he mentioned the impact of the clean, pleasant Icehouse. "My girlfriend invites people to watch, they enjoy the game and they have a good experience in the building, so they want to come back." Only diehards put up with rinks as cramped and cold as Adelaide. I'm getting sick of repeating it. The league needs more people with a lot of money, nous, patience and negotiating skills to fall in love with its game, as happened in Melbourne. It needs new rinks.

The Mustangs have had most of the best chances, but they are being thwarted by excellent Adrenaline import netminder Michael Will. This has become commonplace this season – a hot import goalie thwarting a hot offensive team. On yet another tiny rink, it's all about tips and deflections, and avoiding mistakes, which give your opponents an almost instant scoring chance. With ten minutes to go, Adrenaline, desperate to thwart a three-game losing streak, lead 3–1. Brad Vigon, rolling the dice, puts together an 'all-international' line of Pat O'Kane, Viktor Gibbs-Sjodin and Jeff Grant. This results in an 'All-Australian' line joining Joey Hughes with Jamie Bourke and Brendan McDowell. Ryan later says he had no match-ups for these combinations.

Jack Wolgemuth has been enduring a scoring drought. It is a wonder he is on the ice at all, given that his jaw is broken and he's only playing because he's wearing a cage helmet. Three weeks into what was diagnosed as a six-week injury, he has copped plenty of blows to test the helmet he so hates. After

CHLOE MEIERS, ADELAIDE'S "DO EVERYTHING" ADMINISTRATOR IS UNSURE OF HER OFFICIAL TITLE WITH ADRENALINE, BUT SINCE FALLING IN LOVE WITH HOCKEY VIA THE 2010 OLYMPICS, THE EX-SHOWBIZ SINGER HASN'T MISSED A GAME, AND IN RECENT YEARS SHE HAS BECOME INVOLVED IN DISCUSSIONS WITH THE GOVERNMENT TO TRY TO GET A NEW FACILITY FOR ICE SPORTS IN SOUTH AUSTRALIA. TODAY SHE IS HOSTING A RADIO STATION CROWD. SHE SAYS THAT SHE DOESN'T GET TO WATCH AS MUCH OF THE HOCKEY THESE DAYS AS SHE WOULD LIKE, GIVEN SUCH DUTIES. IN MELBOURNE RECENTLY SHE WAS HOPING TO TAKE IN THE GAME, BUT FORWARD CHARLIE HUBER WAS HURT AND SHE HAD TO DRIVE HIM TO THE HOSPITAL.

Chloe Meiers, do-everything Adrenaline administrator.

scoring with a deft wrist shot from the slot off a face-off to bring the Stangs within a goal, Jack levels the game up with 3.45 left by using his broken head. A back pass to the point from Pat, a searing slapshot from the powerful Viktor and ... the puck smashes into Jack's jaw, right where the plate has been put in, but behind his despised but essential helmet. Time stops, the puck drops off his metal cage to the ice, right on the crease, and he stuffs it in to the net.

Typically, the Mustangs' momentum and self-belief keep growing the longer the third period goes. Their ecstatic travelling horde makes a racket as the previously impassable Will coughs up the go-ahead goal to Pat on a dirty rebound from a Jack Wolgemuth shot, with 1.53 left. Then Jack lobs the puck from inside his defensive zone towards the empty net. Joey Hughes and an Adrenaline defender race back as it slows on the snowy surface, but it trickles and rolls to a stop a couple of inches over the goal line. Stunningly, with 33.8 seconds left, the Mustangs lead 5–3. Jack's scoring drought has been broken by a hat-trick and the Mustangs have scored four goals in ten minutes to steal the crucial win against a fellow finals contender in a rink where they have always struggled. Self-belief, momentum and confidence begat extra effort and never-say-die persistence. Stang (Tristain Cole), the Mustangs' excitable horse-headed mascot races around waving his flag. Fans, grateful they had made the trip – at no small expense – beam and shout. Viktor Gibbs-Sjodin salutes them from centre ice, a few metres away.

Brad Vigon is not putting a lid on it. "That was an awesome win!" he says, grappling with playful seven-year-old son Zander, who is dressed in a men's Mustangs jersey which is comically large for him, a hockey muu muu. The cage goal is all the talk. It is decreed that Jack's girlfriend Natalie, newly arrived in Australia, now has to come on every road trip; she is now officially a good luck charm.

Ryan O'Handley says Adrenaline tightened up when leading and stopped attacking. It's fatal in hockey, at least in the AIHL, another thing I like about the league. "It's like we're scared to win," he says of his team's losing "patch". He bemoans the attitude of some players. "It's not a recreational league anymore. Some people don't realise the commitment that's necessary now."

After such a thrilling win, the Mustangs soundtrack in their bus back to their beachfront accommodation starts, appropriately, with "celebrate life, celebrate your life". Joey Hughes expresses wonder when voluble assistant coach Chuck Connolly's techno requests prove more radical than many of the players half his age. Joey I imagine to have no-frills music tastes; he has the most primitive phone of anyone on the team bus, earning Mick Burslem's approval. Chuck plays a track and instructs listeners to "wait for the drop". He is one of the bench crew who changes into a suit for match day duties – complete with natty orange tie – but his speech is usually on the candid side of informal. When his mode changes from its usual cheery enthusiasm – "I love this, I wouldn't be anywhere else" he says of coaching – to old-fashioned hot gospeller, I imagine he is quite a sight. Viktor Gibbs-Sjodin confirms this. He says he asks Chuck if he is about to fire up, so he can move to the most distant corner of the room. "In Sweden we don't yell," he says.

Viktor also tells us that Swedish hockey is sometimes boring, low-scoring and conservative, approached like soccer. A former NHL draft pick, the powerfully-built forward has shown glimpses of his powers, but you can't help but feel that there could be more to come from him and Jeff Grant. He is generally laid-back, but his on-ice celebrations with the travelling Mustangs crowd today perhaps reveal a growing sense of belonging.

Brad makes an economical announcement to the players as they disembark at the accommodation. "Keep it real. Have a few beers, but we have a game to play tomorrow and top spot is on offer."

The club dinner does what the after-match song demanded, fans, family and staff joyously mingling with players as Mick and physio Andrea Heywood serve lashings of steak and a chicken salad that is fast being refined into a 2014 speciality. These hours are the "payment" for playing in this league: the communal enjoyment of storytelling, a few drinks and the satisfaction of building towards something bigger than the individual.

Joey Hughes tells the stories I listen to the most closely. He says playing in minor pro leagues took "cunning", as most of his meagre wage had to be negotiated, and strapped coaches had many players willing to take a cheaper rate lined up behind any bolshie incumbent. Negotiations best took place after one had a good game, and postponed, using a feigned injury as an excuse, if you just had a shocker. He says some semi-pro players were protected from their misdemeanours by club officials, in the manner of VFL footy stars a generation ago in Melbourne; speeding tickets got taken care of, drunken or drugged escapades were excused. The existence of prima donnas, arrogant and insecure, means a hard-working Aussie could get ahead. Joey says he was first on and last off the ice at training when playing pro. Joey doesn't just bring stories from his pro stint – his simple but ingenious hanging gear-dryer is a hit, several players keen for one after seeing it swing from the balcony ceiling of his unit.

Mustangs president John Belic, always cheerful, is rapt by this win, which confirms his club's league-leading status. He re-states his love of being the underdog. "Fans like us because of that," he says. "We could win ten titles in a row and they'd never admit they were wrong," he says of those who opposed the Mustangs' hasty entry into the league. He mentions a letter he retains which states there was not enough room for two teams in Melbourne. Affable in the main, John is driven by what he feels is an unforgivable snub. But a line of conversation pertaining to music rolls by and he latches on, once again beaming, with the surprising announcement that he once saw legendary, but obscure Melbourne punk band I Spit On Your Gravy play naked. Brad Vigon offers Metallica as the most outré band he has seen.

SUNDAY THE 22ND

ROAD TRIP FOUR:
ADELAIDE ADRENALINE V MELBOURNE
MUSTANGS
DAY TWO

I am up before most of the players, returning to the rink for a chat with Ryan O'Handley. On the way, my cabbie regales me with the big issues of Adelaide, like the extended opening hours for shops, a privileged few of which are now allowed to operate from 11 am to 5 pm on Sundays. These battles were fought in Melbourne 20 years ago. After Melbourne, the proximity of everything – CBD, airport, coast, even rink – is hard to believe. The rink at is right on the fringe of the pretty, arty city at Thebarton, but its grubby surrounds make it feel like a product of a drab outer suburb. The Stepney's shop next door is an inexplicable showroom of expensive sculptural pop-culture kitsch oddities, mostly life-sized. If you need an $895 Elvis, hockey goalie, camel, Bogart or masked spray-painter for your backyard, this is the place for you.

Ryan and I chat in the cold as his sons play, one on the baby rink, one on the main rink. The elder, Morris, scores a hat-trick. He says at the end of a long discussion about how to get a new facility. "We've got to change the attitude from 'This is why we can't do it' to 'this is why we can do it' ". His hockey-mad home town Kenaston, population 300, got a rink built. There are 400 members of Ice Sports South Australia …

As for being an AIHL coach, Ryan's words are similar to those of Brad Vigon and Brent Laver. "The only collateral you have as coach is ice time." But coaches don't have it bad compared to players. One Adrenaline player, a plumber, broke his wrist recently and was banned from the worksite. When the player's sponsorship came in – a duty of each Adrenaline roster member – the club returned it to this financially challenged individual to help him through his lay-off. One of Ryan's crusades is for improved insurance for AIHL clubs and players.

He introduces me to nuggety returning import Brett Liscomb, another SPHL player (Fayetteville Fire Antz) who is starting up an early morning session for high school age kids. "It's a pig of a rink, but it's what we have…" he says of the Ice Arena. Even an import has to be thankful for whatever rink exists in Australia. Brett, 28, guides kids aged from four to eighteen at a hockey school at home in Ontario. He says he knows he is lucky to be in Adelaide. "Someone said to me 'you're in Australia and you've still got hockey?' " Brett likes byes because they afford him an opportunity to see more of the

The Stepney's store next to the rink offers items indispensable to any madman's yard.

country. He says it gets to be a very long season if he doesn't take such breaks, as he heads straight from the Fayetteville season into the AIHL. An import's experience has to be as much about seeing the country as the hockey and he would not be back in Adelaide but for the five or six guys he knows well and hangs out with off-ice, talking about anything but the game. "It's got to be fun. That camadarerie of hockey is the thing you can't replace. It wouldn't be worth it if it wasn't for the friendships." For Brett, the camaraderie extends to guys he has played against. Before a face-off today, he can be seen chatting with Jeff Grant, also an SPHL veteran.

Today's game is a more physical encounter from the outset, the Mustangs skipping out to a two-goal lead before Adelaide star local Greg Oddy, the first of Adrealine's injured players to start filtering back, puts away a goal on the powerplay. As in Canberra, the penalty box is not a box. Here it is two side-by-side trestle benches "separated" by an unfilled water bollard. When Adelaide's Nick Clark and the Mustangs' Sean Jones get concurrent penalties after mixing it up on ice, this open-air arrangement – right next to the fold-out piano accordion grandstand, on the ice of the mini-rink – offers them a chance to continue their discussion about the merits of their respective actions. The attendants at the penalty boxes provide one of many indelible images from this crazy rink. Sober and efficient with managing penalised players of either team, they turn into uber fans when Adelaide scores – utilising an air horn which rests on top of the penalty 'box' bollard. Most volunteers are partisans in this league. And they have to be hardy. I am standing alongside these attendants and the cold from the mini-rink is seeping up, informing my joints of future arthritis.

Unique and innovative: temporary grandstands open up on the 'baby rink' next to the main ice surface.

Adelaide Ice Arena puts you right on top of the action.

Jamie Bourke, sent to the bollards for consecutive penalties in the second period, responds to crowd taunts with the old chestnut "[look at the] scoreboard!". His next rejoinder is "and the ladder!" The score he refers to is 3–1 after an unassisted Pat O'Kane goal, and despite worries they are being sucked into too many penalties, the Mustangs are in charge. As in the first period, a late powerplay goal, this time to Brett Liscomb, reduces the margin to one goal (3–2), but the visitors are setting the pace. It becomes 4–2, then 4-3, and the home team is looking to return the favour from Saturday with a surging finish. But the seemingly tiring Stangs push again to finish off a brilliant travelling weekend with the final two goals to win 6–3, Joey Hughes this time providing the hat-trick, and Pat a brace. They go back to the top of the standings.

This is the game when I realise why Brent Laver rates Joey Hughes the equal of any player in Australia. It isn't just his hat-trick – and an assist. There are times he has three players hanging off him and he retains the puck, or delivers it to an unmarked teammate. He works back as hard as forward. He is strong, fast, brave and smart on the ice. And despite his mad moment against Ice early in the season, he appears to be reformed, avoiding much of the argy bargy and helping calm aggrieved teammates.

The Mustangs top brass have chosen a good weekend to come along. Andy McDowell, John Belic and Brad Vigon share a group hug after the win, having seen a culmination of sorts. Their growing team has shown maturity and composure against a tough opponent in a tough rink. "Wins like that make it all worthwhile," Brad says. "In all my time as a player and a coach I can't ever remember winning both games in Adelaide. You usually go to Adelaide hoping for a split. To leave with six points is a huge effort from the boys."

I ask Ryan what's next for Adelaide and he says "Newcastle". He gets two more players back for that game, but he admits he has to "shake things up". Adrenaline, in the top four for most of the first half of the season, is on a five-game losing streak. "Today wasn't good," he admits.

On the bus to the airport, Brad picks a moment to thank volunteers Mick and Andrea on behalf of the players. John Belic adds "You are hereby guaranteed tenure!" Mick makes the mock ambit salary claim. It's the old volunteer joke, a necessary, satisfying box to be ticked. The players spend their $15 allowance for dinner at the one open 'restaurant', a hamburger palace. Pat gets his hurt hand tended to in the bar. Fraser is told he only got hit in the head, so he's OK.

Maybe it's the good mood following such a joyous trip, maybe my continued exposure to the group has put them at ease, but at that bar, more players open up for a chat. Mustangs skipper Sean Jones says two things hold back Australian hockey – the expense of rinks and the initial expense of gear for players. Of playing in Adelaide, he says systems "go out the window". You just have to adapt on smaller rinks, and work hard. Viktor Gibbs-Sjodin asks about Australian wine, but there is a language issue. I say our shiraz is good, but not too subtle. Viktor doesn't understand that word, and it is hard to think of a better one. He chooses a shiraz anyway. Defenceman Troy Robertson delivers a definitive statement about imports. "They have to prove themselves. We're Aussies. We don't care who you are or how much money you have earned, you have to earn respect." He says Pat being a college player has been a good fit with the young Mustangs list. Troy, a new dad, is just 24 himself.

We chat about the league's idiosyncratic rinks, Troy recalling his favourite Canberra moment. His helmet was ripped off during play near the boards and ended up in the crowd, which gleefully absconded with the offering, transporting it hand over hand over the top of the mob to the highest point in the rink in Heckler's Corner, where it was worn and paraded like the ritual offering of an enemy scalp to a chief from tribal warriors after a successful battle. You don't get that in the NHL.

MONDAY THE 23RD

In between periods of Saturday's Adrenaline v Mustangs match in Adelaide, coaches, fans and sponsors hunched over smartphones, trying to find collective agreement from varying messages about occurrences elsewhere in the country. The Mustangs game became too captivating for many updates during its third period, but there was high drama elsewhere: a shootout in Melbourne between Ice and Brave; and in the second Sydney derby the Dogs squeaking home 2–1 against the eternally competitive Bears, thereby extending the Bears' losing streak to nine games.

In the aftermath of the Mustangs' stunning comeback victory, as the beaming club entourage waited for their charges outside the dressing room, news came through that Ice had prevailed over Canberra in the shootout, a big win for the home team without the absent Jason Baclig and the suspended Matt Armstrong. The tone of Facebook posts and tweets suggested an epic battle and a big crowd. And Thunder, stunningly, had thrashed the North Stars, in Newcastle, 5–0. Brad Vigon said that Thunder would barely lose again, given the quality of their goalie and other imports. The North Stars had humbled Ice at home the previous weekend, and had been the in-form team in the competition. As all season, the only response was: go figure.

Sunday, there was a message I couldn't understand and didn't believe: "Army playing D". I wrote it off as a mistake. Matt Armstrong, returning from suspension, had an assist and a goal early on, after all. Ice led 4–0 then 5–1, if the correspondents I found were to be believed. At a similar time, the Bears were holding out the formerly rampant Thunder 6–5 at home. And in the Ice Dogs/North Stars game, Newcastle had bounced back from the shock of their home ice loss on Saturday to win 4–1 in what amounted to a battle for fourth place in the standings.

After the Mustangs made their raucous travelling contingent louder with another rousing victory over Adrenaline, there were three cheers from their throng. One for the win; the second for the announcement that Ice had lost to Canberra in a shootout after a massive Brave comeback; and the third for the fact that the Stangs were now top of the table.

The resurgent North Stars are now inside the top four, and injury-hit Adelaide have fallen to sixth, still in contention, but in need of some wins, as fourth place shapes as the battle royale for the rest of the season. And I need to call Matt Armstrong to see if he really played defence.

Brad Vigon, son Zander and Pat O'Kane under the ski slope.

"Ice lost, we won and we're on top!" Happy Mustangs.

Brendan McDowell with dad Andy.

FRIDAY THE 27TH

Pat O'Kane's parents Sean and Terry are visiting Melbourne and reveal that their son has subjected them to a "strict regime" of sightseeing. Sean says when a teenager his son responded well to the "almost military" schedule of prep school, which had designated times for study and sport, and when Pat got into the gym at age thirteen, his parents had to set boundaries on how much he did. Are they revealing a fatal Pat O'Kane flaw, finally? No such luck, he just likes things to be organised.

Sean and Terry are involved in international business and are keen travellers, but Sean is part of a coalition trying to counter the brain drain from liveable New Hampshire, the family's home. Pat is one of the talents the campaign will conceivably target. Sean says his son has a bright future. By next August, when he completes his degree at Monash University, his CV will include an MBA, and experience living and playing hockey overseas.

Keen sailor Sean knows there is now a good chance Pat may stay in Australia – because of his relationship with Stephanie as much as his hockey or study. The O'Kane parents, clad in Mustangs jerseys, have become fixtures in the grandstand on this trip, greeted by fellow fans like long-time regulars. In essence they have been, watching Pat's games at all hours via the club's livestreams. Mustangs apparatchik Myles Harris said he became emotional when they wrote, stating how much they appreciated the service. It was a big decision for the Mustangs to commit to livestreams at the start of the season. The fear was that internet coverage could impact crowd figures. But Mustangs crowds have grown even more in 2014 than last year, and for those who can't make it, James Morgan's team has the professionally produced product on hand. Like many visitors, the O'Kanes say they love "easygoing" Australians.

The Mustangs gleefully announced this week that they had overtaken Melbourne Ice with 6448 'likes' to 6363, making them the most 'liked' AIHL team on Facebook. Their renewed commitment to their media coverage is bearing fruit, the fresh content most days creating a sense of momentum which matches the deeds of the team. ATC supremo James Morgan, an Ice fan with strong opinions about how that club is run, says Ice is set in its ways compared to the fledgling Mustangs, and doesn't "reach out as much".

Sean, Terry and Pat O'Kane.

SATURDAY THE 28TH

You can't talk about the cold to North Americans. No Australian city suffers blizzards. In winter, we don't have to get up an hour early to clear the driveway of snow and revive a frigid car and if we pass out drunk on the street on a big night out, we won't be found frozen to death in the morning. But Melbourne punches above its weight as a wintry temperate zone metropolis. The Canada Day weekend at the Icehouse welcomes the Sydney Bears to Melbourne with some world-class inclemency. Heavy rain broken up by bouts of drizzle. Clouds low enough to nuzzle your cheek before they slap you with intrusive, missionary rain. It seems appropriate that the coldest weather of the year should accompany Canada Day celebrations. Canucks who emigrate to Australia come, or stay, because it's warmer here than back home. There are other contributing factors – Aussie spouses and jobs – but I am yet to meet a Canuck who doesn't mention getting away from the cold as a major factor in their decision.

On this Saturday, it is warmer inside the rink than outside. After my recent trips interstate, that fact alone is startling. There's been something gruelling about the bone-invading cold on my travels so far. In Adelaide, the sullen frigid air seeped inside you laced with the sweat and fast-food rink bouquet of decades. It felt like the whole place needed to be peeled open, exposed to summer gales for a month and subjected to a giant air freshener. The Liverpool esky was just damned freezing and proud of it, the lowly temperature getting its own scoreboard.

At the Icehouse this day, AIHL Commissioner Robert Bannerman can be seen living up to his name by smoothing new Travel Alberta advertising stickers on to the boards, welcoming my hockey-friendly *Age* colleague Alana Schetzer with a jersey, and checking in on primary sponsor Air Canada in the VIP area. The arena is filled, Ice comes out in a natty red jersey designed for the occasion, and a large beach ball is bunted around the festive crowd, which is waiting to acclaim their team and the occasion. Many of those gathered have brought teddy bears for a Very Special Kids charity drive. Upon Melbourne Ice's first goal, they are to be thrown on to the ice and gathered by players for delivery to disadvantaged children.

The singer performs a stirring *O Canada*, and a passable *Advance Australia Fair*; the maple leaf flag hangs beneath the Australian flag, which hangs beneath the scoreboard. All is in readiness. Except for the scoreboard, which snubs the festive atmosphere, its malfunction causing a ten-minute delay. It is a portent of what is to come for Ice.

Sporting motivation is rarely complex. In Melbourne, fans of my generation were raised on stories of footy teams invoking an us-against-them mentality based on the flimsiest of evidence, coaches invoking supposed slights from opposition personnel to generate righteous outrage and 'fire-up' their gullible charges. Coaches became ludicrously paranoid and sly with their media-disseminated utterances, aiming to counteract any potentially damaging propaganda, and lay some

The Sydney Bears came to Melbourne on a mission on Canada Day.

potential landmines of their own. It was all ham-fisted theatre, but it often seemed to work. (The fourth estate was only too happy to assist such schoolyard tactics become fond legends.)

Most sportsmen these days require fewer grand lies and fire-and-brimstone speeches and seem to favour more emphasis on game plans, preparation, processes and structures. "Systems" is the word used in hockey circles. But human nature has not evolved since we used rocks as cutlery. Sometimes the most effective motivation remains tribal, primal, emotional, a little bit silly. The Sydney Bears are fired up by the impending Teddy Bear Toss.

They are annoyed by the presumption that Ice will score early, unleashing the pent-up desire of 1000 fans to throw fluffy toys through the air. There is a party waiting to happen and the Bears are necessary but overlooked, like catering staff. The underdogs are back in form, having broken their nine-loss losing streak with a win over the revitalised Perth Thunder. They also pushed Ice all the way in Sydney, and they have a plan.

Melbourne Ice, who had been goofing off in a lacklustre warm-up - I was later informed this didn't perturb their coaches as they play best when relaxed - unsurprisingly concede the first goal, a freak rebound off goalie Jaden Pine-Murphy which ricochets off Ice defenceman Ross Howell. It's a 'dirty' goal, an anomaly scored by a team making infrequent offensive journeys. Bears goalie Daniel Palmkvist is looking solid, but surely it is only a matter of time before Ice replies, the bears get tossed and the home team takes control, no?

No. It takes a very long matter of time for Ice to score. In soccer parlance, the Sydney Bears 'park the bus' in front of their goalie, defending for dear life. Ice gradually find their feet and begin to have the overwhelming share of possession, but with the Bears sitting back and protecting the scoring lanes, and Daniel Palmkvist standing on his head in goal, there is nothing for the recalcitrant scoreboard to display, even if it was working.

Frustrated fans throw a couple of bears at Bears at the end of the second period, in protest at their stymying tactics. Bears' reserve goalie and internet cult figure Luke Read picks up the teddies gleefully. The Bears rope-a-dope works a treat. Rushes; power plays; snapshots from the point; tips from in front; none of it looks like piercing Daniel Palmkvist's defences. The Bears remain utterly committed to their ultra-defensive mission, allowing themselves occasional counter-attacks only if they are offered clear-cut opportunities. They harass and hustle as if playing the entire game on the penalty kill.

Inevitably, sheer persistence and weight of numbers count for something. A semblance of a scoreboard starts appearing

Finally: Ice fans let loose for the teddy bear toss.

intermittently on the big screen, and a speculative shot from the goal line somehow gets past Palmkvist via a complex of skates and sticks. One ugly goal each, 10.32 to go. There's a huge eruption of relief and elation and a gratifying cascade of fluffiness on to the ice, then laughter, and another long delay as the toys are gathered. Surely this was the part where Ice, having fought so hard for so long for their goal, storm home all over the gallant but tiring underdogs?

No. Within a minute of the restart, the Bears convert a half-chance with a perfect wrist shot from the slot, the lead is back to a goal, and Ice is stuck with the same problem that has defeated it for 40 minutes of play: how to beat Bears goalie Daniel Palmkvist. How to hammer a freight train into a keyhole. Rush follows Ice rush, save after save. Army, Ice's outstanding player as a defenceman, is moved to centre in the last four minutes,

Delay of game. Players and volunteers gather the charity donations.

Daniel Palmkvist celebrates.

Melbourne Ice's Rookie's Night.

imposing his will, skating rings around Bears, and his shots are saved by Daniel Palmkvist. He threads passes through the tight Bears defence to teammates open in the slot: their shots are saved by Daniel Palmkvist. You never see him move, he is always where he has to be. Add an empty netter with a minute to go. Sydney Bears 3, Melbourne Ice 1. Three hundred and six teddy bears thrown on the ice, belatedly, and $1300 raised for Very Special Kids.

Consensus afterwards is that Daniel Palmkvist was just too good, and it was just one of those nights when the puck refused to go in the net. Ice had 53 shots to 22, cold comfort in a league with a sudden-death finals series. No team is safely ensconced in the final four now. The Bears have won back-to-back, this time without talismanic skipper Michael Schlamp. The Ice Dogs have just defeated Canberra on the road. Adelaide, down in the dumps after four straight losses, including two at home the previous weekend, has hammered Newcastle 6–2 on the road, Brett Liscomb nabbing three points. In 2014, there are no underdogs.

The bottom-of-the-table Bears remained hard to beat during their run of outs, rarely getting blown away, usually competitive shift-by-shift. It is clear that the Bears players relished the simplicity of their strategy against Ice. They knew what to do at all times. They played as a team, with unstinting effort and discipline. That the party surrounding a bear toss could affect the outcome of so strenuously contested a game seems ludicrous. But it is undeniable. Those paranoid hoary old footy coaches knew something. Sporting empires rise and fall on bounces and decisions made in moments. You have to compete all the time, in every way, to avoid things like fluffy toys from bringing you unstuck.

Post-match at the Harbourtown Hotel, Ice players commence their "rookie night", refusing to let the preceding frustrations ruin their fun. The gleeful Bears eat in their midst, and applaud Jason Baclig's band Haybax along with Ice fans. When Ice first-year players arrive, it is in not in club-issued dark blues, but … suffice to say there is plenty of cross-dressing. And Jeff Smith is kitted up as a six foot six elf. Tradition dictates that each new player is dressed in a costume chosen by the rest of the team, then paraded around the pub in search of donations. It is a cruel and unusual form of busking, but a pretty benign form of hazing given the horror stories one hears from North America, and many of the female fans in particular enjoy the ensembles. There is always one especially fit player whose torso is dressed up with just a bow tie and trousers who attracts the most generous sponsorship. Perhaps I was wrong and Tim Johansson is an exhibitionist, for he is the team's appointed beefcake, done up like a male stripper. Anything too scandalous about the evening takes place after the players leave the pub, at a location far removed from prying eyes. Elder statesmen confer like US presidential bodyguards, making sure arrangements to keep everyone legal and sociable are watertight.

For the rest of us left talking hockey at the pub, it is like a few hours of a road trip, undertaken with fans and staff instead of the players. Emma Poynton, after comparing make-up notes with Jeremy Brown, explains to me why she is pictured on one leg on a hilltop on her Facebook page. The photo was taken on holiday in Greece, when she had a broken ankle. Nothing was going to stop her completing her trip. She is making sure everyone signs an oversized card for Chris Wong, who will miss the rest of the season with the shoulder injury he incurred in Canberra. Johan Steenberg tells me he dreams of helping nurture the first Australian-born NHL goalie. And Robert Bannerman tells me the league is about to announce something big and I will be the first to know. Administrators and coaches of the league and clubs now say this to me all the time. I have arrived as a beat reporter.

Jeff Smith is a six foot six elf on Rookie's Night.

SUNDAY THE 29TH

What was meant to be the Mustangs take on Canada Day has happily become Nathan Walker Day, the Australian hockey community uniting in a spontaneous outpouring of social media celebration after the Sydney-raised winger was picked up in the NHL draft by the Washington Capitals. Early Sunday morning, after catching up with Ice folk, I checked the draft on the internet, and performed a double-take when I saw his name on the nhl.com list at pick 89. He's been picked up, in just the third round! The Capitals traded picks in order to ensure they got "Stormy". I stayed up until the wee hours getting a piece up on theage.com.au and then watching the realisation reach waking Australia. Hours later, the selection is the talk of the Icehouse. Anyone grinning uncontrollably or shaking their head happily is talking about Nathan's drafting. Robert Bannerman is convinced it is a landmark for the sport in Australia. "This is an historic event for Nathan, his family, and Australian ice hockey. It will generate broad awareness for the sport in Australia. It will encourage young kids to come and try ice hockey."

More than a few Ice folk bemoaned getting the assiduous Bears on night one of the road trip, assuming they would party Saturday night, and be tired and less focused for the Mustangs. But on Sunday, it is more of the same. The ever-growing and visually arresting Mustangs crowd fills the stand, the Canadian food on offer sells out before the game, and Daniel Palmkvist is too good for the Stangs shooters. The youthful Bears are neither hungover nor jaded, despite the toll the Saturday game has taken. And they are not as defensive as the previous day. The early exchanges provide good chances for both teams, and sustained forechecking yields the first goal, a tap-in after a wide shot bounces back behind Fraser Carson in the Mustangs net. The Mustangs look rusty, the Bears slick, and more than once the home team fans on chances in the slot, or fails to handle straightforward passes.

It looks like Pat O'Kane is putting on a show to impress his parents. His compelling, direct skating continually disconcerts the Bears defence, which cannot keep up once he crosses the blue line. He levels scores with a minute to go in the first period on the breakaway after a bad change by the Bears. Given the array of scoring talent at the Mustangs' disposal, it is not absurd to expect them to over-run the Bears.

Mustangs brains trust congratulate the Bears.

But they don't. ATC broadcaster James Morgan says the old Bears used to bore teams to sleep, then do their scoring. But Sunday's Bears are vibrant, dangerous, confident. Gun young Aussie Cameron Todd matches Pat's goal with a brilliant individual effort, out-skating the defence and beating Fraser Carson short-side, two minutes into the second period. Up 2–1, the Bears commit further up the expansive rink. Then they don't. Most of the final, 20-minute period they spend clearing their zone, trying to avoid icing, desperately holding on to their lead. The Mustangs push and push, but their attacks lack cohesion and penetration, and they rarely have players in dangerous positions. Daniel Palmkvist is so comfortable at this rink that it may not have made any difference. By game's end, there hasn't been a Mustangs goal for 36 minutes, and the Bears, with less possession, have out-shot the hosts 28 to 27. Palmkvist has saved 77 of 79 shots he has faced for the weekend.

Afterwards, Mick Burslem says the Mustangs came out thinking they had it won. "You can't be on your heels, you have to be on your toes and in their face … We were too passive, too defensive, we worried too much about their style. Let them worry about us when they are playing in our house!" Mick employs brutal honesty, the oldest coaching tactic. He might not always be right, but he doesn't say things unless he believes them. He says he doesn't like all the talk around the club about being on top of the ladder – "just concentrate on the next game" – but he also says the group has to embrace the opportunity before it. "Why not us?" he asks, and increasingly, it seems the answer has as much to do with the Mustangs as any of their opponents.

Sean O'Kane says he's undertaken two trips to Melbourne for no win. He might have to stay!

Elsewhere, Adelaide have arrested their slide with a pair of tough road wins, 6–2 over the North Stars in Newcastle, and a precious 3–2 shootout win over the Dogs at Liverpool. The Ice Dogs have beaten Brave in Canberra on Saturday 4–1. So the away teams have won every game of the weekend. These results prompt Stan Scott, whose Perth Thunder had a weekend off, to write the following: "League gone crazy! At the beginning of this season I tipped that this year's league would be the tightest and hardest fought one yet, and it is proving to be exactly that! Every team is splitting their series, there are no bad teams and everyone is capable of beating each other home or away ... Awesome!!"

TEAM	GP	W	L	D	SOW	SOL	PTS
MUSTANGS	16	9	5	0	0	2	29
ICE	16	7	5	0	3	1	28
BRAVE	15	7	4	0	2	2	27
ICE DOGS	17	8	8	0	0	1	25
ADRENALINE	18	5	8	0	4	1	24
NORTH STARS	15	7	7	0	0	1	22
BEARS	17	6	9	0	1	1	21
THUNDER	14	4	7	0	1	2	16

MONDAY THE 30TH

I catch up with Matt Armstrong after Ice has gone through its roughest patch of the season – in June, they started on top of the ladder, then came three heavy losses, the shootout win and loss against Canberra, and the shock loss to the Bears. They have garnered just six points from 21 on offer. They are now second in the standings, with several teams snapping at their heels. But Matt is unfazed. "To be honest with you I think we're OK at the moment," he says. "Obviously you like to win every game, but that's just not the case this year. I think you learn a lot of lessons losing – what you did right, what you did wrong. I think where we're at right now is alright. We've got a lot to learn by the end of the year."

Matt admits that the team's transition is having an effect. "Our team is going through a bit of a change with the young kids coming through. We've got to get those guys out there and get them experienced and hopefully it will pay off in the future." Past deeds frame Ice's current self-estimation. "I've been here since 2010 and we have such high expectations on ourselves to win and to be the best. I think that's why we've always been such a good team. I can understand why teams like to come in here and try to blow us out, because we're like the [New York] Yankees of the AIHL." For someone so competitive and accustomed to contending for the title, Matt is philosophical about 2014. "I think the future is bright but this year is a learning curve which hopefully we embrace."

He approached Brent with the idea to play defence, a change he has enjoyed. "I felt like I was getting a bit bored. I wanted a new challenge, something different to change it up. It's probably the only time in my life I could probably try this, in a league like this, I think back home people would laugh at me. I really liked having everyone in front of me - watching the play develop. You see the holes open up when you carry the puck up ice. I did feel out of my element at times but that's just because it's a new position."

BY THIS STAGE OF THE SEASON, THE EVER-GROWING ORANGE HORDES ARE AS POWERFUL A FORCE IN THE GRANDSTAND AS ICE FANS.

JULY 2014

SUNDAY THE 6TH

It takes until their last game in the country for Pat O'Kane's parents to see a Mustangs win, a commodity much more plentiful in 2014 than ever before. On Saturday, after Canberra is warmly welcomed by John Belic, the visitors repaid the hospitality by defeating the Stangs 7–4, after leading 5–1, despite being outshot 35–25. It is a familiar story, a strong goalie and rampant import forwards dominating, but on this occasion, local James Byers adds two goals to an Anton Kokkonen hat-trick, and the biggest name, scoring leader Stephen Blunden, is out suspended.

Heading into the Sunday game, the Mustangs have lost two in a row, an unfamiliar situation for them in 2014. They make an emphatic statement, though the scoreline reads 4–3 at game's end. Dominant early, a goal after a giveaway in the slot leaves scores at 1–1 after one period. It remains so after two periods, the Mustangs again monopolising the puck, but struggling to get past their latest import goalie nemesis, Petri Pitkanen. Previously, the Mustangs might have wilted when facing with such debilitating frustration, but this afternoon they just keep coming at Brave, and their powerplay finally clicks. By halfway through the final period, they lead 4–1.

Brave being brave, they irrepressibly fight back, and score the two goals to make the final minutes cook. Even then, the Mustangs have good chances brilliantly saved by the Finnish goalie. At game's end, the numbers tell the story. The Mustangs have won 4–3 on 51 shots to 15. It had taken a mountain to fill a pothole, and the double-header – Brave outscoring the Mustangs 10–8 over the two games – further clouds reckoning of the respective finals chances of the combatants.

Brave chairman Peter Chamberlain says, "This is Ice's place, isn't it?" of the Icehouse, noting the dominating signage and championship banners. But by this stage of the season, the ever-growing orange hordes are as powerful a force in the grandstand as Ice fans. Look from the penalty box up at the grandstand and the venue appears to be the home of the Mustangs, their rollicking crowd loud and bright, loving the ride they are on in 2014. With a tough finish in August featuring three road trips, the Mustangs needed full points today. So far this year, when they have had to dig deep, they have done so.

Post-match, Sean O'Kane tells me about a possible venture in nanotechnology, then banters with Chuck Connolly, saying he is going to watch the next Mustangs game on his computer early in the morning on a boat off Maine. I am not sure which one of them then said "If it's dark, you can drink!" but they concurred on the point.

Early July is no kinder to Ice than the club's tough June. Shutout 4–0 on Saturday in Adelaide, each of its turnovers punished clinically, Ice redoubles its efforts on Sunday, desperate to arrest its slide. They lead 2–0, but concede two goals in the last minute and lose the shootout, the precious single point scant consolation after three points were in their keeping most of the encounter. Now third, Ice next face the Sydney Bears again at home, and they cannot afford another upset if they want to maintain their top-four standing.

After their rough patch, Adelaide Adrenaline have now won four games in a row to get back in the midst of playoff contention. With momentum building and players returning from injury, Adrenaline are only three points off top, but they've played two more games than some rivals. They have a weekend off, then face a season-defining road trip to Brave – who they've already beaten in Canberra this year – and the Bears. Bank six points there, and the Adrenaline will put the frighteners up even the Melbourne teams, which have led the competition for so much of the season.

Perth Thunder will still hold hopes of a grandstand finish bringing them into contention, after winning their home double-header against the North Stars. They will probably need to win every game, but this is the time of year they're meant to be at their best.

The Ice Dogs hold out the Bears 4–2 in a fiery Sydney derby at Liverpool to maintain their finals push. However they will play fellow finals contender Brave at home next week without skipper Robert Malloy, who will be suspended after receiving a game misconduct for a hit that drew blood from Sean Hamilton Steen.

TUESDAY THE 8TH

Talk about hockey in Australia for more than a couple of minutes and the topic turns to rinks. For the league and the sport to continue its growth, more arenas with greater capacities and more modern amenities are required. The common wisdom is that rinks don't make money, and hockey can never be the major driver of an ice rink in this country. If things change, it will be due to some uncommon wisdom, the sort of smarts and passion that saw the Canberra Brave created in fewer days than it took God to create heaven and earth.

Former Melbourne Ice president (2010–2012) Andy Lamrock has a proposal "still on the table" that offers a fundamentally different model for a new rink. "We aim to build a facility that is an elite hockey and ice sports training facility with a schools program associated and a health and fitness program associated with it. Rather than running it as a general session, where people just go for a skate ... every hour would be worked out to be something related to ice sports." Andy's model, which involves several high-profile partners in sporting and construction circles, would not require direct government input, which would not be forthcoming in Victoria because of the existing investment in the Icehouse. It would instead pay its way largely via grants associated with schools programs. With this source of income covering operating costs, the rink would complement, not compete with the Icehouse, and hockey and other ice sports would have first dibs on ice time. Such a venue would also be adaptable enough to accommodate basketball, netball and small to mid-range concerts, adding additional sources of revenue. Andy's vision is for a rink with a greater seating capacity than the Icehouse, also located close to the Melbourne CBD "in the key sporting hubs". He is hopeful that such a business model could be applied around Australia, leading to a network of "ice sports centres of excellence".

If Andy's big picture vision is necessary to create impetus for new ideas, it is also important to accept the feedback of those with practical experience. Two men who know all about getting a rink built in Australia are Ice Hockey Australia president Clive Connelly and banker Andrew Shelton. Clive is a veteran of playing, coaching, managing teams, administration and rink management, and offers guidance to any parties interested in rink development. Andrew is the founder of Ice Sports Australia, the driving force behind the establishment of Melbourne's game-changing Icehouse.

Their key advice for would-be rink-builders:
- The rink must be purpose-built.
- Make sure the government is involved.
- Make it a dual rink facility, so public skating continues while hockey is played.
- Make the building is energy and cost efficient.
- Locate the rink near public transport hubs.

So what does someone trying to build a rink say? Hockey stalwart and businessman Jonathan Cornford, father of Mustangs youngster Ethan, has a rink planned for Pakenham, in Melbourne's outer south-east. He says rinks must follow the energy-efficient example set by Garry Dore's Hunter Ice Skating Stadium in Newcastle. Jonathan's primary hockey love is junior development – he just returned from coaching the Victoria DeFris under-15 team to gold medal success in Newcastle – and his "main reason" for taking on the rink is to provide opportunities for kids to play. "It's in my business plan to give back to the community because there's a lot of kids in the south-east that commit suicide and a lot of kids that have a lot of issues. The main reason I coach is just to get kids across the line as much as I can. Any kids with problems I try to work with them, it's in my nature, and sport's the best thing for them."

Despite his priorities, commercial reality will govern his rink. "You've got to give your prime slots to general skating where you're going to make most of your money and then everything else is secondary." Newcastle rink manager and North Stars general manager/coach Garry Dore concurs. He is sceptical about the capacity for a hockey-only rink to work. "I think hockey's great and it's growing no doubt, but to build a rink that's designed just for hockey, I don't believe it would work. It's not our biggest income by far," he says.

There are two personal qualities Jonathan – critical of some technical aspects of the Icehouse – has in common with Andrew Shelton. Persistence and risk-taking. "It's just something I've always wanted to do. It hasn't been an overnight process, that's for sure, it's been about six years. I'm going to be putting everything on the line, so I'm hoping it works. I'm a bit of a risk-taker; I have multiple businesses, so I don't mind taking a challenge every now and again."

Ringwood's Iceland rink nurtured a generation of stars.

Melbourne's Glaciarium: centrally located rinks work.

St Moritz was a feature of St Kilda until 1982.

ON THE PHONE ANDREW SHELTON HAS THE ASSURANCE OF A PUBLIC SPEAKER AND NEGOTIATOR ACCUSTOMED TO TALKING TO IMPORTANT PEOPLE AND TRYING TO CONVINCE THEM TO DO SOMETHING. WORKING AS A SUCCESSFUL INVESTMENT BANKER FOR JP MORGAN IN NEW YORK WILL DO THAT. IT WILL ALSO EXPOSE YOU AND YOUR FAMILY TO HOCKEY. "MY KIDS HAD GROWN UP PLAYING ICE SPORTS AND WE GOT A LOT OF PLEASURE AS A FAMILY OUT OF THAT." HIS SON KEPT PLAYING HOCKEY AFTER THE SHELTONS RETURNED TO AUSTRALIA, WHERE ANDREW WAS IMPRESSED BY THE "RESILIENCE AND ENTHUSIASM" OF THE HOCKEY COMMUNITY, AND "JUST APPALLED" AT THE QUALITY OF FACILITIES. HE BECAME COMMITTED TO HELP CREATE WHAT EVENTUALLY BECAME THE ICEHOUSE. "THE GOAL FROM THE OUTSET WAS TO BUILD A HIGH-QUALITY FACILITY THAT COULD SURVIVE. ARGUABLY THE ICEHOUSE COST MORE THAN IS DESIRABLE ... BUT WE ENDED UP WITH A GENUINELY WORLD-CLASS FACILITY." ANDREW STUCK AT IT BECAUSE OF THE SUPPORT AND ENTHUSIASM OF THE ICE SPORTS COMMUNITY. BUT WHY BACK HOCKEY SO STRONGLY IN AUSTRALIA? "IT'S A FABULOUS GAME THAT INNATELY APPEALS TO AUSTRALIANS, SO IT'S A MATTER OF OFFERING IT PROPERLY. AND IF THE GAME IS TO DEVELOP AROUND THE COUNTRY THEN WE NEED OTHER FACILITIES OF SIMILAR CHARACTER ELSEWHERE."

THURSDAY THE 10TH

It has been announced that the playoffs will be held in Melbourne, and Brave are arranging tickets for their fans and a place on the 'Brave Bus' to travel to the Icehouse. There is a possibility that Brave might not make the finals, with five teams within four points, and only eleven points between first and last on the standings, but it is prudent to make early arrangements when there are only a thousand seats on offer.

Brave sets its sights on the final weekend of August.

FRIDAY THE 11TH

Australians, Melburnians particularly, love a dress-up. Here, fancy tailoring does not mean stuffy formality, it means a raucous party. Melbourne Ice doesn't deny itself the fun of a glam night. There are six people involved in the organisation of its annual Gala, including Sara Armstrong, and they know what they are doing. At Etihad Stadium, the roofed arena (capacity 55,000) at the gateway to Docklands, guests are directed two levels up to the swish Medallion Club. The men have suited up, and Melbourne Ice's womenfolk have spared no expense. Hair is done, make-up is camera-ready, and some of the dresses reveal young flesh in manners worthy of rich footballer's partners. The tables are adorned with a foam hockey motif. If Ice can be divided into the old guard and the new, this is definitely a night for the new, and young. The Ice family is united in grief for a young fan and volunteer, Dan Oakley who died earlier in the week. But Dan was renowned for enjoying a social life, and this occasion remains festive.

Before we are seated for food and speeches, veteran defenceman Ross Howell, who resembles a rounder-faced Roger Federer, tells me he left Victoria because he had grown sick of the confines of the Oakleigh rink. He said that on occasion, both teams had to skate around and around in order to disperse fog so they could start a game. He went to the Gold Coast and ran into a rink where a massive crack down the middle of the ice forced a forfeit! Having started in Ice's inaugural line-up, he returned this year to play at the comparatively palatial Icehouse.

The MC makes a lame Mustangs joke and the night is underway. The coaches, the team within the team, sit together, with ex-coach Paul 'Jaffa' Watson and his wife Barb. Brent Laver will soon monopolise Jaffa, drawn to the opportunity to talk shop for a couple of hours with his old coach and current mentor. Before he does, Brent reiterates that if his long-term plan for the club works, and a better coaching candidate comes along, he will "buy a beer and a ticket" and join me in the grandstand. His revelations don't stop there. Brent says he was so stunned by the second road trip loss to Adelaide, after he felt Ice played so well, and followed his every instruction, that he didn't address the players after the game. Sunday games in Adelaide involve a rushed departure for the airport, but afterwards Brent was dirty on himself. He said he apologised for his silence to the players at Tuesday training.

The one-off red jerseys from the Canada Day game are in high demand and fetch prices over a thousand dollars at auction. Handsome and popular defenceman Todd Graham

Josh Puls and Barb Watson.

Paul 'Jaffa' Watson and Brent Laver.

and the team's youngest member Sam Hodic assist the auctioneer on stage, answering a few questions, asking a few of each other. The interjections of the rowdy crowd result in a new item being auctioned – a shower with Todd and it is enthusiastically sought by a table of young women. Things are getting pretty bawdy.

As Matt takes up duties as DJ, I get talking to Jaden Pine-Murphy, always one of the friendliest of the Ice squad. "We are so privileged … some locals don't know it," he says of playing for Ice. He says imports like Jeff Smith know how well the club looks after its players. Jaden's satisfaction has been evident in his play this season. The Kiwi has gone from back-up to one of the better performed goalies in the league.

I get to thank Shona Green, Ice and Australian women's star and Ice bench worker, for her participation in the shoot for the *Age* multimedia piece, which was released hours earlier. She tells me that she and Tommy Powell have been an item for twelve years, since they met playing hockey. It follows a pattern: Tommy's dad Alan – an enthusiastic bidder for auction items (though not the shower with Todd) – met his wife when aged seventeen.

Word around the room is that Swedish "accidental import" Tim Johansson is a possibility to return for another season. His girlfriend has a job in Melbourne and is enjoying Australia. James Meredith tells me he got to spend a day with conditioning guru Darren Burgess, largely credited with making Port Adelaide the fittest team in the AFL. Every moment of every Port player's next three years is mapped out … I wonder if hangovers are factored into such meticulous planning.

Back at the coaches table, Barb Watson tells me about her years as the wife of a hockey icon. It was lucky, and essential, that she loved the game herself. She says for most of their lives together, Jaffa was effectively doing two 40-hours a-week jobs, his paid employment and his hockey jobs. Jaffa once said "I was born on the wrong continent", wondering how different his life might have been if he'd been able to make a living out of hockey. Aged nearly 60, Jaffa has played and coached through the toughest period of hockey in Victoria, when the sport was reduced to operating out of Oakleigh. He persisted until the Icehouse opened and presided over Ice's three consecutive titles. But Barb says the past two years since he retired have been the toughest of his life, as he has had to start anew in his paid employment after previously being self-employed. Jaffa still exudes uncomplaining chest-out energy, but this is the time he should be winding down and enjoying his commentary for ATC Productions and Fox Sports. He deserves a reward apart from championship medals for what he has put into the game.

SATURDAY THE 12TH

There are mini-finals now every week, with less than ten games to go. At home to Brave, the Ice Dogs come from 1–3 down after two periods, then 1–4, to win 5–4. Brave pushes hard in the final minutes, but Tim Noting comes up with three big saves and the melee on the final buzzer after another physical game at Liverpool leaves Brave with three suspensions, including leading scorer Stephen Blunden, for next week's crucial home game against Adrenaline, who are hot on their heels in the standings. It's a heartbreaker of a loss, not unlike Ice's last-minute defeat in Adelaide, and the sort of hardship a good team puts behind them if they go on to bigger things. The star for the Ice Dogs, not for the first time in 2014, is former goalie and defender turned forward David Dunwoodie, who nabs a hat-trick. "Dave is a local player who I believe has only ever played in Australia and he finds himself the lone local among a number of very highly capable, highly credentialed imports in the top ten scorers in the league," says Dogs coach Andrew Petrie. "It's been a phenomenal effort."

Andrew is rapt with how his team has been able to pull together a good season after such a tumultuous start. "It speaks volumes about the character of our dressing room," he says. "The commitment, determination and effort to get back in the game, to get the lead and then to protect the lead was exceptional."

With only eight teams, the AIHL often offers rematches of memorable encounters shortly after a famous game. The upstart underdog Bears return to Melbourne two weeks after their heroic double upset of the Melbourne teams, this time playing the Mustangs on Saturday and Ice on Sunday. This close to the finals, with so much on the line and so many lessons learnt this year, the Mustangs broach no further nonsense, hitting the Bears with high-pace attacks from the outset. Bears goalie Daniel Palmkvist is still outstanding, but the Mustangs follow instructions to avoid his glove and move him side to side. The threadbare Bears line-up – they have travelled with only thirteen skaters – offers next to nothing offensively, and the defensive game plan is useless without numbers totally committed to frantic skating. Tired but dogged, the Bears cannot make inroads as long as the Mustangs attack. The Mustangs attack. It ends up 4–0, with the Stangs having pounded Palmkvist with 51 shots, Jamie Bourke scoring the first three goals for the home team. Symbolic of the game is the final goal. The Mustangs have two men in alone on Palmkvist. He makes the save, but Adrian Nash is there to put away the rebound. There's only so much the goalie can do.

At the end of the game, smooth talking Mustangs announcer Greg Spaetgens reads out the stars of the game. "He's from Sweden ... VEEEEKTOR!" An ebullient Viktor Gibbs-Sjodin performs a belly slide along the ice in front of the fans. "He's from Lilydale ... JAMIE BOURKE!"

On the bench, Brad is content, his son Zander sitting on the boards, demanding his attention, inured to all the hockey fuss surrounding them. The coach's next duty will be to play soccer with his sons outside the dressing room. Brad Vigon and Brent Laver have shared notes about beating the Bears. Mick confirms that Brad's message to his players had been distilled to "Attack all night". In doing so, they have achieved the first-ever shutout for Fraser Carson, and for the team.

Viktor Gibbs-Sjodin looks like he is enjoying his hockey in Melbourne.

SUNDAY THE 13TH

Since the Icehouse opened, the most rabid and colourful Melbourne Ice fans have chanted and banged the glass behind the city end goals, proclaiming it, with a large banner attached above them on the Plexiglas, to be the 'South Pole'. Before their encounter with the Bears, Melbourne Ice gathers its pre-game huddle against the glass behind the net in front of these diehards, in recognition of the passing of South Pole regular Dan Oakley. They have a fierce focus to them rarely evident before a game. It seems they can perform when not light-hearted: Ice attacks ceaselessly all night, and the fragile, tired Bears are totally overwhelmed from the first puck drop. Ice put six past them in the first period, from six different players, including defenceman Ross Howell. The fans who wanted a goal so badly on Canada Day now get their feast. Ace goalie Daniel Palmkvist departs after four goals from six shots in six minutes and perennial back-up Luke Read gets to play most of the game.

When the South Pole yells out "Hey Ready, give us a wave!" he obliges, despite the hammering he is taking from Ice shooters.

I'm watching with Jeff Smith, who is out for a game with a groin strain, at ground level on the grandstand corner of the rink. At the outset he says he is a nervous watcher, but there's never any tension in this contest. We talk hockey, but he's distracted by the South Pole. Before he joins them, he says "Fighting stops stickwork," and he points out a couple of cheap slashing incidents in the game that "would have been dealt with" under professional rules. When he returns from his stint with the hardcore fans, he says he told them they needed some new chants, but he looked like he was having fun standing at the back of their noisy behind-goals clump. "If things aren't working, change them," he says, endorsing Brent's line changes. This week Lliam Webster is playing defence, the position his dad Ian thought he was best suited to when he took up the sport.

The Bears, triumphant two weeks prior, are now unravelled, their players losing their cool, their shots tally fewer than Ice's goals tally. The game misconducts picked up by Spencer Austin and Sean Hamilton Steen in the final period ensures the last-placed team will be further weakened for their next game. The lack of resources, on and off the ice, is taking its toll. Underdogs cannot often repeat upset wins - that's why they are underdogs. This is the most forlorn performance at the Icehouse since the Canberra Knights went down 16–0 to Ice in 2013. The final score is 10–1 and Ice have had 54 shots to 21. Luke Read has doggedly stopped 42 of the 48 shots he faced. For Ice, it was a clinical team performance, with nine players scoring. They now need to prove they can beat fellow contenders again, in order to hold on to a finals place in the final six weeks.

MONDAY THE 14TH

Finals tickets have gone on sale to club members today, after the club allocations, and I didn't tarry. Any combination of the current top six teams competing will be worth seeing. Facebook is awash with non-Victorian fans asking about where to stay in Melbourne.

The other big news in Australian hockey is the well-received opening of the international exhibition series in Perth. The first such games played there featured two capacity crowds of 13,500. Plenty of fans are urging those who enjoyed it to see a Thunder game.

Jeff Smith (at rear) visits the South Pole.

SATURDAY THE 19TH

I run into Newcastle boss Garry Dore an hour before the North Stars' game against the Mustangs. He's on his way to get a pre-game coffee. We stand on either side of the barrier to the public rink, fully intending to let each other go, but we end up talking rinks and hockey long enough that the North Stars coach has to abandon his coffee plan and get back to the rooms. He tells me that the Icehouse is the best finals venue at least two years out of every three, because of its venue size and the range of entertainment options nearby. He remains sceptical that a stadium holding two or three thousand fans would be viable anywhere in Australia, including Melbourne. "I wouldn't put my money into taking that risk," he says. "Rinks are hard." Garry is a cheerful but sensible realist, who has run his rink long enough to know the industry pitfalls backwards, but he delivers his verdict hoping someone can disprove his pessimism.

He praises CBR Brave for their effort in putting together a competitive team, but he is concerned about their future. "Canberra and Newcastle in time will struggle, because we're the only clubs in our region. Compare that to Melbourne, where they have four or five local clubs that promote and develop hockey. We've got to get the resources to compete with that, it's very difficult."

It is one of those days at the Icehouse where I am an evangelist, hosting first-timers including Nif, who is visiting from Milan, and my girlfriend Samantha, who has been to one local game before but is fresh enough to hockey to later say she got motion sickness from following the action from end to end. The tennis court head swivel comes about because Nif has reserved primo seats, dead on the red line, offering a perfect view of either end. I haven't yet sat in such a great perch in four years at this venue. Nif has also recruited her daughter Yasemin, her sister Nilgun, and Nilgun's boyfriend Craig. I want hockey to deliver today.

For much of my first three years watching the AIHL, I coaxed friends to take in a game with the enthusiasm of a music fan circulating mix-tapes of a favourite band. I usually say it is a simple if frantic game, and try to leave them to pick up the pace without too much coaching. I start to explain icing – "If you dump the puck ..." then have to define "dump". But pretty soon, everyone seems to have a rudimentary understanding of the basics.

The newcomers enjoy this contest much more than me. There has been a spate of complaints about refereeing around the country in recent weeks, and today it is my turn to be distracted by the officiating, and the lack of communication surrounding it. I hate to bag officials, another vital group doing a great job for the league for minimal payment. Too often, a referee critic is a hot-headed team official or player over-reacting, and the official is eventually vindicated. And hockey has to be the toughest game in the world to officiate, being so fast; it is certainly the most dangerous. But when my friends ask me "what was that penalty for?" and "why has the game stopped?" I have no answers. There are no announcements or explanations as play stops for five and ten minutes at a time, refs and officials talking to everyone but the crowd. Mild-mannered Garry Dore has had a conniption-fit on his bench.

After two periods, down 4–1 and outshot 31 to 17, the North Stars are in trouble. A quick glance at the standings pre-game reveals that this most even of seasons is being decided before our eyes. A pair of road losses here for the North Stars could prove deadly to their chances of making the playoffs. They are seven points off fourth and six off the contending Adrenaline in fifth. They can sense a spluttering season getting away from them.

Seventeen calls in the last period make this the longest game I have ever attended in Australia, the ironic music growing tiresome as players wait to be told who is going in the box, those in the stand none the wiser. "It's usually a lot better than this," I insist to my hockey greenhorns. "It usually flows." They know no better, having never before seen the game live, and they have enjoyed the spectacle, especially the first two periods, when the Mustangs twice scored shorthanded to set up a match-winning 3–0 lead. My girlfriend, a writer, enjoys the term "roughing". Her linguistic amusement is the only good thing about the interrupted final period. The final score? The Mustangs won 6–3. Seven of the nine goals were penalty-related.

At the Mustangs' post-match haunt, the Groovetrain, just upstairs from Ice's Harbourtown Hotel, I listen to the new fans discuss what they liked about the experience. Craig cannot believe that no-one except the referees gets paid. He's trying to compare the speed of the game, and the mingling of playes and officials with fans after the game, to professional footy thirty years ago.

I introduce my crew to Mick Burslem, Andy McDowell and Pat O'Kane. Yasemin and Nif get their photo taken, fan-style, with Pat, who they decide looks like Tom Cruise. Pat pleads guilty to running his parents' time in Australia like a commando mission, and relief that the hectic schedule is completed. He is booked in for a visit home with Stephanie in

January. Receiving high distinctions for his just completed academic work has put him at ease. But that's not enough. He has also booked himself in for a major charity bike ride with sponsor Bryan Jeffrey in December. The first training run is tomorrow morning.

As the womenfolk fuss over the athlete, I consider the game. The Mustangs took another step forward today, I conclude. Now familiar with the feeling of good results, they are repeating the actions which create those results. They again started aggressively, played at a high tempo, putting their opposition on the back foot, and they got the shots off – another 51 of them today.

There's something not quite right with Newcastle, who now appear to have all the pieces they need in place, and play attractive hockey between lapses. The two shorthanded goals conceded within seconds in the first period speak of a fundamental breakdown in teamwork and defensive structures.

New fans remind you how far hockey has to go in Australia. When I asked junior coach and rink-builder Johnathan Cornford about the biggest issue facing the sport, he said "publicity", and I felt a little taken aback. But he is right. Most Australians still don't know that the sport exists in their backyard. Many are barely aware it exists at all. It's a numbers game. And before the game today, Garry Dore was right when he spoke about the impact of the international series, which gets wide exposure, compared to hundreds of individual fans haphazardly converting one by one. The social media explosion is great for the ranks of the sport itself, but it is mostly a conversation among the converted, and in a crowded media landscape people mostly see what they look for.

Craig and I check out the scores in the AFL game in the background. Ubiquitous TV coverage maintains the entrenchment of that football code. It does not need to be explained to anyone in four Australian states, where it shown on prime time free-to-air TV. It also earns the game one billion dollars.

Checking scores from around the country at the end of the second period, I noticed a social media expletive from ATC commentator Stephen White. An Adelaide team bus has rolled over en route to Canberra from Sydney, and four players have been taken to hospital. At the Groovetrain, Ice Hockey Australia boss Clive Connelly revises this to include seven people in all, including coach Ryan O'Handley. All are apparently OK, and being kept under observation as much as being treated, but it is a shock all the same.

Prior to the game, the Mustangs had requested observance of a minute's silence to acknowledge the loss of life due to the Malaysian airlines flight shot down over Ukraine. I think of Nif and Yasemin, just arrived, still jet-lagged, from Italy. Any of us making such a voyage could have been a victim. Anyone of us travelling to a game could have suffered the fate that befell the Adrenaline. "It's a bad stretch of road," Clive says. "I suppose we've been lucky all these years."

THE SOCIAL MEDIA EXPLOSION IS GREAT FOR THE RANKS OF THE SPORT ITSELF, BUT IT IS MOSTLY A CONVERSATION AMONG THE CONVERTED, AND IN A CROWDED MEDIA LANDSCAPE PEOPLE MOSTLY SEE WHAT THEY LOOK FOR.

SUNDAY THE 20TH

The Adrenaline bus accident happened in an instant, but it has had ever-widening repercussions. In its immediate aftermath, the game between their teams postponed indefinitely, Canberra officials rushed to the scene, and then hosted shaken Adelaide players at their venue, transporting them, buying them dinner, putting them up and even supplying clothing as required.

Sunday's Adrenaline game against the Bears is also postponed, and thoughts turn to getting the Adelaide players home as soon as possible. Adrenaline secretary Chloe Meiers attempts to reschedule the club's QANTAS flights from late Sunday night, but is quoted over $4000 to make changes. Cue the social media power of the AIHL community. A campaign urging Qantas to get the team home earlier begins on Saturday night and succeeds late Sunday morning. Chloe ends up getting the players seated together, with no extra charges. The clubs need the games missed rescheduled, as happened with Newcastle's bus breakdown earlier in the year, especially since they are in direct competition for a playoff berth; the proposed game in Canberra was crucial to the chances of both teams. But with a cramped fixture in the final weeks before the playoffs, it won't be easy.

Melbourne Ice lost all seven regular season games to the North Stars in 2012, 2013, and 2014, its only two recent wins over Newcastle coming in the 2011 and 2012 grand finals. That odd confluence of facts makes for a healthy contemporary rivalry, which has built on the foundation of Ice's failure to win a final as the ugly duckling of the competition in the first decade of the century, when it struggled to adapt away from its Oakleigh home base. Aside from the Mustangs, Ice fans are most fired up by the presence of the North Stars.

Within thirty seconds of the start of this game, those fans are rolling their eyes, after North Stars import Cody Danberg scores from the crease – on his team's second good chance. The Ice DJ plays *Nothing Too Serious*, hopefully. The crowd remains unconvinced, subdued until Ice scores shorthanded via Todd Graham halfway through the period. A minute later, with scores 1–1, a scramble in the goal crease leads to some push and shove … and the refs take long minutes to confer with each other and the captains, and the crowd is left in the dark. Garry Dore is throwing his hands up. Eventually a misconduct and a bench minor are amongst the penalties delivered against Newcastle.

Ice fans rallied after the death of mate Dan Oakley.   And Ice players followed suit.

The North Stars are playing like this is their last chance. They equalise after a Jeff Smith deflection gives Ice a 2–1 lead, and their first line is too good for Ice's third line early in the second period, Beau Taylor making it 3–2 to the visitors. The penalties keep coming, including the now familiar misconducts for what I guess to be verbal transgressions. Matt has two goals disallowed, for reasons undisclosed - the first off a face-off, may have involved a high stick. The second was one of the efforts of the year, in which he went coast to coast and wrapped the puck in the net. Best guess was that the net was out. Contentious but unexplained situations continually put the referees in the spotlight, but in the last period, the game refuses to be sidetracked. It is 3–3, and Ice, just a game clear of fifth-placed Adelaide, and Newcastle, striving to keep in the playoff race, will make a thriller of this no matter what.

The North Stars score first in the final period, through promising youngster Hayden Sheard – his second – but Ice level at 4–4 through the deserving Matt Armstrong with 15 minutes left to play. Beau Taylor is dragged down after grabbing a stretch pass coming out of the penalty box, and he is awarded a penalty shot. Dink! He beats Jaden Pine-Murphy but not the post, and it remains 4–4. A minute later, Jeff Smith, the target of so much of Newcastle's penalised behaviour, breaks the deadlock on the powerplay to put Ice ahead 5–4. Subsequently, some of the hardest hits of the season shake the Icehouse, and the frenetic up-and-back thrills a rapt crowd. Ice spurn several powerplay chances to put the game away, then in the final five minutes the North Stars get their chance with two powerplays. They have shot after shot with the man advantage in the final two minutes, Ice reduced to shot-blocking to keep the puck out of the net.

With 28 seconds left, Ice are back to full strength but don't play like it, and the North Stars are still pressing with three seconds to play, with a face-off in their offensive zone. They call a timeout. But there is no miracle from the following puck drop, and the home team has somehow defied its regular season North Stars jinx to shore up, for now, its position in the top four, winning 5–4. It has been a game worthy of a final, an irony surely not lost on frustrated North Stars coach Garry Dore, now unlikely to see action on the last weekend of the season.

"We were only okay in spurts because we broke down at times," says Brent Laver after the game. "But at this time of the year, it's just great to get another three points. It's pretty difficult to get flow in a game with that many penalties, and I think it's something that both teams struggled with." Jeff Smith is an obvious source of praise after so much heavy lifting in the win. "The fact that he's able to do what he does – being physical – yet remaining in total control the whole time is fantastic," Laver says. "To see him do that and score a couple of times is great - he's a great leader."

Jeff Smith himself is pleasantly surprised by his haul this year on the powerplay. "I'm usually known for two goals per season. Everyone's good in this league, the competition is really tight. It's crucial to get these tight games at home".

After the game, I break my Sunday night curfew - the early start at work hurts on Monday mornings - and take in the Ice post-mortem at the Harbourtown Hotel. More than once, Ice insiders there speak of this being a 'development year', despite their aim to be a contender every year. But if Ice can beat Newcastle and Sydney on the road next weekend, they are good enough to win the competition. The North Stars will regain import Chris Wilson and naturalised star Brian Bales and the Dogs are still fighting to qualify for the finals.

Also still in the running for a finals berth are Adelaide, who were poised to re-enter the top four before their frightening bus crash. But the health of everyone affected is the primary concern now, Ryan O'Handley admitting Adrenaline are "pretty rattled, pretty shaken up". They have four players in doubt for their home double-header against the Bears this weekend.

The Ice/North Stars rivalry has been heightened by two recent grand final epics.

Jeff Smith is relishing his role as a forward on Ice powerplays.

MONDAY THE 21ST

The latest video from Canberra Brave media machine: *NOW WE ARE AT THE CROSSROADS. AND THE SEASON IS ON THE LINE.* It's as dramatic as a major motion-picture trailer. Stirring music, an American voiceover exhorting motivational epithets, the headlines of Brave's year appearing ... Then the real star of the show, two minutes in, captain Mark Rummukainen in the Icehouse dressing room between periods. "It's a fuckin' top of the table clash ... first time in history for the fucking Brave, first time in history for a Canberra team. If you need someone else to get you in the game take your fucking stuff off now." Other notable quotes: "Allow your pain to push what you do ... This is the opportunity of a lifetime, never give up. You've got to want to succeed as bad as you want to breathe ..."

They are in a different league to most of the clubs with these offerings, superior to most produced by pro sports.

STEPHEN WHITE'S HOCKEY STORY HAS ELEMENTS TYPICAL OF MANY IN AUSTRALIA. A CHANCE ENCOUNTER WITH THE GAME, IN HIS CASE, FOOTAGE OF THE 1991 STANLEY CUP FINALS, PLANTED AN INSATIABLE CURIOSITY. HE ORIGINALLY PLAYED INLINE. HE HAD TO GIVE THE GAME AWAY WHEN STUDYING. AND HE FELL IN LOVE WITH THE AIHL WHEN HE SAW A GAME AT THE ICEHOUSE. STEPHEN, NEWLY MOVED FROM PERTH, FIGURED GOING TO THE RINK WOULD BE A "GOOD WAY OF MEETING PEOPLE". FOUR YEARS LATER, HE IS A COMMENTATOR ON THE WEEKLY, NATIONALLY TELEVISED FOX SPORTS BROADCAST FROM THE "REALLY TIGHT-KNIT COMMUNITY" OF ATC PRODUCTIONS. HE SAYS IT IS "PHENOMENAL" THAT ATC, WHICH BEGAN WITH JAMES MORGAN SHOOTING FOOTAGE OFF THE ICEHOUSE BALCONY WITH A STEADICAM, NOW FEATURES A FULL CREW, SOUND DESKS, REPLAY MACHINES, AND EIGHT CAMERAS. "I LOVE COMING TO THE ICEHOUSE. THE WHOLE WEEK THAT I SPEND AT MY OTHER JOB AND NOT LIKING IT, I'M THINKING OF THINGS TO SAY ON AIR." HE SAYS HOCKEY COULD REACH THE LEVEL OF BASKETBALL AND NETBALL - "TIER TWO" SPORTS WITH LIVE, FREE-TO-AIR BROADCASTS - WITHIN A DECADE. HE BELIEVES FACILITIES "WILL MAKE OR BREAK" THE SPORT BUT "THE FOUNDATION OF THIS WHOLE LEAGUE IS COMMUNITY, AS WE SAW WITH THE ADELAIDE BUS CRASH".

Stephen White, right, with fellow ATC commentators Michael Clough and Jaffa Watson and ice volunteer Jason Bajada.

FRIDAY THE 25TH

Showbiz sport has reached Melbourne. The Douglas-Webber Cup international exhibitions series, having successfully packed out games in Perth and Brisbane, is about to cram them in at Rod Laver Arena. The great drawcard of the series for people like me, Nathan Walker, will not be playing, his drafting by Washington having changed his priorities. "I was talking to my manager and it's probably not the best thing for me at this present time," he tells me. "I'm currently undergoing contract negotiations with Washington, so I'm trying to keep my mind focused on that and just get through that process." But he's excited by the prospect of thousands of Aussies attending the matches. "It's going to be massive. I mean, you get 20,000 people who have never seen a live hockey game in their life ... I think there's going to be a lot of talk around each of the major cities that the games have been played in and hopefully it can boost hockey and get a lot more kids getting involved in hockey." Despite his brief (three games) involvement with the AIHL, the leftie is aware of his impact. "It's a small community but they're very passionate about hockey ... hopefully me getting drafted can boost that community into getting much bigger," he says. During his off-season at home in Sydney, he has been attending Ice Dogs games and training on steep hills pulling weights, making for some memorable web footage.

The heavily-attended travelling hockey extravaganza offers a foothold for AIHL amateurs, but only off the ice. Photographers Andrew Mercieca and Tania Chalmers, regular Icehouse snappers, are working for the tour. Andrew fell in love with hockey when he saw it for the first time at the second game held at the Icehouse in 2010. He hopes his hockey snaps help form "a way into the media", but he also does it for the players, enjoying their responses to shots he posts on Facebook, blog sites like Hewitt Sports and club and league sites.

The AIHL has helped bloggers, technicians and photographers finding an audience for their talents via social media and the internet. ATC Productions remains the major success story, having parlayed a love of the game, technological virtuosity and theatrical knowledge into a burgeoning sports telecasting business. Their unpaid hockey heroics eventually led to significant paid work such as this tour, and broadcasts of racing, cricket and baseball. ATC Productions boss James Morgan, 28, is in charge of all the audio-visual elements of the exhibition series, and his boss Craig Douglas is effusive. "He's show director now, he's kicked me out of a job! I really want to take him along with me."

The contribution of James to Australian hockey has been enormous. While there had been other attempts to cover games,

THE CONTRIBUTION OF JAMES MORGAN TO AUSTRALIAN HOCKEY HAS BEEN ENORMOUS. THE ADVENT OF ATC PRODUCTIONS HAS TRANSFORMED EXPOSURE OF THE LEAGUE.

the advent of ATC Productions has transformed exposure of the league. James went with a cousin to the first game at the Icehouse after watching ice hockey on TV during the Winter Olympics. An eighteen-year veteran of amateur theatre despite his tender years, Morgan loved the spectacle, but felt the audio quality needed improving. He offered his services. They were accepted. After he "begged, borrowed and stole" some second-hand equipment, taught himself how to make rudimentary broadcasts by scouring university textbooks and broadcasts of other sports, working with volunteers who "hadn't touched a camera", James Morgan managed to piece together coverage of Ice games broadcast in the stadium and online, gaining an audience as far afield as Canada. While maintaining his full-time job as a network engineer, James built ATC into a professional entity which provides footage for Fox Sports. But his work for local hockey remains an invaluable labour of love, without any direct payment. James is a good fit with the Douglas-Webber entrepreneurs, people who can make seemingly outlandish visions into lucrative realities. For these go-getters, problems are just stories to tell later on, once they have been solved. Paid work for Douglas Webber is an indirect reward for ATC's altruism.

Robert Bannerman tells me that after the series openers in Perth, Thunder enjoyed a bump in new ticket sales, merchandise sales, and game enquiries. Newcastle all-rounder Garry Dore compared the effect of the series to when *Disney on Ice* plays the major entertainment centres, and there are suddenly 15 new figure skating students at his rink. "It's a spectacular, it's an event, it's exciting, everyone's going there, and they're seeing a show ..." Garry says. He says Nathan Walker's signing is "awesome for the country, awesome for the sport", but he doesn't expect a major jump in the numbers of youngsters playing ice hockey as a result. "The only people who

Andrew Mercieca, AIHL snapper, snared a role capturing images for the exhibition series.

The sellout crowds for the Douglas Webber international exhibition matches have proved there is curiosity, at the very least, about hockey in Australia.

know Nathan Walker are already playing hockey." He believes this series reaches more people and has a bigger potential effect.

Inside Rod Laver Arena at ground level, just before game time, I look around in astonishment at the crowd banked up to the ceilings in every direction. They are all here to watch hockey. Or fights. But they are here. Resolution Media, the team behind the Ice *Threepeat* video, have created a heart-starting video that airs on a huge scoreboard cube which hangs over centre ice, and with the lights down, and the crowd buying in to the call-and-response hype, it works perfectly. There's sonic boom pyrotechnics, flames, flashing lights, and a pugnacious MC done up as a circus ringmaster, wearing extraordinarily gaudy half-American, half Canadian tails. The production values have risen as Craig Douglas promised, and we are constantly bombarded.

Once the smoke clears and the small rink in the big stadium is occupied by the duelling teams, I am reminded of the phenomenon that sometimes afflicts gripping Icehouse games – everyone is too transfixed or stunned by the speed of the game to make a noise. This is anathema to the organisers of this event, but one senses that any converts to the game will be won over in these interregnums when the athletes are the show, and the contest for the puck is most gripping. Somewhere in these thousands of people is a kid watching who will nag his parents to take him to hockey school.

The power and skill level is well above the AIHL, and it makes you think of a factory conveyor belt, where oddments are tossed aside, and only the most perfectly formed product progresses, the reality of professional sport all over the world. No-one on the ice is anything less than six feet, there are no

James Morgan gets out from behind the cameras. He says volunteering has provided most of his opportunities.

anomalous skilled little men like Pat O'Kane or Jason Baclig evading the big hits.

Ice alumni Matt Armstrong and Todd Graham have scored tickets, and Matt puts me straight. "It's not size, it's talent," he says of the smooth movers on display. He says his sizeable mate Todd should be out there. "He's as good as any of these guys." He is also amazed by how many people are at the game. By game's end, I am talking AIHL with Matt. He feels the Ice kids are learning what's required. "We are a chance," he concedes.

Nathan Walker is briefly introduced during a stoppage in play, but the Australian element to the occasion is minimal. There are AIHL folk dotted throughout the stadium in ancillary roles, but the league is not mentioned, and is unseen. Mustangs president John Belic will tell me later that he and fans of both Melbourne teams handed out thousands of fliers to attendees to promote local games. And Mustangs social media guru Myles Harris has run a Facebook ad and tweet campaign targeting a 10 kilometre radius around the arena. The series is undoubtedly useful for hockey awareness in Australia, but it also feels like a missed opportunity. The promoters are not obliged to showcase the local league, of course – this is business – and they are selling Canada v America, not Australian hockey, which few of the patrons know exists. But the massive crowd both vindicates and depresses an AIHL fan.

There are reports of an NHL game being courted for Sydney. But if a percentage of attendees want to try out local hockey after seeing the big-time, will they want to traipse an hour west to join 100 fans at cold Liverpool? There are no frills at an AIHL game; you have to love the game itself, not the trappings.

A columnist at my newspaper, an erudite ex-footballer, has made it to the show. I tell him he should take in a local game featuring Todd Graham, and introduce them. His *Sunday Age* piece, which will be the most prominent article about hockey in his paper all year, starts with the old chestnut about going to a fight and a hockey game breaking out, and is mostly about the brawling.

SATURDAY THE 26TH

ROAD TRIP FIVE: NEWCASTLE NORTH STARS V MELBOURNE ICE
DAY ONE

This weekend, CBR Brave need to get points out of the tough road-trip double in Perth. Ice gets the North Stars on the rebound in Newcastle, and then the Liverpool test against the Dogs on Sunday, and the battered Adrenaline host the Bears twice in Adelaide.

So it's time to learn about Norse mythology, specifically the invasion of Scotland by the Vikings. In the rental car from Newcastle airport, Ice club patron Josh Puls has asked Johan Steenberg to enlighten us about this aspect of his Scandinavian heritage. The Swedish yolie coach doesn't waste time putting us straight: "They took a lot of mushrooms and went bananas." End of history lesson. So it's back to the year-long Odd Couple bickering in the front seat, driver Tom Harward and passenger Johan resuming normal service. The moment we touch down, the abuse and leg-pulling commences. I can't imagine their floorshow is anywhere near as entertaining in Melbourne. On the

JOHAN STEENBERG'S REPEATED PHRASE, ALMOST A MOTTO, IS "YOU HAVE TO HAVE FUN". THIS PHILOSOPHY IS IN HAPPY COINCIDENCE WITH THIS YEAR'S ICE TEAM.

road with a select captive audience, optimum bullshit session conditions are realised. Josh goads the double-act from the back seat, adding timely leading questions like the history request and: "What did we do before you came along, Johan?" Johan shakes his head sympathetically. "Must have been tough," he replies. Johan's repeated phrase, almost a motto, is "You have to have fun". This philosophy is in happy coincidence with this year's Ice team, which is also committed to that crucial three letter word. To bait Johan, Tom threatens to give Gustaf a Finnish jersey for his 22nd birthday tomorrow. "I wouldn't go to sleep tonight if I was you," Johan responds. Tom is known as "newt' amongst the group, as it already had a Tom (Powell). Tom Harward is the "new Tom"...

Our path to the rink from the airport, from Newcastle's northern fringe to its southern edge, makes the city of 350,000 feel like it consists largely of outer suburbs. The waterfront CBD, modest but revitalised in recent years, is by-passed. Newcastle is a big town or a small city, depending how you define these things. The region's psyche – fierce civic pride co-existing with defensive defiance – speaks of the massive shadow cast by nearby Sydney.

The North Stars are welcoming. From the moment they recognise me until game time, I am talking with someone, from Garry Dore, who I first see selling tickets in the box office, to media manager and club stalwart Pete Lambert to Michael Smith, another diligent media operator. These friendly folk are also sure of themselves, for good reason - Newcastle are four-time champs and have never finished lower than fourth. Their rink is second only to the Icehouse as a hockey centre – it even has glass around the rink, a luxury in Australian hockey – and it doesn't hurt that the general manager and head coach is the rink manager. Their volunteer organisation is extensive and talented – Pete tells me there are sixteen people involved in their media offerings, and they do a lot of the little things right, like promoting their popular and engaging mascot Marty the Moose.

Even a well-managed Aussie rink is full of idiosyncrasies. The Hunter Ice Skating Stadium's unexplained Euro ski chalet chic decorating scheme features miniature alpine roofs and flags of

Marty The Moose making friends in Newcastle.

Ice staff prepare; Josh Puls captures the warm-up.

Gear-drying is an inexact science on the road.

Newcastle volunteers Greg Rickford, Beth Smith, Michael Smith and Peter Lambert.

many nations, and a picture of a log fire burns inexplicably on a small video screen on the petite platform above the team benches. The 2008 championship banner hangs modestly. Pubescent cheerleaders hand out programs and form a guard of honour in the dark when the team comes on the ice, and each (North Stars) goal is announced by Garry's wife Leanne as belonging to a sponsor. There is a playful gaggle of middle-aged, pink-hat wearing lawn bowlers here today, and they gambol gleefully with mascot Marty, more enthusiastic about the hyperactive big head than the kids. It's the sort of place where that seems appropriate. Grannies and pre-teens are as likely to be yelling here as adolescent boys, and opposing teams get polite applause when they skate on.

The North Stars, well-covered by local radio, TV and newspapers, have more sponsors on their jersey than I have ever seen, but not the names of the players. They belong to their community, commercially and spiritually, and that populace turns up in good numbers, wearing the colours and making their voices heard. The rink accommodates them with rudimentary wooden bench-terraces, five deep on one wing and three deep behind the goal opposite the entrance, with standing room behind the entrance goals. The surface itself is a good size, similar to the Sydney Ice Arena, neither as large as the Icehouse nor as pokey as the hit-and ricochet-shoeboxes in Adelaide and Liverpool. When Newcastle hosted Ice in the 2012 grand final, the North Stars fans created a din that reverberated off the well-insulated walls, a force that supercharged their players and make victory seem inevitable.

All of the above generally lends itself to a strong home-ice advantage for Newcastle, but in 2014, they didn't win here until June, and overall have only triumphed three times from twelve attempts. In between such mysterious underperformance, the North Stars have had some strong wins.

Three minutes into the game, naturalised North Star forward Adam Geric stuffs in the first goal on a powerplay, and the tinsel-waving teen dancers celebrate. Ice create chances as good in the subsequent minutes, but they are running into another wall, import goalie Harrison May. Ice forward Jeremy Brown shows why he is going places in junior hockey in Canada by setting up Tommy Powell for the equaliser with skill, but mostly repeated efforts – not three or four of them, but five, six, seven. He's a strong skater, checks aggressively, and reads the play quicker than most, but it is this level of determination and his fitness which sets Jeremy apart. Cody Danberg deflects a slapshot against the run of play for the go-ahead goal, and Matt Armstrong rattles the crossbar shortly thereafter. After

Newcastle volunteer Louis Wetini doesn't feel the cold.

a period, it is 2–1 to the North Stars, and the pattern is well established – this will be a fast, open, clean game, governed by excellent refereeing, and Ice will have more of the play, take more shots and never really look like winning, finding either Harrison May or the post in their way. The North Stars owe their fans a win, and they will take their chances. There is a mutual respect between these proud teams and clubs, and it generally makes for this kind of hockey between them: fierce, intense, but without rancour.

In the first intermission, Brave Chairman Peter Chamberlain rings, agitated. The league has been unable to reschedule the two games lost to the Adelaide bus crash, and have deemed the games "cancelled" and not forfeited – requiring a new rule made on the run. The upshot is that all teams involved will be granted one point each for the games they missed, and the games will not count for suspensions, meaning two key Brave players have been flown to Perth for nothing, as they aren't allowed to suit up against Thunder.

Army scores upon the game's resumption, and Ice dominate for ten minutes without further score ... so Newcastle score to regain their one-goal lead with sixteen seconds left in the second stanza, after barely firing a shot for ten minutes. 3–2 to Newcastle. Recorded crowd noise piped through the speakers assists the live response of contented fans.

Garry Dore tells me in the second break that one of the problems the league has is that many of the players are now of a calibre that they know the game better than the referees - and people like himself. "These are pro players, I'm just old-school," he says humbly. "That's what people want to see, they want to see the sport fast, with no whistles. There's nothing vicious going on out there between these teams."

Statistics can obfuscate, but these numbers say it all: Ice have seventeen shots for zero goals in the final period, and thirty eight overall. Newcastle, twenty-four shots overall, has five shots on target in the final period and scores one goal. Final score: 4–2 to Newcastle. Ice has converted few of its many chances; the North Stars have made the most of theirs. It has been entertaining game which both teams leave with some satisfaction. Ice know their effort was there, the opposing goalie was hot and "these things happen". Newcastle won.

At game's end, Ice seem to be moving on from the loss quickly, but lurking is the spectre of a phenomenon all clubs fear - a final in which the dominant team loses purely because a goalie has a great night.

In Adelaide, the home team is defying injury and a hat-trick from Bears import Sean Hamilton Steen on the way to a

6–4 win, with young Australian representative Wehebe Darge
upstaging the imports with a four-goal haul, one of the best
individual performances of the season. In Perth, Canberra's two
remaining first-liners, Mathieu Ouellette and Anton Kokkonen
more than compensate for the absence of the suspended
Stephen Blunden, with six of the seven points in their team's
tense 3–1 win over Thunder.

Ice now needs to win on Sunday to remain in the top four,
but there's no panic. In the car on the way to the night's
accommodation, the banter resumes. When Johan is called
upon to shut up by Tom, he says "I always speak", both an
undeniable truth and a credo he lives by. To prove it, he then
dubs his club patron "Posh Yosh".

At the night's digs, road manager Ian Webster delivers
a restaurant-quality feast which meets with widespread
satisfaction. Over dinner, a more serious Johan admits it's been
tough at times being Gustaf Huth's coach, landlord and mentor,
handling calls from Sweden at 2 am. Coaches compare notes
about Facebook critics and pub experts telling them how to
do their jobs. Brent Laver reiterates that his primary task is to
turn boys into men. He says he wishes he could have done an
apprenticeship under Brad Vigon. He often surprises me, but
this will not be the last statement that provides an unexpected
insight tonight. Gustaf's birthday is celebrated with a cake, a
song and the players chanting 'HUUUUUTH' like Icehouse
fans. He is truly moved, and seeing it is moving. This has
been a tough, but rewarding journey for him, poor health
and unexpected on-ice travails testing his mettle. Josh holds
Gustaf's attention and looks him in the eye as he shakes his
hand and thanks him for being a part of the club.

Brent sits at the side of the central table in the small room,
inconspicuously picking players off from the noisy meal for
intimate yet public chats. These are the moments when he does
his coaching, as he probes, listens, encourages and advises his
players. Prior to today's game, in downtime, he toyed with the
ultra-conscientious Marcus Wong. "When were you planning
to tell me Wongy?" (Concerned look from Marcus.) "About
playing last night ..." Marcus looked mortified, thinking he had
let Brent and the team down by playing in the local competition
late on Friday night. But Brent was kidding; it didn't bother
him at all. He knows Marcus. After completing a scholarship
in Chile in the off-season, the diminutive defenceman was so
concerned about being late for a pre-season training session,

Ice escape their rooms between periods.

Merchandise remains a crucial money spinner for AIHL clubs.

Garry Dore catches up with Ice veteran Jason Baclig.

due to a delayed flight, that he rang Brent from Sydney airport. If there is anything to worry about with Marcus, it is that he needs to loosen up. Now Brent tells driven but reserved Jeremy Brown that he is a leader without knowing it, having great "buy-in" with his peers, despite not being vocal.

The club's reaction to today's loss is philosophical, and the conversation tonight starts at thoughtful and goes deeper. Ian Webster and I drift into discussion of intuition in decision-making, especially when determining character in recruitment. Brent joins us, the last of his player conferences completed. He says that there is a gap between stimulus and response where many of us make mistakes. It is the place where white-line fever exists, and occasionally claims otherwise rational people such as Joey Hughes. He is aware that his players know that their coach also suffered from this malaise as a younger man.

Brent speaks of the "no ego" martial art practices, rooted in Buddhism, which enabled him to gain self-control and now underpin his coaching. Now too busy for the "grounding" Monday night classes he has attended for years, Brent says his coaching is a way of continuing his practices, for he has graduated from pupil to teacher. He is not interested in the prestige of attaining various belts, but admits that "high-end" practitioners achieve things that he wouldn't believe if he had not seen them.

He's come a long way from when he was a kid dealing with being the son of a homicide cop, or the young man who only felt "safe" at the rink or on the footy field. Brent's candour and his calm, down-to-earth demeanour make the discussion of such matters riveting and utterly credible. His practices concentrate not on the accumulation of knowledge or status,

but understanding based on self-awareness. They are about
clarifying and stripping away as much as learning new tricks.
They focus on that which is most relevant and most important,
and aims to keep it central. It is an approach that applies
whether one is a poet or a plumber.

He is impressed by Ice committeeman Bernie O'Brien,
who used titles instead of names during a contentious
discussion, defusing the debate and keeping it on topic, not
about personalities. It is a tactic he will now use in business
as well as sport. Brent's manner is testament to his practices,
his teachings subtle, his influence grasped incrementally by
those open enough to accept it, his insights born of personal
exploration and discipline. He lives this stuff; these are not
platitudes on offer. We go so far as to discuss our tentative
cosmologies – Brent suspects one force behind all, with various
manifestations. He talks about all of this over a bottle or two
of red with the voice and vocabulary of a guy you could meet
at a suburban pub. He has integrated what is often considered
esoteric work into his everyday dealings with the world. He
doesn't preach or aim to convert anyone to anything, and shuns
the self-satisfied virtuosity of some people proficient in martial
arts. No ego. That's what informs his role as a teacher, a man
manager, and a coach.

"What does success look like?" he asks. "How are we to be
judged?" I know he is wary of the trappings of Melbourne Ice's
past glories that are draped across the Icehouse. He is not so
pie-eyed as to think his job is all about intangibles and personal
development – results count as well – and he is now worried
Ice could miss the finals, with Adrenaline and Brave winning
today, but it cannot be denied, Brent is most interested in
"making young men the best version of themselves". He takes
the club's mission statement seriously. It is *his* mission. "In 30
years, when Mitch Humphries meets me on the street with
his twelve-year-old son, and, regardless of championships, he
knows that this time with Ice had an impact ... to me that's
success ..." Brent describes 2014 as a "culture change mission"
for Ice, which endured a "toxic" 2013. "At the start of the season,
we said to each other making the finals would be a win." He
says the league should aim to get to a stage where everything is
paid for, but no more. Payment of players would make things
easier for the coaches, but it would not be good for the league.

Late in the night, late in this year of travelling and talking on
these trips, we have seen off every other player and staff member
and we get to the crux of the matter. Brent sees a pivotal
decision coming up for Ice. "When Jason and Army get PR
[permanent residency], I can get in another gun set of imports

and put another banner on the wall, but is that really success?" Brent is more concerned with improving pathways for junior talent. He would like to help develop an academy that provides players for both Melbourne clubs, using Next Level Hockey, a director of which is former Ice star, now Mustangs linchpin Joey Hughes. Brent's garage doors company is a Next Level sponsor.

Brent's vision is clear, but I wonder if it is too demanding of a club in an expensive national amateur sporting competition where many rivals cannot afford loftier goals than getting a team on the ice. As Brent says himself, less resourced teams will grasp any advantage they can. But Melbourne Ice is lucky. It has the rink, the fans, the governance structure, and the published desire to amount to more than a successful sports team. The permanent residency decision will prove defining. Making it more tricky is the fact that Matt Armstrong and Jason Baclig are now in their thirties, and whilst still elite players, they are not the superpowers of the league they once were; and each year's crop of AIHL imports is faster and more skilful. Matt and Jason lifted the standards at the club, and helped create its golden era, but now it is this be-spectacled, quietly-spoken coach who is holding the club to account.

Would any professional sporting club give a damn about such high ideals? Yes, most of them. But not one I have encountered would make a decision that put that the personal development of young players ahead of another banner on the wall. To them sport is business. It's all about winning. Brent believes developing character and winning are intertwined, or should be, and it is pointless to have one without the other. It is the best conversation I have ever had with a sportsperson and when I take my leave – at 4 am – desperate to capture some notes, I go to my cabin thinking there is a reason for sport and this book to exist beyond the fact that they are fun.

‘

BRENT LAVER'S MANNER IS TESTAMENT TO HIS PRACTICES, HIS TEACHINGS SUBTLE, HIS INFLUENCE GRASPED INCREMENTALLY BY THOSE OPEN ENOUGH TO ACCEPT THEM, HIS INSIGHTS BORN OF PERSONAL EXPLORATION AND DISCIPLINE.

SUNDAY THE 27TH

ROAD TRIP FIVE:
SYDNEY ICE DOGS V MELBOURNE ICE
DAY TWO

I said to Matt Armstrong last night that this game will define where we are going in the next five years. He agrees, but I realise he has misunderstood. I was talking about the match facing my AFL team Collingwood today, whom he also notionally supports. He was talking about Melbourne Ice. Suddenly I understand how high the stakes are for Ice in this Sunday game at Liverpool.

Johan says Ice players need to aim low on Ice Dogs goalie Tim Noting, as only Lliam Webster and Matt have shots powerful enough to beat him top shelf (high in the net). Jeremy Brown certainly won't get a chance to get added to the list of powerful shooters - it is revealed that he is playing with a fractured wrist, and he will barely be able to pass, let alone shoot with any power.

On the three-hour trip to Liverpool across the ridiculously scenic north of Sydney, all cliffs and hills and inlets, Posh Yosh tries on the Yolie Coach with questions and stories about mythical local creatures drop-bears and bunyips. The ranks of Australia's imaginary fauna are well populated, testament to our love of a piss-take. Johan is handing out Greek-style Fremantle anchovies from an esky. He breaks into the banter to sincerely thank Tom for organising Gustaf's birthday celebrations. Then it's back to business. He explains my nickname for him – 'Supercoach' – to Tom and Josh, saying "it makes sense". When Johan's stream of consciousness drifts back to hockey, he says training was misery when he and Glenn Laver took it earlier in pre-season, before Brent had arrived. "I wondered what I was doing," he admits. And he took it personally earlier in the season when Ice went badly. I forget this regime is young, and Brent, Johan, and Tom are all new to their roles as coaches and manager. Before dozing, Johan has the last word, not surprisingly. "Today is the day," he says. Up ahead, the hand of Jeff Smith surfs in the slipstream out the window of the player bus. It is a typically exuberant New South Wales day, clouds scared out of the state, a vivid blue sky competing for attention with the steep-sided waterways.

I tell Josh Puls that Brent feels Pat O'Kane has changed the model for AIHL recruiting, and more clubs will now target college graduates. Josh, beside me in the back seat, says Ice applies "The Muppet Test" to its recruiting. "If Wayne Gretzky came to us with a bad attitude, we wouldn't take him. Too many people put in too much time, blood, sweat and tears, not to mention money, for us to have dickheads."

Upon arrival, I repeat my circumnavigation of Liverpool Catholic Club, this time enticed by car park activity at the adjacent pokies function palace. It's the annual Doll and Bears show, of course. Hundreds of stallholders have been sharing and selling their toys in one of the main rooms, and they're now packing their cars with fluffy merchandise. There are passions and economies out here beyond the imagination of an inner-city type.

Prior to the huddle, Jeff Smith drifts to the boards and taps hands through the netting with the Ice Dogs' chief heckler. I would want to be six foot six if I was doing that, the hardcore of the Dogs barrackers are fearsome, their chanting endless and vitriolic. One of their number, nearly as big as Jeff, has a hillbilly beard and shuffles along in a dressing gown. "Graham, you're a fat prick. You're a fat bastard," is an example of his contributions. I'm not too proud to admit that I failed you, dear reader – I didn't go and talk to him and his compatriots. For all that, the Dogs

Portable nativity van, Liverpool Catholic Club car park.

See the light.

The LCC complex is about more than the ice rink.

The LCC rink is cold, white and loud.

fans never do more than heckle without elegance, and in my experience, they don't hassle opposing fans. They are crude and rough, but they have a code.

With stakes high, and a few more souls in than usual, the atmosphere is martial in the Liverpool echo chamber. During the first period I write the following note: "Collective impression is of people yelling 'FIGHT FIGHT FIGHT!!!' " Ice Dog forward David Dunwoodie is smaller than most of the players he targets, but he's a fast moving mini-tank, ramming with intent to hurt. His rattling checks set the tone for the most physical AIHL game I've ever seen, and the skills executed and restraint shown under this aggressive pressure from both teams is exhilarating. The more heated the clashes, the more important discipline becomes. Ice scores halfway through the first period, Matt getting down on his knee to first-time a short pass past Tim Noting on the powerplay. Brian Funes scores the only goal of a tough second period, also with the man advantage, and it feels like the final period is a referendum on Ice's season. Are they a contender in 2014? It is an unscripted drama, and a ferocious test of the group. There are few fans, critical or backslapping, to satisfy or disappoint, no trappings of home; they have only each other to rely upon. There is not a player on the ice, regardless of size, who is not delivering fierce, grinding checks; both teams are absolutely committed. The dressing-gown fan slams a drum, his group having changed ends at each break. It is now six degrees, the contest having heated the room from its starting point at a bracing three degrees.

Both goalies are making huge saves on breakaways; the Dogs hit the post after a giveaway, and the tempo continues to rise, odd-man rushes coming in waves from both teams. For nearly thirteen minutes, the pot is boiling. And it is one of Brent's 'kids' who breaks the 1–1 deadlock, Austin McKenzie hustling off the boards and snapping near side … and going top

Where is it? Ice Dogs and Ice players search for the puck at Liverpool.

shelf to beat the previously impassable Noting. It is 2–1 with 7.35 to play. With five minutes left, Lliam Webster and David Dunwoodie inevitably get penalised after spending the entire game crunching each other.

Players are now shot-blocking, something rarely seen outside AIHL finals. Noting makes a big save and the Dogs force Ice back in their zone, a superb lateral goalfront pass from Simon Barg to John Clewlow, a powerful, high wrist shot, and its back level at 2–2. We could be at Madison Square Gardens or the MCG or Rod Laver Arena now - it is loud, the passion of the fans matching that of the players. Every rush is bringing a scoring chance. With 1.33 remaining, Ice converts one of those many chances, Jeremy Brown setting up Jason Baclig with a sublime two-on-one pass, Jason's finish unstoppable. 3–2. My insightful note from this moment? "Wow!" All the dollars spent traipsing around the country this year are worth it at this moment, seeing such great sport so far from home.

Andrew Petrie calls a timeout with 56 seconds left. The Dogs press, Ice desperately slings the puck down the ice, but receives no respite, as the icing call brings a face-off back near their net. The Dogs look as likely to score now as at any stage all day, they are such a potent outfit, but somehow the visitors hold them out, and Ice have won.

Jeff applauds the rowdy fans behind the goals, who have reacted to their narrow loss by singing, "*Always look on the bright side of life.*" Lliam says later he enjoyed them calling him 'Mordor'. Jaden Pine-Murphy got a laugh out of the abuse that ensued every time he took off his helmet and revealed his well groomed locks.

I may not know hockey inside out, but I know enough about sport to know that I have just seen two finalists, both of whom are capable of winning the title. This experience was so brutal, so intense, that it is hard to think of it as just a game. Brent's reaction confirms my ranking of this as one of the best contests of the season. "That eighteen seconds of euphoria at the end is what it's all about," he exclaims as the players enter their toilet/dressing rooms. "That's the hit, it's hockey heroin." He says he will remember this moment if he gets in strife for spending too much time on hockey. Austin McKenzie – who Jeff awarded the team's ceremonial helmet as best player – and Jeremy Brown were as important as much more experienced players, making this game a personal vindication for Brent. He says he now knows what the "triggers" are for his team.

Andrew Petrie, grinning as always, grants that it was a great game, but says "it could have been better!" He has the look of someone who knows his team will live to fight another day.

It was not a good sign for the Sydney Bears that injured import Dane Ludolph was at Liverpool watching the Ice v Ice Dogs game with AIHL Commissioner Robert Bannerman, rather than in Adelaide, where his team battled Adrenaline. It was the 300th game of Australian and Adelaide legend Greg Oddy, and Adrenaline scored three unanswered goals in the second and third periods to record a fitting 8–1 win to honour their most celebrated player.

Canberra swept their double-header with Perth in another tense encounter in the west, converting two of their eight powerplays while conceding only one themselves in winning 5–3. Perth fought back to within a goal twice after being 3–0 down at the end of the first period. Too often this season, Perth has fallen just short. It will cost them a chance to back up their incredible effort in making the finals last season, just their second in the competition.

In the intermissions at Liverpool, Robert was unflappable about criticism of the league's bus crash points decision, saying there hadn't been a rule in place to handle such a situation, which hadn't arisen in the previous 14 years of the league's existence. There had been extensive negotiations to get the games re-scheduled, but the parties had not been able to reach agreement. "We gave them a chance to work it out, and then we had to make a decision. We'll do it better next time," he says. A buffer is likely to be built into the fixture to accommodate any postponements, as it proved impossible to get a midweek game organised due to the work commitments of players. (The Icehouse, roughly halfway between both clubs, was offered as a midweek compromise measure.) There has been no word from Adelaide, but Brave still sound like they might take further action, Peter Chamberlain saying their insurance policy covered losses due to a forfeit, but could not cover a rule that did not exist at the start of the season. Robert says all parties have to bend a little in unforeseen circumstances. "If the strict letter of the law was always applied, CBR wouldn't exist."

TEAM	GP	W	L	D	SOW	SOL	PTS
MUSTANGS	20	12	6	0	0	2	38
ICE	22	10	7	0	3	2	38
BRAVE	21	10	6	1	2	2	37
ADRENALINE	24	8	8	2	5	1	37
ICE DOGS	22	11	9	0	1	1	36
NORTH STARS	21	8	11	0	0	2	26
THUNDER	20	7	10	0	1	2	25
BEARS	24	6	15	1	1	1	22

TUESDAY THE 29TH

Most Mondays after road trips I have taken as leave days in order to write up the experience. This time, as an experiment, I went to work as usual, starting my shift at 7 am. You may argue this is far from a scientific study, given I am a 47-year-old, wine-drinking desk jockey, not a super-fit twenty-something hockey player. But I figure after two-and-a-half hours sleep on Saturday night and four hours Sunday night, my mental weariness might mimic the tiredness experienced by players forced back into the "real" world Mondays after playing two games interstate.

By 9 am, I'm resorting to my first ever "energy" drink. My weariness is immediately evident to bemused co-workers. My voice is octaves lower. I usually find my rhythm pretty quickly on hectic Monday mornings, but today I continually forget what I'm doing, or intend to do. Repetitive cut-and-paste jobs require repeating after I paste the same item twice and forget others. I come-to repeatedly, wondering what I was just doing. I am yawning so widely that my epiglottis threatens to pop and my jaw wants to dislocate. My mind is definitely dislocated; I'm an alien in my own brain and a stranger to my colleagues. But responsibilities and the 'Mother' drink kick in and I find a way through the shift.

It is Tuesday that's the real problem. The cumulative torpor after a second busy shift feels like altitude sickness or severe jet lag. I berate myself to do more, but the weariness grows. I feel like gravity has been turned up in every space I occupy, out to crunch me like a car-squashing machine in a scrap-metal yard, and I'm of a mind to give in, as only being horizontal offers any prospect of relief. My motivation is down, I am slightly melancholy …

I'm still awaiting funding for a comprehensive study of AIHL work tiredness which satisfies internationally accepted standards. But my anecdotal conclusion is this: replicating the demands of an AIHL player made me feel like I had pneumonia.

Pat O'Kane posts on Facebook that he is in a relationship with his girlfriend Stephanie. There is a barrage of response, including this from his coach Brad Vigon: "What about us?"

WEDNESDAY THE 30TH

Nathan Walker is not the only young Australian who has
spent extended stints overseas in pursuit of his hockey dream.
Many locals good enough to play for Australian Ice Hockey
League teams have some sort of experience playing in North
America. Some have been at it for years. Last Saturday, dynamic
North Stars forward Beau Taylor was opposed to powerful Ice
defender Todd Graham at the Hunter Ice Skating Stadium. Beau
has been going back and forth to Canada for 10 years; Todd has
been travelling to North America since 2006.

Todd Graham's father Terry says he could write a book about
the travails of an aspiring hockey player who is not from the
US or Canada trying to get an opportunity in those nations.
Many leagues have restricted opportunities for non-North
American "imports", fearful of a European invasion. Then there
are visa hassles, arcane academic strictures, and occasionally
goons taking the place of less ferocious players. There are
unscrupulous agents who take hundreds of dollars from
desperate prospects who want access to try-out camps, where
there are hundreds of other similar prospects. And if you are
from a nation that plays a lower level at world championships,
or play lower than division one college hockey, even some of the
most assiduous talent spotters are unlikely to ever know you
exist. Terry Graham says it is only Todd's passion to play at the
highest possible level that has seen him perservere through all
these tribulations, criss-crossing America.

Beau Taylor says it's "a little scary" to consider that he's been
going back and forth for a decade. "But it's the sacrifice you
have to make if you want to keep playing hockey and I get to
play hockey twelve months of the year." Beau started out with
the goal of bettering his hockey by playing more "and I kept
going with it and going with it". Apart from sporting ambition,
it is education behind such persistence. Beau says "I'm getting
my schooling paid for and I'm getting to play great hockey at
the same time. That was always a major goal of mine. I had
opportunities to maybe play pro at 20, 21, but my main focus
was to get my degree and play hockey at the same time." Now
aged 24, Beau studies at the University of Alberta's Augustana
campus in Camrose, a small prairie town. Todd Graham, 23, is
a business student at Buffalo State College. Both Todd and Beau
are forthright and confident and look you in the eye during
conversation. To have prospered in their field, they had to be
self-reliant, leaving them quietly assured.

Beau, while ambitious and talented, is realistic about his
hockey career. He says he has "a couple of years" before he has

to ponder whether to pursue a career in advertising or marketing. "After three years of school I would like to go play pro and use it as an excuse to travel." He has England, France and Italy on his list of countries to visit for "just a couple of years, to see what professional hockey is all about". Whatever happens, he will keep returning to playing in the AIHL, not just because it enables him to keep playing in his "off-season", but out of loyalty. "Garry Dore and Newcastle have done nothing but great things for me, they've helped me out a lot over the years. I want to make sure I keep coming back to play for Garry and the Newcastle North Stars. They've got a great club here and it's a bonus to come back and keep playing for four months."

Terry Graham says that he and wife Janine didn't push their son Todd into the tough life of an aspiring hockey player – they just provided "money and a taxi service". But they make sure he is comfortable when he returns each year, early in the AIHL season, flying from Coffs Harbour to Melbourne to "settle him in".

Todd Graham, like Beau Taylor, plays as many AIHL games as his commitments at Buffalo State College permit. Apart from playing with their mates, there is a sporting reason for the two young stars playing through the northern summer. Quite simply, the Australian league keeps providing challenging hockey. "It is getting better every year. The difference from my first year here to now is just huge," Beau says. "There's not just one line anymore. There's a lot more Australian talent coming through, so you can't just win with imports anymore. You've got to make sure those second and third lines have good Australian players."

'THE LOT OF AN ASPIRING AUSTRALIAN HOCKEY PLAYER IN NORTH AMERICA? VISA WRANGLES; ARCANE ACADEMIC STRICTURES; GOONS AND UNSCRUPULOUS AGENTS.

THURSDAY THE 31ST

Matt Armstrong could be forgiven for thinking Australia is not that warm. When he isn't playing or training for Melbourne Ice, he is otherwise occupied at the Icehouse. It is luxuriously comfortable compared to other Australian rinks, but it's still cool, and he spends a hell of a lot of time there. Before training tonight, he is teaching, conducting an off-ice shooting class for two eager adult pupils. To do this, he has converted a function room into 'Sniper's Alley', complete with a vinyl surface to shoot off, and a net surrounded by camouflage netting, boards and tarps to protect the walls. A hint as to the original use of the room is provided by a group of girls coming through to enter a backroom to blow up party balloons. The comical fluff-it sounds this creates set another challenge for the shooters, who are trying to hone technical lessons into instinct. The whole elaborate set-up must be removed every Friday so birthday parties for novice skaters can take over the room.

Matt is not surprisingly a good coach. He has natural authority derived from ability, self-confidence and a no-nonsense manner. He tells it as it is, and he is consistent, equally blunt about shortcomings and successes, his yes or no dependant purely on outcomes.

As we gather pucks for another session, he reveals that the recent sale of the Icehouse had many of its employees worried. In his case, visa requirements demand an applicant be employed continually at one workplace for two years, and he was two months short when O'Brien's catering took over the lease two days ago. But initial meetings have allayed fears, everyone has retained their jobs, and there is considerable optimism about what the new bosses will do with the venue.

One of the shooters has earplugs in, a wise accessory. Even off-ice, hitting a puck is a violent, noisy act, and requires a number of moving parts in synch with each other. It takes me back to my father trying to teach me skating basics as a kid. I remember his exasperated cries of "bend your knees". I was always too stiff, I could feel it myself. I had a notion that puberty would somehow magically unlock my joints. As Matt teaches the wrist shot, I remember that there are no magical transformations when learning skills, just hard work, practice, and occasionally, a moment when you realise that you have improved a little.

Matt films the shooters on his phone, then shows them the footage, helping them understand what he's asking of them. One of the shooters is trying too hard. The more he tries to bend his knees as Matt requests, to shoot from the legs, the more upright he becomes, the reactive mind at work. His compatriot, a determined, focused businessman, has improved with every instruction and adjustment, now lifting the puck after being unable to at the start of the session. The other pupil, powerful but linear, executes fitfully.

"There you go," Matt says when he nails it. But there's no false encouragement when he fails. That helps no-one. It also adds satisfaction to eventual success. When the student is high-fived by Matt, he knows he has nailed it, and the pleasure is intensified, cementing the correct execution. Matt knows what is required: hundreds and hundreds of hours of practising the right technique, over a lifetime. That's how his slapshot gets to look so powerful yet effortless. If these guys love it enough to work hard enough on what he has taught them, they will feel thrill-of-improvement moments. If not, they will remain hit-and-miss merchants. All he can do is pass on the knowledge.

There are those who never lose the need to improve, to test their bodies and minds with these simple but addictive puzzles of grip, stance, weight transfer, and timing. It is why old men die on rinks and playing fields, maddened and thrilled by the mysteries of the perfect shot long after their bodies can best achieve them. Apart from the companionship of playing with friends, it is the challenges of execution that keep us beholden to a sport.

Part of me is burning to get back on the ice, after watching all these great players and games. But my ineptitude will drive me nuts after being a competent kid, and I will not have the dedication to improve enough. The voice yelling 'bend your knees' is now mine, and I need it for making better sentences, not perfecting passing plays and old man dekes.

The stiff shooter persists and persists. Finally, he starts slapping the puck consistently. It was puck positioning all along, they have unravelled the mystery. Ya Boi!

Matt Armstrong passing on his knowledge in Sniper's Alley.

Best of rivals: Matt Armstrong, Pat O'Kane, Brent Laver and Brad Vigon.

THURSDAY THE 31ST (EVENING

At Mustangs training John Belic is cheerful and hockey manager Andy McDowell is earnest. John is bemused by his underdog team's new status. "We're the golden-haired, blue-eyed boy at the moment." He is happily rueful regarding the challenges of volunteer staff. "You can't sack them and say there are twenty like them waiting to do the job, because there isn't." Andy has the recent refereeing complaints on his mind, and the less-than-perfect relationship between the league and Ice Hockey Australia. There will be frank discussions at the end of the season. It's a sign of how fraught such matters can be that even John and Andy disagree about the flexibility of either body. Andy would like a 'hockey' figure on the AIHL board.

But Andy is not just concerned about political or administrative issues. He wants the Mustangs to bed down their finals position as soon as possible. "What if we don't make it?" he asks. "We've done everything right, but sport can be cruel." The Stangs are on top but have three road trips to come. If they now have the slump every other contender has endured, they'll be touch and go for the playoffs.

I have arranged for Matt, Pat and the coaches of their two Melbourne teams to be shot together by photographer Tania Chalmers. There are a few interested onlookers as the rivals meet in the corridor beneath the Icehouse grandstand, between the two teams' dressing rooms. "Yank, Yank, Canadian …" Andy cracks, doing the roll call. Brad protests, saying in his broad Californian accent that he is as Australian as anyone. "I was in a vegemite commercial!" (True.)

CBR Brave are still aggrieved by the bus crash points decision. A statement they have released reads, "we believe this decision creates a points imbalance that is unfair of these teams involved and the wider league." A full statement is promised. As it stands, Adelaide is fourth, but has played two more games than the fifth-placed Ice Dogs

AUGUST 2014

SATURDAY THE 2ND

For Australian Ice Hockey League fans, when their teams hit the road, it's the internet or bust in the search for game-day information. There is no billion-dollar broadcast deal guaranteeing spiffy live coverage. Unless ATC Productions is covering the game you seek, you're in the hands of club volunteers manning the cameras, computers and microphones. Today, CBR Brave are playing the North Stars in a crucial clash in Canberra. Not surprisingly, the enterprising Brave have a live feed, despite the challenges of their cheek-by-jowl arena. My ageing and not so trusty desktop computer handles the webcast without complaint, and I'm pleasantly surprised by the quality of the picture.

Like most things technological in the AIHL, live feeds are rapidly advancing. On this Saturday afternoon, the access the CBR feed provides is intimate to the point of intrusion. The ice is a bright white and the players are in high contrast. A camera at one corner offers an alternative perspective as well as great shots of Heckler's Corner and the first floor bar behind the entrance end net. The presentation is admirable, but the remaining amateur touches are reassuringly quirky, thus reflecting where the AIHL currently teeters – somewhere between semi-pro efficiency and precarious grassroots improvisation.

At the end of the first period, the screen is set to a simple graphic, but the audio, reassuringly, is still live; the swish and drone of the circulating Zamboni is heard, mixed with the distant, muffled pop-throb of the rink PA. When the lone commentator Geoff Koop returns, the watcher is thrown into the action. Geoff is no minimalist. Trying to capture each significant pass or collision, he is often at fever pitch. There are rough edges: he doesn't know some North Stars players, and there are some passages that narky media-watchers would deride if this was a professional broadcast. ("That was a good pass to Kokkonen but it doesn't reach him.") But you know what he means and he keeps up with the play in an entertaining and appropriately upbeat manner. This is a fast-moving game after all, effort is required and appreciated. And he's on his own; no special comments offsider to ease the load.

Vivid: Ascension Sports coverage of Brave.

Brave could become an AIHL juggernaut.

Geoff is partisan, but not heinously so, following the North American model where most games are covered by "home" commentators providing a service primarily for fans of that team. In the third period, Geoff is under no illusions as to the altered balance of power. "They've come out the better of the two teams," he says of the North Stars, who are 1-2 down after six minutes. Brave survive after goalie Petri Pitkanen is stranded face-first on the ice metres out of his net. "How on earth didn't they score with Pitkanen five miles out ... I'll never know!" Geoff screams. North Stars Brian Bales and Cody Danberg in particular are causing havoc, and the game is picking up tempo by the moment. With nine minutes left, I consider just how hard good hockey commentary is, especially on a small rink. There's so much to watch, so much to assess – is that take-away more important than this tip pass or that interception?

The feed starts pixelating briefly, as if sensing the rising tension. After a week spent debating the league decision to award it only one point for the game missed because of the Adelaide bus crash, Canberra's finals chances hang by a thread. Newcastle, further back in the standings but still beating top teams, is even closer to the brink. At stoppages the crowd can be heard, ecstatic with urging. The fans can be seen in many shots as well. One section near the blue line seems to be constantly dancing. Among it is a man with what looks like a massive white puck-head. I can't check, because the action moves on ...

Inevitably, a perfect Cody Danberg pass to the backdoor leads to a tap-in North Stars goal. It's 2–2 with eight minutes to play, and Geoff's cracking voice is an apt accompaniment for the frantic final minutes. When Newcastle's Tim Stanger beats Petri Pitkanen, only to strike iron, Brave coach Matti Luomo has seen enough. With five minutes left, Newcastle look the likely winners, and he calls a timeout to change the momentum.

Petri Pitkanen makes a huge save on a point-blank shot with fewer than four minutes left. Soon afterwards, Geoff says: "Both teams have a chance to win this if they want". They want. It is great hockey, chance after thrilling chance. Appropriately a microphone gets CRUNCHED somewhere – the loud, crinkling, sonic equivalent of being checked into the boards. Appropriately, Geoff's valiant voice is struggling. At one point we hear a throat-clearing cough clearly meant to be off-microphone. He knows these final minutes will be tough. Anton Kokkonen takes the puck mid-ice after a seemingly minor Newcastle error on a line change, and he's in two-on-one with the prolific Stephen Blunden in the slot. The defenceman does well to force Anton to shoot from a more acute angle, but he buries it over North Star goalie Harrison May's shoulder. Brave lead 3-2 with 1.39 left to play. "Is there anything the Finnish superstar cannot do?" Geoff asks of the airwaves. Every club has a player they think the league underrates. Kokkonen is that player for Brave. It is one of many key moments in the CBR season. Given the exacting, dramatic nature of this campaign, it is likely there will be more if they are to make it, but this is surely one of the biggest. CBR Brave rose from the ashes of a team that existed to survive, and to entertain lucratively, but rarely to contend. They don't just want to be in the league, they want to win it. They want to inspire and thank the people who resurrected hockey in the ACT by commencing a new era of excellence.

North Star Beau Taylor's near-side shot is saved and Anton Kokkonen hits the post with an empty net shot. There's some clock resetting to add some suspense with seven seconds left. "Barring some sort of miracle, Brave might go top of the table," says Geoff. There is no miracle. Brave tie up the puck in the corner, Petri Pitkanen with his pad against the post guarding against a freak bounce. And then there is an outpouring of euphoria, not the least from Geoff. "THIS IS MASSIVE!" he cries. But he is not denying the visitors. "A monumental effort from the Newcastle North Stars. They deserved something but they'll get nothing. CBR has stolen this. It was an amazing game." 3-2 Canberra.

Geoff is hitting all the right notes – this was a "pulsating" clash, and a shootout would have been more fitting. But this is how things have gone for the two teams this year. Newcastle has somehow missed their key moments, and Brave has taken control of theirs. It adds up to the points which keep one team in finals contention, and the other wondering why they probably won't be there, despite being capable of beating all those in the top four. As coaches have said more than once this year: "That's hockey."

The previously indiscernible stadium PA announcer is now loud and clear over the livestream. "How about a hand for your CEE BEE ARRR BRAAAAAVVVEEEE!" Then a refrain familiar from team buses: "At the end of the day, some you win, some you lose ..." It's a pop song that understands the phrase "That's hockey". Sometimes you play better and lose. Sometimes everything goes in the net. It's something fans can better understand these days, thanks to the growing number of livestreams. The league should embrace this service, for there is no substitute for seeing the game yourself.

As for the Mustangs game against Thunder in Perth ... There is no live feed of this game, which is to be broadcast the following Thursday on Fox Sport. "SCORES!!!!" is the first Twitter message I see from the Mustangs press corps. It is 3-1 after two periods in the west. The latest-first style of Twitter informs us of a Sean Jones goal from a Vinnie Hughes pass, and then some argy-bargy as the teams left the ice through the same entrance.

It also sounds like talismanic Mustangs import Viktor Gibbs-Sjodin has copped a big hit. Stopping his bleeding seems a major issue, and a game misconduct for checking to the head has been issued to Perth's Ric Del Basso. The Mustangs tweets are exemplary – plenty of time and score references, basics are everything in this pithy medium. When fans get too caught up in the moment and neglect such fundamentals, it gets very frustrating. AIHL live-feed gurus often try to balance delivery of just-the-facts-please with responses to those asking questions or conversing. Interactivity must run second while we seek the score, I say, this is primarily a service for those without sight and sound of the game. The Mustangs go above and beyond, including news of penalties, wandering goalies and shorthanded saves, giving a good sense of the game's big moments.

It is one of the new, rare talents of the modern sports environment, this capacity to convey a frenetic game by typing quickly and accurately on a tiny screen. The only time I tried, I missed goals and major penalties as I struggled to correct clumsy errors that would have rendered my offering incomprehensible. By the time I sent it out, it was outdated. The Mustangs' Twitter feed is like the Canberra commentary – passionately partisan, yet informative, from warm-up to puck drop to final minutes. But after being able to watch a game and make your mind up about the action, reading tweets to follow a game is a strange melange of the progressive and the antiquated, like an elite form of 1930s telegram.

Perth's take on the game is different. For them it was all about the big hit on Viktor Gibbs-Sjodin halfway through the second period, with scores tied 1-1, which they - and some neutral observers – considered a fair hit that had an unfortunate, and accidental outcome, in Viktor's concussion. During the ensuing powerplay, the Mustangs scored the game's final two goals. Mustangs import Jeff Grant takes exception to a Perth Thunder Facebook post about the incident. Cue a week of impassioned social media debate.

SUNDAY THE 3RD

Perth Thunder are not going quietly, but they are going out of finals contention, it seems. Once again, they lose a game they have led. Their second loss to the Mustangs at home extends their losing streak to five games, and the visitors' winning streak to five games. Perth led 2-0 and 3-2 in the first period, but conceded five of the last six goals to go down 7-4.

It is the time of the season when the teams in the top four stop losing, and those with little hope of making the last weekend start to struggle. Brave smash the Bears 12-4 at Baulkham Hills, Stephen Blunden adding six goals to his scoring title quest, and Anton Kokkonen and Mathieu Oullette tallying five assists each. That first line is surely one of the best import scoring machines ever assembled in the AIHL.

It was a penalty-strewn game in Newcastle, where the North Stars recovered from their Saturday disappointment in Canberra with a 5-3 win over the Ice Dogs. Five players were issued misconducts and there were 28 items on the penalty sheet.

MONDAY THE 4TH

Fraser Carson's dad Jeremy explains why his son became a goalie thus: "He was a shithead." By this, the elder Carson means aggressive young Fraser incurred too many penalties when playing as a skater in inline hockey, leading to his banishment to the net. It's the same story for Bears goalie and AIHL cult figure Luke Read. He says he was an "ADHD kind of kid" with endless energy, always getting into trouble playing roller hockey in Wollongong. Made a goalie as a twelve-year-old, he thrived within his "own little area". By the age of thirteen, he was playing in every age group at an interstate representative carnival, including seniors. "I played all day and you still couldn't wear me out!" he says. A year later he was on the ice and representing New South Wales. It was the start of an addiction which survived a hiatus when he followed his dad, Jim Read, the 'Peter Brock of drag racing' on to that circuit after he left school.

He's now in one of the most unenviable positions in worldwide hockey, as back-up goalie to a gun import for a New South Wales AIHL team, because once he has played three AIHL games, he is ineligible to play at the next level down, the East Coast Super League. The rule is intended to promote the ECSL's younger players, but proves brutal for the Bears and Dogs towards the end of seasons, when injuries bite; they are often left struggling to find replacement players. For Luke, it means it is hard for him to get regular hockey if he is not in goal for the Bears at the highest level. "It takes you a good three games to really get up to speed," Luke says of the gap between the AIHL and the ECSL. "It's a good league for the kids, but you either play AIHL or ECSL and you can't hedge your bets at my age."

Luke has to be resilient. The Bears started the year strongly, and had a high point in June with their heroic wins in Melbourne, but they have fallen away since, injuries restricting them to one fit import and road trips undertaken with only 11 skaters. Luke has taken over from injured star Daniel Palmkvist at the toughest possible juncture. "Other people might think the wheels have fallen off, looking at the scores, but as long as I know what went wrong and what I have to do to fix it, I'm happy," he says. He's looking for himself and the team to win "little battles" at the moment. "We need a good start, if the other team gets the first two goals we don't play catch-up hockey too well. After the bad run we've had the last couple of years, we think 'here we go again'."

Luke says the Bears "got into a bit of a funk" when they lost nine games in a row. "A lot of the games we lost we were right in them, pick up a win or two and things would have been different." Injuries bit, coach Vlad Rubes was away, and the losses mounted, but Luke is far from downbeat about the club's prospects. "We do have good kids coming through and we have played a style of hockey that you do want to come and play now. We have showed we are a team that with a bit of work could be successful."

Luke says playing in the AIHL takes a toll, especially on those who have to go to work, but the attitude of players is the league's greatest asset. "All the guys that are playing in our league are in it for the right reasons; they love the game and they're dedicated and they're happy to sacrifice for it. That's what separates us from a lot of sports in Australia, that's why our fans love it so much, because we are such normal people. I can guarantee I've got less money than the people in the grandstand, but they put you on a pedestal like you are a superstar. The biggest thing I have noticed is the fans really respect the players."

Luke's engagement with fans in person and on Facebook has been warmly received by the AIHL community. It led to a talented fan mocking up a "Commissioner Luke Read" poster. The notion is not so far-fetched. "Later on, down the track, I would like to be involved, when I can't play anymore. That's something that I would be 100 percent interested in doing. It deserves 100 percent of your attention, so I wouldn't be so selfish as to tackle something like that until I was finished."

Luke believes that hockey must be "regional" in New South Wales, in order to gain passionate support. His solution is to base teams in places like his hometown Wollongong, or the town of Bathurst, areas with decent population bases, but less entertainment options. "In sleepy places, people really get behind their teams." He believes the Bears would do well at Penrith, further away from Sydney, but partisan and well-populated, or at Macquarie in the inner north. New South Wales sports fans want to identify with a local entity. "In Sydney if your team is on top of the ladder and leading the competition and looking like they're hot to trot, you'll get all the extra fans," he says. But when they lose a few games, other distractions beckon.

He has anecdotal evidence of the attraction of hockey from his work at Wollongong Hospital. "I get chatting and I have never had anybody not be interested when you tell them you play ice hockey. It's a bit of a fantasy sport. They say 'Oh wow, they play that game here? That taboo game? That barbaric sport? Tell me when it's on, I'll come watch!' It's got a real fascination, especially when you tell them you're the goalie. They ask, 'what did you do to become that person? What did you do wrong?!' "

"Commissioner" Luke Read.

FRIDAY THE 8TH

CBR Brave has sent out a press release announcing that it has finalised agreements "that will see key imports Stephen Blunden, Mathieu Ouellette and Petri Pitkanen signed on for the remainder of the 2014 season". I was unaware that this was necessary, but the European season begins the week after the AIHL finals, and the club may not have previously considered the need to have their stars around for the last weekend in August.

"There has been speculation over recent weeks about the early departure of key imports and the board has been working closely with the players and their clubs in France and Finland to negotiate a positive outcome," the release reads. I bet those were difficult negotiations, an amateur team trying to cut fine the arrival of a player going to a professional club. The release continues: "Given the pressure under which the team roster was put together at the start of the season, we've been aware that some of our imports had commitments elsewhere from mid-August. Obviously the guys want to finish what they started with us here and we are very keen to keep the squad together until the end of the season."

The Dogs will be missing two-point-a-game import John Clewlow, Australian national team representative Billy Cliff and regular forward Richard Tesarik due to suspension for tomorrow's match away to the Sydney Bears. It's rather important news. The Bears are yet to beat the Dogs in three attempts this season, but they have pushed them all the way in their last two outings, get their biggest crowds for these "Battles of Sydney", and surely will want to raise a Saturday effort to retrieve some heart from a declining campaign.

Every finals aspirant will be nervous heading into a pivotal set of matches this weekend. Adelaide Adrenaline, fourth, must get points out of its double-header with Ice in Melbourne. One point behind Ice and one point ahead of the Dogs, Adelaide has played two more games than Ice and one more than the Dogs. After this weekend, they have only a home double-header against Brave next weekend in which to shore up their position in the top four. Ice has six games to play, but they are all at home.

The Dogs play three of their five remaining games against Perth, now all but out of contention, plus the should-win fixture today against the Bears. Their only game against a current top four team is at home in the season's final match-up against the Mustangs.

The Mustangs are sitting pretty for now, on the crest of a five-game winning streak, seven points clear of the drop-out zone. But today, a week after the draining trip to Perth, they are on another plane, to play the second-placed Brave. They have yet another trip in two weeks, to Newcastle and Sydney. None of those games are gimmes. And the small matter of the Melbourne Derby intervenes next Thursday. They need at least one more win to be secure.

CBR Brave, on a four-game winning streak, has a straightforward fixture from here: two games at home to the Mustangs, two away to Adrenaline, and a final away game against the Bears, whom they trounced 12–4 last week. Grant that as a win, and they would need only four points from their four games against fellow contenders to make the finals in a year in which they were initially made extinct.

The increased scrutiny on the league spreads complaints about refereeing more quickly and more widely, making life harder for the officials. In recent weeks, at least one game has been controversial. "We fight to get all these people to our games," one aggrieved coach told me. "We have to give them a product worthy of their time. We have to let the game flow and get them microphones so people know what's going on."

Currently the referees are under the jurisdiction of Ice Hockey Australia. The sport's governing body receives funding from the International Ice Hockey Federation to run junior development and representative teams. Its avowed concern is with the players, the grassroots and national teams. The league, overwhelmingly the point of contact for people who watch the game in Australia, operates under IIHF rules and supplies the national team's players. The IHA and the AIHL both insist they can do without the other, but say they try to get along.

There are conflicting points of view about what would happen if the AIHL went out on its own, without IHA sanctioning, which would enable it to hire referees as it pleased, and exercise the option of bringing in import referees to lift standards and educate as overseas players do for AIHL teams. Would AIHL players be ruled ineligible to play for Australia? Who would the players support?

Broadly put, the AIHL leadership is un-funded; white collar; media-friendly and adept with social media; entrepreneurial; corporate-friendly; technologically astute; and young. Again generalising, the IHA is minimally funded; blue-collar; less media and social media savvy; more experienced with, passionate and knowledgeable about grassroots hockey; more conservative; and older. Put the good qualities of each body together and you have the perfect Australian hockey intelligence.

Ideally, the sport's showpiece league and its umbrella organisation would complement each other. The good news is that both bodies – which both possess dedicated, down-to-earth souls, as hard as the other might find that to believe – realise that a parting of the ways is not ideal.

Perth coach Stan Scott's timely missives have been a highlight of the season. Here he details the longest journey for a game of Australian domestic hockey. "We are in Newcastle and ready for a challenge. We are down a few players this trip and [Andrew] Cox and [Jordy] Kyros who took a later flight have been diverted to Brisbane. So it will be tight when they get here, hopefully fit for the game. Either way it's play your best and play on! We want everything we can take from this weekend, we feel we haven't done our best lately, or had much luck, but we are wise enough to know it can't all be easy so it's time to dig in and grind it out."

WE FIGHT TO GET ALL THESE PEOPLE TO OUR GAMES. WE HAVE TO LET THE GAME FLOW AND GET THEM MICROPHONES SO PEOPLE KNOW WHAT'S GOING ON.

SATURDAY THE 9TH

The AIHL's super Saturday provided no upset results. After an often confounding season, the standings were upheld. Newcastle, marginally ahead of Perth, traded goals all night before Chris Wilson fired the 5–4 winner with seven seconds left to play. Perth had fought back to level the game four times.

The Ice Dogs scored four times in the first and final periods to dispatch the Sydney Bears 8–0. Though many might have hoped for a tight contest between the Harbour City rivals, the main surprise was not the result but the player who did the bulk of the scoring. With three key Dogs sidelined by suspensions, Shane Southwood, who had scored one goal in 21 games, added five – and an assist – to spearhead the comfortable win. Luke Read had just 11 skaters in front of him today.

The two top-four encounters also went according to rankings. The Mustangs controlled their first versus second game against Brave in Canberra, a Joey Hughes hat-trick the highlight of a 4–2 win in which they had 40 shots to eighteen. Ice Dogs coach Andrew Petrie said on Saturday morning that the secret to beating Brave was matching the output of its stellar first import line. Of that storied high-scoring trio, Stephen Blunden and Anton Kokkonen recorded points. But their compatriot Mathieu Ouellette injured his knee. Does Canberra have the depth to maintain its title tilt? The win made the Mustangs the first team to qualify for the finals. Their proud declaration of this fact on social media earned a tweet of congratulations from the official Detroit Red Wings site.

In Melbourne, Ice overcame a sluggish first period to beat Adelaide 4–2. Having been read the riot act at the first intermission when trailing 1-0, their renewed aggression was evident from the outset of the second stanza. A contentious penalty on Josef Rezek with 1.45 to play effectively killed any hopes of a last-minute rally from Adrenaline. Ice had lost in Adelaide after leading 2-0 with a minute to play. The game-ending powerplay ensured they would not face the prospect of a nerve-jangling repeat on home ice. Post-game, Brent Laver was philosophical about the need for a wake-up call after one stanza. "They need it jovial, this group. If they are joking and there's banter and they are giving each other shit, you know they are switched on. If they are quiet and looking at the ground, we're nervous, something's wrong ..."

The spectre of the much-anticipated final Melbourne derby next Thursday cannot be denied, Brent wondering aloud how the Mustangs will handle their first finals series, given their lack of experience. It has been a rapid ascent from easybeat and little brother to title favourite. You get the sense that Ice is revelling in being the underdog after four years as the team everyone in the league set their sights upon. I recall Brad Vigon's words about expectations after the Mustangs were overpowered by the physical Ice Dogs way back in May. At that point, the official line was that they were aiming to make finals. But you couldn't help but surmise that behind closed doors, senior Mustangs were saying, or at least thinking "We can win this thing."

There is no shying away from the big picture this Saturday night. The Mustangs have made it. Ice now needs only two points from the five remaining games to qualify. Beat Adelaide again tomorrow and they are in. "It would be awesome for the competition if we finished one and two and made the final," Brent says, expressing what many in Melbourne are hoping for. Former Ice president Andy Lamrock predicted such a final as early as April. I say that Brave making it would also be a great outcome, and Brent agrees. In footy parlance, he isn't "getting ahead of himself". If Adelaide win on Sunday, the entire scenario is deconstructed. After a surprising season proper, fatigue, resources and depth have started to sort out the contenders.

SUNDAY THE 10TH

Today, Adelaide has to win to stay alive; Ice can make the playoffs if they win. Ryan O'Handley chews his gum fiercely, arms crossed, on his bench. Brent, Glenn Mayer and Johan Steenberg stick close together on the Ice bench. Greg Oddy is back for Adelaide, and he has duly scored with a canny wraparound late in the second period. It is 1–1 going into the final twenty minutes. The third lines are getting less ice time. Penalties are coming, the tension overflowing. The misconducts being handed out might attest to the players and referees losing their cool.

I am losing my cool. Halfway through the final period, I write "too much Green Day." Even musical choices get a hammering when the game is tight. Adrenaline are leaving it all on the ice, the passion overflowing. Powerplays abound, and Lliam Webster scores with a special, taking the puck from defence, employing a toe drag and shooting off-stride through the legs of a defenceman and the goalie. 2–1. Adelaide are another team aggrieved by Jeff Smith. There is the now customary long break as penalty complexities are cleared up, tick-tock music sounding. To Ryan, it must sound like his season, which has been beset by accidents and injuries, is being counted down. He desperately needs discipline from his charges, but infractions keep coming, and Ice gets another powerplay goal, off post and goalie skate, to make it 3–1.

Adelaide loses its rhythm and intensity, then its discipline – Sean Greer is thrown out of the game after attacking Sean Hamilton in the middle of play. It is a chaotic finish. Will makes some big saves, two Ice goals are disallowed, Matt gets a penalty after rushing the net. When it is four-on-three with six minutes left and the score still 3–1, commentator Stephen White asks for a turnstile to be installed in the penalty box.

Adelaide kills that penalty, and then gets one last chance, its own powerplay, to keep its season alive. But Ice's chances shorthanded are just as good as Adelaide's, and Greg Oddy and David Chubb get misconducts in the final thirty seconds as the frustration becomes too much. It is frantic, frustrating, compelling, and over. Ice has won 3–1 and joined the Mustangs as a confirmed finalist. Adelaide, more than likely, will miss the finals.

Adrenaline's Sean Greer is displeased with Sean Hamilton ...

As if to underscore the importance of discipline, the Ice Dogs, still missing two suspended players, are thrashed 8–2 at home by Perth Thunder. It's a hell of an effort from the travelling team after losing in the final seven seconds the previous night. All hail the circuitous route – the late-arriving Jordy Kyros and Andrew Cox are the stars of the game, with four points each.

In Canberra, Brave win 4–2 to crucially split their home stand against the Mustangs, in a fierce game in which Joey Hughes has a tooth pushed into his gum. Try telling him that it is a dead rubber for the already qualified Mustangs. Being Joey, he also scored two goals.

... but Ice's Sean is content.

THURSDAY THE 14TH

Thursday night Melbourne derbies suit me; it's the end of my working week and I can't think of anything better than going to the Icehouse to watch a game between these red-hot rivals. I kill a little time after knock-off with a haircut. I mention hockey and the barber recalls the beloved St Moritz rink in St Kilda, burnt down in 1982. "It was great. Put on the tubes and it was easy to pick up a girl. You'd get a date to the pictures no problem if you took them for a spin." He's interested in the hockey, says why don't you publicise it a bit, I could put up a poster in my shop; a lot of people come in here ...

It's a distractingly spectacular sunset, a pre-spring treat, and as I approach the Docklands, walking from the CBD over the railway, the Observation Wheel, all lit up, looks to me like a giant marketing finger pointing down, proclaiming HOCKEY HERE! I heed the direction.

Both Melbourne teams have qualified for the finals, but the final derby is psychologically vital. Ice has to prove it can match and contain the Mustangs. The Mustangs need to prove their 8–3 drubbing of Ice in the last derby was a turning point in the balance of power between the two teams.

This game doesn't need any more publicity, it needs more room. With mates Jon (first local game), Gav (second game) and Kristian (regular), we try all corners of the stadium, but wherever we stand we can barely see a thing. Jon couldn't knock off until just before game time, so our options are limited. To have a good view of this one, you needed to be here an hour and a half early, guarding your position as avidly as the players do the puck on the ice. The Mustangs fans have turned up like never before, making this easily the biggest crowd at one of their home games. Many of their diehards have embraced a Viking theme with their outfits in honour of Viktor Gibbs-Sjodin. Attending an orange game is becoming a fun event.

Early in the game, it is as tense as a final, with the first goal – a huge Matt Armstrong slapshot from the point on the powerplay – not coming until five minutes into the second

Get in early at a Melbourne derby.

What is the balance of power between these rivals?

Ice's Mitch Humphries and Austin McKenzie.

Jamie Bourke inverted.

period. Four minutes later, not long after I have finished telling Gavin about this book, Pat replies for the Mustangs with an elite top-shelf wrist shot. Thank you gentlemen! The search for a place to watch might offer the greenhorns different viewpoints of the occasion, but I'm a little flummoxed by the time we settle on the South Pole end of standing room, with the score 1-1 at the final intermission.

The final period is a Mustangs nightmare. Jason Baclig scores five-hole, two minutes in, and Mitch Humphries makes it 3–1 with 12 minutes remaining, with a shoulder high wrist shot - it is clear the instruction has been to target the top corners of Fraser Carson's net. The Mustangs spurn a powerplay opportunity shortly thereafter. The rest of the game is summed up by what then appears on the gamesheet: Joey Hughes, his dental issues thoroughly probed by Ice opponents, two penalties; Jamie Bourke, five minutes for spearing and a game misconduct; Vinnie Hughes and Viktor Gibbs-Sjodin, roughing penalties. Emotions boil over, control is lost, it gets messy.

There are also two more powerplay goals to Ice, meaning they have scored three times on special teams and four times

Joey Hughes heads to the penalty box.

in the final period for a 5–1 victory, almost as comprehensive a win as the Mustangs achieved in the previous derby. If there was a manual on what not to do against Ice, the Mustangs have just written it with this capitulation. The Ice fans are beside themselves, the previous 8–3 loss now categorised as an aberration. In their minds, they still have it over their little brother, having won three of the year's four derbies, and former Ice players are the ones who lost their cool in the final minutes. The Mustangs end the game with three men in the penalty box. "There's only one team in Melbourne," the South Pole chant. Undeterred, the big orange contingent gives their humbled team a standing ovation.

There can be no hiding now for Melbourne Ice. They are a contender for the title, a fact they have to face. After the game, Brent says it was his team's best win of the year. "We've answered a few questions; they will be asking a few questions." My friend Jon gleefully observes that the hardcore fans in any sport are "scumbags", having enjoyed the South Pole's sarcasm.

I have been reading Malcolm Gladwell's *David and Goliath*, which points out that the bigger entity in a contest is often misrepresented as more likely to win, as size has its disadvantages. Goliath is vulnerable. The Mustangs identify Ice as Goliath, but Ice itself is somewhat schizophrenic about its identity. Ice diehards from the Oakleigh years haven't shaken an underdog mentality; cocky newcomers have only ever known championships and the successful Icehouse years. 'Goliath' has been helplessly vulnerable at times this year, but has also at times appeared formidable and complete, as it did tonight. 'David' was not a tiny weakling tonight; it was the top-of-the-table team, fast, young, strong and confident and well-supported. But inexplicably the Mustangs reverted to playing like a self-doubting kid.

At the pub after the game James Meredith says he woke up wanting to be at the rink, that's how big this game was for Melbourne Ice. It is confirmed that Ice's 2013 coach and long-time stalwart Sandy Gardner went to the team's rooms at the end of the second period. A four-goal final period makes that look like an efficacious visit.

The Yarra Cup is passed around Ice diehards. It is an impressive silver bowl which is handed over to the fans of the winning derby team by the fans of the losing team. It is an institution wholly created by the supporters and not officially endorsed by the clubs, but Emma Poynton says she mentioned it in a pre-match speech, and the players happily pose for photos with South Pole fans and the trophy. Brent mentions the abuse that club staff face when times get tough. When I sympathise, he says, "It's kind of cool that someone cares enough about ice hockey in Australia to go on Facebook like that!"

I introduce my mate Jon to Johan. The last I hear, they are comparing notes about the apparently heinous Australian customs practice of confiscating incoming chewing tobacco products. They have somehow bonded over the bureaucratic challenge of bringing Swedish snuff into Australia. This project is expanding my range of conversation topics.

Chaos at the South Pole.

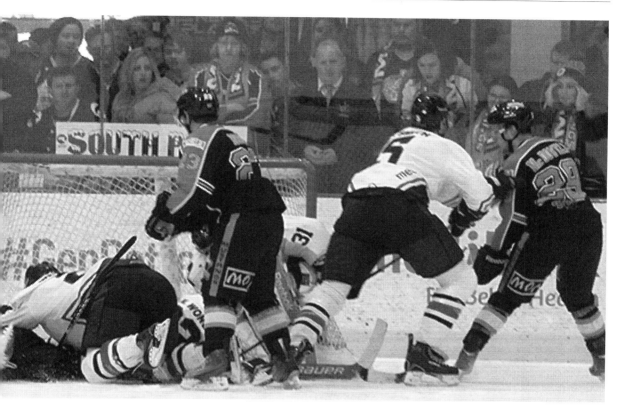

Ice and the Mustangs. Metres apart, and drawn to each other.

SATURDAY THE 16TH

Finishing my long walk from home to the Icehouse for the game between the Mustangs and Newcastle, I run into a North Stars player. It is Victoria, BC-born forward Adam Geric, formerly of the Saskatoon Blades. He tells me that he has been flying from the Gold Coast to play with the North Stars since the Gold Coast Blue Tongues were wound up three years ago, but he is finishing his studies and will be returning to Canada at the end of the year. He won't be playing "anything serious" after the next two weeks with the North Stars. All over. He is just 25-years-old. 'Real life' is beckoning.

It is not an intense game after all the high-stakes drama of recent weeks. There are few contentious hits or calls, the play open on the big rink. The Mustangs have Michael James in goal and are suiting up a couple of players who haven't had ice time recently, with injury and suspension biting, and the need to keep the full squad up to pace with the finals looming. Mustangs fans have embraced today's rockabilly theme and the Atomic Hi Tones rock the house before the game and in breaks. The Mustangs off-ice crew has again created a festive atmosphere for fans at the rink. There is a real sense of momentum about the energetic young club.

The Ice brains trust is scouting the game and they relay the words of North Stars veteran John F Kennedy: "You can't win on talent alone anymore in this league". It recalls Ryan O'Handley's verdict earlier in the year. Ambitious young clubs are overturning the long-established league order.

The Mustangs prosper as the North Stars try to unsettle Pat O'Kane. To quote *Get Smart* "That trick never works!" Pat draws three penalties, and ends up with two goals and two assists, as does Viktor Gibbs-Sjodin. After trailing 1–0 at the end of the first period, the Mustangs flow, scoring the next four goals en route to a crowd-pleasing 6–3 win. It is a matter of holding form and staying fit. It was probably also a matter of winning the final home game before the playoffs. Players hand over their jerseys to sponsors at game's end in an annual bonding ritual.

For Newcastle, the loss is part of a tame end to a perplexing season. They had chances to press for the final playoff vacancy, but couldn't raise their best hockey at the right time, or consistently enough. They're just off the pace and won't make it for the first time in their history. There's a sense of weariness about them, a resignation. When you miss the finals, even a 28-game season is long. They need to regroup.

The social media bush telegraph brings weirdly ironic news. Canberra's luggage has been lost on their journey to Adelaide, and the game has been postponed. There is some sort of wicked karmic transportation tangle between these teams. The show eventually goes on, and Adrenaline, clearly the best team in danger of missing the playoffs, dominates, winning 5–2 on 38 shots to 22, Australian stars Greg Oddy and Wehebe Darge scoring two goals each. Adelaide remains two points behind the Ice Dogs, but has only one game to play.

Under pressure, the Ice Dogs dig deep in Perth, scoring three goals in the final period, all from their super-fit scoring star Simon Barg, to win 3–1. The defending champs, after losing coaches and administrators to resignations then players to suspension during the year, have taken thirteen men, all they could afford, to Western Australia and overturned a 1–0 deficit. They have two more chances to get the two points they need to claim the final playoff position.

SUNDAY THE 17TH

The Mustangs had a rockabilly band. Ice simply releases a beach ball into the grandstand as pre-match entertainment. But its real playoff celebration is the spontaneous undertaking of fans, who have printed *Free Jeff Smith* posters and plastered them all over the glass – and on the front of the Zamboni – to acclaim their popular import. They make this Jeff Smith Day. The atmosphere is similar to Saturday at the Mustangs game, a festive, relaxed vibe helping create an open, penalty-free affair in which Newcastle start well but run out of gas. Ice doesn't score until just before the end of the first period, but they do so at regular intervals thereafter, and the crowd gets its fun by odd means, such as goalie Jaden Pine-Murphy being credited with a goal as the result of a beneficent ricochet.

Jeff Smith finds friends all over the globe.

The big defenceman is last on and last off the ice.

Ice players mingle with fans post match.

In the final period, I sit with James Morgan and his wife (and fellow ATC worker) Shelley in the middle of the Ice member's area. It is one of the few times he has been able to watch Ice as a punter since that fateful first game he attended five years ago. Emma Poynton tells us Matt Armstrong is on 99 goals for Ice, adding some suspense to proceedings as we will him to bring up his hundredth Australian goal. It looks like we will be in luck. Matt is at his best, curving down the ice, linking up and taking the puck deep, then back-checking, laying checks and going all the way again. Both Matt and Lliam Webster, after their stints in defence, are now again playing as forwards. It brings to mind racehorses being schooled over steeplechases to freshen them for flat racing. Such moves have also improved Ice's versatility and lessened its reliance on individuals. Brent has said he will not mess with the line-up in these final games: this will be the team that contests Ice's semi-final.

Matt's second goal of the game, which gets him to the milestone, receives due acclaim because South Pole leader DJ Ferris has taken over the microphone, and he knows how to use it. However, when Army gets called for hooking an opponent despite skating alone metres from anyone, the limits of Ferris' professionalism are reached - the announcer is so astonished that he calls the penalty "two minutes for icing" at first. When he corrects himself, he can't suppress laughter. Army is just as amazed as he enters the penalty box.

With two late goals, the score blows out to 7–2. At game's end Jeff Smith joins regulars Lliam Webster and Tommy Powell in slamming into the glass in front of the fans, the customary Ice reaction after an Icehouse win. Brent wanted discipline from his players and no injuries and he got that. Everyone else wanted a party and got it. It's not fun for the North Stars and will surely fuel their revival next season.

Elsewhere, more important games are being played. Adelaide, finishing their season strongly, again handle Brave comfortably, winning 6-2 after leading 4-0. But the Ice Dogs repeat their strong Saturday effort against Perth. After trailing 2–1 at the first break and 3–2 at the second break, the Dogs storm home with the game's final four goals, to win 6–3 and qualify for the playoffs. Without those four unanswered goals, they would have had to beat the Mustangs in their final game of the season at home next Sunday.

With one round of games left, it is settled. The Mustangs, Ice, Brave and the Ice Dogs will contest the 2014 AIHL finals. Only the order of the standings can change – Ice or the Mustangs will finish on top and Brave or the Dogs can finish third or fourth. With the playoffs consisting of first versus fourth and second versus third, the two Melbourne teams, pacesetters all season, will not meet again unless it is in the grand final.

FRIDAY THE 22ND

This is my ultimate Suburban Tour. I am trudging back to Oakleigh's Olympic rink for the first time since 1981. Back then, it was the smallest and dingiest of several Melbourne rinks, home to the Hakoah club, which had a light blue jersey I now realise I admire for its hue and simplicity. Back then, a patient parent would have been driving me to games. Today, it is a long walk from Huntingdale railway station past Huntingdale golf course and an abandoned quarry or sand farm, now an immense, haphazardly fenced, overgrown hole. It means factories and busy roads, seventeen kilometres from the Melbourne CBD. Out here, the 'burbs are a grid gone large. North, South and Centre Roads traverse the sandbelt creating large blocks meant for frantic cars, not pedestrians.

Not too far down the road from a typically massive green Bunnings hardware complex, flanked by a scrap metal shop, and set back from Centre Road with a hopeful car park out front, the rink looks proud but battered, showing its 43 years. The Ice Hockey Victoria website acclaims it as the longest running rink in one location in Australia. This building, this business, this hockey institution is a survivor, like the sport itself.

There is still public skating, but these days it feels like the place exists because of Next Level Hockey, the brainchild of Mustangs star Joey Hughes and hockey veteran Tony Theobald. They have created a tiny, highly efficient office-pro shop hutch in a triangle of space in a high corner of the rink, and their programmes – from learn-to-skate group classes to supervised adult scrimmages – provide much of the rink's traffic.

For Joey, starting a hockey school and pro shop in Melbourne was the alternative to a precarious existence as a minor pro player in the Southern Professional Hockey League in America. In 2009, he took the plunge into the uncertainties of small business not far from his Springvale roots, after over a decade overseas playing hockey and studying. Tony had coached since 1994 and they shared a vision to improve Australian hockey from the grass roots up. The grass roots are misshapen and scarred in this frigid rink. The floor is uneven, the boards wavy and low, weathered like driftwood, the overhead heating poles are rusted relics that have long since given in to the dark cold, the terraces of rubber, timber and concrete are deeply scarred, and the half-dozen rows of plastic seating perfunctory and stained.

But the ice surface, however small, is not too bad. It is a rink, a precious rink, and as I add layers listening to Tony and watching Joey begin his Friday night classes, it's hard not to be grateful, and feel some affection for this decayed building. It feels like it got very old very soon, and then settled, content to live hurt if promised it would not be killed. Original owner Graham Argue sold the premises on the condition it remained an ice rink for another 25 years. That time is long since up, but it seems safe from development for now, thanks to the passion of Next Level.

Joey is fit, athletic, and healthy. With dark hair and dark eyes – the Hughes boys have a combination of Irish and Chilean parentage – he looks like a 1970s hotshot who should be the team playboy, but he has been with his girlfriend for years and loves coaching kids as much as scoring goals in the AIHL. He is both proud and modest, laid-back and passionate. I suspect he has often been misunderstood, literally because of his accent, an amalgam of Australian and Canadian pronunciations, but generally because of his occasional lack of impulse control during AIHL games, and the penalties that have followed. But like many hockey players, off-ice he is mild-mannered. If you play a sport which pushes you to the brink, perhaps you need less drama off the playing arena.

Joey has the attention of the foundation kids as he asks them to "take a knee" and listen at the start of their session. "You're going to play contact this year, yes? Well someone is going to put you on your arse ..." (If they don't learn the following drill, about keeping their heads up when accepting a pass).

The rink management helped Next Level out when they started; now Next Level guarantees payment for sessions regardless of numbers. When 90 novices come through on a Friday, everyone is happy, but it is a tough way to make a living. The company hopes to expand to the proposed new rink at Pakenham on the city's extreme south-eastern fringe, but it will maintain programs at Oakleigh. Among the clients tonight is a mum whose husband played hockey. Her kids have taken beginner's classes, now she's following suit. Every weekend they skate at Oakleigh on Saturday and the Icehouse on Sundays. "You can't get anywhere with one hour on ice a week," Tony says. Next Level helps kids get up to eight hours per week of productive ice time, and they monitor students to avoid burn-out, as some keen youngsters come for dawn sessions several times a week.

As Joey takes a huge class through c-cuts and balancing on one skate, Next Level social media guru Damien 'Damo' Newland asks me "Getting cold yet?" The disarming Welshman is about to run a fourteen kilometre fun run in hockey gear to raise money for charity, but he admits that he is doing it as much to raise awareness of Next Level. He has just been photographed for a newspaper promotion. Damo was brought to hockey by his

Oakleigh's Olympic rink is still valuable in its twilight.

A precious surface.

Joey Hughes in his office/pro shop, which utilises every inch.

wife and kids, then Joey said for him to have a go. "I have never seen anyone with his enthusiasm," Damo says of Joey. "He comes home from Perth, 6 am, after one hour's sleep; he gets here not even looking tired, he leaves that at the door. He's passionate about it. Those kids have to see what it takes if they want to make it to the AIHL. They're still going to have jobs they have to go to."

Joey is yelling "the stick is not a tripod!" to an intermediate class. It is 8 pm, my breath is a cloud before me, and being an inactive watcher, I am not sure how much more of the cold I can take. The coach, star, teacher demonstrates a move so elegantly, performing a kind of skating fleur-de-lis that his pupils laugh. Damo provides the final word. "I like that we start here. I like slumming it a little as you learn."

I end this pilgrimage to my youth encouraged. It's a rink we need. If it wasn't for the passion to play, and teach, in buildings like this, there would be no hockey for people like me to watch in the comfortable Icehouse. Decrepit, frigid Oakleigh measures the sacrifice it takes for hockey to exist in Melbourne and Australia.

Move, or freeze.

SATURDAY THE 23RD

ROAD TRIP SIX:
NEWCASTLE NORTH STARS V MELBOURNE MUSTANGS
DAY ONE

Joey Hughes's older brother Vinnie is keen to play AIHL for as long as possible. He says his mates in old-timers hockey think he is due to join them "any day now". "I'm only 33!" he announces, feigning outrage. "I don't qualify for another two years!"

Both Hughes brothers understandably kept their distance from me earlier in the year. Their club had advised it, and there had been a lot of attention on them when they first started pulling on orange, not blue-and-white jerseys. They wanted to earn the trust of their teammates, and downplay all the attention on themselves. And they would have wanted to size up this writer-type hanging around. But something has convinced Vinnie that he can relax and chat to me. Though I have not sought it, I'm lucky this has happened. He is genial company and a great hockey-loving storyteller. I'm in for bit of a treat on this final trip with the Mustangs to Newcastle and Sydney.

Vinnie tells me that hockey was a saviour for his mother. "Joey and I used to fight ferociously all the time as boys. Mum saw us quietly watching *Mighty Ducks* and she asked 'Do you like ice hockey? Do you want to play?'" Next thing the brawlers knew, a trip to Oakleigh had been arranged. Be here at this time. But mum, the boys cried, we don't know how to skate! Just be there, she replied. Finding an activity that would occupy two boisterous boys was vital. They would learn to skate! And they did. Vinnie became a fixture of local hockey, and Joey became an Australian pioneer overseas. The Hughes boys are the product of a tough environment - the streets of Springvale were gang-ruled when they grew up, their family life was sometimes turbulent and Oakleigh was hardly a haven for shrinking violets. Vinnie says there were "a lot of broken bones and a lot of fights" in the suburban rink when it was an AIHL venue. "Players got frustrated. Teams used to hate coming to Oakleigh ... Now with the Icehouse we're Hockeytown!" he says with wonder. In those days, Melbourne was the ugly duckling, struggling with a poor rink and small crowds, and New South Wales was the country's hockey power-base.

After I left Oakleigh last night, two hours into Joey's night of classes and games, he had another four hours of hockey tuition to come. He was up past 1 am, but says simply of today's travels "You've got to be ready to go." The Hughes boys remind me that this is a game played by tough people, and physical self-sacrifice is still part of their code. There are non-negotiables around loyalty and standing up for your teammates or siblings. Vinnie says when the state's rinks shrank to just Oakleigh, Victorian hockey lost half of its players. "People said 'why bother?'" The Hughes brothers were part of the hardy group who kept playing. Those Who Stayed. Those who could not do without it. They really are hockey tragics.

When the Mustangs land in Newcastle on this final trip of the AIHL season, there is announcement from the pilot requesting cabin staff to "disarm doors and cross check". Hockey terminology infiltrating aeroplane protocols? I'm in deep now. There is a relaxed, business-like feeling to this journey, with a place in the finals sewn up. The exciting prospect of the playoffs lurk just beyond these two games for the Mustangs, an undeniable fact so long a dream, then an expectation.

The team will be heading straight to the rink from the plane, but there's enough time to realise Mick Burslem has perfected his 2014 chicken salad. It has enough flavour and protein for satisfaction, but enough goodness and lightness to nourish athletes pre-game. The two team buses stop on a gravel-and-puddles-roadside not far from the airport, Mick places a massive tub of the salad on the spare tyre between bus one and its trailer, and the procession of hungry Mustangs grab a bowl and fork and dig in.

Mascots combine forces for charity.

The team has no suspensions or injuries, but Jamie Bourke and Viktor Gibbs-Sjodin have been left at home, 'rested' in the modern parlance. In Jamie's case, it is undoubtedly to avoid conflicts that could see him miss a final through suspension. Viktor had that concussion in Perth and returned shortly thereafter for the derby. He probably doesn't need to further test his health with unnecessary games. They seem wise decisions from Brad Vigon, and it enables a couple of his big squad to get some more ice time.

Outside the Hunter Ice Skating Stadium, the crowd-to-be and Mustangs players huddle under the veranda roof as heavy rain pours down before the gates open. "We left sunny Melbourne for this," someone quips. Fraser Carson shares news about Mathieu Ouellette's knee injury and rumours that fellow Brave ace Anton Kokkonen has to go home to Finland before the finals, as players try to work out which team they would rather play in their semi-final. Players talk like fans at times like this, and there is little separation between the two groups as the Mustangs play one of their endless "keep–up" soccer ball games, an activity which blends competition and co-operation, the collective trying to keep the ball from touching the ground.

Beau Taylor is shorn for charity pre-match.

Alongside, goalie Michael James warms up with the most extreme deep-lunge groin stretches I have ever seen, bouncing displays of limb-defying flexibility that make me feel as if I'm made of concrete. Fraser Carson, who sometimes sounds like a grizzled veteran rather than a promising kid, pooh-poohs stretching. He's fit, but not interested in having the elasticity of a gymnast.

The crowd comes well-prepared in Newcastle – they carry seat padding, blankets, blue-sequinned hats. The early-bird diehards bring the air of a primary school craft market, home-decorated, face-painted, the generations mixing, plenty of grandparents keen to snag their favourite seat alongside tiny kids. The under-veranda crowd are getting a whiff of the inescapable odour of a season – after 27 games, the sweat is winning despite the use of many deodorant gimmicks, and the players' gear reeks. North Stars veteran Ray Sheffield pushes politely through the crowd. A seven-year-old says "Hi Ray," sizing him up, then asks, "Ray, do you have a son?"

We are let in at 4.30 pm, half an hour before game-time, and on the terraces there is an unpacking ritual: find your patch, establish your territory, then start adding North Stars-themed clothing layers. *Come On Feel The Noise* blurts on to the PA. Mascot Marty the Moose is photographed by Australian hockey's pre-eminent snapper Mark Bradford, and Garry Dore goes from selling tickets in the box office to instructing the dressing room. The pre-game ceremony is elaborate and extended, including the shearing of Beau Taylor's flowing locks for charity, but eventually a young choir gently sings the national anthem and we're away.

The Mustangs play at a decent tempo and score the first two goals, and the North Stars appear a little flat, but I am more transfixed by the figure in the penalty box than the game. Louis Wetini, father of North Stars forward Matt is manning the penalty box in singlet, shorts and thongs. I am wearing four layers of clothes including a scarf. Louis is a manly apparition from a world where whales are wrestled before breakfast and frostbite can be conquered with a scoff.

The game is entertaining enough, if not for the home team, which finds it hard to score, and struggles to contain the Mustangs. The visitors are not flirting with their form, and their resolve to maintain high minimum levels, or their inability to drop them, is most impressive. The most salient matters, from the Mustangs' point of view, are the performances of Michael James, excellent in net; Adrian Nash, playing just his ninth game of the year, who is lively as always and records a goal and an assist; and the goal of seventeen-year-old Ethan Cornford in

Newcastle stalwart Peter Lambert calls the action.

Newcastle's international decorating theme.

Newcastle, a family in victory or defeat.

the final period. Coach Brad Vigon cannot ask for more – the "fringe" players excel and no-one gets hurt or suspended. The 4–1 win maintains Mustang momentum and ends a deflating North Stars season.

Between periods, Garry Dore reveals that he is about to step down as North Stars coach. He wears too many hats at present, as general manager, coach and rink manager, which leaves him doing all of them less thoroughly than he would prefer. He only intended to coach for one year – it's now been three years. He would like to be out in the crowd glad-handing potential sponsors. It is likely an experienced team member will take over the coaching. Garry hopes to expand his facility to create more space and seating above the benches, and possibly a licensed bar. He's looking for another activity that can draw some more people into his building to pay for the development.

It feels like the game has been an interruption to North Star family rituals. John Kennedy gets a bucketful of ice water thrown over him – the "ice bucket challenge" for charity that is August's fad in the way that the "#nek nomination" belonged to January. Then kids, spouses, figure skaters, officials and volunteers join the players on the ice for a large annual group portrait shot by Mark Bradford.

The Mustangs are satisfied. Fraser Carson, back-up tonight, high-fives Chuck Connolly, who agrees that this is a good win. They are both happy that Perth has beaten Melbourne Ice in a shootout at the Icehouse. In their final game of the season, the Bears suffer yet another narrow loss, at home to Canberra, losing 3–2 after a scoreless final period.

The booze stop en route to our digs, always capable of providing local insights, offers a teen cashier dressed in a lion onesie, who says the following: "Locals here like their pinot chilled. I know. Weird." Everything about the stop is weird.

Vinnie and Joey Hughes, Mustangs.

Back at the holiday camp accommodation post-match, the hearty communal meal takes place in a large, smoky fluoro-lit room, then a handful of players, sponsor Bryan and his fiancé Debbie and the Mustangs staff convene in the coaches' cabin, the backdrop a silenced TV chronicling the comeback AFL win of Hawthorn over former nemesis Geelong. The Mustangs trip to Perth I missed at the start of the month has passed into legend. Extended Mustangs family members went along and the team won both games, but it seems the coach's Saturday night Latvian joke-telling session is the source of the weekend's infamy. On this more low-key Saturday night on the coastal fringes of Newcastle, Brad Vigon reprises a few of his favourites, shaking his head in disbelief.

"Latvian #1: Knock knock

Latvian #2: Who there? I kid! I see you, we burn door for warming."

Or how about:

"Two Latvian look at sun. Is not sun, but nuclear reactor meltdown. Latvian happy because maybe now warm enough to plant potato."

Those are the tamer examples safe for consumption in this family publication. But Brad isn't all jokes and laughs. He says his wife told him to write down the club's aims for the upcoming season. He looks up exactly what was agreed to on his Latvian joke-provider smartphone. The objectives sound pretty similar to Brent's goals - consolidate a good culture and make the playoffs.

When talk turns to Melbourne Ice, Brad reveals that he was very disappointed with how he was treated when he was a candidate for the senior coaching job there after eight years at the club as a player and assistant coach. He didn't feel he was offered the same terms as an international candidate and disagreed strongly with a policy that made family members of coaches buy a ticket to get a seat. The day after Ice's offer, Andy McDowell approached him. He says he was surprised by how at home he felt discussing his future position with the team he

VINNIE HUGHES SAYS HE USES LESSONS LEARNED IN HOCKEY EVERYDAY ... THE SPORT GAVE HIM CONFIDENCE, COMMUNICATION SKILLS, "PEOPLE KNOWLEDGE" AND LEADERSHIP SKILLS.

said was "painted as the devil" by Ice. Such matters are never cut and dried and Brad is as effusive about people like Josh Puls - "a great guy" - as he is critical of some others then involved with the club. The key figures from either club don't even agree among themselves about their adversaries on the other side. However, this night reminds me that for some key personnel there is genuine feeling behind the rivalry.

Everyone in the room agrees there were high expectations at the start of the season. The room praises Mick Burslem's blast after the Ice Dogs loss. "As an older man you know how fast it goes," he says of why he felt it necessary to address the playing group. Mick relays the news about Mustang Jack McCoy, his stepson and Ken McCoy's son, who damaged his eye playing inline hockey last summer, costing him any chance at playing this season. There were fears during the week that surgery had not worked and more would be required, but it was just a blood clot, and a change of medication was all that was required. Ken was due to travel on this trip, but stayed home because of the setback. Jack is 24, and played 22 games last season.

Skipper Sean Jones takes up my question about permanent residency. If you start as an import, you should stay one, simple, he says. He is passionate about the development of Australian hockey. The feeling around the room is that the Mustangs do more than their Ice rivals to support local and junior hockey, and all AIHL clubs need to do more for the grassroots. When Brad muses aloud about what a locals-only Melbourne team would look like, combining the best Australians from Ice and the Mustangs, Sean laughs. "We'd kill each other before we got to the ice!"

Brad admits he is resting Jamie Bourke because the Ice Dogs would try to "suck him in". It prompts Chuck to recall one of his favourite coaching moments, when he refused to give a junior team pucks for the pre-game warm-up. "If you want it, get it in the game!" he told his charges, who included Jamie. They were wide-eyed at the audacious gambit, but duly hungry for the puck once the game commenced.

Vinnie Hughes is not as forthcoming as Brad about his departure from Ice, the team he captained to two championships. He really doesn't want to rake over those coals.

But he is rollicking, grinning good company as he talks hockey, it is clearly his comfort zone. Hockey has meant more than fun on the weekend to the Hughes boys. He speaks of Oakleigh as a saviour, not just a ramshackle rink. He is thankful to current IHA president Clive Connelly for "kicking his ass" and supporting him as a kid. He says he uses lessons learned in hockey every day in his business; the sport gave him confidence, communication skills, "people knowledge" and leadership skills. When he became a boss, stepping into areas he didn't understand, which clients assumed he knew about, he said yes to the challenges, then worked them out on the fly, something he would not have been able to do without the lessons he had learned from hockey. Hockey self-knowledge has helped him cool hotheads at work, and deal with his own frustrations. He organises his life so he can play, and now that he has an extended hockey social network which his family enjoys, he is not intending to depart any time too soon, even if the eventual prospect of the old-timers appeals. My guess is that one of the main attractions of that culture is its three interstate road trips a year, preserving the pleasures of Saturday nights like this, spent talking hockey.

"I have to say that I take everyone at face value and everyone is nice to me," Vinnie says. He puts the "backstabbing" that goes with minor sport behind him, and he is philosophical about the breakdown of some relationships, and even teams. Inevitably, some things run their course. Vinnie has a new lease of life as a player for the Mustangs, unburdened of captaincy and the responsibilities of mentoring and being on top of club politics. He is fresher after a big off-season and a regime of two off-ice gym sessions and two myotherapy sessions per week in addition to training. A veteran cannot get by on smarts alone these days; the league is fitter and faster by the year. He says his harried mum was "very smart" to get him and Joey into hockey.

SUNDAY THE 24TH

ROAD TRIP SIX:
SYDNEY ICE DOGS V MELBOURNE MUSTANGS
DAY TWO

Jack Wolgemuth at home in
Alaska.

In the food hall at breakfast – the second-last meal Mick
Burslem will provide for the Mustangs this season – Jack
Wolgemuth talks about life in Alaska. He says Australia is
"such a good place, so relaxed" and he has loved his time here
– enough to have returned for a second stint – but the pull of
home is strong. He speaks of his 55 cousins, and the remote
community strife where they live; even troubled Alaskan
kids have the benefit of elite survival skills to cope with their
beautiful, harsh environment. Jack's dad runs a grocery
business in Barrow, "two blocks from the Arctic Ocean", a
business dependent on skidoos and small planes. Jack plans to
get his pilot's licence. "How much freer can you be?" he asks,
contemplating flying over the Arctic Circle.

Freedom appeals, responsibilities beckon, and he and
girlfriend Natalie are missing home. Having endured so many
consecutive winters, they are keen to experience the fabled
heat of an Australian summer, but they may not be able to stay
around long enough. When at home, Jack does logistics for
the family business, mostly from Anchorage, the northern US
state's capital and biggest city. I mention that I am a fan of some
of the TV shows now based in Alaska. It says much about laid-
back Jack that he prefers the "true documentaries" about Alaska
to the contrived reality shows. Laconic, slow-talking, curious, a
traveller, Jack, like Jeff Smith, is a model import. He chats with
Chuck and I for so long that he is last to the nearby beach for
'recovery'. Nothing hurries Jack, on or off the rink.

As the stragglers make their way to the Pacific Ocean, I
notice Ethan Cornford is wearing the honrary orange Mustangs
construction helmet after scoring his first AIHL goal the day
before. In this older company, he is quiet, bashful, and grins
occasionally, believably seventeen. When he neglects to wear the
helmet later on, gnarly old veteran Fraser Carson calls him out,
demanding he put the headwear back on straight away, only
half-joking.

In Australia, the finals are too brief for the cultivation of
playoff beards. The Mustangs stopped shaving from the point
they qualified for the finals. The Hughes brothers, naturally
hirsute, have lustrous black moustaches on the go. When Joey
takes off for the beach wearing reflector sunglasses, Chuck

Connolly calls him Pablo Escobar. There is a definite seventies flavour to the entire hockey endeavour in Australia. Sometimes it feels as if I was never away!

When the group have had their swim, I grab my pre-finals chat with Pat O'Kane. Discussion starts at that pivotal 7–2 loss to the Ice Dogs in Liverpool, back in May. "It wasn't really necessarily the loss, it was just everything going on around then," he says. "Guys weren't happy with situations going on away from hockey and everyone brought their issues to hockey, and it just wasn't fun. Guys weren't getting along, some guys weren't buying in. It was a struggle going to practice. You wondered 'who's going to get upset tonight?' and 'who's not going to put in the effort tonight?' Brad wasn't happy and that made me worry, because I didn't want him to call it quits. I said to him 'don't do it, you've put in so much effort, you can't give up on us now'."

Pat says Mick didn't yell at the group when he addressed them after that loss Ice Dogs, he just laid down some home truths, and it carried weight coming from him. "You could see he was passionate about it. And this is a guy who really has no ties to the team besides Jack McCoy, who is not even around this year. He just loves it, he comes on his own time, drives us, cooks for us, takes care of us. And after he spoke to us, I think we all took a look in the mirror and said 'Why are we here?' And then things started picking up."

Pat remains steadfast about the player selection issue. "I just don't understand the mindset that if you're not playing you complain about it. If you're not playing, you should be working harder than the guys who are playing. I think there's a different culture here because it's not so cut-throat like it is back home. It's such a small sport here that a lot of these guys haven't had to compete for their spots growing up. Whereas guys like Jack and Jeff and Joey and myself, if you weren't performing or you were complaining or something off the ice was bugging you, you'd just get cut."

As for the AIHL, he is another who believes the lack of good facilities is holding back the league. "The sport is growing and it's growing fast, but there's a ceiling right now. You need more places. Because it's going to stop, it's going to plateau."

He agrees with Sean Jones that "if you're an import to start, you're an import for good". "It's a shame because obviously you want the best players you can get, but at the same time you want Australian players to come through."

Pat now wants to be an Australian resident, not for hockey, "just for my life". "My visa ends August 30 of next year, so I need to figure out what I am going to do next, because I'd really

THE SPORT IS GROWING AND ITS GROWING FAST, BUT THERE'S A CEILING RIGHT NOW. YOU NEED MORE FACILITIES. BECAUSE ITS GOING TO STOP, ITS GOING TO PLATEAU - PAT O'KANE.

like to stay." It's a bureaucratic challenge to become a permanent resident of Australia, and Pat is going to take some advice from Chuck's dad, who works in the field. But his claims are strong. By the time his visa comes up, he will present as a clean-cut, well-regarded applicant, under the age of 30, from an English-speaking country, who possesses a Master's Degree from an Australian university, has an Australian girlfriend and a secure job. Plus he's a candidate for Pope and could pass for Simon The Likeable played by Tom Cruise. Sounds like a good case.

Given his international business education, what does he see as the AIHL's future? "I don't think it could go any higher. With the facilities, it couldn't go semi-professional or anything. Each team would need a rink comparable to the Icehouse or Newcastle ... I don't think the teams have nearly enough money to do that. I like it. I'm not out here to go to the NHL. Just try to be the best amateur league you can be ..."

This Mustangs group consists of true sports nuts. The only thing required to keep them occupied is a ball, which means competition, and a game, often improvised on the spot. Outside the airport, underneath the Newcastle veranda in the rain, and now on the driveways between cabins at the holiday camp, they play, endlessly. This morning, time is killed by the throwing of a miniature American Football, which has a tail that makes it look like a torpedo.

When we stop the buses for lunch in the car park of an outer suburban baseball field, the team's battered orange soccer ball comes out. It took a direct hit from a vehicle the night before at Newcastle, and Joey Hughes tends running repairs, wrapping the sacred sphere with a mummy bandage of stick tape. The Mustangs have not presented as a superstitious bunch, but they're desperate to get this slashed, cracked, squashed, ripped square pumpkin through their final pre-game keep-up sessions of the year. They hope there will be two more after today. At this hour-long stop, an inexplicable shelter which covers heads but not legs offers a novel site for a stand-up cards game. But there is still plenty of time to chat. For the AIHL lifestyle to appeal, you have to love the game, yes, but you also have to enjoy the company of your teammates.

On this bus voyage to Liverpool, Mustangs import Jeff Grant has a bit to get off his chest, and maybe it could only be said

Joey Hughes affects running repairs to the keep-up ball.

Keep-up: competitive and co-operative.

Identification by legs only.

to an outsider. He says the AIHL is undergoing an "identity crisis" and must decide what it wants to be. "There's so much they could do to improve that doesn't cost much money," he says, frustration palpable. It's the little things Jeff is talking about, like letting the opposition know exact running times and sticking to them, and providing water and towels in penalty boxes. And the not-so little things, like security for players when they enter and leave the ice. "The little things make you feel like a pro ..." he says, insisting much of which he speaks is a matter of organisation and achievable protocols, not massive investment. He also believes Australian referees are not keeping pace with bigger, stronger, faster players and need help from imports and players who have just finished playing. "People need to decide what they're doing it for, they need to get serious ..." His point is that minor professional hockey is not glamorous or lucrative, and it is not an easy lifestyle, but because it does the little things right, it respects the players. He wants a professional attitude to the amateur game here. It is, I guess, what Pat is talking about when he speaks of the 'next step' for the league.

Jeff has a lot to decide in the next few weeks. There is the prospect of an opportunity helping to start up the Australian distribution of his uncle's specialty vodka. This was going to be his last year of hockey, but if this job materialises, it would utilise his marketing degree, and possibly see him continue playing for the Mustangs. In the next two weeks, his future employment, accommodation, and nation of residence is up for grabs, not to mention the AIHL championship. Jeff is grateful to the game of hockey for the opportunities it has provided him, especially to travel the world. He says it helped him come out of his shell. So it is little wonder he wants to spread the hockey gospel. Jeff may not yet have yet fully embraced the relaxed (or slacker) Australian "she'll be right" ethos, but his motives are admirable. To Jeff, it is important to "respect the game".

This is my third trip to Liverpool, and the first time I enter the Liverpool Catholic Club proper. At the core of the sprawling complex of restaurants and bars and function rooms and auditoriums and clubs and playing fields and mini-golf courses and gyms and a seemingly forgotten ice rink is the pokie machine room, which generates income necessary for all of the above from the pockets of the club's members and guests. It is a clumsy form of taxation which can damage already difficult lives, yet it provides comforts and facilities. Everyone here on this Sunday afternoon is old and overweight. A lone motoring

The Ice Dogs finish their last home game with a get-together.

The view from behind the glass, upstairs at Liverpool.

The Liverpool Catholic Club. interior.

Time to close ranks before finals.

enthusiast watches a telecast of a V8 race, no other soul within 60 metres. Rugby league games go unwatched. The atmosphere is muffled, placid, people talking quietly in small groups, or not at all. I get a reasonably priced burger, having signed in as a temporary member, and marvel at the elaborate expenditure that has provided TVs, water features, lounges, bingo rooms, children's games room, and lavishly advertised upcoming entertainment, including an electric violin player, magicians, impersonators and comedians.

The vision of providing an entire world for members is breathtaking. The LCC offers holidays for members and a free member's bus servicing surrounding streets. It says it is donating "much more than required under legislation" to local charity and community organisations.

In the calming grey corridor between the meals area and the main rooms, glass cabinets house myriad sporting trophies, from darts to soccer. And stunningly, there is the towering, silver Goodall Cup, in all its shiny, Stanley-Cup-imitating glory. It is easily the grandest trophy housed by this odd West Sydney palace of dreams, but it is of no more importance here than the fishing club's honour roll. The literature put out quarterly by the LCC, glossy and comprehensive, doesn't mention the Ice Dogs or the AIHL, instead devoting its ice hockey page to the LCC Saints junior team, but here is the national league's trophy. Amongst the other clubs given as much space as the LCC Saints, and more than the Ice Dogs, are the following: Bocce; BMX; Double C Toastmaster, Quilters, and Southern Cross Pipes and Drums. A national ice hockey league team may not be its major priority, but, like Oakleigh, the Liverpool Catholic

Club provides a precious rink, so hockey is another beneficiary of pokies fund-raising.

The Ice Dogs have pulled out all stops for their final home game, and the queue for the always delayed entry to the rink is longer than usual. The Mustangs have finished preparations with one more bout of keep-up on the rugby field out the front. Mick Burslem, then Jeff Grant address the players.

It's a conundrum, this game, a dead rubber in which there is more to lose than gain - injuries and suspension in this final contest of the AIHL season disqualify a player from next week's playoffs, the reason for so much toil. The Mustangs need to erase the memory of their listless 7–2 loss here earlier in the season. The Ice Dogs never take a backward step. Both teams will be keen to maintain momentum going into the deciders, and keen to deny each other a motivational advantage. After all, they may meet again in a semi-final.

It's the biggest crowd I've seen in the LCC esky, the ribald choir behind the net supplanted with extra Dogs fans and a good portion of Mustangs fans, the shallow terraces filled and loud. The game is fast and fierce from the outset, the narrow confines and the natural competitiveness of the teams immediately banishing any thought of the players going through the motions. Joey Hughes appears the focus of the heaviest hits, and he draws two penalties in the first period, the second a high slash. The Mustangs lead 1–0 and 2–1 in the first period, Pat's powerplay slapshot from the slot and Jack Wolgemuth's Barg-esque finish from a stretch pass keeping them ahead. The Mustangs kill off four penalties in the second period, including a patch of five-on-three, yet outshoot the hosts 12-8, forcing several big saves from Tim Noting, and it remains 2–1 at the second intermission. Jeff Grant has been the Mustangs' best player, reliable in defence, and feeding the puck to forwards, choosing deft and game-opening options.

In the break, Chris Kubara, the tall, white-haired father of Ice Dogs forward Tyler, shows me the upstairs gym viewing area, a neglected vantage point behind a spectacular wall of glass. There are two rows of seats up here, offering a fine view, and behind that, a spacious sprung board gym. Chris says the rink has scope for expansion, and opening up of the wall opposite is on the to-do list of the LCC. That would mean a decent grandstand, a kiosk, and proper change rooms for teams. He says the project was next in line for the LCC, but a car park renovation took precedence. Chris also says there is glass available for the Liverpool rink, for free, but all renovations must be approved by the

TEAM	GP	W	L	D	SOW	SOL	PTS
MUSTANGS	28	17	8	0	0	3	54
ICE	28	14	8	0	3	3	51
BRAVE	28	14	9	1	2	2	49
ICE DOGS	28	14	11	0	2	1	47
ADRENALINE	28	10	10	2	5	1	43
NORTH STARS	28	11	15	0	0	2	35
THUNDER	28	9	15	0	2	2	33
BEARS	28	6	19	1	1	1	22

LCC management. With its 17 clubs, the LCC has many competing projects.

Chris is one of the few Australians ever drawn to hockey by comparative ease of access. His sons were playing inline hockey near Wollongong when their rink closed, forcing the Kubaras to travel to distant, inland Penrith. On one such long journey, they passed the Liverpool ice rink, an hour closer to home. Chris asked his boys if they were interested in transferring their hockey passion on to ice, they said 'yeah!' and some expensive purchases from the "Bank of Dad" later, the Kubaras became ice hockey devotees.

Chris says dissatisfied players, volunteers and parents have approached him about challenging for the job as Ice Dogs president. He wants to know more details about the finances and constitution of the Ice Dogs before he makes his decision.

The Dogs equalise early in the third period, unleashing a barrage of air horns. Brendan McDowell responds for the Mustangs within two minutes to make it 3–2, then Ice Dog star Simon Barg taps in at the end of a rush to claim the league scoring title by a single point from CBR Brave star Stephen Blunden. The final fifteen minutes demonstrates why these two teams are finalists, every player laying checks as hard as they can, and scoring chances coming thick and fast. 'COME ON YOU DOGS!' sounds throughout the period. Joey is involved in two more heavy clashes in succession, but number 21 keeps his cool.

Vinnie Hughes and David Dunwoodie are awarded double minors. The atmosphere is combustible, but the game, so often contrary, offers only a 3–3 tie, and a shootout. The fans get their win when Paul Baranzelli scores for the Dogs and Joey's slapshot goes wide, earning him plenty of advice from Ice Dogs players as he skates back to his bench.

The Ice Dogs gather for their end-of-season team photo, convinced that they can defend their title. The Mustangs hurriedly prepare for the rush to the airport. "See you in Melbourne," Mick Burslem says to Ice Dogs fans as he packs.

The finals match-ups are confirmed. Perth has beaten Melbourne 3–2 in the day's other game, so the Mustangs have remained on top of the standings and will face the Ice Dogs in the first semi-final, while Ice will play Brave in the later evening final.

The rush to the airport is delayed a little by Mick circling three times (a 1080?) at the main motorway roundabout, as Chuck searches his phone to confirm that we have to go left to avoid

GF	GA	DIFF	WIN %	POINTS%
108	88	20	60.71%	64.29%
104	88	16	60.71%	60.71%
106	89	17	57.14%	58.33%
116	97	19	57.14%	55.95%
94	90	4	53.57%	51.19%
87	106	-19	39.29%	41.67%
94	94	0	39.29%	39.29%
68	125	-57	25.00%	26.19%

ending up in Canberra, and instead proceed to Sydney and its airport. I could have put them straight, as I did a 720 with Ice at the same roundabout on another trip, but another voice would not have been appreciated in that centrifugal decision-making process, which was entertaining back-seat drivers like Fraser Carson.

The final flight of the year is delayed, dismaying news for many, but perfect for me. I have taken Monday off and these minutes at the end of trips are the best time to talk to players: an extra pint in the airport bar is ideal. Brent Laver calls while I am ordering that beverage, confirming there are no casualties from his team's two losses to Perth and asking about the news from the Mustangs. "If we don't win it, I hope it's them," he says. Fraser Carson cannot imbibe as he has to drive home from the airport and is still on P-plates (zero alcohol required). They serve us only one before the bar closes, which means I get to see one of the defining images of the season.

At 10.20 pm Sunday night, after two games of hockey and hours of bus travel over the previous 36 hours, the ball games are not complete for the Mustangs. Six to eight players form a tight circle in the middle of the walkway near our gate playing an arcane made-up-on-the-spot form of downball utilising the square-tiled floor. Mick Burslem is happy to observe that Vinnie, 33, and Joey, 30, are two of the most enthusiastic participants. He says the Mustangs played a good final round. "They have the feeling of a group with destiny on their agenda," he says.

I ask Mick what he said to the players before today's game. He says he told them that, unlike the last time they visited Liverpool, they had now proved themselves to be the best team, not just in their own building, but in the competition.

One more game during the flight delay.

Goodbye regular season. What lies ahead?

TUESDAY THE 26TH

Something happened while we were in New South Wales. At first it seemed it was stealing the limelight from finals week, but now, as with many things this year, it feels like it happened at exactly the right moment. On Saturday night, Ice and Thunder played an entertaining game at the Icehouse. Ice fought back from 1–3 down to outshoot Perth 46–17 and force a shootout at 4–4. Perth goalie Mathieu Dugas underlined his reputation around the league as one of its elite net-minders. But in the shootout Jaden Pine-Murphy proved just as tough to get past, the tie-breaker extending to 11 shots without settling the game.

This meant Perth was moving beyond its regular shootout snipers in search of the sudden death winner. Up stepped Ric Del Basso. He had played as a forward this day for the first time all year. He moved in straight at Jaden, at pace, and fired a wrist shot hard from the high slot, not a typical shootout ploy. Perhaps pulling the trigger so early without any moves surprised Jaden. The powerful shot beat the Ice goalie and Perth had won. It was time to celebrate. So Ric turned back up the ice ... gathered pace ... then crouched ... and performed a headstand, skidding on his helmet, then tumbling over into a half-somersault before being embraced by his ecstatic teammates.

ATC Productions caught the headstand on its livestream and it soon became the biggest 'story' in my four years covering the league. You Tube video of the stunt was shared hundreds of thousands of times. Most major sports agencies ran the footage and/or a story about the reckless celebration. Bleacher Report; Romanian websites; CBS; and Australian TV news services and current affairs programs all featured what Stan Scott would want known as the "Delly Celly". By early September, it had been viewed 626,364 times.

ATC commentator Michael Clough was chuffed. "Hands up if you've ever been quoted (credited or not) in *The Washington Post*?" he asked cyberspace. Poster Abigail Louise summed up the feelings of hockey fans: "Cool isn't it! It's funny to see some comments from around the world where they say they didn't even know we played ice hockey here." Amy Fulton on the Mustangs website wrote: "Thanks to Ric Del Basso of the Perth Thunder and his imaginative goal celebration, the whole world has joined in the build up to the biggest weekend of the year in Australian ice hockey."

James Morgan yet again burned the midnight oil to circulate what he knew would be in-demand footage. "Nine News Melbourne (via Tony Jones) carried it first for us on the Sunday night and it took off since then. We know it's been shown on Network Seven, *Footy Classified* last night, *The Project*, and made it into the (US, ESPN) *SportsCenter* Top 10 Plays, which is new ground for the AIHL and has been a goal of ours for ages. Even today – days after the incident – I'm getting enquiries from the major North American networks seeking permission to show the footage to their audience. The Twitter response has been crazy and is still going - there's got to easily be 10+ million people at home and abroad that now know we do ice hockey in Australia on the big stage." Perth Thunder social media manager Paul Rewell was also excited by the exposure. "We're getting new FB fans aplenty at the moment and our website is being bombed, which is all good ... amazing how something so innocently impulsive turns into something we just couldn't buy if we wanted to ..." As Yahoo Sports *Puck Daddy* blogger Greg Wyshynski puts it: "Man, Australian hockey is weird."

I speak to Ric Del Basso on Tuesday, after his celebration has become famous. The former Thunder co-owner is a little bemused about getting interviewed by international agencies "at the wrong times", but graciously chats about it one more time. "It's pretty funny. There's not really much to say. They ask 'How did you do it?' I say 'I put the puck in the net. I got on my head!' "

The most exposed moment in Aussie hockey history: The Delly Celly, as captured by ATC Productions.

There was a little more to it than that, however. He has performed the headstand "a few times a year" since seeing it when he travelled to a Pursuit of Excellence camp in Canada, where it was performed by an American. "Ever since then we've been doing it at training and having a bit of a laugh about it. I guess you just wait for that moment to do it spontaneously ... and I don't think you could get much better than a point like that – after you win the game in the penalty shootout. I thought, screw it, it's going to happen."

There was something about the exuberance of the celebration that suited Perth, and the league. Despite being borderline dangerous, it was enterprising and irreverent. Social media analyst Myles Harris, whose business it is to understand such things, wrote about the impact of the Delly Celly at length on his Hewitt Sports platform, when it had only been viewed 65,000 times. He started by pointing out that the footage had worked because ATC Productions had been able to shoot without a net in their way. Most AIHL rinks have nets, not glass, and are constrained by insurance policies from pulling them back. Myles urged the league to investigate legal disclaimers on tickets so they could pull back nets and improve TV and livestream coverage. "There is a sticking point with most things hockey down under. This is all a bit new and scary to most," he wrote. "There is a large community of hockey lovers worldwide who love the game, love anything about the game, and love consuming content related to it. We need to be in that conversation. We need AIHL content to be on those networks and circulated around."

In 2013, the big story had been when a referee got crunched at the Icehouse and ATC commentator Stephen White had taken over as replacement linesman. No-one could remember a commentator joining the fray as an official. Again, footage provided by ATC proved the catalyst for precious exposure.

In a media-saturated world, the Delly Celly could be seen as a scratch on the surface, with the Zamboni of daily media production coming to quickly wash it away. But Myles believes repeated exposure grants a cumulative effect. Yes, it is the "the dinky things" about the AIHL that get noticed, he concedes, but beggars can't be choosers in a country where the major football codes demand 95 per cent of air time and "a few smart systems and processes in place ... can get a lot of eyes on the league quickly".

Meanwhile, James Morgan tells me he has turned his attention to beefing up his company's coverage of the finals weekend. "It's an exciting time to be a hockey fan. I am steeling myself for one last push. It will be like a road trip at home, wall-to-wall work and fun." Eight cameras, presentations during intermissions ... James is always looking to expand, to do something new and better. "The league is at the crossroads. This could be a high watermark. Or base camp. I think the league needs to clamp down on the teams a bit and build themselves a more sustainable environment. Get a co-ordinated PR effort, generate themselves an income stream."

Even those off the ice have finals nerves, that combination of dread and can't-wait anticipation that give sudden death deciders their vicious glamour. The reaction to the Delly Celly somehow raises the stakes at the start of a long, exciting week.

2014 AIHL Finals

Semi Final 1
Mustangs v Sydney Ice Dogs
Saturday 30 August, 3.30pm

Semi Final 2
Melbourne Ice v CBR Brave
Saturday 30 August, Saturday 6.30pm

Grand Final
Sunday 31 August, 3pm

WEDNESDAY THE 27TH

The four teams contesting the sudden death finals series this weekend are understandably confident that they will take out the title. Each has beaten the other throughout the season and each has a credible contender's story.

The Dogs withstood early-season coaching and administrative upheaval and a 1–5 opening, and have won three games in a row, including a defeat of their semi-final opponent the Mustangs last Sunday. CBR Brave have munched every challenge thrown at it in its inaugural season, and in four visits to the finals venue, Melbourne's Icehouse, have lost only once in regulation time. Melbourne Ice has blended emerging and established talent into a unit which led the league for long periods of the season. And the Melbourne Mustangs were deserved minor premiers, after improving steeply and consistently over the past two seasons.

The finals ought to be the best-attended and most passionately supported in the fourteen-year history of the growing league. All seats have already been sold, and there is a large travelling contingent from north of the border. The quality of the finalists can be ascertained by a glance at the teams that didn't make it. Adelaide, Perth Thunder, Newcastle North Stars and the Sydney Bears were good enough to beat the top four at various stages of the season.

Ice Dogs coach Andrew Petrie says the Ice Dogs will put their heart and soul into their semi-final and take it from there. The teams has flights home booked for Monday afternoon. "We're planning as though we're going to be there," he says of Sunday's decider. Andrew has immense respect for his first opponent, however, saying that he thought the final game of the year between the Mustangs and the Dogs last week was as good a game as he had seen all year. "Their structure and adherence to systems is far and away better than any other team. Other teams have strong first lines and strong powerplays, but across the board, five on five, they're as well-drilled a team as I've seen," Petrie said Tuesday night. He is maintaining the same routines which have served his team all year, trying to keep the weekend "as normal as possible".

Finals newcomers CBR Brave are taking a different approach. After a season in which mishaps with two bus trips and an airline flight postponed or cancelled games, they will take no chances and travel to Melbourne Friday morning. This will enable the first-time finalists a chance to get reacquainted

> IT'S THE BIGGEST GAME OF OUR CAREERS. THIS IS NOT GOING TO HAPPEN EVERY YEAR ... WE'RE EXCITED BY THE OPPORTUNITY.
> - MARK RUMMUKAINEN

with the Icehouse during a training session, and will ensure they will be settled in Melbourne on the day of their big game. Brave captain Mark Rummukainen describes his team's semi-final as the "biggest game of the season, the biggest game of our careers. This is not going to happen every year ... we're excited by the opportunity."

Canberra will fear nothing in a season in which it cheated death. Their passionate juggernaut has defied all expectations thanks to the most taxing training regime in the league and brilliant recruiting of experienced locals and high-quality imports. Mark says the team's early success – "beyond everyone's expectations" – caused a quick turnaround in attitude. "Once the element of surprise was gone, we developed a new mentality. When we had the mid-season blues and dropped games ... it would have been easy to say 'here we go again'," he says. "But we said 'we've done so much together, we can get out of this little funk. If we get back to what we were doing we can turn it around. We passed that test, no-one freaked out. We said 'we're better than this'. It's definitely a new club, a new culture."

Tellingly, Mustangs forward Jamie Bourke, rested from the final round against the Ice Dogs, says self-discipline will be the key to the Mustangs'

What they're fighting for: The Sydney Ice Dogs with the 2013 Goodall Cup.

chances. "It's going to be awesome to play in front of so many people. It'll be bigger than Melbourne Ice games. The feel around the club is that if we play our game we'll win," Bourke tells the Mustangs website. "Keeping out of the box is going to be crucial this weekend. It's going to be the key for us doing well. Five-on-five [hockey] is where we are at our best. Our strength is that we have three good lines that we need to take advantage of, where a lot of teams rely heavily on one or two lines." Line-mate Pat O'Kane says it is a "one-game season" now. "We're just going to give it everything. Just play the entire 50 minutes and give it everything we have, then see how we go."

WEDNESDAY THE 27TH (2)

The best shot of 2014 CBR Bravehearts fans, in full face-painted glory, has been taken by communications and social media consultant Jessica Schumman. I liaise with Jessica about her involvement with Brave, and her story appears emblematic of their amazing season.

Braveheart boys.

"The first game I attended was probably round two or three. My husband and I are best mates with the Ascension Sports Australia guys and they were streaming the games. I would tag along to the first few games. The Brave team approached the Ascension guys in week four [Perth double-header] asking if they knew anyone who could tweet live from games. They suggested me, the Brave handed over the Twitter password and it went from there. I knew nothing about ice hockey and am still learning at every game. The momentum has been great! It's certainly brought about a new following for ice hockey and a new belief in the power of community. It has been about anyone and everyone who has wanted to help, volunteer, contribute money or time, and dedicate their spirit or their home. There have been no cliques, no judgement and no exclusion. And that's what I have loved about being involved with the Brave."

Jessica is due to travel to Melbourne along with 180 other Brave fans on buses. "I'll be tweeting live from the Brave game for the team and I'll be looking after the Brave fans on the bus to Melbourne on Saturday," she says.

In Brave's latest video *The Underdog Story*, back-up goalie Brad Hunt is quoted: "When you feel cared about, you perform. I've never had a season like this in 20 years."

THURSDAY THE 28TH

I am meeting the leaders of the Icehouse's unofficial cheer squads at the nearby Harbourtown Hotel hours before the final training sessions of the Mustangs and Ice. Though Melbourne derbies get passionate in the stands, their most visible supporters are sensible. "It's not actually that bad between us!" says Adam 'Nads' Van Bael, head honcho of the Mustangs' unofficial fans group the Stable of the rivalry with Ice's fan group the South Pole. "We're at opposite ends of the rink. It's more the random fans that cause issues. You get the ones who are heavily European football-influenced and they think that we should be throwing flares at each other. Online they're full on."

South Pole boss Dee J Ferris says the only issues come from "fringe dwellers". Stable stalwart Samuel Hohneck says the two Melbourne fan groups "hook into each other", but it's "these people who aren't really connected to any of us ... they're the ones getting real heated about things."

"We've worked pretty hard to still keep it civil with each other. We'll chant: 'I'll see you in the car park', but we'd rather see you in the pub!" Ferris jokes. But his statement sums up the attitude of everyone present. Occasionally the wrong thing gets said, or rather yelled, but they are all hockey lovers, and they want to enjoy the rivalry, not have a literally violent or genuinely abusive environment. "I heckle Ice players, then I remember that I actually like them personally and I feel bad for about two seconds," says Nads. "Then they do something else and it's OK!" He bemoans the fact that Matt Armstrong has hung up his "fancy" white skates, reducing the ammunition he has to hurl at the Ice star. "We all hit each other up on Facebook ... but at the end of the day we're all in it for the same thing, and that's love of the game, love of the teams," says Samuel.

It is the accessibility to players and administrators which still impresses and amazes these fun-loving über-fans. Nads says he was a little "starstruck" at first and kept his distance from players on road trips. "But then you start getting along with trainers and they go 'oh no, come in' and you have a drink after the game and at the airport." Damian Bright was the first Mustangs player Nads met at an after-match function. He now sponsors the defenceman, and sees him socially; they are mates. Ferris has experienced the same welcome from Ice. "You're kind of not expecting it. They open the door and the next thing the president is there, the committee is there, players are there and shit's getting loose! I used to think it was a cop-out that people, when asked 'what do you like best about Melbourne Ice?' would say: 'it's the family atmosphere'. But it is like a family. You come as a fan, then you meet friends and all of a sudden, bang, the whole team is your family."

Nads is frustrated by those who blindly advocate an AIHL rush to growth. "I don't understand why all of a sudden people are saying: 'Why isn't it at Rod Laver Arena every week?' You start getting tens of thousands of people in and you're going to lose the element of going back to the pub and talking to the guys." Sam agrees. "Bit by bit the sport is getting bigger. Maybe the Icehouse isn't big enough, but at the same time the sport itself isn't big enough. Once a season a derby at Rod Laver (Arena) would be amazing. But it would probably be more beneficial to increase the other rinks first. Stabilise everyone else, get the crowds ..."

Ferris came to hockey in 2010, when he heard an ad on radio, surely some of the best money ever spent by the Icehouse. "I got about ten of my mates together, we cruised down and probably ten minutes into the first period I bought two memberships, a jersey and a hockey stick ... I've been here ever since." Nads had been an NHL fan. He was brought to his first game by Ice fans. "I've always been anti the blue team, so I didn't follow Ice. I think the Mustangs came up as a suggested page when they were doing exhibition games, then I came to the first game."

Both fan leaders are keen on building the growing culture of the rivalry, and excited by the development of the sport they love. "I remember when we first started going you'd be lucky if two or three bays were three quarters full (at Mustangs games)," recalls Nads. "Now even lower end games the place is packed. I see people from school and say 'how long have you been into hockey?' and they say they found out about it on Facebook or something. It's growing immensely."

DJ Ferris, Adam "Nads" Van Bael, Samuel Hochneck, Justin Kuyken and Bradley Lynch taper for the finals.

They are all aware that they might be enjoying a golden age of the game in Melbourne. Sam says he was taken aback when the drum he takes to every game was signed by the entire Mustangs line-up, including the President, as a sign of appreciation. "That drum is one of my most prized possessions, dumb as it sounds. It's little things like that. If you start a fan club for an AFL team they don't care." "That's the kind of thing we're going to lose as the sport gets bigger," opines Ferris. "This kind of thing will never be seen again by the future generation of hockey fans."

Because they have access to the players and administrators, these supporters understand the realities of the league. "The whole pay-to-play situation, I think that's what drives away so many of these players," says Sam. "You've got that generation of players now who are moving into having kids, saving for houses, buying houses and it comes down to financially moving on with their life or their 'amateur career'."

All present are hoping for an all-Melbourne decider, and predicting it. "I think the ultimate win for this year would be a Melbourne-Melbourne grand final and the Mustangs come out on top," Sam says. "I think there's nothing more that will build Melbourne ice hockey than not only to have grand final but for the underdog to take it out."

Ferris has to depart for a DJ shift. The Mustangs fans are off to watch training, after dinner at the Groovetrain and maybe another beer or three. The rivals part, keen for each other's company over finals weekend.

THURSDAY THE 28TH (2)

At the end of the first period of the final Melbourne derby, I strayed near the Mustangs bench, in search of a photo. I ran into Stangs forward Andrew Fitzgerald on the stairwell behind the bench. "What have you done to yourself?" I asked, smiling, full of the exhilaration of the occasion.

Then I saw his eyes. The affable 24-year-old forward, who is usually smiling, was close to tears. His arm was in a sling. He had damaged his shoulder in a big hit in a corner, which few people had noticed. He was going to miss the rest of the season. There was no mistaking the diagnosis: 'Fitzy' is a myotherapist. He had 'done' his other shoulder in a similar hit. The look in his eye said: "No, there is no hope".

Two weeks later, almost to the minute, 8.30 pm on a Thursday night, we are sitting not far from where I encountered Andrew that fateful night. He is smiling as he usually does. But he remains crestfallen. "It is frustrating. You definitely want to be part of the team, especially in finals, the first time in finals. And I've been with the Mustangs since we started four years ago. We've hit our goal and you're not part of it, or you're part of it but you're not playing. I started when I was seven, and there's a few guys on the team I have played with since then."

Such an injury costs more than finals appearances. "I'm not working. It's lucky I teach pilates. But there's no hands-on myotherapy work." In two weeks he sees the surgeon, and in all likelihood he will go under the knife shortly thereafter, which will mean he misses three months of work. He is partly covered by fundamental insurance taken out by the league, but he knows he's in for a financial hit. "It's getting to that stage now, especially being a little older and living out of home and renting and trying to save for a house, it does impact. If I go and get this fixed, do I just not come back next year and play local league? You're still at risk of being injured but it's just not at that high level."

Andrew is trying to stay involved. "I just go down and have a bit of a chat to the guys, see what the feel is. I'll have a chat with Brad and see if I can dress for the finals, just to be on the bench. I'll see if that is an option or if not. If not, I'll just sit with my parents in the crowd."

He feels that the "chemistry" between the Mustangs foundation kids will be of benefit in the finals. "You don't have to think what the other player's going to do, you just know. The coach sometimes yells at you for not talking enough, but when you've played with a guy for fifteen years you just know what he's going to do!" Everything has been accelerating for the Mustangs in their rapid ascent over the past two seasons. Attendance has "gone through the roof". Off the ice attention is also increasing. "This year more so than ever, social media has played a big part. It's the first year where we're saying 'OK, maybe we shouldn't accept everybody who asks to be your friend'. We started to filter that a bit more."

To Andrew, the number one issue facing Australian hockey is "definitely" the lack of good facilities. After 17 years in the sport, he has played in the fancy Icehouse at AIHL level, for only three seasons. He has played 51 Mustangs games in total. The future is long when you are 24. But mortgage payments beckon.

Injured Mustangs forward Andrew Fitzgerald.

THURSDAY THE 28TH (3)

A few metres away across the grandstand, Melbourne Ice forward Austin McKenzie is watching the Mustangs train ahead of his team's final session of the season. He says he has been excited by the "camaraderie of the group" this year, after Ice made a concerted attempt to unify. "There just seems to be no conflicts, everybody seems to be on the same page, everybody is here for the same cause. We come to the rink and we want to be here, we enjoy being here."

Austin confirms that Ice had a big wake-up call last season. "Check your egos at the door," is the message that emerged. "We're happy to spend time with any number of guys on the team and we all just get along. I don't know, something has just clicked and it feels good."

Some people, wherever they live, are predisposed to hockey. Austin, from Frankston, is one of them. He tried Aussie Rules and soccer and "just didn't have the same passion" for them as for hockey. "When I first started my parents didn't even think ice hockey existed in Australia. Because I said to them straight off that I was really interested in this. I played inline for a long time and then made a natural progression to ice hockey and I've really never looked back, I've loved it since I started."

Eventually Austin tried his luck overseas, moving to the Ontario Hockey Academy on his own, when he was 15. "From growing up being the go-to player, the top guy in my age group ... You go over and play in Canada and you're a middle-of-the-pack to low standard of player and you have to change the whole way you play. It's just a big slap in the face. You're not the best. That was a huge thing for me when I went over there. Once you accept that fact and you realise it, you're able to continue to develop to become a better player." Most AIHL-class locals have now had experience overseas and learnt this indispensable lesson. "I had my 18th birthday over there, so I pretty much became an adult and independent by myself. It forces you to grow up and mature

Rising Ice forward Austin McKenzie.

pretty quickly."

Now that he is back in Australia, Austin looks to imports to help continue his development. "Personally, they set the standard for myself. The majority of them [imports] these days have played some type of professional hockey, which is what we all aspired to when we were growing up. It gives you an idea of where you want to be at, where you should be at."

Austin has thrived under Brent Laver, his points-scoring and influence increasing with the more responsibility he has been given. He appreciates his coach's support. "It makes you want to improve, it makes you want to strive to be better, it makes you want to make an impact on the team. You want to be a go-to guy, you want to be able to be relied upon."

Austin knows many of the Mustangs. Is the Melbourne rivalry all it is cracked up to be? "No the rivalry is definitely there. I'm great friends with a lot of the guys on the Mustangs and I think that's really good. We're great friends off the ice. On the ice it's completely different. So, so many players I grew up alongside or against are playing with the Mustangs. I absolutely have a blast playing the Mustangs, the rivalry is definitely there on and off the ice. As soon as gameday comes around we're not great friends, but as soon as the final siren goes we're all back."

I'm glad I didn't drink with the fans at Harbourtown. The final training sessions of the Mustangs and Ice are a merry-go-round of excited personalities and vivid impressions and I need my faculties clear-windowed. After speaking with Andrew Fitzgerald and Austin McKenzie, I find some news on my phone about Ice's line-up. Ice goalie Gustaf Huth is out of the playoffs, having been diagnosed with "an eye and an ear infection, which affects his vision and balance, and therefore his ability to perform the duties of a goaltender at the highest levels." I remember Gustaf missing games in Perth back in April with an ailment which sounds very similar. He's never had a clear run at it on this trip, ending up playing eleven games through a combination of his ill-health and Jaden Pine-Murphy's fine form. It has been an incredible experience for the 22-year-old Swede, nonetheless. Johan, his landlord and housemate, is also laid low by illness, and is conspicuously absent at the Ice training session.

Watching their charges train, Mustangs management are contemplating Brad Vigon's final choice of personnel for the weekend. Andrew McDowell doesn't envy the coach his job of telling those who have missed out. He has a quote ready if aggrieved personnel approach him: "Oh, you want the complaints department!"

"There's always a hard luck story this time of year," says Mick Burslem. Fraser Carson's dad Jeremy notes that Pat O'Kane has missed half a lecture to be on time for this training session. "He never does that. He's not a local, but he wants this as much as anyone." Andy McDowell is happy to have the Dogs in the semis. He thinks Brave could be very hard to beat when they are on an "emotional high" on Saturday, but if they win they might fall flat on Sunday.

Ice players arrived early so they could have a 45-minute session with Anthony Klarica, the sports psychologist from the reigning AFL premier Hawthorn, who helped Ice set their goals at their pre-season training camp. Afterwards, I have a brief chat with Matt Armstrong, asking him what changed for Ice over the course of the year. "I would have to say maturity. As a team obviously at the start of the season we were still trying to feel people out, fill lines out, and we've been learning lessons throughout the year. I would like to say we had a perfect season, but we didn't. We were up and down, but I think we learnt a lot of lessons doing that." He says beating the Ice Dogs in Sydney in July was the "turning point" to Ice's season. In 2013, Ice couldn't beat the physical Dogs anywhere, let alone away from home. On that July Sunday in 2014, they were coming off a loss in Newcastle and their only win of the month had been over the listing Bears at home. "There was a bit of a losing streak so we needed to turn things around in order to keep ourselves in the playoff hunt. The coach put it on us to work hard together and get the job done that night. So it was a gritty win." Matt says Ice plays the same in all of its wins - with input from all comers. If they do that again, he believes they can get past Brave.

At the end of the Mustangs training session, hardcore fans and insiders afford the squad generous applause. It is the first time all year I've heard anything like it at a training session. "This week has gone glacially slowly," says coach Brad Vigon. He's putting the finals team up on Facebook on Friday, as usual. He says the temptation is to try a new drill, to cover something else, one more thing, just in case. But if it isn't right by now, you're just confusing things and introducing doubt.

I meet his Ice counterpart Brent Laver not long after. He is glad to have work to keep him busy tomorrow. "We are as ready as we could be, we've got into a position to give ourselves the best opportunity," he says. He also "just wants it to start". Ice go on to the rink with an exuberant whoop. Their session is assured, fast and loud. As usual for Ice, it's as much about maintaining high spirits as fine-tuning strategy. Chris Wong, who has been out of the line-up since round nine, May 31, when his shoulder was crunched in Canberra, gets on the ice, obviously still ginger, but part of the team.

Ice patron Josh Puls is also watching training. Close to the bench, he's a touch stately, in a long overcoat and scarf over his suit. What is a patron, I ask? Is it defined in the Ice constitution? Josh

PRIOR TO 2014, THE MUSTANGS HAD WINNING RECORDS AGAINST ONLY THE CANBERRA KNIGHTS AND THE SYDNEY BEARS, AND THEY HAD ONLY BEATEN MELBOURNE ICE AND THE SYDNEY ICE DOGS ONCE IN REGULATION TIME.

says the role of patron was the idea of his presidential successor Andy Lamrock. The committee came to him with the idea and he was honoured to accept. He only goes on road trips if asked by the coach – and hadn't done so for a couple of years because of the demands of his employment, including an overseas posting. Otherwise, the role is what he makes of it, a fascinating paradox for the advocate of proper governance. The designation would be meaningless if the patron didn't possess Josh's qualities.

He jokes that when Ferris introduced him to new South Pole leader Benny - when Ferris was needed as announcer – he started asking questions of Benny like: "Who are you? What do you believe?" He wants to get to the essence of a person, it's a compulsion.

"I am so proud of the team this year because it has been a values-based effort," he says. Watching his happy 'kids', I agree with his contention that they are "ready and confident". Josh differs from the fans at the pub by saying that the "stress" of a Melbourne Derby final would be too much for him. He would prefer to play any other team than the Mustangs if Ice make the decider. He likens it to Collingwood being in an AFL grand final – the idea they could win is so bad that he would prefer they didn't make it, even though the joy of beating them would be so great.

Josh makes his customary "Come on Melbourne!" cry at end of training. He hasn't found need to alter it since the second Melbourne team joined the competition. Ice finishes training at 10.40 pm, twenty minutes early. There is nothing to be gained by more practice. It is time to decide the winner of the 2014 season.

Josh introduces me to Stephanie, his sister, who was media officer for the club in Oakleigh days when there were only newspapers to court, with their coveted, limited spaces. Well-mannered, witty people, the Puls siblings are also staunch and passionate, an ideal combination for club leadership. They are as likely to ask a question as give an opinion, to listen as to speak. Yet they are up for a chat, old-fashioned conversationalists curious about the eternal verities, the only topics that never go out of style, regardless of facilities or technologies. Personality. Character.

Josh, like Mick Burslem's partner Colleen Nash, and the Websters, demands to give me a ride home.

FRIDAY THE 29TH

The ever-innovative Brave are getting a feel for the Icehouse with a late afternoon training run. Ice insider Ian Webster and trainer James Meredith are also in attendance. Ian says "CBR are good for the league and great for the sport". Ice love making the finals a commando mission; James has a busy couple of days ahead of him, this scouting session the first part of it.

For CBR Brave Chairman Peter Chamberlain, sitting halfway up the grandstand watching his charges prepare for their first finals series, there is time for some reflection on an incredible season. "Early in the year we thought we don't have to win a game as long as we don't have any blowouts. Then probably after game two or three, it was about doing better than we did last year, which was not difficult: two wins. Then it was 'hang on, maybe we can win more games than we've ever won before'. Achieved that. Then we reset that goal about six or seven weeks out to 'finals or bust'. If we didn't make the finals with where we were, it was going to be a failure of a season." The Brave brains trust went to the team with that attitude and "to a man" they agreed. Finals or bust. And like every other target Brave set this year, it was achieved. No bust. Now what?

"Finals are a whole different experience," Peter says. "You get a couple of lucky calls and all of a sudden you've won a grand final. You miss one here, you miss one there, hit a post instead of putting the puck in the net, and you're out in straight sets. Now it's really about performing at our best, and what will be, will be."

One player who could be forgiven for not performing at his best is hobbled star forward Mathieu Ouellette, who has torn the anterior cruciate ligament in his knee, a setback usually requiring months of rehabilitation. But Peter says Mathieu has previously recovered miraculously from a similar injury, he has trained twice this week and his knee has been expertly strapped. Mathieu has a "bit of a limited range of motion", Peter concedes, but if he can walk after training he will be playing against Ice in the semi-final.

Peter believes his squad matches up well with Ice and he's expecting a fast, exciting game of hockey in their semi-final. If Brave gets past Ice, there's the daunting prospect of the Mustangs ("stellar" this year) or the Ice Dogs, something of a bogey team for CBR in 2014. However, it is a fact of life for someone in Peter's position that he has to look much further ahead than the attention-hogging finals. And thankfully for

Old mates: Ice's Tom Harward and Mustang Andy McDowell.

Brave, the executive has already signed trainer and team builder Lee Campbell and marketing gurus Coordinate for the upcoming season. Ensuring a sustainable future comes down to principles being followed by all the successful clubs. "You look at the top three teams this year and you look at their administration, their volunteers, their governance and all those little things they do ... The top three teams all do that very, very well. Then you've got the Sydney Ice Dogs who've just got a very capable team they've put together and one or two guys doing a hell of a lot of work to keep them going."

Not surprisingly, given how successful Brave's marketing has been, Peter believes it should be a priority for the entire league. "I think the league needs to employ a marketing team that would work on behalf of all clubs and provide all clubs with the help to gain further funds and better exposure. If you put money into something like a marketing team you're going to create more money again."

Peter is in talks with his rink and the government about improving safety and seating and installing plexiglas around the arena. While upgrading the facility is crucial for Brave, there is another big issue. "Recruitment will be the big one for us for the next three years. We have a lack of depth in younger players. There's not a whole lot of hockey that gets played at a reasonable level over the age of sixteen through to the age of about 20 in Canberra."

It's a measure of Brave's appeal to its community that Peter feels his club had *too many* volunteers earlier in the year, a rare problem. "So we're very much taking a leaf out of John Belic's book from the Mustangs for next year and you won't get to be an official volunteer without basically going through an interview process and earning a job."

On my way out of the Icehouse, I run into Robert Bannerman. The commissioner is tired, and he's angry. The promotional material for placement at the rink has not arrived, for the second day in a row. The last opening on the Henke rink, where sponsor's logos need to be stuck to the boards, is gone, and the rink is now booked solid until 1.00am. And then from 6am. If the material arrives, he will, for the second year in a row, spend his finals-eve sticking banners on the boards in the middle of the night. The AIHL is nothing if not hands-on. But Robert sighs, then relaxes. "I hope the fans just see hockey [and not the effort that goes into it] and drink lots of beer."

Lee Campbell marshalls the Brave troops at the Icehouse.

SATURDAY THE 30TH
SEMI-FINALS

The warmest, most exuberant weather of the winter greets hockey fans entering Docklands for the semi-finals. Cloudless, still, bright, the scene demands a carnival atmosphere, and the gathering tribes provide it. The rink surrounds – a gaudy mini-fun-fair, guarded by a [model] Tyrannosaurus Rex, beneath an observation wheel, overseeing a pub – make it hard to frown. The ATC crew are roving the precinct like digital minstrels, accosting hockey fans, who are asked to watch the Del Basso headstand celebration on an iPad and provide an alternative commentary for the cameras. James Morgan, Jaffa Watson, Michael Clough, Stephen White and crew are all gleaming with enjoyment, revelling in this day, trying to enhance it as much as possible. I can tell they know exactly how I feel from their question: "How much did you sleep last night?" It was four hours for me, luxurious compared to Robert Bannerman, who was here until 3.30am sticking those overdue banners on the boards, or ATC, who were setting up their new-fangled finals features. None of us are playing the games, and not all of us are barracking for a specific team, but we are all heavily invested in trying to capture whatever is about to happen.

I'm told the big issue of the week has been the referees refusing to wear microphones. They wore them briefly at the start of the season, and it enhanced the broadcasts. Jaffa is sympathetic, saying they needed time to practice with them before being put under scrutiny during the finals. James Morgan is not impressed – hearing the rationale behind decisions adds depth to the coverage, and anything too blue will be edited out of the Fox Sports replays. There will be a significant live audience on the internet today, however, especially in Canberra.

There's an element of joyful ordeal about finals. My week has been overloaded with hockey, just as I wanted it, but there is a drilling need for it all to start. One's veins are stale from unused adrenaline. You peak before the event starts, then you're too consumed to register your exhaustion. The super-fit players who best resist this insidious affliction – a weariness born of too much alertness – will win. The grand final is a distant journey that cannot be contemplated until today's explorations of uncharted territory have been completed. As happens with the best travel experiences, this weekend's minutes are hours, they are so filled with novelty and action.

On Facebook this morning the Mustangs offered: "Today is the day we have been waiting for. Today is the day we go further than we've ever gone before!" Canberra and the Mustangs have gone further than before just by playing finals. Their fans are not missing the moment. A rebel merchandise stall operates out of a shopping trolley on the Dinosaur commons opposite the rink entrance, selling vividly orange Mustangs FINALS T-shirts. Busloads of Bravehearts wander to their second bay eyrie in full garb, one or two going so far as donning kilts, many extravagantly face-painted. The tiger-suit fan has his feline head, but he is also clad in tartan. If former quasi-Aussie Mel Gibson had not taken on Scottish history in a blockbuster drama at the end of the film age, an ice hockey semi-final in Melbourne, Australia would not have been decorated by a Highland warrior theme unintended by management when they revived the club, with ingenuity and defiance, much like a fierce Scottish clan. God bless popular culture.

Ice and Mustangs fans are already standing behind the South Pole goals, heavily adorned. Chintzy top hats are in vogue for Ice fans; Stangs fans have ramped up their eye-threateningly vivid orange. John Belic on Facebook: "Regardless of the game results this weekend one thing is certain, this [season] has been a truly amazing experience …"

The ATC crew roams the Icehouse precinct.

The Mustangs rebel merch stand opposite the rink.

Sasky Stewart untangles the AIHL finals.

Early, I am drawn to the hallway under the stand, where the four teams have their dressing rooms. Its gatekeepers are Stavros, a genial Stangs fan volunteer, and Sasky Stewart, the "first lady of Australian hockey" as named by Yahoo's *Puck Daddy* blog and a *Hockey Night in Canada* commentator. Sasky is small, with a splash of bright orange hair, and she does not stop talking and moving – fidgeting, flashing her hands about elaborately, practically dancing on the spot as we have our overdue first conversation. Sasky is well named – she embodies 'sass'. Her responsibility today is the administration of a tangle of lanyards for players and officials, but being located so centrally, she fields questions about warm-ups, game times and "the running sheet" from coaches, players and officials, which she handles with aplomb. Andrew Petrie, wired, expectant, says in his charming, wry way, "You are the source of all truth?" Sasky replies: "If I don't know it, I'll find it out for you".

Sasky worked for the league for two years in 2010-2011, and clearly has event-planning abilities she could put on her CV alongside her digital marketing expertise and legal training. Such energetic, enthusiastic, multi-talented individuals are gold to volunteer organisations and seem drawn to hockey of late. But Sasky has been around longer than most. She fell in love with the sport when watching a Stanley Cup playoff match in 2003. A star who was knocked out returned to score the winning goal. Immediately she felt "this is the greatest game in the world!" Hailing from rural Queensland, the most non-hockey environment imaginable, Sasky first encountered the local brand via the late lamented Gold Coast Blue Tongues, whom she chronicled with a book of photographs in 2008. She has been involved with the Mustangs just this year since moving to Melbourne, but has completely embraced the orange. She returns to Canada shortly, after several previous stints in the home of hockey. Chatting to her, I have fluked into the nerve centre of semi-final day.

John Belic comes by and adds a live quote to his morning statement. "It's like my wedding day. It'll be over like that, and I'll be saying 'What happened?' " He's also smiling broadly. Ice junior Sam Hodic, who probably won't get shifts today, is blithely confident. "We'll do it today and then tomorrow," he says. Why wouldn't you be confident when you are freshly 18? He has just started playing without a cage helmet.

Ice team manager Tom Harward's excitement is less obvious, but a wry grin from him equals uncontrolled hysteria from anyone else. He says Ice will be getting rubdowns during the first semi-final, upstairs in the gym. James Meredith has brought in four colleagues and extra tables. Tom has the air of someone confident his team is doing all the right things to ensure success.

I leave Sasky to her duties and join Kristian at our seats, which turn out to be on the red line, halfway up the stand, perfect. I have never sat in the belly of the beast like this. It feels ordained.

The sound system booms "Who Let the Dogs Out?" as the Ice Dogs go through their pre-match paces at the south end. Down here, the bass is fearsome.

Things are different for the finals. The platform at the rink's far left is occupied by bright lighting rectangles where the Fox commentators complete their pre-game chat. The VIP area stretches around either side of the penalty box opposite the grandstand, tables adorned with miniature cardboard player cut-outs. And instead of a sponsor or volunteer dropping the puck, here is hockey's man of the year himself, Nathan Walker. Robert Bannerman introduces him as "the man who put Aussie hockey on the map", and he receives thunderous, unanimous applause, maybe the first clue to just how much his personal achievement has meant to the real local hockey fans. Walker's presence having united the crowd, it is now time for division.

Puck drop, first semi-final, Mustangs v Ice Dogs. It's everything one expects, immediately. The Dogs hit hard, the Mustangs skate hard. The fans call *"Darryl!"* – and local identity Darryl Hamilton is not reffing, and it's an offside, the linesman's call – but the call offers a chance for a laugh to break the tension.

Mustang forward Brendan McDowell hits the crossbar, then there's a weird bounce, a big rebound and Jeff Grant slams home a goal from the high slot. 1–0 to the Mustangs less than five minutes in. Fraser Carson makes his first save shortly thereafter, and the local fans are buoyant. The Dogs ice the puck four times, and Jamie Bourke has three hacks at a loose puck in Tim Noting's crease, the Swedish net-minder diving full length, creating a swishing chaos which somehow keeps the puck out of the net. It slides past the goal slowly, like a sullen teenager trying to act cool.

Ian Webster catches up with Nathan Walker.

The NHL draftee's second job? Puck-dropper.

The vivid Mustangs end of the Icehouse.

Then Sydney score. It doesn't matter how much possession you dominate if you cough the puck up mid-ice. Halfway through the period, the Dogs accept the Mustangs donation, race in on a two-on-one and Mitch Bye flips the puck over Fraser Carson's shoulder to level the scores at one. Momentum shifts entirely, and the Dogs press, forcing a huge save from Fraser. There's a penalty on the play, and early in the subsequent powerplay, Ice Dogs import John Clewlow uses a short, sharp pass from behind the net to set up David Dunwoodie, who snipes it home from close range. Goal. The Ice Dogs lead the Mustangs 2–1. The Mustangs spurn their own powerplay opportunity before the break. They go to the rooms at the end of the first period having outshot the Dogs 13–8, but trailing 1–2. Thus the pattern of the match is established. Whatever the home town Mustangs do to delight their raucous mob, the defiant, efficient Dogs match to amplify their small but vocal contingent.

The drama meets all expectations. After so many people looked forward to this final so much, knowing there was so little between the teams, it feels unavoidable. The teams cannot escape each other's competitive embrace, or the gravity of the high stakes on offer, and their fierce push-me-pull-you is creating a thrilling equilibrium. At the start of the second period, the Mustangs strike through Jamie Bourke, who glides clear and buries a wrist shot past Tim Noting's ear, then Joey Hughes pulls the puck out of a goalmouth scramble and flings it into the net on the powerplay, the goalie left sprawled and grasping. 3–2 Mustangs.

The Stang, who, having removed his horse's head, is Tristain Cole, turns and faces his constituency, "WE ARE …" "MUSTANGS!" comes the reply, over and over. The room is at a simmer. The refereeing is exemplary, no pedantic calls interrupting the increasing tempo. Here comes that end-to-end hockey we were expecting, good chances at the end of each team's rushes. Here's Vinnie Hughes diving full length to get a stick on a half-chance stretch pass. Here's Fraser Carson roaming out of his net all too fearlessly for nervous Mustangs fans. Here's Sean Jones in alone on Tim Noting but almost too close too soon, and stopped.

I write the note "Joey saved, huge pressure. They need to convert," but the Mustangs do not score. That would be too easy; this is going to the wire. The Mustangs go in after two periods leading 3–2, and there is confidence on their portion of the terrace. Between periods, ATC vox pops are the only entertainment apart from booming music, which gives the fans some respite, and a chance to discuss the state of their dreams.

THE TEAMS CANNOT ESCAPE EACH OTHER'S COMPETITIVE EMBRACE, OR THE GRAVITY OF THE HIGH STAKES ON OFFER, AND THEIR FIERCE PUSH-ME-PULL-YOU IS CREATING A THRILLING EQUILIBRIUM.

No-one wants their attention taken from the contest.

Mustangs' dreams feel foolish early in the third. The Dogs throw a renewed effort at the hosts, and for the first time in the game, the Mustangs are just holding on. Retiring scoring superstar Simon Barg is working triple time, his brilliant first line pushing hard against the Mustangs' third line. Inevitably, there's a big rebound on a good slapshot and John Clewlow is right on the angle to slap it into the net before Fraser can get across. 3–3.

The Mustangs are going to have to do something special to win now. As a final should be, it is a searching test. They finally get some action on Noting's net, Brendan McDowell just missing; then a lethal pass just eludes Jamie Bourke's stick when he is wide open. But the brilliant provocateur will still have his say. With 11.21 left, scores tied at three, Jamie Bourke slashes Tim Noting. There's nothing much in it, but it's needless, and deserves sanction. But has Jamie's infamous volatility worked in his team's favour? David Dunwoodie flies the flag and also gets penalised. It's four on four instead of a powerplay for the Dogs, just when they had the Mustangs worried.

I see Ice's Ian Webster and Johan Steenberg – sporting a tightly wound scarf around his sore throat – on the balcony above the South Pole, watching intently, silent. The rest of the rink is hollering, gasping, shuddering. You could pick-pocket every crowd member at this moment, so focused is their attention. At 9.37, Ice Dog Aussie young gun Billy Cliff hits the post. At 8.33, Simon Barg looks to have been tripped while charging mid-ice, and Andrew Petrie stands on the top of the boards demanding the call. Life-loving, charming and wry is Andrew. And also remarkably dexterous, it seems. Twenty seconds later the Mustangs surge back, Pat O'Kane's hustle and Jamie Bourke's superb backhand pass setting up Viktor Gibbs-Sjodin in the high slot. He's been given space - an Ice Dog change gone wrong? Viktor smashes a one-timer and it sears past Tim Noting.

4–3 Mustangs, 8.10 to go. It feels like the Mustangs have come through the flames. They now have questions for the Ice Dogs to answer. And at 6.45, it is again Pat O'Kane with the grunt work, Jamie Bourke with the exquisite backhand pass, a short one this time, and Viktor Gibbs-Sjodin with the finish, this time a deft backhand. Import to Aussie to Import. Glorious hockey, three touches in close through a desperate, well positioned defence, the goalie pulled from one post to the other. 5–3. There is Mustangs delirium in the stands. Surely the final five minutes are for celebration, with the Dogs looking flat after the double strike.

THE FIRST SEMI-FINAL PITS FAIRYTALE AGAINST FAIRYTALE.

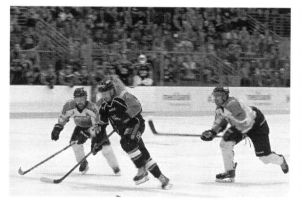

The first semi-final remained up for grabs until its final seconds.

But to use the phrase now familiar to me from years of working in breaking online news, there is "More To Come". With three minutes left, Andrew Petrie pulls his goalie to gain the man advantage. The resulting pressure draws a Mustangs penalty, and the Dogs coach calls a timeout. It is the perfect call. His charges regroup, with nothing to lose, and a two-man advantage, and Simon Barg stuffs in his ugliest, but most important goal of the season. The Mustangs lead 5–4 with 2.11 remaining. The Icehouse rocks, many Ice fans supporting their arch-rivals. The Mustangs, the attacking force that loves to keep moving forward as fast as possible, must defend for all they are worth if they are to make the grand final. This simple truth tests them completely. Can they hold their nerve, their discipline?

The Dogs, with the extra skater, but an empty net, must be patient but frantic in search of the equaliser. Viktor Gibbs-Sjodin blocks a shot with 1.20 left. He's playing his heart out performing at a higher level than at any time during the year. It is aeons until 0.39, when the Mustangs are called for icing. The tension makes Kristian and I laugh and shake our heads. It's a "How good is this?" moment. The Stangs neutralise the draw, and somehow Viktor finds Jamie Bourke mid-ice. A defenceman tries to go with him, but the born forward kills a second or two then he sends the puck into the empty net from outside the blue line, and the Mustangs into the grand final. 6–4.

The bedlam that erupts means it is probably a good thing the upstarts did not have the game won earlier. There are only 36 seconds of untroubled bliss left in game time, then a few minutes as the players shake hands and acknowledge the grateful, ecstatic crowd as *Glory Days* plays; it could not have been a better outcome for the Mustangs. They got the win, slaying a mighty foe after being tested in every way, and they didn't get to be rock stars for too long.

Downstairs, Nathan Walker is chatting to Brent Laver and Ice team doctor Peter Moores as I rush to grab some words from the victors. I overhear him say "I am usually back by now". He leaves September 7 to start his Washington Capitals adventure. While he is here, he is getting around all the teams, a class act. At the Mustangs enclave, everyone is excited, beaming, confident. Pat confesses that he was nervous, and had "hard hands" early in the game. You could run the rink off the energy buzzing between fans, players and officials outside the rooms.

Interviewed moments later, Mustangs captain Sean Jones admits his team was nervous in their first final. "We got that first goal, but then they scored one and we were gripping the sticks a bit tight." However, the team now has the firepower and strategies to stop one goal becoming a disaster. "In the early years getting scored on meant a team was starting to run over us and one turned into two turned into three turned into four and we couldn't seem to stop that flow. Ever since Brad came on board, we can score just as many as they score. If they score one, it's heads up, back to work next shift."

Sean was impressed with his team's willingness to put their bodies on the line for the cause in the final minutes, when they chose to block shots when outnumbered by two men. It is these sorts of sacrifices which will determine their fate. "We got to this point by doing what we know how to do, what we've worked on all year," he says. "All of a sudden Joey doesn't need to do it all himself or we don't need the defencemen taking it all the way and scoring ... because that's not what Mustangs hockey is. Keep doing the little things and hopefully we get the 'W' tomorrow."

The Mustangs will try to keep things as normal as possible ahead of their grand final. Teams meditate upon semis for a week, but have less than 24 hours to get their heads around the decider, perhaps a blessing. Sean says the players do notice the support they are getting. "I definitely noticed it when the Viktor chant went up after he scored! I think we have some of the best fans that I've seen; especially considering it's such a small sport in Australia ... You look up and see a sea of orange. There's nothing better after getting a goal than hearing that roar."

Kristian and I regroup upstairs in the St Moritz bar, alongside the ATC crew. Jaffa Watson is a kid in a candy store, his love of hockey palpable. I ask him about mentoring Brent. "Can't fault his character and as a coach he's going to get better and better," he says. Fascinatingly, he reveals that Brent had the same dark night of the soul moment during the season as Brad. "There was a moment when Brent said 'What am I doing here? I'm missing my kids' sport and the players are not listening to me'." Brent's despair seems way behind him now. Jaffa has been asked down to the rooms prior to the game. I ask why Brent wanted him there. Jaffa replies, "He said 'because you're an old fart and it'll make them laugh!' "

I make a pass through the teams area, and Brent is chatting with Andrew Petrie, old friends and opponents catching up, minutes before the former's first AIHL final as coach, an hour after the latter's first AIHL (losing) final as coach.

Announcer Greg Spaetgens' usually soothing voice sounds under pressure during the warm-ups for the second semi-final, six 'WOOOOOS!' after Mustangs goals during the preceding thriller perhaps stretching his vocal limits. Ice fans are chanting

"Go Ice Go" five minutes before the puck drop, and the CBR contingent, occupying a bay usually the Ice's preserve, are rowdy and joyous. The "SOUTH POLE" signs are adhered to the glass, and Lachlan Bell has responded to social media suggestions and dubbed the opposite corner "THE BELL END" with a large banner. Designated Brave fans march down to ice level and hold signs up to their bay. Ice's cyborg-like mascot does the same for the home team. Then he joins president Emma Poynton and a nine-year-old girl in whacking a drum to syncopate the chanting. Amid it all, there are ardent Ice types who still choose to yell "there's only one team in Melbourne!" I notice for the first time that the new ten foot tall Ice player banners have been hidden from view. The Ice's championship banners are prominent enough, hanging next to the scoreboard. Everyone knows they are the league superpower.

I'm looking for signs. Austin McKenzie goes to the bench exhaling hugely, obviously keyed up. The Canberra bench eyes only its own players during the warm-up. The Ice brains trust also watches the Brave. They have prepared their charges as best they can, there's nothing more they can do with them. With more Brave fans than Ice Dog fans in the building and with all four teams fully settled in, the Icehouse is as noisy as I can remember, and we're underway in the second semi-final.

Ice hit Canberra's stellar first line with its youth first; Lliam Webster, Tim Johansson and Jeremy Brown taking first shift, Jason Baclig and Matt Armstrong held back. This year, they are no longer automatically the first line, Brent shifting responsibility to his emerging players. But all the ploys in the world can't stop big, fast CBR star Stephen Blunden. Only Jaden Pine Murphy in the Ice net can. Brave's powerful Canuck somehow gets free in the slot and an open net beckons, but the Ice goalie gets across. Austin is called for an elbow after front-on contact and the CBR powerplay forces saves from "JPM!" which the Ice fans chant after each big save.

Another brilliant Blunden rush is saved, and then Matty rushes back just as potently. "Pitstop!" yell the Canberra fans as their net-minder is pressed into action. It's a pulsating start, with Brave having the better chances. Halfway into the period, Sean Hamilton cracks a slapshot from the point and Tommy Powell is perfectly placed to tip it in. Unstoppable, even for Brave MVP Petri Pitkanen. Against the run of play, Ice lead 1–0.

JPM saves on a Chris McPhail backhand. Is it getting frustrating for Canberra? Matthew Harvey shoves a prone Ice player and gets penalised. The Ice powerplay, best in the league, gets its first chance. And it converts. Tommy, seemingly marooned deep on the goal line, slaps a laser pass through traffic to Todd Graham at the far post. He smashes it past Pitstop from close range, again an unstoppable shot, and Ice lead 2–0 with six minutes left in the first period. Tommy's assist was breathtaking.

Jeff Smith takes a penalty with five minutes remaining. Cue the *"Free Jeff Smith!"* chant, more spontaneous than the orchestrated barracking, and more vociferously indulged by the happy Ice mob. As I watch the CBR stars push for their opening goal, I marvel at Mathieu Ouellette. Slight, crouched, he looks more like a Flemish romantic painter than an elite sportsman, but despite his serious knee injury he glides to great effect, regardless of whatever pain he is feeling. The CBR powerplay has no great effect, however, and there is a huge roar as Jeff is freed from the penalty box.

It is 2–0 to Ice after one period. Ice have had nine shots, Canberra seven. I run into Brad Vigon in the kiosk queue. I say Brave are still in it. "But the Ice goals were really good," Brad says. "It looks like it will be Ice." He says the Mustangs showed composure in their third period. He looks drained yet energised. He's staying switched on, so much more to do. On the way back to my seat, Brave boss Peter Chamberlain says "We're still in it. We've come back from further behind than this." After the season we've had, I am loath to make predictions, but Brave feel like they are doing it on emotion. Today Ice are pretty emotional as well.

The second period opens with Petri Pitkanen forced into a massive pad save. Then CBR gets just what they need, a powerplay, less than two minutes in. But Ice are diligent, team-aware, brisk. They survive their short-handed stint, then Tim Johansson, fresh out of the box, picks up a bouncing puck and tears off on a two-on-one, laying it off perfectly for Matty, who fires it home. Regulation play expertly executed. Ice lead 3–0 four minutes into the second period. They have taken half-chances and scored, and defended stoutly in the face of fierce early attacks. Suddenly their tails are up. Jeremy drives the net. Tim, almost too fast for himself, hurtles menacingly. Ice play like they know another goal now means the game is over. But Stephen Blunden scores! Of course he does, from a nothing angle, moving from behind the net, near-post. 3–1 Ice. The score now accurately reflects the game.

Ice's young-gun line featuring Tim and Jeremy is causing havoc, their aggressive skating ruffling Brave's defence. Another Matthew Harvey penalty. You just can't give Ice this many powerplays. Tommy and Jeremy combine to set up Jeff in his now customary position, close to the net. He takes the millisecond available to pick the right corner. 4–1 to Ice, with eight minutes left in the second period. The South Pole erupts. This goal is a triumph for Brent Laver. Jeff Smith never played forward before this year, and late-arriving Jeremy has become one of the most potent and complete young players in the league. The Ice powerplay unit which scored that goal was unrecognisable from the previous season.

Now there is no doubt Canberra are frustrated. Matt pick-pockets Stephen Blunden at centre ice and the big forward chases him down, and runs through him while he's on his knee. It's nothing vicious, but it is untoward, a rush of blood. Penalty. The better controlled teams are winning these finals. Stephen gets out of the box and reoffends almost immediately. 4–1, 2.18 to go, second period. The room knows this is the moment the former triple champions can win it. Jeremy Brown tries a toe drag. Pitkanen comes up with a big save. Jason Baclig hits the post. Todd Graham can't ... quite ... get ... his stick down on a rebound ... Canberra survive. It remains 4–1 after two periods.

Brave know they can come back, they have done it here before. But Ice will be ready this time. And Canberra cannot afford any more penalties. In the second intermission, I meet

Loud, colourful and passionate: the Ice v Brave semi-final was the most watched in AIHL history.

ubiquitous internet presence Eric Scaresbrook, a first-year fan who has travelled from Sydney. He is sitting but a few seats down; Nick Place is a few seats behind; John Belic a few seats to the left; I am surrounded by hardcore hockey folk. Eric supports the Bears, as evidenced by his red jersey, appropriate given his girth and beard, which makes him resemble an amiable giant of the woods. I wonder if somewhere in the Canadian wilderness a grizzly is wearing an Eric Scaresbrook jersey. Eric is delivering video updates period by period, and will go on to document the finals forensically. Writing about Melbourne, he applauds trams, and the proximity of the Icehouse to the city, and he likes that the hockey community can direct him, connect him to new friends and inform him which pub to go to after the game. Fans this committed this soon are a growing fact of the AIHL. Eric is interviewing players and coaches and chatting with league bosses months after knowing next to nothing about the sport.

On Facebook, Sydney Ice Dogs captain Robert Malloy has already addressed his team's demise. "On behalf of the playing group, thanks to all the volunteers, fans, coaching staff and sponsors that helped throughout the season. It's been a wild ride and we are sorry the cup is not coming back to Sydney. I'm proud of my boys and preparation for next season starts now. Thanks for sticking with us through the dramas. We will be better next year. See you next season. Go Doggies." The Dogs' "preparation for next season" is starting with a hard-earned beer behind the goals, near the Zamboni exit, next to the VIPs. At the first finals series I attended, beaten semi-finalists high-tailed it out of town pronto. This year, everyone wants to be around each other. Everyone wants to see what is going to happen. Everyone wants some more of the racket this big crowd is making.

CBR Brave is asking where people are watching the livestream, a suitably canny question from this progressive club. The answers include Cairns (far north Australia, hundreds of miles from a rink); Germany; Samoa; Czech Republic; Finland, and of course Canada.

Though Ice has out-shot Brave 27–13 and it has been the better team, there is an unresolved tension in the game. The third period is not keen to determine anything in a hurry. It isn't until nearly halfway through the period that there are any more really definite goal-scoring chances for Ice. But Ice are conceding few clear-cut chances themselves. Their three-goal buffer is enough, they don't have to over-commit. They are teaming together superbly. Brave refuse to give in, or even acknowledge the deficit, and their efforts are unrelenting, but

IT WAS ALL ABOUT GETTING TO THE GRAND FINAL FOR THESE GUYS, AMATEUR SPORTSMEN WHO PRESENT LIKE PROFESSIONALS AND PUT THEIR HEART AND SOUL INTO EVERYTHING THEY DO - BRENT LAVER.

the penalties come again as time runs out. The powerplay loosens up both teams. Brave have a gilt-edged shorthanded chance, which leads to a counter-attacking rush. Both goalies are excelling. With 3.17 to go, on the powerplay, and after Anton Kokkonen has been given a game-ending misconduct, Tim Johansson tips in from the crease and it is 5–1. We are in for a derby decider. With 1.36 to play, Jeremy feeds a pass from behind the net and Tommy Powell goes down on one knee from a couple of metres and closing to first-time it into the net for the cherry on top. It is Tommy's hat-trick goal, and Ice's fourth powerplay goal from five opportunities. Canberra, reduced to three men at times in the final minutes, will know where to start their inquest.

The Ice fans are chanting "MELBOURNE". The Mustangs fans are adding "MUSTANGS". It is on already. Ice has won 6–1 to make the grand final against the Melbourne Mustangs. Mid-ice, Canberra players raise their sticks to acknowledge their fans, but supporters of every club take the chance to applaud them for a landmark season. Ice fans deliriously receive their heroes. Jaffa high-fives fans and friends through the glass behind the commentary box. Backstage soon after, Brent jokes that the derby finale is "all for the book!" Metres away, Nathan Walker consoles Mark Rummukainen. A beaming Josh Puls congratulates his coaching staff, saying to Brent: "That is the most fun I can remember having!" He looks like a rapt kid.

Brent tells me that he went back to basics to get a grip on the finals, re-convening with assistant coach Glenn Mayer to assess Ice's season. "It was all about getting to the grand final for these guys, amateur sportsmen who present like professionals and put their heart and soul into everything they do. It was just about giving them the opportunity to be involved in something that's going to be incredible. I mean this derby is just going to be the biggest thing for a long time in Australian hockey and definitely Victorian hockey." Brent sounds almost wonderstruck about where Ice find themselves, and tonight's experience. "Just the noise, the feeling ... I'm just now full of anticipation for what tomorrow holds. I had tingles going up the back of the neck when I drove down the street and saw blue and orange people everywhere. You just can't help but be excited and feel incredibly privileged that you get a chance to be part of it in some small way." His personal preparation won't be restful. "I won't sleep. We'll get straight into recovery, we'll look at tonight's Mustangs game straight away. We just start trying to prepare mentally to go again." Brent praises James Meredith's "phenomenal" work with the team. "To be honest it went to script. In some funny way it all came together." That regime will be replicated tomorrow ahead of the 3pm final.

I ask Brent how he felt after the meeting with sports psychologist Anthony Klarica on Thursday night. "I drove away from that incredibly satisfied just with a small sense of ... relief. The feedback that was coming back through Anthony, I couldn't help but feel that we've made an impact. In some small way we've given something to these guys. That's what today was, you could see it the way they are together. They've really bought in."

Lliam Webster
and Tommy
Powell celebrate
victory in their
customary
manner.

The CBR Brave bay; Josh Puls and Brent Laver celebrate "buy-in".

CBR Brave thanks its fans, and the entire league returns the love.

SATURDAY THE 30TH
SEMI-FINALS (EVENING)

Ice players are preparing meticulously, having been fed at the rink, then transported to Port Melbourne beach for a late night recovery session in the dark and cold. The Mustangs have gone home after socialising briefly, keeping with routine.

Nonetheless, at the Groovetrain restaurant near the Icehouse, there are plenty of AIHL types having a meal and a drink and discussing all things hockey. They are interrupted when Brave players file in, to a standing ovation. CBR have booked an end of the venue and there's nothing but pride in their team's performance despite the disappointing result today.

Brave skipper Mark Rummukainen hails the club's travelling fans, who he believes are the best in the league and the giant strides taken in 2014 by the team. "The biggest thing for us [this year] was the fresh start," he says. "We've got a new board running things and it really gave us a new outlook and a different attitude to everything. This year the guys in the front office really pushed us to win and that has flowed right down to the guys on the ice who want to do everything they can to make that happen. Most of all, it's been a fun year and great ride. We just want to keep it going into next season."

The first person I speak to at the post semi-finals shindig is Mustangs fan leader Nads. By way of greeting, he says "FUUUUUUUUUCK!" He's not being gratuitously blasphemous: the word is uttered in awe of the prospect of the Melbourne derby as grand final, unthinkable to most fans last year, a foolish dream earlier this season. He tells me that during the Mustangs semi-final, Ice South Pole president Ferris went to the Stable, heart of the Mustangs cheer squad, and Nads went to the South Pole, in order to reverse Mustangs fortunes. The Stangs scored, so they stayed in their respective positions. Nads notes enviously that things can be said at the South Pole standing room area that cannot be uttered in the Stable, where the fan is surrounded by the president, children and player's wives.

At the bar, I chat with Nads, Kristian, John Belic, Stan Scott and Perth Thunder co-owner Rob Cox. Two fans, a president, and two team co-owners: it's the AIHL way. Stan gives the lowdown on the "Delly Celly". He says Ric Del Basso had practiced it many times at training, on newly slickened ice, just after the Zamboni finished its sweep. "It was one of his worst efforts!" Stan says of Ric's now famous Icehouse inversion. The ice was snowy, being the end of the game, making it more difficult.

Stan and John gleefully swap stories about the Stang, the league's most visible and interventionist mascot. Stan jokes, "I came here a couple of years ago and there are a couple of hundred people in the rink and a horse's head went by me when I was alone on the bench. I thought 'what the fuck am I doing with my life?!' " John says the Stang is about to retire, needing to spend more time with his kids. He loves Tristain Cole's fervour, and happily tells of trying to keep his mascot's enthusiasm harnessed, using a palms-down gesture meant to convey "simmer down!" He recalls that the Stang went too far once when hassling players in the penalty box. Greg Spaetgens, in the middle of making an announcement, interrupted himself to cry "Stang!" like a stern Dad admonishing a wayward pet. The Stang duly bowed his equine head and desisted.

We won't turn anyone away at the Mustangs, John says proudly. Everyone has a place, everyone finds their role, everyone can be involved. He warms to his theme. "There's no us and them with the Mustangs. It's one for all and all for one." John tells new players that sponsors and fans enable them to get on the ice, so they are to be considered equals. The access fans like Nads enjoy is proof of the policy. It may become more difficult to uphold as the club grows, but it is a strong spiritual basis for a sports club, delivering new fans a hefty serve of one of the buzz-phrases of the year: buy-in.

Stan wants his 2013 star Michael Forney to return to Perth for five years in a job as Western Australian ice sports co-ordinator, a role which currently does not exist. Stan has dreams and makes them grow. He is an entrepreneur, an ideas man. His positivity makes him great company and one of the most popular men in the league. Those with opposing points of view still like him. He believes a 3000-seat stadium would fill up for AIHL hockey "tomorrow" in Perth if available, citing the 27,000 fans who showed up for the international series, which he embraced much more wholeheartedly than any other club in Australia. He believes hockey can do what basketball did in the nineties, with free-to-air TV deals and sellout crowds at 15,000-seat stadiums.

While I am talking hockey with Stan and Rob, John is telling Kristian, who admits to a soft spot for the Mustangs despite being an Ice fan, that "morally" he should barrack for the orange club. John once again details the infamous letter which told him that there wasn't enough talent for two teams in Melbourne. John says he is going to ritually burn that letter when the Mustangs win. He doesn't say that will be tomorrow but it is clear that is the moment he dreams of, as much as the raising of the cup.

Stan has the opposite approach to John's person-by-person recruitment, backing the "big splash" of the international series to expose the game to as many people as possible. He says the massive viewership for incidents like the Delly Celly can be leveraged to land a major sponsor. The AIHL has gone from next-to-nothing to over $200,000 in various sponsorships in a couple of years, which he hails as a tremendous effort. But Stan envisions a major naming rights quantum leap. One sponsor tipping a million dollars per year would take care of the operating costs of every club. Stan Scott is assuredly one of the AIHL's visionary optimists.

Heads high: Brave's 2014 post-mortem was anything but sombre.

SUNDAY THE 31TH
GRAND FINAL

After all the anticipation, and the long, rich Saturday hockey feast, grand final day feels abrupt. As soon as I hit the rink surrounds, I'm saying hello to people. It brings home how many new friends I've made during this project. The further into this league I've gone, the more rewarding it has become. I decide not to haunt the players and coaches under the grandstand today - we have already discussed this electrifying situation, the fifth derby as decider, there is little more to say. As Brent said last night, we just need this game played. So I circumnavigate the rink and visit the toff's section, the VIP area beneath the scoreboard, in order to say hello to commissioner Alex Lata. She is due to leave the country to get married, and because she competed in a half-marathon triathlon last weekend, had her hen's party last night. That meant guest Sara Armstrong had a difficult balancing act, trying to check Twitter for score updates from Ice's semi-final while doing her best to "be there" for Alex's big night.

The VIP section consists of tables just behind the glass at ground level. It would be nothing special but for the great view of the action and in particular the grandstand crowd opposite. One of the unexpected outcomes of having the stand on only one side of the rink at the Icehouse is that most fans don't get to see the extent of the gathering they help form. A gigantic mirror is needed. On this weekend, with the bays packed with the league's loudest, most involved, most colourful fans, the view is indeed privileged.

There is an anteroom for sponsors decked out with four life-sized cardboard cut-outs of AIHL players. Robert Bannerman introduces me to some of the league's benefactors. I realise later that as a hockey-friendly representative from the mainstream media, I'm effectively part of the package the AIHL offers such people, and I should have visited earlier and stayed longer. I still don't fully grasp my position despite my gratitude for the access I've enjoyed.

On the way back, I run into Jeff Klinck, the referee who I first met at 4.30 in the morning at the Imperial Hotel watching the Olympic semi-final between Canada and the US. Then I say hello again to Terry and Janine Graham, Ice defender Todd's parents, who I first met at Liverpool. Terry says whatever the result this fixture is great for hockey. Then there's a grinning but nervous DJ Ferris and journalist Ellie Marie Watts, down from Newcastle. Ice's designer-in-residence Nigel Sherwin is joining the South Pole crew, freed from usual volunteer duties on the door. Ludicrously generous Nigel didn't just offer assistance with this book, he designed everything from Facebook and table banners to advertising hoardings that now festoon the boards of the rink. I wish him all the best. My hand is sore from handshakes, and as a result of Nigel's promotion, for the first time in my life I am experiencing what many of these players and coaches must be getting used to – people I don't know saying hello to me and knowing my name.

I encounter Johan Steenberg, still rugged up to ward off a virus. "This is the best thing that could have happened to Australian ice hockey. If this doesn't get 30 seconds on the TV news ..." he says. (It will not). People greet me and ask 'When will the book be out?' and 'Who are you barracking for?' Nick Place is one of them. He has just blogged that Melbourne fans must get off the fence and choose a team in this grand final. He grudgingly accepts that a journalist can 'barrack for the story'. But the fact is, I am truly unsure of who I want to win. How could I wish disappointment upon Mick Burslem, or Brent Laver, or Emma Poynton or John Belic, or Ian Webster or

Big stakes: a Melbourne derby decider was unthinkable a year ago.

Andy McDowell? Why would I favour Pat O'Kane more than Matt Armstrong or Jaden Pine-Murphy over Fraser Carson? I like and respect them all and both clubs have been open and generous with me. Primarily I am barracking for Australian hockey to thrive. That said, these playoffs feel right for the league, because they feature three of the most stable, financially viable clubs, units resourced by talented, committed volunteers and creative administrators. They set a good example, and in sport, the teams that win set the agenda others mimic. Better to have the best-run clubs winning, not just the best teams.

The other question we are all asking each other is: 'What is going to happen today?' I just answer "overtime". It is hard to imagine that one of these teams could dominate the other with both so heavily motivated and invested. Previous games shouldn't count for much, but the Mustangs must keep their composure and not get penalties as they did in the final derby just two and a half weeks ago. As the younger team with less finals experience, they are more of an unknown quantity and have more to prove. Ice must bring the commanding, not feckless version of themselves; both have been on evidence at different times during the season. The respective semi-finals offer reasons to select either team. The Mustangs had the harder game, but overcame a strong opponent playing well, which must provide confidence, and they have the extra few hours of rest. Ice were at their best and should be self-assured after such a crisp, complete effort. Repeat that, and they will be hard to beat.

I utilise the tunnel under the grandstand to get to my seat. I am either starting to let my privileged status go to my head, or I am feeling comfortable around off-limits spaces. It is intense at the Ice end. Brent and I share a fierce handshake, saying little. The playing group emits an eerie "whoop!" It is a desperate war cry more than an expression of exuberance. This is serious for the fun team. They are pent-up. The Mustangs are already out. I watch Mick and co. proceed to the bench.

As I get to my seat, the drama has a hold of me. I feel like I'm about to play myself. Am I good enough? Can I do this? I have a year of writing and note-taking behind me, a good 'preparation'. Like a player, I have to trust my ability, work hard, stay alert and take my chances ... I wish I had a coach, and a huddle to go to, but I do have Kristian beside me. I ask him to shake my hand. "Will the letter get burned?" he asks, grinning. The anthem is upon us. The players stand on their respective blue lines gazing up at the scoreboard.

Jack McCoy, missing all year from the Mustangs line-up because of his eye injury, stands with Rod Johns, impassively

> IF COACHES PICK UP THAT THEIR TEAM'S MINDSET IS AMISS, THEY ARE USUALLY POWERLESS TO CHANGE IT. WHICH GROUP WILL GALVANISE, WHICH WILL DOUBT?

watching his childhood mates prepare for the biggest game of their lives. On the Ice bench, Brent is chewing hard. The best anthem of the year is completed, the last bars drowned out by the traditional roar from the impatient, but edgy crowd. It's to be former teammates Joey Hughes and Lliam Webster contesting the first face-off.

Grand finals in the sports I have seen are primarily psychological tortures. The stakes are so high that the effect on the groups is impossible to predict. If coaches pick up that their team's mindset is amiss, they are usually powerless to change it. Which group will galvanise, which will doubt? The vagaries of group-think are often beyond all plans and preparation. Address the elephant in the room and sometimes you inflate it. Fans, coaches, even the players themselves are in the grip of mystical forces. Will the nervousness give or take energy from your team?

At the start of this final, Ice, the more experienced team, more accustomed to finals pressure, look like they went to inhale a deep breath and got hit in the solar plexus. The Mustangs stymie their every move, and most Ice rushes die before they cross the red line. The Mustangs are hardly making major inroads either, there is a care to their play, but they are focused and full-lunged in their defence. Ice look like they have been rushed on to the ice two hours early and they are forced to chase.

As part of my rink rounds pre-match, James Morgan set up my laptop in the ATC Productions communications hub next to the bar – a high-ceilinged tangle of cords and impressive

screens and scopes and loudly activating walkie-talkies. The
ATC tech-heads and commentators bantered, playful abuse and
yellled instructions creating a happy chaos. 'Jaffa' addressed the
crew like a coach as he departed for the interview platform at
the far end of the rink, announcing "Will beats skill!"

The Mustangs have the will. They also have the skill. Ice
cannot stick a pass. They ice the puck when not under pressure.
They shoot high on Fraser Carson, as they did to good effect
in the last derby, but these shots are not from close range, they
are telegraphed from outside the blue line. Ice appear listless,
disconnected. The Mustangs are composed and methodical,
disallowing any easy opportunities and forechecking fiercely,
even when shorthanded. Ice has no space or time; they look
like they need a time-out. They look like they need to go back
to the rooms and come out again, minds cleared. But there's no
respite. The Mustangs start making inroads into the Ice zone,
Jack Wolgemuth taking the puck the length of the ice, forcing a
panicky icing.

Then the stellar line of Pat O'Kane, Jamie Bourke and Viktor
Gibbs-Sjodin break through, with the latter getting a pass on
the goal line, then simply weaving between three defenders to
stuff the puck in with a wraparound from the crease. Ice's three
nearby would-be defenders looked rooted to the spot.

1–0 up, the Mustangs third line makes it a good five minutes
for the Stangs, and they are building momentum, their
unleashed crowd roaring. Brendan McDowell's clever pass sets
up Stangs skipper Sean Jones, who goes close. The resulting
goalmouth scrum sees Sean and Marcus Wong ejected for two
minutes, then Vinnie Hughes concedes the first powerplay after
Jeremy Brown puts on one of Ice's few good moves in attack.
But the best powerplay in the league is suddenly a shambles,
conceding scoring chances, and Ice is then called for having too
many men on the ice. To end the period, Jaden Pine-Murphy
makes a big save on a powerful Pat O'Kane slap-shot.

There have been only nine shots between the teams as they
felt each other out in the first stanza. Ice have had just three
shots, as impotent a fifteen minutes as they have experienced
since their first game of the year, when they were grossly
undermanned.

As the Ice brains trust search for the smelling salts in the
break, fans are treated to recorded interviews in which patrons
are asked for their highlight of the season. Greg Spaetgens says
it was having Nathan Walker receive such a great ovation when
he was introduced prior to the semi-final. The final interviewee
is Brent Laver. "It hasn't happened yet," he says, smilingly
calmly. "At six o'clock I'll answer that for you."

On the odd little balcony above the South Pole, Ian Webster, in shorts as always, sits alone, with arms crossed, inscrutable, overlooking the scene. He can't like what he sees at the start of the second period. Ice get another powerplay, but they are lucky to escape with the score still 0–1, Jeff Grant helping set up two chances that the Stangs penalty-killers nearly convert. Then referee Rick West goes down, after copping a puck to the chin. Trying to use the delay to game-changing effect, Ice President Emma Poynton stands on the stairwell facing her constituents and bangs a drum to try to get some Ice noise happening. Straight from the face-off at Ice's end, a Pat O'Kane pass sends Jamie Bourke off to the races. The cheeky, volatile forward has been dangerous all weekend after an ineffectual and ill-disciplined final derby, and a week off from the Sydney trip. Riling Ice fans and players, especially Jeff Smith, he is also playing brilliantly, somehow dancing on the tightrope he often falls off. Chased desperately, he remains a step ahead on the breakaway, then fires a wicked wrist shot over Jaden Pine-Murphy's shoulder.

2–0 for the Mustangs. The grand final just won't flow. Jeff Smith lays a big hit on Joey Hughes in front of the Mustangs bench and play stops once more as the injured Mustangs forward is assisted by medical staff. The 'neutrals' in the crowd figure the stoppage ought to favour the faltering Ice, enable them to regroup, and it should disadvantage the usually fluent Mustangs. A handful of the less evolved Ice fans abuse Joey. The Mustangs fans roar and chant his name when he gets to his feet. He will be assessed in the dressing room, but soon return. The atmosphere for a few minutes is intense, Ice fans finding voice. 'Go Ice Go' and 'Let's Go Mustangs' compete for the airwaves like a disjointed round sung by a mad choir.

'GO ICE GO' AND 'LET'S GO MUSTANGS' COMPETE FOR THE AIRWAVES LIKE A DISJOINTED ROUND SUNG BY A MAD CHOIR.

The Mustangs denied Ice time and space, to devastating effect.

The confounding final becomes shocking a minute later. Jamie Bourke menaces near the goal line, and Viktor Gibbs-Sjodin somehow hacks the rebound past a crowded defence. It's a "dirty goal", that valuable item so cherished by Brad earlier in the year. The Mustangs are doing everything right. 3–0 with ten minutes to go in the second period. Not even Mustangs fans believed this was going to be a rout. Both sets of fans wait for Ice to get rolling. But Tommy Powell, outstanding on Saturday, is subdued. Lliam Webster likewise. Austin McKenzie flies into play but doesn't get hold of the puck. Tim Johansson scorches across the ice to little effect. Even Jason Baclig and Matt Armstrong appear shackled. Only Jeremy Brown seems immune to the Ice malaise. The consummate team player, his incisive raids are to no avail without a partner-in-crime. The Mustangs are always in position; they concede no odd man rushes, no stretch passes, they win face-offs. They keep pressing themselves.

Ice just have to score. Another powerplay. Viktor pins them Ice their own end with superbly defiant forechecking. Then comes the big chance, finally: the open net gapes as Jason Baclig swoops on a big rebound ... But the puck bounces awkwardly, and he hits it wide. There's more words and push and shove between Jamie Bourke, well beneath six feet, and huge Jeff Smith. Bourke points at the scoreboard, his trademark move this year. Ice know the score: it reads now or never. Jeremy Brown drives hard and pulls the save of the match from Fraser, a lunging pad way out from the net. The first end-to-end play drives the crowd into a frenzy. With 2.17 left in the second period, Pat O'Kane scoots down the right wing, and from a poor angle, beyond the circle, rips a wrist shot past Jaden Pine-Murphy. 4–0. Definitive. Now it cannot be denied. Unless Ice can reverse the flow of a mighty river, the Mustangs will be champions.

The game provides another "last chance" when Viktor Gibbs-Sjodin is sent to the penalty box just after the re-start. Then Jack Wolgemuth is called as well. Five on three. The Stangs hold firm, Fraser making some fine saves. Ice go off at the end of the second period looking dispirited and baffled. The Mustangs fans give their charges a standing ovation. Twenty minutes to go to glory. Bottom to top in two years.

Icehouse hero Andrew Shelton calls me during the intermission. It will be impossible to meet – his rink is too crowded. I tell him to enjoy the occasion. This is vindication, writ large. All the years he spent pushing for this rink to be built … The entire weekend has run smoothly and thrillingly for fans, who have loved it loudly in person and on social media.

Within seconds of the start of the third period, the few remaining doubters are silenced. Pat steals the puck off Matt at centre ice and supplies Viktor, who is playing at a different level to any time during the season. He smashes a slapshot first time from the slot high past Jaden Pine-Murphy. 5–0. The Mustangs are not just getting the result they want; this is complete domination, a humbling of their arch-rival. Greg Spaetgens announces the goal and emits his trademark Canucks 'wooooo!' – perhaps not kosher for the announcer at what is not a Mustangs home game – but the massed response sounds like a freight-train whistle, and this afternoon has become a Mustangs party, a massive existential affirmation. Before our eyes, the next power of the league is being confirmed.

At 17.13 Jason Baclig sets up Ice skipper Lliam Webster, who powers the puck past Fraser from the slot. The Ice goal emphasises how few good scoring opportunities Ice have had and reminds one of their brilliance on Saturday, which seems as distant as 2013. In finals, eras end, seismic shifts occur. "Twelve hours is a long time in sport," Brent will muse shortly after the game. Ice went from command to capitulation in that span.

Mitch Humphries delivers a poor check from behind, and Nice Guy Pat O'Kane takes exception, pushing him against the glass. A huge save from Jaden Pine Murphy denies the Stangs, whose fans have risen to their feet in premature celebration. You can hardly blame them – all their dreams are coming true, everything they wanted but did not expect. On the Mustangs bench, Brad Vigon, a picture of tense urgency, yells to be heard by Brendan McDowell. I lip read "keep it simple".

The Mustangs are holding Ice at arm's length. Lliam gets a shot off and he hurtles in for a rebound that never comes. Fraser pats him on the shins as he hands the puck over to the ref. The incredible, the hard-to-believe now unfolds slowly. Another Ice powerplay, and Matt Armstrong hits the post with a sharp wrist shot. Little response from the crowd for the best chance Ice will have. There will be no miracles. Sean Hamilton joins the fray and injects some energy. But Ice are less than the sum of their parts. The Stang holds up a life-sized cardboard cut-out of Fraser to the delight of the Mustangs crowd. Ice fans watch and wait for the end, placid, a few lone voices still defiant. Team and fans reflect each other's disbelief.

With 2.45 left, Vinnie Hughes whacks a slapshot and Andrew Belic tips it past Jaden Pine-Murphy. The icing on the cake: a third line local's goal. 6–1. It is the same score as for Ice's defeat of Brave in its semi-final, but this game has been more one-sided. The Stangs are now in full party mode. The players on the bench turn their backs on play to take in the crowd. (Mick later tells me he instructed them to do so.) Pat finds Tracy Carson (Fraser's mum) and gives a subtle thumbs-up, smiling broadly. The players start hugging each other.

Then the Icehouse counts down ... and the season is all over. "The Melbourne Mustangs have defeated Melbourne Ice 6–1 in the grand final of the Australian Ice Hockey League to win their first Goodall Cup." Try that sentence on. Yes, it fits. It has occurred. They had the will, and the skill. Fraser was superb in goals; Viktor, Jamie and Pat were dazzling up front, and every member of the squad turned in a brilliant, disciplined defensive effort. They achieved everything they set out to do. They rose to the occasion; Ice did not. As Mick said early in the year, elite sport is brutal. The clamour is magnificent, many of the Stangs fans split open by joy. The players hurtle towards Fraser and pin him to the glass at the north end, right in front of where beaten semi-finalists the Ice Dogs and Brave are sharing a beer. The teams shake hands at centre ice, then skate past each other's bench. Several get heartfelt bear hugs from their beaten brethren, not just just perfunctory shakes. Pat in particular is embraced with feeling by the Ice coaches.

John Belic and Andrew McDowell embrace, unwilling to let go, trying to squeeze more out of their long-awaited triumph. Andrew Fitzgerald, arm still strapped, beams. Finally freed from the pile-up of grateful teammates, Fraser accelerates towards the boards and leaps up at Mick Burslem for an aggressively emotional hug. Mick is equal to the embrace – he

Baffled, stunned. Ice players feel the pain of playoff defeat.

From top left: Ice Dog David Dunwoodie, Australian player of the year; Mustangs skipper Sean Jones with the spoils; Brad Vigon and Chuck Connolly weigh the silverware; John Belic and Andy McDowell celebrate; the Ice brains trust congratulates Brad Vigon: Mick Burslem the winner.

Little brother no more: the Mustangs are champions.

holds his goalie and verbal sparring partner over the boards and shakes him jubilantly. They look like a war-separated couple reunited at a railway station.

Jaffa, who has been high-fiving various Mustangs from behind the glass of the commentary booth, emerges to hug a Mustangs insider. Brad Vigon's ubiquitous, tiny son Zander demands moustachioed, be-suited Mustangs boss Rod Johns reach down from the bench to high-five him.

For an unpaid league, the awards are impressive. Sponsor Skater's Network's cheques for finals MVP "VEEEEEEKTTTTOOOOOORRRRR Gibbs-Sjodin - as he is announced by Greg - and for local player of the year, Ice Dog David Dunwoodie, are a not-inconsequential $1000. Jeremy Brown is named rookie of the year. He skates out dutifully from the disconsolate Ice crew, most of whom are on one knee on their blue line. Genial Jack Wolgemuth meanders out to great acclaim, to accept the gong as the league's defenceman of the year. The CBR bay erupts when Petri Pitkanen is named goalie of the year. Simon Barg accepts his award as league MVP with a very young baby swaddled in his arms.

With the Mustangs players and coaching staff awaiting the spoils on the ice, their partners and volunteers flood the bench, appropriately claiming the previously sacrosanct domain of insiders and combatants to get the best view of the ceremony. Soon enough, the players are being called out to receive their medals. A few idiots yell at the introduction of the Hughes brothers, but they are drowned out by the affirming clamour from the Mustangs fans. There is selfishness, small-mindedness and pettiness in this league, like any other, but it usually does not prevail. Sean Jones is called forward to accept and lift the glinting silver Cup. He does so with a roar, quickly taking it into the Mustangs fold, and the downcast Ice players can finally seek the sanctuary of the dressing room.

Joey gets the Cup above his head and does a lap of the rink, showing it off to the crowd, grinning widely widely. Vinnie is next. He is well-practiced, having lifted it three times for Ice. He takes it straight towards the Mustangs stronghold. CBR's Peter Chamberlain tells me we have the "right result". He says the final was like his team's semi-final. Ice missed a couple of early chances, then just couldn't get anything going. He looks forward to seeing a huge Mustangs banner up on the wall alongside the Ice premierships. By the next day, a fan will have mocked up a design of the prospective banner and posted it online.

What follows is my lasting image of the Mustangs for 2014. Following the presentations, after I have briefly chatted to a gracious and drained Brent in a lonely corner under the stand, I return to seek a few more words. The ice surface has turned orange. Players and fans are mingling on the ice surface in their street shoes, hugging, getting photos taken, ogling and grasping the Cup. The spontaneous rink invasion typifies the down-to-earth ethos of the club John Belic proudly championed the night before. The fans had clearly taken him at his word - they

Clockwise from top: Jaffa and Barb Watson in the midst of the after-party: the orange haze descends on the ice after the Mustangs win; Bears and Ice Dogs fans unite in Melbourne: Johan Steenberg, Brent Laver and Mick Burslem; Nath Tanner vows to return Vinnie Hughes premiership meallion; Nath Tanner vows to return Vinnie Hughes' premiership medallion; Brad Vigon arms himself with the Goodall Cup.

'THE MUSTANGS HAD THE WILL AND THE SKILL. THEY ACHIEVED EVERYTHING THEY SET OUT TO DO. THEY ROSE TO THE OCCASION; ICE DID NOT. AS MICK BURSLEM SAID EARLY IN THE YEAR, ELITE SPORT IS BRUTAL.

had taken ownership of this triumph. Facebook will be flooded with images from these blissful orange Icehouse minutes.

Greg Spaetgens, strolling amongst the throng with a microphone, makes a couple of half-hearted attempts to encourage the mob to move off the ice and into the after-party behind the penalty boxes. Should someone slip and hit their head ... But Australian hockey, exuberant and informal, is blessed once again. The elated, egalitarian orange mob gets their fill of on-ice celebration safely. It is my first time on the ice all season, as for most others out there. It feels appropriate somehow. Civilians wander agape, attaching themselves to each other, the spectacle now, not the watchers. It is a kind of ritual unification. The huge clump of rapt Mustangs exemplifies much of what is great, and possibly unsustainable, about Australian hockey.

I have to file for *The Age* so I miss the scenes in the dressing room, when John Belic reads out the letter in which it is stated that there is not enough talent in Victoria to form a second team. He gets his moment of bitter vindication. Then the party starts in earnest.

Brad Vigon seems stunned by what he has just witnessed, this "total team effort". He says such a win had not seemed even remotely possible. "I knew that we had a good squad but we were still growing, still developing and our goal was just to be in the top four. So to win the minor premiership was completely baffling to us. We knew looking at everybody that we matched up pretty well against them. For the guys to come out tonight and play the way they did, put everything on the line and really stay within the structure of the game-plan and really stay disciplined, it was awesome. I never expected that we'd beat them like that. I just think that the guys were almost like animals tonight. They were hungry animals and they were chasing down every puck and they were putting their bodies on the line."

Before I file, I get the moment I need. Mick Burslem, overwhelmed, comes off the ice, as if in need of respite. I take my phone out to take a photo which captures his emotion, and he half-heartedly tries to evade me. I insist, with an instinctual ferocity that shocks me. This soft tough guy is moved to tears by the achievement of the group of boys, now men he has driven around for years. He has a green-and-gold AIHL champion's medallion around his neck. It makes me teary to see his joy, and I didn't know Mick a few months ago. I have been emotional a number of times this weekend, excited by what Australian hockey is presenting. I implore Mick, redundantly, to enjoy the night. "Mate, it's not going to be one night. I told these boys I was going to celebrate through them if they pulled it off!" He's a man of his word - he will be having a good time. I give him a bear hug and move off.

This takes me past the desolate Ice zone. The dressing room door is locked. Emma, on her own, is distraught, the polar opposite of Mick. I can only offer a consoling hand on the shoulder. I shake Josh's hand, no words forthcoming. He attempts a smile, but he is shaken. Worst nightmares enacted. The sum of the human condition has not been altered by events of the preceding hours, but these dedicated stalwarts are shattered. It wouldn't have mattered so much if Ice had played to the best of their ability and been vanquished. Brent says, "They just never settled". Ice's deer-in-the-headlights performance is a mystery. It feels wrong to move on, but the deadline beckons.

My lasting image of the AIHL season emerges after I quickly file my story. The area between the two rinks has become hockey heaven. Players, fans and officials from the finalists mingle happily. Enough time has passed that some of the more emotionally sturdy Ice folk have joined the throng. Everything someone says is pertinent, every greeting is noteworthy. Mustangs administrator Rod Johns, a former Ice official and former Ice Hockey Victoria President, analyses the contest, consciously measured, but utterly immersed. Brent and Brad share a chat and a beer; Johan takes pictures of Mustangs folk with the Cup; Brave guys talk to Dogs ... I bounce between conversations, rolled around the large area like a puck in a scrimmage. One voice says that the Dogs were right on the verge of taking their semi-final when David Dunwoodie retaliated to Jamie Bourke and got penalised, and the balance of power swung back to the Stangs ... Everything could have been completely different ...

Matt and Pat greet each other with a big hug, and have an arm around each other's shoulders for many minutes as they chat. They make golfing plans for the summer. Taking in the scene, hockey foes mingling, Matt says, "This is what it's all about." He also says "God, I hate losing", but I think I'm the only one who hears. And almost as an aside, he explains what just happened. "They wanted it more."

I know these minutes are precious – the winners and losers will soon disperse to their respective corners of the country. Here is the cream of the year's talent, gathered together like never before. Robert Bannerman, eyeing the big crowd, jokes that the beer sales from this simple venture may match the revenue from the entire finals weekend. He goes on to muse about the future. The league has come to the end of a three-year plan and now has to steer a course for the next three years. He says that both the league and Ice Hockey Australia have been guilty of being "emotional and stubborn" at times, but makes conciliatory sounds, saying they need each other and will find common ground and a way to get on. His words give me hope that the divide can be broached. Surely this well-run, strongly attended finals series will remind all parties of the necessity of rapprochement. The opportunity for hockey is too great ...

Jaffa's wife Barb, beaming, tells me of her love for the hockey community that so baffled her when she met Jaffa as a sixteen-year-old. She couldn't understand why he was sharing a beer after the game with men who had been trying to belt her guy during the preceding contest. She had wanted to hit them!

I take a photo of a Mustangs fan who has an orange scar painted on his face; the ATC Productions crew prepare for commentator Michael Clough's bucks' party, still gathering cords and packing black bags of gear; Andy McDowell shakes my hand firmly and tells me it is his greatest moment in 37 years in the sport. He says he is so proud of the Mustangs boys, and he does not need to find any more words, his awestricken, utterly euphoric expression saying it all. Eric Scaresbrook carries the life-sized cut-out of Bears star Thomas Schlamp. He can't take it back to Sydney, but he knows a local Bears fan who will appreciate it. The Goodall Cup is filled and drunk from in the midst of Peter Chamberlain and Mark Rummukainen and David Dunwoodie and Simon Barg and fans and sponsors and commissioners and volunteers.

There is a champion, but as Barb Watson says, the hockey community is the biggest winner from this weekend. The wisest and most fun-loving of that family gather around the Mustangs, sharing their achievement. The efforts of everyone here, including opponents, made that accomplishment great, and sweet. For a little while, the grand final is a shared triumph, with an orange core. The Mustangs will soon get their time with the trophy and their people and their memories, but for now they are the epicentre of the league, but still a part of it. It feels like there is little this roomful of people couldn't achieve. This is not true of course - the world and its realities lie in wait.

But for this delightful hour, Australian hockey, having come so far, and facing such big challenges, can just enjoy its own company, assured that whatever happens, it is a great sporting competition and a wonderful community, here and now. For an hour or two, Melbourne, Australia is the site of the best hockey high in the world.

'THERE IS A CHAMPION, BUT AS BARB WATSON SAYS, THE HOCKEY COMMUNITY IS THE BIGGEST WINNER FROM FINALS WEEKEND.

OCTOBER 2014

THURSDAY THE 2ND

I wasn't really sure why Joey Hughes had got in contact. But the Hughes men are central to this story, and they have plenty to say about hockey after a lifetime in love with the game in two countries. Vinnie opened up in Newcastle: now it was Joey's turn. We meet at noon at Oakleigh on a school holiday Thursday, Joey propping his damaged leg in front of him, his back to the ice, which is covered with tottering kids.

Joey has played most of his hockey in the North American system, where designated fighters are the norm and every player is expected to be aggressive. Any strong contact demands retaliation or a player's commitment to the team is questioned. This relentlessly violent style was not natural to Joey, he tells me – he had never been a fan of dirty hockey, despite his history of mixing it up – but he willingly did his coach's bidding to survive. One of those coaches had offered to sharpen his stick for him, demanding he hook an opponent. "Leave splinters in," had been the mentor's call. Joey has a phrase for the state of mind this conditioning creates: Hockey Ego. It's not a matter of egotism per se, more a super-aggressive attitude. Touch me or my teammate and we will come back at you, immediately, with full force. It's a hair-trigger, pack mentality that fully exploits one's natural volatility. It leaves him amazed at the provocations shrugged off by Australian Rules footballers. "They just run off!" he says of heavy body contact in the local football code – which would precipitate a response in North American hockey.

Joey is talking to me because he has been trying to tame his Hockey Ego in this past season for the Mustangs. He was rapt for the group and club when the Stangs took out the title. But personally, he was pleased because, on the whole, he had conquered his demons and maintained his discipline. He has been on nothing less than a mission of personal transformation. Central to this mission was the 'story' he told himself about himself as a player and person.

Personal, team and business issues became so fraught for Joey that he stepped away from Ice midway through 2013. For the first time in his life, hockey had ceased to be fun. In hindsight, he realises that he needed time away from the game in order to fix this. He does not want to go into details about

Joey Hughes broke his leg during the grand final.

specific issues involved in his departure. And he doesn't want to express any bitterness. In fact, he wants to distance himself from the notion of bitterness. He wants to talk about the "stories he created" which had caused him and others grief.

Joey flatly states that his 'kick' against Chris Wong in the first derby of 2014 had been a lapse into Hockey Ego, and those who tried to justify it had been wrong. He was happy to "take ownership" of the moments he lost self-control, because he could not progress without completely honest self-assessment. This was the reason he insisted upon playing in full in the final match against the Ice Dogs on the road, a dead rubber in which Viktor Gibbs-Sjodin and Jamie Bourke were rested.

With the Dogs pounding him with a physical and verbal onslaught, Joey was doing no less than testing his self-resolve. He passed that test, but in doing so he sustained a rib injury that required painkillers. He kept that quiet going into the finals the following week, but at a cost. When Joey was hit heavily during the second period of the grand final, stopping play for several minutes, the full extent of his injuries were not immediately apparent. And he couldn't take any more painkillers. So the newly disciplined Joey Hughes played the final period of the decider against his old team barely able to put weight on his left leg, with the aid of two panadol and two aspirin. He had broken his leg and torn his quad muscle from its moorings in two places. A month later, he is one day off crutches, and he has just tested his quad injuries by trying the stairs to his office nook. The whole process of rehabilitation will take over three months.

During the season, perceptive Mustangs teammate Brendan McDowell, noting how quiet the star recruit was between periods, asked Joey if he re-taped his stick at every intermission. Yes was the answer. The tape ritual kept Joey from getting too caught up in the banter and gee-ups. He now needed calm to focus on what he had to do in the next period, how he wanted to play. It was almost a form of mediation, utilising a methodical, repetitious activity to keep one's mind out of the emotional realm. Joey used the resources provided by his two clubs to effect his change. He turned to Hawthorn football club psychologist Anthony Klarica, used by Brent Laver for Ice. And he paid heed to club sponsor Bryan Jeffrey from MOAT Mental Health Services, condensing Bryan's suggestions to a single activating word: 'cortex'. Be in the game, in the doing-not-thinking space, not in the emotional realm. Calm down, re-assess, and gain control of your story. One word helps re-start the process to alter one's hard-wiring.

Much of what Joey has learnt from the viciousness and glory of hockey he is applying to himself as "life lessons". As Joey speaks about his struggle to reinvent himself, I feel for Brad Vigon, who must have thought his star recruit was aloof early in the season. Joey said that Brad had been keen to seek his input when he came on board, and Joey's need for a quiet role could have been misinterpreted. Yet he says, "Brad did more for me this year than any other coach ever, as a person and a player."

Joey says that he rang every Ice team member at the end of 2013 to apologise for leaving. He had broken his word to be there for them throughout the season. The Hughes boys do not break a pledge lightly. Aussie boys from tough backgrounds often trust slowly, but then absolutely. He tells me that he has no trophy room. "It's not about awards; it's about enjoying your teammates and playing for something together ... knowing teammates have your back." Hockey, for all it has given him and cost him, is bigger than championships and clubs. More than once he comes to the phrase "reality check" and laughs. He has had a few recently. The game in Australia provides them for free all the time.

Friendly and startlingly candid all afternoon, Joey leaves me with firm words. Don't make your book about rivalries or bitterness. It's not about the Mustangs and Ice, or the Hughes brothers.

"Make it about hockey."

IN 2014, JOEY HUGHES HAS BEEN ON NOTHING LESS THAN A MISSION OF PERSONAL TRANSFORMATION.

The teacher learnt as much as his pupils in 2013-2014.

EPILOGUE

DECEMBER 2014

Jeff Smith is back playing in the English Elite Ice Hockey League with the Braehead Clan, of Renfrew, Scotland, after the Dutch League collapsed. Holland placed ninth at the 2000 Olympics, but the subsequent demise of the national team has apparently made it difficult for the country's professional league, the Eredivisie, to attract sufficient sponsorship. It is amazing to think that the amateur Australian league is more stable.

James Morgan and wife Shelley have welcomed their first-born, Jack, into the world. So far it hasn't slowed James down. ATC Productions is working on the TV show *Manspace*; for the Australian Baseball League; and on boxing and horse-racing. James says he receives enquiries about their services every day. "Who knows? I might even have to leave my day job," he says. ATC, like the AIHL, is looking at "incremental improvements" to its hockey coverage in 2015, which means qualifying for "Frequent Flyer Platinum". "I'll be involved with hockey for as long as it will have me," he tells me. Those words are worth a lot of money to the league.

Mustangs assistant coach **Mark "Chuck" Connolly** has stepped aside. He is "very happy and content" with his last four years in the game, which netted a local premiership with the Demons, a state Brown title and the Mustangs' Goodall Cup victory. In a tough work year off-ice he had four jobs, and the travel from his rural home to training became too exacting. "What else was there to do with this team other than win another cup? The team finished ninth two years ago and the rest is history. We had so many firsts this season and some can never be repeated. The game was good to me and I wanted nothing more from it. Working with Brad was a thrill and I felt the time was just right."

Joey Hughes is back on the ice, teaching and training at Next Level, his leg on the mend, his passion for teaching hockey as strong as ever.

Young Mustangs local **Andrew Fitzgerald** will most likely miss the 2015 season. His right shoulder, injured just before the finals, is healing, but he needs the plate in his previously injured left shoulder removed. He may play locally for the Blackhawks, and he is planning to add a physiotherapy degree to his qualifications in myotherapy and Pilates.

Young Ice star **Jeremy Brown** left Australia within a day of the grand final, and faced a training run within hours of arriving in Montreal. Another couple of days later he was named captain of his Canadian Junior Hockey League team the Sherbrooke Cougars. Five days after being Ice's best player in its grand final demise, he recorded his first points and penalty minutes of his next season in a 3–2 win over Granby.

Chris Kubara has not found the information he needed to commit to offer himself as an alternative president of the Sydney Ice Dogs. His three sons are playing overseas, Ice Dog **Tyler Kubara** with the San Diego Gulls team alongside Sydney Bears star **Cameron Todd**.

Ace Australian goalie **Anthony Kimlin**, a native of Ipswich, Queensland, is living in Toronto and will not be returning to the AIHL in 2015. He says he remains keen to do so in the future.

Nathan Walker has been plying his wares with the Washington Capital's AHL affiliate the Hershey Bears. He was reassigned to Hershey's East Coast Hockey League affiliate the South Carolina Stingrays, but after two games, in which he scored an assist and a match-winning goal, he was recalled to Hershey.

Former Ice president **Andy Lamrock** said in September that there has been "big movement" on a possible new rink in Melbourne.

Joey Hughes may not want this book to be about bitterness, but that emotion is part of the story wherever there is a club and two opinions on how to run it. **Emma Poynton** has decided not to renominate for the presidency of **Melbourne Ice**, citing "constant campaigning" against her, and saying she is "pretty shattered, pretty disappointed how it ended up". Emma was offered a job as podiatrist with AFL club the Western Bulldogs in July, a great professional fillip, and it was made clear she would not be able to continue with her Ice role if she accepted. "If you had said it to me a year ago, I would have said no, no, no, I want to stay with the hockey." But it hasn't been "all rainbows and roses" at Ice. "I would have liked to have gone further and done a bit more, but there's just too many roadblocks and people resisting change. There's a fear of new people and a fear of change which ultimately stops progression ... and that's where the Mustangs will overrun Melbourne Ice if we're not careful."

Emma is still organising medical appointments and jobs for players and vows to continue assisting them. "I'll just be a member, I'll be a fan, I'll be there when I can." Emma will continue in her role as national women's team manager, and

'BETTER FAN ENGAGEMENT, BETTER GAME-DAY
EXPERIENCES AND BETTER COMMUNICATION OF THE
LEAGUE'S POSITIONS ON KEY TOPICS ARE PRIORITIES
FOR THE UPCOMING SEASON.

playing summer and winter hockey. She believes the structures put in place by the new Melbourne Ice coaching staff are bearing fruit in the development of young talent.

Bernie O'Brien, Emma's replacement as Ice president, recognises that some older members of the club who survived the privations of Oakleigh have trouble with some of the changes the club is going through, and he wants Ice to better recognise its history. However, his planning is mostly concentrated on delegation and consultation in order to refresh the club's mission statement and improve its social media, game-day experience and sponsorship, all of which will involve more change, all of which Emma thought necessary. Bernie freely admits that the Mustangs "surpassed" his club off the ice in such matters in 2014, but he says he already has able volunteers working on improvements. Though he has no desire to create a "super team", and wants an even competition and better junior development, there is currently no commitment from Ice to voluntarily retain **Jason Baclig** and **Matt Armstrong** as imports if they are granted permanent Australian residency.

As it turns out, the seemingly endless voyage towards PR is not over for Jason and Matt. They needed only a few more weeks of consistent employment at the Icehouse to qualify for their visas when the lease changed at the rink in August. Despite initial assurances that the change would not affect their applications, there were subsequent concerns. They are working

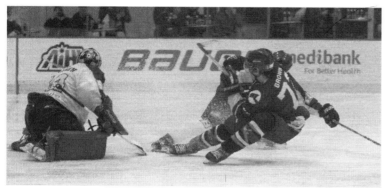

Top left: Mustangs bliss; Top left middle: Jeremy Brown is making waves in Canadian junior hockey; Top right: Stephen Blunden sacrificed a pro contract; Middle left: the Bears may be going home; Middle right: Sasky Stewart is working for the NHL; Middle far right: the AIHL is working more with the NHL; Bottom: Canberra's penalty box - quaint, but is it sustainable?

at the same place performing the same tasks so the lawyers now employed on their behalf seem to have a strong case, but the wait continues. Matt made a three-week trip home for a family wedding and is now back in the groove of teaching skating and hockey to all ages and levels of ability at the Icehouse. There are no positions currently available in the fire brigade, and Matt is aware of how difficult it will be to start a career there, but that ambition remains on his radar. He turns interviewer when the topic moves to Ice's season, and the grand final. He asks what I thought about the team's year. "Good season, bad day," is my response. Though he was gracious immediately after the loss, it's clear that the collective failure to perform in the grand final still bemuses him. "If it had been a thriller, a 3–2 loss in overtime, you wouldn't mind so much ..."

The response of **Brent Laver** to Melbourne Ice's 6–1 grand final humbling was a grudging "eight or nine" days off, then two five-hour meetings with the coaching staff, a six-question quiz of players, and the compilation of a fifteen-page document appraising all of the above and proposing the way forward. Part of that progression is an acknowledgement that he must not be so obsessive about coaching as it is impacting his family. But he has basically not stopped since the grand final. His conclusions from his exhaustive analysis? He needs to communicate more with his senior players, and not fall back on the "out" of being bashful about his hockey achievements and knowledge. And it's time for the second phase of the master plan – the players feel 'safe' and unified, now they need (and want) more of a kick up the backside. The theme for the upcoming year will be "It's not about what you feel; it's about how you act." Performance will dictate opportunity. Ice will also emulate the Mustangs by opening up their long pre-season – which began in mid-November – to more local players, offering the club a chance to assess fringe talent and improve competition for positions, and also providing more of a link to grassroots hockey. Brent, who has a son starting through junior ranks, is acutely aware of the need to provide clearly defined opportunities for local players. Reprising his "What does success look like?" query of his club, he expands it to the national team. "Have we suddenly jumped up the rankings by three divisions?"

The off-season is, unsurprisingly, more settled for the contented champions the Melbourne Mustangs. The club's hockey operations boss **Andy McDowell** "couldn't be happier" that imports **Jeff Grant**, **Viktor Gibbs-Sjodin** and **Pat O'Kane** are all returning for another season. **Jack Wolgemuth** is "starting life" in Alaska, despite the spontaneous chant that arose at the club's presentation night begging him for 'one more year'. The Stangs will be seeking just a single defenceman from overseas this summer to replace the much-loved dual club-champion.

The Mustangs enjoyed their win. "We really did milk it! I have never been involved with anything in my life that made so many people happy," Andy says of the "fantastic" parties and get-togethers they had in the weeks following their first grand final win. But his players were worn out by their campaign and he doesn't want them on the ice until the New Year. At the Icehouse to watch his sister play in the national women's league, **Fraser Carson** backed this delayed start to the pre-season by saying, "I didn't want to see this place until January!" Andy says of his roster, "We do not need players; we've got plenty of players." Their deep pool of local talent may be buttressed in 2015 by the return of **Jack McCoy**. His eyesight is not yet back to 100 per cent, but he is back playing inline hockey and is due to commence pre-season training with his old mates.

Andy insists everyone at the club is "very, very realistic" about the challenge in defending their title, and "definitely back to earth". "We're staying focused; it's not going to our heads." He says the club is "just starting to learn" how to operate in the AIHL.

Pat O'Kane is relaxed. It is a word he repeats a number of times, as if trying to believe that a tough few months are over. His least favoured subjects had to be endured during the AIHL finals and until recently, but exams are now finished and he can just "go to work, come home and just sit there" if he pleases, an unlikely prospect. The slacker took a day off from the gym to recover from premiership celebrations. One day.

Pat is as frank as ever about his team. "If I had my way, I'd weed out a few people ..." he says. "It's time for some guys to stop playing and that's more because of their attitude than their ability."

However, Pat knows that not everyone is as fervent about hockey as himself. "I live for it, but you can't expect someone to do that when they work and have their own lives." He understands because he is anticipating the day when work intervenes to stop him playing. "We'll start with this year and I'm not promising anything else," he says of his future career. He believes it is the Mustangs players who are crazy about hockey who will keep them in contention. "I think we have enough guys on the team that are so passionate about it that it will be addictive. You look at a guy like Joey Hughes – I've never met a guy so passionate about it and it just spreads. I think the

I HAVE NEVER BEEN INVOLVED WITH ANYTHING ... THAT MADE SO MANY PEOPLE HAPPY, ANDY MCDOWELL SAYS OF THE MUSTANGS PREMIERSHIP.

drive and the fire are still there and I think we should be playing with the fear of failing because the only way we can go is down."

Pat doesn't know whether he will be living in Australia beyond graduation next year. Girlfriend Stephanie is prepared to travel, and Pat's degree in international business could lead to opportunities elsewhere. Here is the mindset of the happy migrant in a confusing nutshell: "It's not so much that I want to stay, it's that I don't want to leave. I'm afraid if I leave, I wouldn't come back; it's a big move."

Pat and Stephanie are travelling to visit Pat's parents in New Hampshire in January. He laughs as he says that Steph is preparing for the cold. "She thinks it will be cold, but it will be *freezing!*" he says. A measure of their bond is that Stephanie's mum put on a Thanksgiving feast for Pat, complete with the Carsons as guests.

Pat played this season as he did his first, flat out, as if every game was his last. I am sure this has always been his wont, but it is appropriate in Australia. "I've really enjoyed it, because it's all a bonus; I shouldn't be playing. If I didn't love it, if I wasn't so passionate about it, I wouldn't do it. I wouldn't do it just as a hobby. If I'm going to do something I'm going to do it 100 per cent, that's why I go to the gym so much and I choose to avoid other things. Basically everything I do is with hockey in mind, so when that mindset changes I'll stop playing. Right now, I'm still dedicated and still want to be the best I can be, so I'll keep playing."

Reflecting on what he is looking for in his next assistant coach, title-winning Mustangs coach **Brad Vigon** defines the unique challenge of leading an AIHL team. Chuck Connolly's replacement must be reliable, willing to make every session, and have sufficient hockey knowledge. But most importantly, he must understand Australian hockey culture. The best, most well-credentialed coach from overseas will fail dismally if he doesn't win the hearts and minds of the playing roster, particularly the locals. "If they [Australian players] like you, they will run through walls for you. If they don't like you, they wouldn't piss on you if you were on fire."

Brad emails potential import players a blunt list of Australian hockey realities, ensuring they know that the facilities, coaching and standard of hockey will not be what they are used to. "All we have to sell is the experience of playing in Australia," he tells me. No matter how much you try to warn newcomers, the Australian scene can be a shock. Emma Poynton calls it the "hockey bag test". "When is the last time you carried your own hockey bag?" she asked potential imports. "We don't have people to do that! What are you used to? Because this is Aussie hockey."

Brad reveals that he "had it out" with all of his most talented players, except for Pat, during the just-completed season. He had to demand "buy-in" of his stars, who were all frustrated for various reasons early in the season. Even if they thought they knew better, they had to do things the coach's way for the good of the team. Brad also needed them to relax, have fun, and have faith that everything would come together. Some were trying too hard, feeling they had to do it all themselves. Some had called out the coach or teammates at practice or on the bench.

"I ended up having to be a real hard guy, which is not me," Brad admits. He recalls shaking, he was so "amped up" on the drive to one important player meeting. But he did the tough thing, so did his players, and the championship was the reward. "We knew we had the talent," he says of 2014. "It all came together when everybody was enjoying their hockey. I thought if it did come together, we wouldn't be able to do anything but win." All of Brad's elite talents were playing for the team, in peak form, when it mattered.

The late start for the Mustangs will ensure the players are hungry for hockey. They start in the gym in mid-January and on the ice later that month. They are following similar patterns to last year in many things, but because they are now champions "with a target on their backs" Brad is under no illusions that a different type of season awaits. "We've just got to be aware that teams are coming for us now. There will be a few minor changes to the strategies, but it will be about making sure we come to play every game."

Robert Bannerman loves his AIHL job, but realises the workload he has been sustaining is not realistic. He has been working at a day job where he takes important calls early in the day and at night, from either end of the earth. He will soon have to hire and delegate, like the clubs and associations, in order to keep up with the demands of the growing AIHL. But listen to him talk about his vision for a revenue-raising pre-season All Stars game and the impending onset of another sponsor (uncovered through his "Canadian mafia" network), and his meeting with a legendary Australian broadcasting guru, and you can't help but feel that unless his personal circumstances change, he will have his hand firmly on the tiller for another year at least.

Robert's report to stakeholders at the season's end included the following:

"75 000 fans were entertained at AIHL games, a 25% attendance growth compared to 2013. Our Facebook community jumped from 8,700 fans to 17,944, Twitter followers increased by 1,416, from 3,000 to 4,416. Fox Sports broadcasts helped the league reach more than 475,000 unique Australians via television. Melbourne Mustangs and CBR Brave live streamed games for the first time, total revenue increased 20% over the previous year and we generated 32% more profit compared to 2013. New partners, coupled with a bigger finals series, fuelled our revenue and profit increases."

For all the numbers and Robert's corporate expertise, the league's foremost administrator loves the rough edges of Australian hockey – he beckoned me towards the Hecklers in Canberra – and he is a realist. If the league's relationship with the IHA is not working, he suggests the parties take a year off from each other, before reconvening. After all, there ought to be little overlap in the jurisdiction of the two bodies – the league is about putting out a "quality entertainment product" and the national body is charged with junior development and the national team.

The unflappable commissioner has taken AIHL sponsorship to significant levels from next to zero, and he has overseen a period of unprecedented growth. He is rapt that the work towards reinstating a team in Queensland is way ahead of schedule: the rinks and Ice Hockey Queensland are keen for an AIHL team and the next step is to find some leaders with money and administrative nous to form a club. He is working on building a relationship with the NHL, and he has strengthened the coverage of hockey on the Fox Sports website. Better fan engagement, better game-day experiences and better communication of the league's positions on key topics are among his priorities for the upcoming season. Robert's strengths are obvious enough that even critical opponents often concede his abilities. If he seeks a new 'day' job, his work with the AIHL will make for pretty impressive reading on his CV. But you get the feeling he would like to make his unpaid work his full-time job, like many of the players and coaches.

Sasky Stewart arrived in Toronto via Rockhampton, November 20. It only took her a month to land a job in the NHL war room, as In-Game Social Media Coordinator. All you can say is that the sport's elite professional body knows what it is doing.

After his AIHL season ended, Bears net-minder **Luke Read** starred at an inline hockey tournament. But of more interest to me is the fact that when he visited Melbourne, he was able to camp on **Tristain Cole's** backyard lawn, showcasing a practical benefit of the socially connected hockey community.

At **Perth Thunder**, coach and general manager **Stan Scott** is still working on the possible return of **Michael Forney**. He has meetings with people in high places scheduled. He says the former ECHL star is keen to live and work in Perth, "sooner or later, for five years". Stan didn't want to take over as coach again eight games into 2014, and is again coach-hunting, hoping to announce a new incumbent before Christmas. Coaching as well as being general manager, and moving house twice, was "insanely difficult" in 2014, he confesses. "Nothing else in your life gets proper attention," he says of the murderous regime, made worse by Perth's uniquely exacting travel demands. "You can't do anything to the best of your abilities, you feel like you have underachieved."

Like Newcastle's Garry Dore, Stan sees himself as better suited to the general manager's role. Smart operators like Garry and Stan want to be dealing with "game-days, sponsorships and monitoring outgoings", rather than a defender's laceration or the team's ailing powerplay, or the girlfriend troubles of an import.

Always keen to bring the most talented players possible to Perth, Stan is tempering his expectations of his next crop, weighing up the benefits of having a star if he cannot make it until too late into the season because of playoffs at home. "The best pros want to bring something for others, not just get something for themselves," he says of what he is looking for. They have to understand that locals don't play for a living, and show them due respect. They need to mentor someone, even just one individual.

Stan says he was not happy with the culture of his three-year-old club early in 2014. Bad results were coinciding with a bad culture, destroying what he had meticulously constructed with his young locals in the previous years. He says a decline in such standards is a cancer that is best treated "early, not later". He remains confident his developing young leaders will create a sustainable culture and a hockey juggernaut in the west.

The other team that had a ground-breaking year, **CBR Brave**, has to replace a stellar group of imports, three of whom finished second, third and fourth in the league scoring standings. **Matthieu Ouellette** missed the subsequent northern hemisphere season due to his knee injury and **Stephen Blunden** sacrificed a professional contract with Reims when he re-signed to play (obviously unexpected) finals with Brave. He eventually ended up with another contract in France, but the dedication of those imports can be measured by their sacrifices.

Their legacy is that a higher grade of import than ever before is now queuing up to play for Canberra in 2015. The playing ranks could also be bolstered by a couple of high-profile Australian signings; however, the club, which based so much of its on-ice success on togetherness and fitness resulting from its extensive training regime, now has to weigh up whether it can accommodate a "fly-in, fly-out" star.

There are ongoing talks about new rink developments. Of more importance is the short to medium term future of their current home, which is the subjects of ongoing talks with rink management. Brave has launched a junior team in the New South Wales League, the first step in trying to better leverage its popularity and its relationship with Ice Hockey ACT to ensure more local talent comes through the ranks.

The biggest news of the off-season was the resignation of Sydney Ice Dogs coach **Andrew Petrie** in late September. He was named as replacement for departing **Newcastle North Stars** coach **Garry Dore** less than a week later. Garry, still rink manager, co-owner and North Stars general manager, is bullish about the upcoming season and "excited about the future". He says the North Stars are "going 100 miles an hour" to return to the final weekend of the season and says Andrew is an "impact coach" who will be the "icing on the cake" for his club. He says 2014 was a wake-up call for his organisation: while his team had the capacity to go further this year, it now knows it has to pick up its efforts. "You can't go through the motions and get there," he says of the modern AIHL. The North Stars have a naturalised goalie lined up to play alongside Aussie 21-year-old **Josh Broekmann**, and will get **Beau Taylor** back earlier in the 2015 season than this year, when his education in North America took precedence.

Garry believes the AIHL must welcome the "plateau" which will follow its rapid growth in the past couple of seasons. "We've come along in leaps and bounds, it's now time for everyone to settle and take care of their backyard for a year or two. It's important to stabilise – finances are still an issue – then we can step up again in two years." He sees the readmission of a Queensland team as paramount.

Personally, he admits the lifting of the coaching load is "noticeable" and he feels relieved. Garry is now meeting business groups and sponsors and he is busy planning, devoting himself to building the North Stars organisation. The happy family of the north sounds energised and ready for another title tilt.

Adelaide Adrenaline coach **Ryan O'Handley** is making a "contingency plan" for a successor. His sons, nine and eleven years old, enjoy him coaching Adrenaline, but they also enjoy him being at their games instead of on road trips. Ryan is thrilled that two IHA and national team stalwarts, **Kevin Brown** and **Don Rurak**, have come on board at Adelaide. Their exact roles will be defined at the club's annual general meeting, but Don has already represented the club at the AIHL's AGM, and their experience and expertise will beef up the administrative know-how of the club and enable Ryan and his coaching staff to focus on hockey "instead of putting out fires". There is a lot of work going on to establish a new ice rink in South Australia, and Ryan continues to hear "rumblings" about it, but there appears to be nothing official on the horizon. He says despite the current venue having no more room for more spectators, the club must push for more corporate and government support.

On the ice, Ryan is keen for one more year because he is desperate to get back to the finals. Adrenaline won eight of their final ten games, "playing some fantastic hockey", and the bus accident impacted their season heavily, leaving the players feeling they have "unfinished business". Ryan believes his team was good enough to make the finals, but he is unsure if they would have got past the Mustangs, whom he thought were the team to beat from early in the season.

There's a volunteer coming on board to beef up the flimsy Adrenaline social media presence. "It was social media that got us home from Canberra after the bus crash. They weren't going to budge," Ryan says of the successful campaign waged by Chloe Meiers and embraced by the AIHL community, which resulted in Qantas allowing a change of flights without greater expense. He says it's important to engage the community and reinforce Adrenaline's identity in Adelaide.

Ryan is excited about the prospects of the national team, due to play in Iceland in April, saying his squad, bolstered by several new faces, including Jamie Bourke and Robert Malloy, is young and has firepower, speed and depth.

Several of the players in the Australian team are **Sydney Ice Dogs** who appear set to play for another team in 2015. Captain **Robert Malloy** and forward **Mitch Bye** are Newcastle-bound, highly-rated national representative **Paul Baranzelli** is reportedly joining Melbourne Ice, Australian player of the year **David Dunwoodie** is joining CBR Brave, and several other Dogs players are weighing up their futures.

It's fair to say that in the off-season the Ice Dogs are in disarray. Robert Bannerman, though remarkably calm about the internal turmoil at the club and hopeful of an amicable outcome, is disappointed at the intransigence on both sides of the split and adamant that the last-minute dispensations CBR Brave received cannot be repeated. In any case, he said disgruntled Ice Dogs volunteers and players are currently incapable of forming another team that will satisfy league criteria. The row proves the reality of player power. A remarkable amount of senior Dogs players are tipped to withhold their talents. If they do so, their old club will struggle. Robert is counting on some compromises coming over summer. Incumbent president **Shane Rose** did not respond to requests for an interview.

WAYNE HELLYER BELIEVES A RETURN TO MACQUARIE WOULD BE A GAME- CHANGER NOT JUST FOR HIS CLUB, BUT FOR THE SPORT IN AUSTRALIA.

Though the Dogs brouhaha is the worst news of the off-season, Sydney has also provided its best news. **Sydney Bears** president **Wayne Hellyer** can once again see "light at the end of the tunnel" for his club. The Bears are hoping to play at the Macquarie rink, their original home, as soon as 2016. "It is where our people, our members, our club have always been based and we'd like to move back there," says Wayne.

The Bears' preferred venue is part of the Macquarie Shopping Centre in Sydney's north, 23 minutes' drive from the CBD. The canny local council demanded a recreational facility be included in plans when the centre was first developed, and the rink must continue as part of the owner's obligations. As it happens, current owner, financial services giant AMP, appears keen to revitalise the time-worn arena and embrace a "premium team in a premium league". They are currently deciding between two groups vying for the right to redevelop the venue.

The Bears will play at Penrith in the far west in 2015, but if the more hockey-friendly consortium gets the nod for the Macquarie renovations, works will be undertaken in time for the Bears to return home the following year. Wayne says the rink was highly successful in its prime, with public skating packed out from 6 am until 2 am, shift-workers frequenting even the latest sessions. The Bears had good crowds in the 2000-capacity stadium, and he recalls a time when the "riot police" were called to deal with overcrowding at a world championships fixture.

He says returning to Macquarie could "totally change" his club, rewarding existing sponsors and enticing new backers; and having a "premier rink" competing against the Icehouse in Melbourne would mean more clientele, bigger sponsors and more awareness of the league. He believes it could be a game-changer not just for his club, but for the sport in Australia.

Jonathan Cornford is understandably reluctant to discuss his potential rink at **Pakenham** in Melbourne's outer south-east. He believes in caution when discussing business matters, and getting a rink built in Australia is a supreme test of patience, a trial by red tape. However, he has been granted permits, and expects to commence work early in 2015. The planning application includes reference to AIHL games being played at the venue and an "ambition" to host senior and junior world championship tournaments. Until the slab is poured and the "major recreational facility" becomes a tangible reality, no one in the hockey community will rejoice, but the onset of a new rink in a major growth corridor would be a huge step forward for the sport.

Two months after the end of its best-ever season, the AIHL is understandably enthused about its next, but there is little prospect of major short-term change. Every club I have spoken to outside Melbourne has talked of possible developments and expansions of their rinks. However, I would not be surprised if nothing happens in 2015.

The AIHL will not be able to court more fans without providing more seats and better "experiences". If the venues do not expand soon, the progress of this thriving hockey outpost will halt. No use getting more people interested via your media deal and snazzy social media presentations if there is nowhere for people to sit, or if a trip to the loo makes first-timers gag.

In this phase before venues materialise or transform – or not – the sport will continue to improve on the ice, because the teams are so competitive and full of motivated individuals. Most league- and club-runners are focused on improving the "game-day experience" of the fans they already have. More varied entertainment between periods, fewer long unexplained referee delays, better announcers, more amusing and stimulating music; these are all things they can affect relatively cheaply.

The next couple of years shape as a period of consolidation for the AIHL. Personally, I lean to the side of the visionary optimists rather than the pessimist realists in assessing the future of the competition and the sport in Australia. The game is now played at the highest standard in Australian history, thanks to this league. Sponsorships, media coverage and crowds have improved more in each of the past four years than they did in my first fifteen years in the sport.

I believe the Bears getting a good stadium in a better location is bigger news than the political in-fighting besetting the Ice Dogs. I reckon properly run teams spreading the load will prosper; those reliant on or ruled by individuals will eventually fade. To my eyes, there are more good, smart people than self-serving autocrats in the AIHL; there are more people who love the sport as much as their clubs than in most sporting competitions; and there are few national leagues anywhere with players as self-sacrificing.

I'm with the big-picture dreamers and doers like Andy Lamrock and Stan Scott. Build it and they will come. Fifteen hundred to two thousand regulars at a game of hockey in Perth is wholly achievable. Melbourne could do with a stadium that seats 2500 to 3000, maybe more long-term, and Newcastle could probably fit another couple of hundred at least if it was expanded. Adelaide could double its current crowd in a bigger, newer venue. Canberra has not exhausted its support base. Queensland is a proven, essential market. And Sydney can still be won over with the right product in the right place.

It's a great dream, made all the more enticing by the remarkable progress of Victorian hockey since the onset of the Icehouse. Hockey has the capacity to grow from novelty to a niche staple in Australia. It is poised on the brink of emergence. A huge opportunity awaits a rich, smart hockey lover …

But whatever happens, I'm glad I'm back, regardless of whether another rink gets built or another Australian gets converted to the game. The AIHL is good, bloody good, just as it is now.

The site for the Pakenham rink. Plans are in, permits approved ...

GLOSSARY of hockey terms

Assist: Credit given to a player who shoots, passes or deflects the puck to the scorer of a goal. Two assists can be awarded per goal. (The NHL's greatest scorer, Wayne Gretzky, "The Great One", scored 894 goals and had 1963 assists in his twenty-year career.)

Bantam: Put simply, in most of North America the following terms denote hockey age groups: Atom: under 11 years of age; Peewee: under 13 years of age; Bantam: under 15 years of age; Midget: under 18 years of age; Juvenile: under 20 years of age; Junior: under 21 years of age.

Blue line: Lines at either end of the rink separating offensive zone from the center ice neutral zone.

Breakaway: When a player with the puck has no defending opponents, except for the goaltender, between themself and the opposing goal.

Celly: An elaborate goal celebration.

Check: Defensive technique aimed at impeding an opponent with possession of the puck. If not performed correctly, a check can result in a penalty. The most common form of check involves contact using the hips and shoulders.

Cross-checking: Checking an opponent with the shaft of the stick held in both hands. Should incur a penalty.

Defenceman: One of two players positioned further back on the ice than the forwards. A defenceman's primary job is to stop their opponents from scoring.

Deke: Fooling an opponent with a faked move when in possession of the puck (from "decoy"). Like a "baulk" in Australian Rules football.

Delay of game: A deliberately caused stoppage of play; the player is penalised with a minor penalty.

Empty net goal: A goal scored when the opposing goalie is not on the ice, usually at the end of a game when the trailing team replaces its goalie to get an extra attacker on the ice.

Face-off: The method used to begin play at the beginning of a period or after a stoppage of play. One player from each team attempts to gain control of the puck after it is dropped between their sticks by an official.

Five-hole: The space between a goaltender's legs. The number five is used because goal-scoring targets are defined as top left and right (one and two), lower left and right (three and four), and between the legs (five-hole).

Five on three: When one team has had two players sent to the penalty box. This leaves the opponent with five skaters to the penalised team's three.

Forechecking: Pressuring defenders in the offensive zone in order to gain control of the puck and set up a scoring opportunity. AFL teams adapted this idea and called it the "forward press".

Full strength: When both teams have five skaters and one goaltender on the ice.

Game misconduct: A penalty that results in a player being ejected from the game. In the AIHL, this also incurs a mandatory one-game suspension.

Goalie: (Goaltender). Player whose whose job is to prevent the opposing team from scoring goals by blocking shots with various parts of his body.

Goon: A player whose main role is to fight and/or intimidate.

Grinder: A player valued more for hard work and checking skills than scoring ability, who often sets up goal opportunities.

Icing: Icing occurs when a player shoots the puck across both the centre red line and the opposing team's goal line without the puck going into the net or being able to be touched by an opposing player. Play is stopped, then resumed with a face-off in the defending zone of the team that committed the infraction.

Line: A left-winger, centre and right-winger, a team's main attackers. The first line is generally the main scoring threat, and the third line (fourth in North America) is more defensive, aiming to give the stars a rest without much expectation of scoring themselves.

Linesman: An official responsible for conducting most face-offs and for calling off-side and icing infractions. Can call some penalties. Usually two linesmen on the ice during a game.

Misconduct: A penalty where the offending player is ruled off the ice for ten minutes, but may be substituted for on the ice. Often imposed for abuse of an official.

NHL: The National Hockey League. The elite professional league in North America, pinnacle of the sport worldwide.

Net-minder: A goalie.

Odd-man rush: When a team enters the attacking zone and outnumbers the opposing players in the zone – usually a three-on-two or a two-on-one.

One-timer: Shooting the puck directly off a pass without first stopping it.

Open Net: When a player shoots the puck at the net with the goalie off the ice or out of position.

Penalty box: The area where a player sits to serve a penalty.

Penalty shot: A type of penalty awarded when a team loses a clear scoring opportunity on a breakaway because of a foul committed by an opposing player. A player from the non-offending team is given an attempt to score a goal without opposition from any defending players except the goaltender.

Playoff beard: The superstitious practice of a hockey player not shaving off his facial hair during the playoffs, consequently growing a (usually unkempt) beard.

The point: A player in the opponent's end zone at the junction of the blue line with the boards. It is usually occupied by defencemen. The point man must help keep the puck in the attacking zone and contribute to attacks, often with long-range shots, but he must also be the first line of defence when the opponent starts to counter-attack.

Powerplay: A situation in which one team has a temporary numerical advantage because the other team has had one or more players placed in the penalty box.

Puck: Vulcanised rubber disc that operates as the playing piece like a ball in other sports.

Rebound: When the puck bounces off a goalie, a player, or the net after a shot on goal.

Rec. League: Hockey played for fun by adults, often without leagues, referees and teams and with limitations on body contact.

Referee: The official in charge of the game, who is responsible for calling penalties and starting and stopping play.

Saucer pass: An airborne pass from one player to another, sometimes landing on the ice right next to the teammate's stick. The puck resembles a flying saucer in mid-air.

Rush: A team's movement towards an attack on goal, which might start in their own zone.

Screened shot: A shot that the goaltender cannot see due to other players obscuring his view.

Shift: The time a player, line or defensive pairing is on the ice before being replaced by another. Most coaches want their team's shifts to last no longer than 45 seconds. Players fatigue rapidly, but recover quickly.

Shorthanded: When a team has fewer players on the ice than the opposing team as a result of a penalty or penalties.

Shootout: A series of alternating penalty shots by both teams to determine the winner after a game ends in a tie. Shootouts are usually best of three; if scores are still tied, they become sudden death. All tied AIHL games go to a shootout.

Slapshot: A hard shot, featuring a big wind up, where the shooter hits the puck hard to generate great pace. Often used by defencemen further out from goal near the blue line in order to attract tips and deflections from forwards, or rebounds from the goalie.

Slapshot: Title of a comedy drama motion picture written by Nancy Dowd which hilariously captured the unglamorous world of the minor-pro hockey scene in the late 1970s. A cult classic and staple of travelling teams on buses.

Slashing: A common penalty. Contacting an opponent's body or stick with one's own stick as a result of a swinging or chopping motion.

Spearing: A serious penalty. Jabbing an opponent with the blade of the hockey stick. If picked up by a referee, it will be penalised by at least a four-minute stay in the penalty box.

Slot: The area on the rink directly in front of the goaltender between the face-off circles on each side. It is the optimum position to score from, so should be most heavily defended.

Sniper: A player with a powerful, accurate shot who converts a lot of goal-scoring opportunities.

Stretch pass: A long pass that allows one's team to move out of their defensive zone and start a rush; often causes a breakaway.

"Standing on his head": A goalie who plays extremely well and makes spectacular saves, keeping his team in a game.

Toe drag: A move performed by an attacker by dragging the puck on the ice with the toe of the stick blade, which quickly pulls the puck back towards the forward, out of the defender's reach.

Top shelf: The upper area of the goal, just below the net's crossbar and above the goaltender's shoulders.

Two-way forward: A forward who is proficient at defending as well as attacking.

Wrap around: Scoring a goal by reaching from behind the net.

Wrist shot: A quick shot made by snapping the wrists forward when the puck is against the stick blade. Uses more of a shoving or throwing motion than the heavy contact of a slapshot.

Zamboni: The brand name of the most famous of the ice-resurfacing vehicles that smooth and clean the ice before the game and between periods.

GLOSSARY of Australian terms

AFL: The Australian Football League, professional national league of the indigenous game. See Footy.

Bogan: The closest comparable North American term would be "white trash", but here's the Oxford definition: "depreciative term for an unfashionable, uncouth, or unsophisticated person, especially of low social status". And here's the take from the Macquarie Dictionary: "person, generally from an outer suburb of a city or town and from a lower socio-economic background, viewed as uncultured".

Derby: A match between two rival teams from the same city or region.

Esky: An icebox or portable cooler.

Footy: Australian Rules Football, the game indigenous to Australia played and passionately supported predominantly in its southern states, Tasmania, Victoria, South Australia and Western Australia. Not to be confused with the English games of rugby and rugby league, predominantly played in New South Wales and Queensland.

Hoon: A lout or hooligan, especially a young man who drives recklessly.

Import: Non-Australian player in the AIHL. Each team is allowed six imports on their roster, but only four can play in any single game.

MCG: The Melbourne Cricket Ground. Massive (capacity 100,017) and beloved sporting stadium in the centre of Melbourne. Its main business is AFL games in winter, cricket playing a major role on only a handful of summer days.

Oakleigh (rink): Smallest, oldest Australian ice rink, in the Melbourne suburb of Oakleigh. For a long time it was the only rink in that city.

Peter Brock: Champion Australian motor racing driver, a hero in the 1970s and 1980s.

Piss-take: An act of mockery

Sledge/sledging: In Canadian: chirping. Verbal abuse aimed to unsettle and opponent.

theage.com.au: Website of Melbourne mainstream newspaper *The Age*.

Vegemite: Salty black Australian spread, made from used brewer's yeast.

PHOTO CREDITS

Thank you to all of the AIHL's dedicated photographers, especially: Mark Bradford, Jack Geraghty, Tania Chalmers, Andrew Mercieca, Paul Rewell, Reverend William A Stewart, Paul Furness, Peter Podlaha, Ben Southall, Matt Wragg.

THANKS & ACKNOWLEDGEMENTS

I hope that it is evident from the preceding pages that I had a ball writing this book, and reporting on the AIHL for the past four years. Australian hockey folk are open, friendly and accommodating and their generosity has been inspiring. In effect, the book is my thank you, using 121,000 words instead of two, to all the people who put on such a captivating show without getting paid a brass razoo. Thank you volunteers, fans, Facebook ranters, players, coaches, presidents and administrators; if I leave out a specific mention of your name here rest assured that I am grateful to anyone who has helped put on a game, and everyone who talked hockey with me over the past five years.

Thanks to the Melbourne Mustangs and Melbourne Ice for allowing me access to their road trips and their clubs. To the players and staff members, I appreciate you putting up with an interloper. I loved every minute and learnt a lot.

May blessings most glorious be bestowed upon the two men who put up with my company, calls and texts for a year. Pat O'Kane: I am not Catholic so I might not

get a vote, but I hereby put it on the record that I endorse your candidacy for Pope. You are a gentleman and it was a pleasure to share part of your journey. You and yours deserve the best.

Matt and Sara Armstrong, thanks for your friendly support of this project, your company before and after it, and your forthright viewpoints throughout. Melbourne is better for you being here; hockey is much better for your dedicated, fun-loving input.

To Brent Laver and Brad Vigon, I think it is obvious that I became as fascinated by your journeys as by the players' stories during the course of this project. Your generosity, candour and vision for your clubs and the sport are at the heart of this book. Hockey is lucky to have you, and I am glad you stuck it out when the going got tough. You are class acts.

Thank you to the people I probably spoke to more than any coach or player, the off-ice staff of the Mustangs and Ice. You trusted me, and drank the most wine with me; I hope this work does you all justice. Cheers to the inimitable Ian Webster; the irrepressible Johan Steenberg; the redoubtable Tom

Harward; the charming Josh Puls; the convivial Chuck Connolly; the affable James Meredith; and the one and only Mick Burslem.

Thank you AIHL Commissioners, especially Tyler Lovering (at the outset a few years ago), Peter Lambert, Alex Hamilton and Robert Bannerman. You have always picked up the phone when I have called, and I have always enjoyed having a chat with you socially and professionally. Robert, the book would not have been the same without your input.

Thank you James Morgan for sharing your verve, wit, and energy. Conversation with you never fails to toss up new ideas, the best recommendation of a chat I can imagine.

Nigel Sherwin, your generosity was so outrageous I had to mention it in the book proper! You exemplify the importance to the league of volunteers with professional skills.

Thank you also to gregarious Garry Dore, who always took my calls despite having twenty-seven jobs; Ryan O'Handley, whose friendly enthusiasm has me considering a trip to Iceland; Stan Scott, whose energectic vision makes me want to start a petition to the WA sports minister; Andrew Petrie, who the North Stars are lucky to have; and Peter Chamberlain, who CBR Brave are lucky to have.

Thanks Val Webster and Colleen Nash those for the life-saving rides home after road trips, late Sunday nights.

Myles Harris, who showed me some of the mysterious byways of social media, thanks for your generosity and digital sagacity.

The top brass of AIHL clubs are very down-to-earth despite facing some stressful political and financial challenges. Whatever was going on behind the scenes, you always treated me kindly and cordially. Thanks Emma Poynton, John Belic and Andy McDowell, who I bugged the most, and also Wayne Hellyer, Shane Rose, Ross Noga, and John Raut.

Thanks to Andy Lamrock for such enthusiastic support of my reporting when you were Ice president, and your continued engagement since. Good luck with the rink dreams.

Thank you AIHL website editor Andrew McMurtry for all your cheerfully delivered assistance.

Mark Rummukainen and Joey and Vinnie Hughes did more heavy lifting than many other players in this work; thanks for your time, words and your play.

Thanks Nathan Walker for taking all the long distance phone calls. Good luck with your NHL dreams, you will always know you are doing your utmost to get there.

The Age didn't just pay me a wage for 11 years, it helped develop skills necessary for projects like this, and provided me with a suite of great friends. Thank you everyone who supported me there, and in particular the friendly and professional Alex Lavelle and Scott Spits for supporting my minor sport love affair.

A cast of stellar photographers have lifted this book and saved it from showcasing any more of my limited snapping skills. Thanks to Tania Chalmers, Andrew Mercicea, Jack Geraghty, Mark Bradford, Paul Rewell, Rev William A Stewart, Paul Furness, Peter Podlaha, and Ben Southall for responding to my numerous requests and delivering such great pictures.

Designer Marija Ercegovac made this work look good. I literally could not have made a book that did justice to the subject and contributors without you, thank you so much.

Thanks to editor Sue Harvey for cleaning up the text and good luck with your own project.

Thank you Kristian Schafer for sharing the seasons, and your erudite proofing, from long before deadlines loomed. No author can do without such a generous, articulate mate.

Thanks to my brother Craig for bringing me back to hockey. I hope in the years to come we get to watch more games together with your sons, at the Icehouse and Pakenham.

To friends and family who support what may appear quixotic 'career decisions', thank you. Your backing enables me to be back myself.

Thank you lover, your love and understanding of the writing life enables me to follow my own advice: Keep Going.

LINKS & FURTHER READING

DEAR READER,

If you enjoyed this work, please consider offering a review of it on amazon.com, goodreads.com or on any social media outlet. This work's success is entirely at the mercy of word of mouth and your endorsement is crucial. If you like it, say so! You will have the heartfelt gratitude of an increasingly improversished writer.

For more about my writing and image-making, including past and future projects, go to: **willbrodie.com**

For more on this book, including image galleries and silly articles based on its index entries: **realitycheckhockeybook.com**

- AIHL:
theaihl.com
The Australian Ice Hockey League site: scores, stats, news and features.

- NHL:
nhl.com
The world's best league now features social media input from Australian Sasky Stewart.

- Hewitt Sports:
hewittsports.com
Bloggers cover the AIHL.

- Puck Daddy:
sports.yahoo.com/blogs/nhl-puck-daddy/
Comprehensive, up-to-date blog which has featured Aussie hockey.

- The Hockey News:
thehockeynews.com
Follow this magazine's Facebook feed for (mostly NHL) updates

- Sean McIndoe:
grantland.com/contributors/sean-mcindoe
Down Goes Brown blogger and *Grantland* columnist always worth a read

- Nick Does Hockey:
nickdoeshockey.com
Nick Place takes up hockey - at the age of 45.

Originally, *Reality Check* was intended as a book based on not just Australian hockey, but my impressions of the sport after taking an epic journey through North America. Logistics precluded the international odyssey, but in preparation for that would-be book, I read and watched a lot of hockey-related material, which stood me in good stead for this book. (Keep in mind that I was as interested in lower tier hockey as the NHL)

Here's a few items I heartily recommend:

Books:

***Zamboni Rodeo* by Jason Cohen**
A picaresque portrait of minor-pro hockey in Texas at the end of the 1990s. Hilarious, horrifying, utterly compelling.

***Tropic of Hockey* by Dave Bidini**
A funny, perceptive writer chases hockey in places way more exotic than Australia. An insightful delight.

***Gretzky's Tears* by Stephen Brunt**
The departure of Wayne Gretzky for Hollywood told with intelligence and objectivity.

***They Don't Play Hockey in Heaven* by Ken Baker**
An entertaining chronicle of a unique comeback, and a great portrait of life on the fringes of a minor-pro franchise.

***Journeyman* by Sean Pronger**
NHL without the glitter, by a player funny and humble enough to make the title a badge of honour.

***The Making of Slapshot* by Jonathan Jackson**
If you like behind the scenes showbiz stories, and hockey, this is pure candy.

TV series:

***Ice: Road To Threepeat* by Resolution Media**

Must-see six-part fly-on-the-wall documentary heralded a new era in the AIHL.

INDEX

21010236R00191

Printed in Great Britain
by Amazon